Alpha
Teach Yourself

French

in 24 hours

ALPHA

A Pearson Education Company

Alpha Teach Yourself French in 24 Hours

Copyright © 2001 by Dr. William Griffin

International Standard Book Number: 0-02-864173-6
Library of Congress Catalog Card Number: 2001089690

Printed in the United States of America

First printing: 2001

04   03   02   4   3   2

Note: This publication contains the opinions and ideas of its author. It is intended to provide helpful and informative material on the subject matter covered. It is sold with the understanding that the author and publisher are not engaged in rendering professional services in the book. If the reader requires personal assistance or advice, a competent professional should be consulted.

The author and publisher specifically disclaim any responsibility for any liability, loss, or risk, personal or otherwise, which is incurred as a consequence, directly or indirectly, of the use and application of any of the contents of this book.

Trademarks

All terms mentioned in this book that are known to be or are suspected of being trademarks or service marks have been appropriately capitalized. Alpha Books and Pearson Education cannot attest to the accuracy of this information. Use of a term in this book should not be regarded as affecting the validity of any trademark or service mark.

ACQUISITIONS EDITOR
Mike Sanders

DEVELOPMENT EDITOR
Tom Stevens

SENIOR PRODUCTION EDITOR
Christy Wagner

COPY EDITOR
Rachel Lopez

INDEXER
Angie Bess

PRODUCTION
Angela Calvert
Svetlana Dominguez

COVER DESIGNER
Alan Clements

BOOK DESIGNER
Gary Adair

MANAGING EDITOR
Jennifer Chisholm

PRODUCT MANAGER
Phil Kitchel

PUBLISHER
Marie Butler-Knight

Overview

Contents

Part II The Present and the Future

Hour 5 Express Yourself in the Present Indicative   79

Part III The Past

Part VI The Real World

Appendixes

About the Author

Dr. William (Bill) Griffin is a Professor of French at Appalachian State University located in Boone, North Carolina. He completed his Ph.D. in French at the University of Alabama, Tuscaloosa, Alabama, after studying at the University of North Carolina, Chapel Hill; l'Université de Lyon, France; and Appalachian State University. Dr. Griffin started teaching at Boone, North Carolina, in 1978, in the Interdisciplinary Studies residential college program (Watauga College). In 1990 he moved to the Department of Foreign Languages and Literatures, where he served as Chairperson from 1990 to 1996. Since 1996 he has taught French at all levels and regularly directs a summer study abroad program to Angers, France. Dr. Griffin and his wife, Diane, reside in Boone, deep in the Blue Ridge Mountains of North Carolina.

Dedication

I dedicate this book to my wife Diane, who encourages and supports me as only she knows when and how to do, and to my two sons, Evans and Blake, all of whom give joy to my life and meaning to my work.

Acknowledgments

Special thanks to friends Steve and Jim, who gave words of encouragement and confidence when they were needed; and my mother Sabra Griffin, whose faith and pride in me have never faltered.

Thanks also to Dr. Sixto E. Torres for finding released time for me to complete this project, and for his understanding during many days when I was hard to find at the office; and to my agent Jessica Faust, who encouraged me from the start and stuck with me to the end. Finally, to Dr. Michael Lane, for his excellent technical assistance and editing of the final manuscript.

Introduction

This work is intended for beginning learners of French who wish to master the basic elements of the language without enrolling in a formal course.

Alpha Teach Yourself French in 24 Hours contains 24 hours, or lessons, each of which can be read in an hour's time. New elements of the language are introduced in each hour, building on the information presented in previous hours. Working through the text on a daily basis, you will cover all the elements of the French language necessary to read and communicate orally with native speakers at a comfortable degree of fluency.

The 24 hours are divided into six parts. The first three parts stress the learning of basic structures of the language and the present and past tenses of verbs. The next three parts continue to stress the main grammatical elements of French and introduce a wide range of vocabulary so you can discuss numerous topics.

Part 1, "The Basics" (Hours 1 through 4), deals with the basic structure of a French sentence, the use of nouns and adjectives, and conjugating most verbs in the present tense.

Part 2, "The Present and the Future" (Hours 5 through 8), covers language used in everyday speech, such as talking about time and the weather, expressing emotions through the use of the subjunctive mood, and using the future tense.

Part 3, "The Past" (Hours 9 through 12), introduces the major past tenses and negative expressions. In this part you'll also learn about linking ideas through the use of conjunctions and pronouns.

Part 4, "Leisure Time" (Hours 13 through 16), introduces more vocabulary and useful language, focusing on how you spend your leisure time. The main vocabulary presented in this part centers on free time, things around the house, and going places (travel and vacation).

Part 5, "Stepping Out" (Hours 17 through 20), focuses on what you do outside the home. Vocabulary and structures dealing with eating out, working, shopping, and campus life are presented in this part.

Part 6, "The Real World" (Hours 21 through 24), is the final part of the book and offers advice, vocabulary, and examples of language dealing with real-world communication such as writing letters, conducting business, dealing with emergencies, and reading and enjoying the arts and literature.

Each hour contains cross-references, tips, shortcuts, and warning sidebars to assist you through the learning process. Here are the indicators used in this book:

 FYI FYIs provide extra information that isn't immediately relevant to the task at hand.

JUST A MINUTE

 Just a Minute sidebars offer advice or teach an easier way to do something.

PROCEED WITH CAUTION

Proceed with Caution boxes are warnings. They warn you about potential problems and help you steer clear of trouble.

STRICTLY DEFINED

Strictly Defined boxes offer definitions and explanations of usage for words you might not know.

TIME SAVER

Time Saver sidebars give you a faster way to do something.

GO TO ▶
These sidebars give you cross-references to another chapter or section in the book to learn more about a particular topic.

As you proceed through the book, remember these basic language-learning tips:

- Keep a notebook divided into sections by hours. In your notebook, write down difficult structures, grammar rules, examples of things you want to learn to say, and vocabulary items. The more you write, the more you'll remember.

- Say things out loud. Even if at first you're not sure about your accent, try to read the examples aloud and listen to your voice as you repeat sentences and phrases. Use the Internet to find sites with sound files you can download and listen to native speakers to learn the rhythm and intonation of French.

- Although the lessons are intended to be covered in one hour each day, don't feel pressed to spend just 60 minutes on each lesson. Take the time you need to master the material.

- Avoid translating as much as possible. Many examples are given in the context of things the French say but have no English equivalent. Learn these items in context and avoid asking the question "What does this mean in English?"

And finally, enjoy yourself. Relax. The more at ease you are, or as the French say, the more *décontracté* you are, the easier you will remember things, and the longer they will stay with you. So, let's go! *Allons-y!*

PART I

The Basics

HOUR 1
Saying It Right

CHAPTER SUMMARY

LESSON PLAN:

In this hour you will learn ...

- How to say the French alphabet.
- How to pronounce combinations of sounds.
- How to count from 0 to 10.
- How to link sounds, known as *liaison.*
- How to reproduce the rhythm of French.
- How to pronounce some common exceptions.

Pronouncing French often is considered the most difficult part of learning the language, and it's best to start with hardest part first. Keep in mind that spoken French comes in many forms and many accents. The accent of Paris is not the same as the accent in southern France or in Quebec, or for that matter in Morocco, Cameroon, or Senegal. However, the Parisian accent generally is considered the standard, and that's what you will learn here.

Also, French has many sounds that are close to, but not exactly like, English sounds. This hour will alert you to the major differences in pronunciation that can lead to major misunderstandings. However, when the distinction between the English sound and the French sound is minimal, you can fall back on your English.

One more caveat before you begin: Because learning to speak any foreign language requires that you hear it spoken, some links to Web sites where you can hear native speakers using the language are suggested at the end of the hour. You can find many others using the search function of your Web browser.

PRONUNCIATION

Learning to pronounce French correctly requires that you first learn the basic sounds of the language as represented by the alphabet and then learn how these sounds may change when combined within words and phrases. As is true in English, the same French vowels and consonants may be pronounced differently depending on where they fall in a word or phrase. So, first let's learn the alphabet sounds, then work on how these sounds change in combination with other sounds. Then we'll talk about several sounds called "nasals" that are unique to French.

SAYING THE ALPHABET

The French alphabet has 26 letters, just like English; however, with the addition of diacritical marks, or accents, some vowels (*a*, *e*, *i*, *o*, and *u*) are pronounced differently. In addition, French consonants tend to be crisper and shorter than their English counterparts.

FYI There are five accent marks used in French: acute accent (´), grave accent (`), circumflex accent (ˆ), diaeresis (¨), and the cedilla (¸), used only on the letter *c*. Most often an accent will change the pronunciation of a letter; however, the following accented letters are used only to distinguish spelling between two words with different meanings: *à, î, ù*. For example: *où* means "where" and *ou* means "or"; *à* means "at" and *a* means "has." A dieresis over the letters *i* or *e* means that the letter is pronounced as a unique sound: *naïf, Noël*.

Although there are many subtle differences between French and English sounds, you can approximate the native sound using the following table. When saying the English word provided as a guide to pronouncing the French letter, be sure to cut short the sound and not glide into the following vowel sound so that you create what is called a *diphthong*, which is rare in French. For example, the sound of the French vowel *a* is *ah*, and not (as in English) *ay-ee* (a diphthong in English). The same holds true when pronouncing consonants; for example, the French *b* is pronounced as a quick *bay*, not *bay-ee*, and so forth. Also, *b* and *p* are not *explosive* as they are in English; that is, when you say "Paul" or "Bob" in French, you should feel no air escape when you place your hand close to your lips.

PROCEED WITH CAUTION

When used in combination with vowels, most French consonants are pronounced very similarly to their English equivalent, but have a distinct sound when said in the alphabet. Also, you need to know how the alphabet sounds to spell important words such as your English name. You can hear the alphabet at www.helio.org/education/french/pronunciation/alphabet.html.

Letter	Sound	French Word	Close English Equivalent (for Vowels)
a	ah	ma, ta, la	a in "father"
b	bay (Remember: -ay is a crisp English a sound.)		
c	say		
d	day		
e	euh	ce, de, le	a in "along"
f	eff		
g	jay (g is pronounced more like the English j.)		
h	osh		
i	ee	si, il, ami	ee in "see"
j	gee (j is pronounced more like the English g.)		
k	kah		
l	ell		
m	emm		
n	enn		
o	o	robe, mode	like the o in "hone"
p	pay (Keep the sound crisp, without expelling air.)		
q	kew		
r	err		
s	ess		
t	tay		
u	oo (No true English equivalent. See the following Just a Minute.)		
v	vay		
w	dooble-vay		
x	eeks		
y	ee-grek		
z	zed		

Now that you know the alphabet, you can work on some of the sounds that are distinctly French. Here is a list of the most common accented letters and their close English equivalents:

- *â*   Pronounced more open than the French *a* (*ah*), as in the English words "par," "palm," "parch."

- *ç*   Pronounced like *s*.

- *é*   Pronounced like the *a* in "take" but shorter and crisper.

- *è*   Pronounced like the *e* in "set."

- *ê*   Pronounced like the *e* in "set."

- *ô*   Pronounced like the *o* in "go."

- *ï, ë*   The dieresis indicates that the letter is pronounced separately; you probably use the words "Noël" and "naïve." These two words are pronounced almost the same in French and English.

JUST A MINUTE

Surely the two most difficult sounds in French are *r* and *u*. To say the French *u*, round your lips tightly and say the English *e*. As for the French *r*, well, you might have felt where it originates only while gargling! You really need to hear these sounds to say them correctly, but give it a try by practicing the word "rue," first gargling the *r* then pursing your lips to get the *u*.

COMBINATIONS OF SOUNDS

In addition to the sounds that letters have in the alphabet and the sounds of the accented letters, certain combinations of letters (vowels and consonants) have distinctive sounds. Here are the most common ones:

- *ai*   Pronounced the same as *è*, like the *e* in "set," but when *ai* is followed by *l*, it is pronounced *ah-yuh*, as in *travail* (*tra-vah-yuh*).

- *au*   Pronounced like *o* in "open."

- *eu*   Pronounced like the first *e* in "handkerchief." The *eu* in both *eur* and *oeur* is pronounced the same way: *ehrr*.

- *euil*   Pronounced *euh-yah*. Try saying the French word for "armchair," *fauteuil*, pronounced *fo-teuh-yah*.

- *oi*   Pronounced *waa*. Try saying the French word for "me," *moi*, pronounced *mwaa*.

- **ou** Pronounced like the *ou* in "soup" or *oo* in "goose." Try saying the French word for "you," pronounced *vous*.

- **ui** Pronounced usually as two sounds—*oo-ee*; but *oui* is pronounced *wee* (one sound, meaning "yes"). Try pronouncing the French *suite*, pronounced *soo-eet*, similar to the English "sweet."

- **er** Pronounced like *é*, as in "take" when at the end of a word; the *r* is silent. However: *hier* ("yesterday") is pronounced *ee-yer*, with the *r* pronounced (true of most one-syllable words).

- **et** Pronounced *è*, as in the *e* of "set." Note that *et* ("and") and *est* ("is") are slightly different sounds—*è* and *é*, respectively. (The *t* of *et* and the *st* of *est* are silent.)

As mentioned, most French consonants resemble their English equivalents, but there are a few special cases when this is not true. The following are the major ones:

- **c** Pronounced like *k* before *a*, *o*, and *u* as in "cake," and pronounced like *s* before *e* and *i* as in "Cicero."

- **g** Soft before *e* and *i*, as in "gym"; it is hard before *a*, *o*, and *u*, as in the English "Galvaston" and "gobble."

- **h** Always silent. There are no exceptions; just imagine it's not there except to spell things: *thé* is pronounced *tay*.

- **ch** Almost always pronounced like the *sh* in "sham."

- **ll** Most often pronounced as a *yuh* sound, as in the words *fille* (*fee-yuh*) and *famille* (*fah-mee-yuh*).

- **s** Pronounced *z* between two vowels, as in *cousin*; *ss* is pronounced *s*, as in "base"; *s* is almost never pronounced at the end of a word, even for plurals.

- **-tion** At the end of a word is pronounced as if the *ti* were an *s* (not *sh*), as *see-on*, said crisply as one syllable.

JUST A MINUTE

You're beginning to see why French pronunciation can cause problems! But wait—there's some relief at hand. The consonants *d*, *n*, *p*, *s*, *t*, and *x* generally are not pronounced when at the end of a word. Moreover, some consonants (*b*, *g*, *j*, *k*, *q*, *v*, *w*, and *z*) are rarely or never located at the end of a word. However, *c*, *r*, *f*, *l* (CaReFuL!) may or may not be pronounced. And remember, *h* is always silent! In the following hours, pronunciation exceptions will be indicated when necessary.

NASAL SOUNDS

Now for those sounds that, when learned correctly, will really make you feel French—the nasals. No, you don't have to pinch your nose or have a bad cold to reproduce them, but it won't hurt to start thinking a bit snooty. After all, you should feel somewhat superior—you are learning French!

PROCEED WITH CAUTION

The nasal sounds are so unique to French that the fonts for most computers don't have a symbol for them. Your French dictionary will indicate them with a tilde (˜) over the appropriate vowel sound as follows: Ø̃, ç̃, Ẽ, Ã, for *un, on, in,* and *an,* respectively. See the explanation about the International Phonetic Alphabet in the next section.

Nasal sounds are produced partially through the nose, but not as dramatically as you might think. Technically there are four nasal sounds represented by these spellings: *un/um; on/om; in/im/yn/ym/ain/aim/ein/eim;* and *an/am/en/em.* Your first reaction might be to wonder how so many combinations of letters can represent only four sounds. Well, in truth they represent only three sounds in current speech. The nasal *un/um* generally has been subsumed into that long list of nasals beginning with *i.* The classic way to teach the nasal sounds has been to use the phrase: *un bon vin blanc* ("a good white wine"). Each word contains a single and distinct nasal. However, because most Parisians pronounce *un* just like *in,* the phrase becomes "*in*" *bon vin blanc.*

FYI   There really are no English equivalents for the French nasal sounds and there's no precise way to describe how to say them. They are best modeled by a native speaker. You can hear them pronounced at virga.org/cvf/index.html.

THE INTERNATIONAL PHONETIC ALPHABET

As you continue through the hours ahead, you will need to confirm the pronunciation of new words or review your phonetics by using a good dictionary. All French/English dictionaries will provide the pronunciation of words using the International Phonetic Alphabet, or the IPA. A basic knowledge of this phonetic notation will be indispensable to your study of any language, but it is especially useful for French because there are so many exceptions to the rules and even exceptions to exceptions.

At first glance, the IPA might appear daunting, but in the beginning you need only to be able to check the vowel sounds in French because the consonants often resemble English. The following is what the IPA vowel chart looks like.

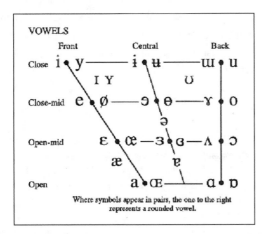

The IPA may be freely copied on condition that acknowledgement is made to the International Phonetic Association (c/o Department of Linguistics, University of Victoria, Victoria, British Columbia, Canada). See the full chart at www2.arts.gla.ac.uk/IPA/fullchart.html.

(Courtesy of the International Phonetic Association)

The IPA represents French vowels as shown in the following figure.

French vowels and nasals in IPA notation.

Written	Phonetic Symbol	Near English Equivalent
a	[a]	(ah)
à	[ɑ]	(par)
e	[ɛ] or [ə]	(euh)
è	[ɛ]	(like the e in set)
é	[e]	(like the a in take)
i	[i]	(ee)
o	[o] or	(like the o in go)
	[ɔ]	(like the o in lot)
ô	[o]	(like the o in go)
u	[u] or	(like the oe in shoe)
	[y]	(no equivalent)
Nasals		
un	[œ̃]	(no equivalent)
on	[ɔ̃]	(no equivalent)
un	[ɑ̃]	(no equivalent)
an	[ɛ̃]	(no equivalent)

FYI You can access sound files of the IPA from the University of Lausanne, Switzerland (www.unil.ch/ling/phonetique/api2-eng.html), to practice the difficult nasal sounds *r, u, ou.*

Linking Words and Phrases: Liaison

Everyone who hears a French song or sees a French movie is immediately struck by the musical quality of this *Romance language*. One of the principal reasons that French sounds so melodious is that words, like syllables, are rarely pronounced in isolation. Words, phrases, and sometimes whole sentences tend to meld together or elide so that often it is difficult for the beginner to distinguish where one word or sentence stops and another begins. This lyrical melding of words and phrases happens a lot in French and is called *liaison*.

JUST A MINUTE

We call languages that evolved from Latin "Romance languages" not because they are particularly romantic, but rather because they evolved from the language spoken by the Romans. French, Spanish, Italian, and Portuguese are the principal European Romance languages. Due to a similar heritage in Latin, the grammar and vocabulary of these languages have much in common.

Liaison occurs when the final consonant of a word is "carried over" and pronounced with a following vowel. Here's one common example: To ask someone how he or she is doing, you say *Comment allez-vous?* which sounds like *com-on-tallay-voo?* The *t* of *comment* carries over to the next word, which begins with a vowel. However, if you just want to say "What?" you say *Comment?* pronounced as *com-on?*; here the *t* is silent!

Some liaisons are required; others are not. Careful speakers (including professors, politicians, and TV announcers) use them more often than necessary for effect or just to play with the beauty of the language; popular speech tends to keep only the ones required for distinguishing between the singular and plural of words. In songs and poetry—even in popular renditions—all possible liaisons are used. You will learn in the course of the following hours which are which; for now, here are five essential liaisons (which, if you don't make them, can cause confusion):

- Between plural subjects and verbs: *ils ont* (*ilzon* means "they have").
- Between most verbs ending in *s*, *x*, *d*, or *t* and the following word if it begins with a vowel: *il peut aller* (*ilpeutalay* means "he can go").
- After numbers ending in *s*, *x*, or *t* (see the "Numbers from Zero to Ten" section later in this hour).

- After the verb form *est* ("is").
- After plural articles when the following word begins with a vowel: *les exemples* (*lay-zegzampl*).

However, there are two instances in which the liaison is never used:

- After *et* (the conjunction "and").
- Before an aspirate *h* at the beginning of a word; these words are indicated in every dictionary by an asterisk (*); for example, *les *hibou* (*lay-iboo*, not *lay-ziboo*): "the owls." You will learn more about the aspirate *h* in Hour 2, "Describing Things."

PROCEED WITH CAUTION

Learning when and where to use a liaison also requires that you hear the language spoken. For example, some Parisians say *pas encore* (which means "not yet") as *pazenkor;* others say *pa enkor*. Such usage often is a matter of personal choice or regional accent. However, making the wrong liaison at the wrong time also can cause humorous or embarrassing blunders. You will be alerted in future hours of important instances when you must or must not make a liaison.

NUMBERS FROM ZERO TO TEN

So what do numbers have to do with pronunciation? Well, first of all, it's very useful to be able to count from 0 to 10; but also, learning these numbers will demonstrate how sounds can change in French depending on where they are located. Counting from 0 to 10 in English means learning to pronounce 11 words that are always pronounced the same way; in French, the pronunciation of the numbers can change significantly depending on whether the following word begins with a vowel or a consonant.

First, here are the numbers as you would pronounce them when counting from 0 to 10 (the sounds are represented using near-English equivalents):

- 0   *zéro* (*zay-row*)
- 1   *un* (a nasal)
- 2   *deux* (like the *i* sound in "dirty")
- 3   *trois* (like the *wa* in "waddle")
- 4   *quatre* (like the *a* in "father")
- 5   *cinq* (a nasal)

- **6** *six* (like the *ea* in "easy")
- **7** *sept* (like the *e* in "set")
- **8** *huit* (like the *wee* in "sweet")
- **9** *neuf* (note that the *eu* in *deux* and *neuf* are different sounds)
- **10** *dix* (like the *ie* in "piece" or the *ea* in "peace")

That's simple enough. But now see what happens when the numbers are followed by nouns. Notice that the final consonants *x* and *s* are pronounced as *z* when followed by a vowel, whereas *q* and *t* become silent before a consonant, except for the number 7.

PROCEED WITH CAUTION

The masculine noun *monsieur* is a very common word for mister, sir, or man. Its pronunciation is exceptional: *m'sjO* (*m's'euh*).

- **1** *un* (nasal) *une mademoiselle* (non-nasal)
- **2** *deux messieurs* (*deu*) *deux exemples* (*deuz*)
- **3** *trois messieurs* (*trwa*) *trois exemples* (*trwaz*)
- **4** *quatre messieurs* (*katr*) *quatre exemples* (*katr*; no difference)
- **5** *cinq messieurs* (nasal, *q* is silent) *cinq exemples* (*sank* contains the nasal *ẽ*; *q* is pronounced as *k*)
- **6** *six messieurs* (*see*) *six exemples* (*seez*)
- **7** *sept messieurs* (*s`t*) *sept exemples* (no difference)
- **8** *huit messieurs* (*oowee*) *huit exemples* (*ooweet*)
- **9** *neuf messieurs* (*neuf*) *neuf exemples* (*neuv*)
- **10** *dix messieurs* (*dee*) *dix exemples* (*deez*)

PROCEED WITH CAUTION

Neuf is pronounced *neuf* at the end of a word group. Before the words *ans* ("years") and *heures* ("hours") it is pronounced *neuv*.

INTONATION

The liaison is not the only element that adds musicality to spoken French. Other elements, such as intonation and rhythm, give the language a distinctive singsong quality. Intonation refers to the rise and fall of the voice; rhythm refers to the cadence of speech. Of these two elements, intonation is the easiest to illustrate. When we ask a question in English, the tenor (meaning general direction) of our voice rises slightly at the end of the sentence and can be illustrated as follows:

Where are you ↑going↑?

This slight rise in the voice at the end of a sentence indicates that the speaker has finished asking a question and now is waiting for a reply. The response can be illustrated as follows:

I'm going ↓home↓.

In the response, the voice drops slightly to indicate that the answer is complete and the speaker has nothing more to say. This is a simple example of intonation. However, in French, intonation plays a major role in almost every sentence, not just in asking questions. Typically, the voice rises slightly at the end of every sentence, and often at the end of phrases within the sentence, as if the speaker were never quite finished speaking.

TIME SAVER

To practice intonation, choose a French movie on tape and find a moment of conversation. Rather than trying to understand what is being said, play and replay the same scene and imitate the intonation of the speech by humming along with the dialog. (You might want to do this in private!)

Another very important element of French intonation is the use of stress within words and word groups. In English, as you can see marked in any dictionary, words are "stressed," or "accented," on certain syllables. Often the point at which we stress a word can change its meaning. For example, in the following sentence misplacing the accents can be both humorous and confusing: He wanted to contest the contest because he was not content with the content.

A native speaker rarely has problems with such words because English pronunciation is so firmly based on stressed and unstressed syllables. The problem in speaking French is that French has *no* stressed syllables. Every syllable of the word *déclaration*, for example, carries the same stress. Compare the English and the French pronunciation of these words:

Constitution in French is pronounced *cõ-stee-too-ssion*, and all syllables receive the same stress.

"Constitution" in English is pronounced *CON-sti-TOO-shun*, and the first and third syllables are stressed.

PROCEED WITH CAUTION

Be careful to not confuse the French accents (´, `, and ^) with a stress mark. The French accent changes the quality (sound) of the vowel but does not indicate stress.

On the level of the sentence, the stress on individual words also differs significantly between English and French. Consider this example of differences in stress when asking an emphatic question:

English: *What* (the heck) are you doing? (strong stress on the first word)

French *Qu'est-ce que vous faites?* (*kesskavooFET*) (mild stress on the final word)

RHYTHM

Rhythm is closely related to intonation but refers primarily to the cadence of speech; that is, how quickly words or parts of sentences are said. In English, we have words or merely sounds such as "well," "hmmm," "eh," and so forth that permit us to slow down the conversation and think ahead before continuing. As you might imagine, French is replete with such interjections. Some words in French, as in English, serve no purpose except to fill space while the speaker decides what to say next.

Knowing when to pause and when to interject comes with listening and practice. The following table shows a few simple interjections you can use almost immediately. Notice that some are full words; others are merely sounds.

Interjections

French	English
Hein? (nasal)	Huh? What? (useful but not very polite for getting someone to repeat something)
Quoi? (*kwa*)	What? (also impolite)
Bof? (*bof*)	Well …, doesn't matter to me …, hmmm …
Bien … (nasal)	Okay, so next …
Quand même (*kanmem*)	All the same …
Pardon (*par-dō*)	Excuse me, pardon, could you repeat that?
S'il vous plaît (*seel-voo-play*)	Please? Come again? Repeat?

COMMON EXCEPTIONS

Now that you've been exposed to the most common sounds of French, have seen some near-English equivalents to those sounds (where possible), and have familiarized yourself with the IPA, it's time to consider some of the exceptions to the rules. This also is a good time to learn some basic vocabulary, because even though you've not yet heard them spoken, you've learned some guidelines for how to pronounce the words you see.

PROPER NOUNS

Let's start with some place names. As is true in most languages, the pronunciation of French geographical names tends to be unpredictable. See the following table. Near-English equivalents appear in parentheses.

French	Phonetic	English
la France	(frans)	France
Paris	(pari)	Paris
Bruxelles	(broox-el)	Brussels
Rome	(roam)	Rome
les États-Unis	(layz-aytah-zunee)	United States
la Nouvelle-Orléans	(lah-noo-vel-or-lay-an)	New Orleans
l'Angleterre	(langle-tare)	England
Londres	(lon-dra)	London
l'Allemagne	(lal-man-ya)	Germany
la Suisse	(lah-soo-ess)	Switzerland
le Canada	(le-kah-nah-dah)	Canada
Montréal	(mon-ray-al)	Montreal
le Québec	(le-kay-bek)	Quebec

LEARN SOME COMMON NOUNS

The following table is a list of some common nouns divided into categories. Practice your pronunciation by reading the words aloud. When you come to one that seems difficult, look up the phonetic rendering of it in your dictionary.

Travel	English	Food	English	Clothing	English
un avion	plane	*un repas*	meal	*une robe*	dress
un train	train	*un dîner*	dinner	*un pantalon*	pants
une voiture	car	*le pain*	bread	*une chemise*	shirt
un taxi	taxi	*le vin*	wine	*un chapeau*	hat
un bus	bus	*le fromage*	cheese	*une écharpe*	scarf
le métro	subway	*le thé*	tea	*une ceinture*	belt
un car	large bus	*la bière*	beer	*une chaussure*	shoe
un vélo	bicycle	*la viande*	meat	*une chaussette*	sock
un hôtel	hotel	*le porc*	pork	*une cravate*	tie
une chambre	room	*le bifteck*	beef	*les lunettes*	glasses
l'aéroport	airport	*les légumes*	vegetables		
la gare	train station				

LISTEN TO NATIVE SPEAKERS

Finding sound files on the Internet provided by native French speakers is becoming easier. Two excellent sites to begin with are Laura K. Lawless's French page at french.about.com and Bob Peckam's Famous French Links at www.utm.edu/departments/french/french.html.

HOUR'S UP!

You made it successfully through the first hour—well done! You've gotten through the hardest part, pronunciation; from here you will build a working vocabulary and learn the basic structures of French, helping you to converse comfortably with native speakers. However, before you continue, let's review some of the key materials in Hour 1.

1. True or False: The letters *e*, *é*, and *è* are all pronounced the same way.

2. True or False: An accent in French indicates a syllable to be stressed.

3. True or False: The sound of *an* and *am* in French is the same.

4. True or False: The letters *b* and *p* are pronounced the same in both French and English.

5. Which of the following English place names most closely resembles its French equivalent in pronunciation?

    a. Paris

    b. Montreal

    c. Rome

    d. Quebec

6. Which of the following letters is never pronounced in French?

    a. *t*

    b. *x*

    c. *w*

    d. *h*

7. Which of the following word groups does not contain a liaison?

    a. *deux enfants*

    b. *huit élèves*

    c. *trois hiboux*

    d. *Il est absent*

8. With which of the following words does *chanté* rhyme?

    a. *hier*

    b. *chanter*

    c. *ballet*

    d. *très*

9. Which of the following numbers does not change pronunciation when followed by a vowel?

    a. *huit* (8)

    b. *sept* (7)

    c. *six* (6)

    d. *trois* (3)

10. According to most learners, the most difficult French sound(s) for an English speaker to reproduce are …

    a. *r*

    b. *u*

    c. nasals

    d. all of the above

QUIZ

HOUR 2

Describing Things

CHAPTER SUMMARY

LESSON PLAN:
In this hour you will learn ...

- How to determine the gender of nouns and adjectives.
- How to use subject pronouns.
- How to use the definite and indefinite articles.
- How to make nouns and adjectives agree.
- How to make nouns and adjectives plural.
- How to count from 11 to 69.

Nouns are words that refer to people, places, things, animals, or ideas such as "man," "woman," "city," "Paris," "cup," "airplane," "dog," "cat," "love," "beauty." Nouns in English that designate a specific person or place (Paris or Susan, for instance) are called proper nouns and are always capitalized; however, this will not always be true in French. Pronouns are used to replace nouns, often as a way of avoiding repetition.

LEARN THE GENDER OF NOUNS

All nouns in French are either masculine or feminine in gender. There are no neuter nouns in French. English nouns don't really have a grammatical gender, but some nouns clearly connote feminine or masculine persons or animals; for instance, "man," "boy," and "rooster" are masculine; "woman," "girl," and "hen" are feminine. All other nouns are considered neuter nouns; that is, English speakers don't think of a tree, a book, or a car as being masculine or feminine.

In French, the gender sometimes will be obvious (*femme* [woman] is feminine; *homme* [man] is masculine), but most often gender will be unpredictable (*arbre* [tree] is masculine; *voiture* [car] is feminine). As you proceed from this hour forward, focus on learning the gender of the noun as you learn each word. Say the words out loud and copy them into your own vocabulary notebook with masculine words in one column and feminine words in another. You also might want to color-code the columns for an extra visual cue.

Rules for capitalization and punctuation are conventional by language; that is, they arise out of customary usage by native speakers. Therefore, these rules differ greatly among languages. Specific differences between French and English rules of capitalization and punctuation will be presented as the need arises.

RECOGNIZE MASCULINE NOUNS

Generally, nouns referring specifically to masculine persons or animals are masculine in French. When a noun refers generally to persons or animals, you must learn its gender; for example, *une personne* (a person, in general) and *une bête* (a beast, an animal, in general) are always feminine, whether they refer to a male or a female.

 For now, simply say the masculine article *un* along with the noun. The feminine article for "a" is *une* (see the following table).

Here is a short list of common words preceded by the masculine article *un* meaning "a/an." Use the pronunciation rules provided in Hour 1, "Saying It Right," to guide you in saying the words out loud. The best way to learn the gender of a word is to say it aloud and then write it down.

Masculine Nouns Representing Masculine Persons or Animals

French	English	Pronunciation Tips
un garçon	a boy	ç is pronounced s
un monsieur	a man, sir	*mon* is pronounced as *m'*
un fils	a son	the *l* is silent; the *s* is pronounced
un gosse	a (male) child	pronounce *ss* as *s*
un enfant	a (male) infant	*en* and *an* are the same nasal sound
un homme	a man	*h* is silent: *un-omme*
un père	a father	pronounced like the English "pear"
un frère	a brother	rhymes with *père*
un oncle	an uncle	*on* is a nasal, thus *on-kle*
un roi	a king	pronounced *rwah*
un coq	a rooster	*q* is prounced as *k*
un taureau	a bull	pronounced *toe-roe*

Although the only sure way to learn the gender of a new noun is to look it up in a dictionary, you will notice that certain noun endings will give you a clue to gender. The following table shows some common endings for masculine nouns, but the golden rule of gender is when it doubt, check your dictionary.

PROCEED WITH CAUTION

Some nouns that are spelled the same way have a completely different meaning depending on the gender. Always check your dictionary.

Masculine Noun Endings

Nouns Ending In	Examples	English
-on	patron	owner
	carton	carton
	mouton	sheep
	démon	demon
-isme	classicisme	classicism
	catholicisme	catholicism
	journalisme	journalism
-age	ménage	housework
	louage	renting
	naufrage	shipwreck
	chauffage	heating
-eau	chapeau	hat
	château	chateau
	bateau	boat
a consonant	lac	lake
	vin	wine
	bar	bar
	lit	bed
	riz	rice

With rare exceptions, geographic names that do not end with the letter *e* are masculine—*le Japon, le Chili,* and *le Nebraska* all are masculine. The major exception is *le Mexique,* which ends in *e* but is masculine. Conversely, with rare exceptions, all geographic place names that end with the letter *e* are feminine—*la France, la Belgique, la Suisse, la Floride, la Californie.*

RECOGNIZE FEMININE NOUNS

Nouns referring to female persons also are generally feminine. The feminine article is *une*.

Feminine Nouns Representing Feminine Persons or Animals

French	English	Pronunciation Tips
une fille	a girl, daughter	pronounced *fee-ya*
une madame	a lady	pronounced *ma-dam*
une gosse	a (female) child	pronounce *ss* as *s*
une enfant	a (female) infant	final *t* is silent
une femme	a woman, wife	pronounced *fah-m'*
une mère	a mother	pronounced *mare*
une sœur	a sister	final *r* is pronounced
une tante	an aunt	*t* followed by *e* is pronounced
une reine	a queen	*in* followed by *e* is not nasal
une poule	a hen	*oo*, pronounced similiar to *oo* in the English "pool"
une vache	a cow	pronounced *vah-sh*

As is true with masculine nouns, there are some endings that can help you recognize feminine nouns.

Feminine Noun Endings

Nouns Ending In	Examples	English
-aison	*saison*	season
	raison	reason
	comparaison	comparison
-ière	*dernière*	last
	soupière	soup tureen
	prisonière	(female) prisoner
-tte, -lle	*galette*	pancake
	étiquette	label
	brochette	kabab
	coquille	shell
	ville	city

Nouns Ending In	Examples	English
-é	*beauté*	beauty
	volonté	will
	charité	charity
-tion	*constitution*	constitution
	déclaration	declaration
	institution	institution

PROCEED WITH CAUTION

French, like English, is filled with *homophones,* words that sound alike but have different meanings such as "tale" and "tail." The words *un maire* (a mayor), *une mer* (a sea), and *une mère* (a mother) are pronounced alike, but are distinguished partly by gender, partly by context.

LEARN NOUNS WITH ONE OR TWO GENDERS

Many nouns in French have both a masculine and a feminine forms depending, of course, on whether they refer to a male or a female. Some are spelled the same way in both forms, distinguished only by the gender of the article; others change both the article and the ending of the word. The following table is a list of some common nouns in these categories:

French	English
un professeur	a teacher (female or male)
un architecte	an architect (female or male)
un médecin	a doctor (female or male)
un ingénieur	an engineer (female or male)
un agent de police	a policewoman or a policeman
un membre	a member (female or male)
un auteur	an author (female or male)
une personne	a person (male or female)
un assistant/une assistante	an assistant
un avocat/une avocate	a lawyer
un/une athlète	an athlete
un acteur/une actrice	an actor/an actress
un vendeur/une vendeuse	a salesperson
un cousin/une cousine	a cousin

FYI In Canadian French one says: *un professeur/une professeure, un agent/une agente* (agent); *un auteur/une auteure* (author), *un maire/une mairesse* (mayor/mayoress), *un écrivain/une écrivaine* (writer).

Nouns designating titles (such as *un président, un ambassadeur,* and *un général*) also must be used with caution. Traditionally, the feminine forms of these nouns (*présidente, ambassadrice, générale*) have been used to designate the wife of the man holding the title. Thus, *Madame la générale* refers to the General's wife. However, this usage is fading. Today, especially among younger persons, *une présidente* and *une ambassadrice* clearly refer to a female president or ambassador.

Some nouns have both a masculine and a feminine form, and the meaning of the noun changes completely depending on the gender. The following table lists a few of the most common:

Nouns Whose Meanings Change According to Their Gender

Masculine	English	Feminine	English
un critique	a critic	*une critique*	a criticism
un mode	a mode	*une mode*	a fashion
le vase	the vase	*la vase*	the mud
le poste	the post/job	*la poste*	the mail
un livre	a book	*une livre*	a pound

When a noun has both a masculine and feminine form, the endings typically change as follows:

- *-eur* changes to *-euse* or *-trice*.
- *-er* changes to *-ère*.
- If a noun ends in a consonant, add an *e*.

RECOGNIZE THE SUBJECT PRONOUNS

The importance of gender in French will become increasingly apparent as you proceed through the coming hours. At this point, a couple of quick examples using pronouns will demonstrate how the gender of a noun controls the structure of a French sentence. You will learn more about pronouns in Hour 7, "Describe Your Surroundings."

A pronoun is a word that stands for a noun (pro + noun). In English, there are nine subject pronouns that can be used as the subject of a sentence: I, you, he, she, it, we, you, they, and one. In French, there also are nine subject pronouns: *je, tu, il, elle, nous, vous, ils, elles, on*. You can see that, in addition to he/she (*il/elle*), French has masculine and feminine forms for the plural, *ils* and *elles*. In addition, some of the other pronouns (such as *tu, nous, vous*) can be either masculine or feminine depending on the gender of the person to whom the pronoun refers. Finally, *il* and *elle* also can mean "it" when referring to masculine or feminine things.

Note in the following examples how the adjectives in the first sentences are all in agreement with the nouns (masculine/feminine, singular/plural). In the second sentences, the subject pronoun agrees with the subject noun it replaces.

- *Pierre est un petit garçon. Il est américain.* (Peter is a small boy. He's American.)
- *Marie est une petite femme. Elle est américaine.* (Mary is a small woman. She's American.)
- *Voilà trois petits garçons. Ils sont américains.* (There are three small boys. They are American.)
- *Voilà trois petites femmes. Elles sont américaines.* (There are three small women. They are American.)

STRICTLY DEFINED

Voilà means "Here it is!" or "There it is!" when used alone. It also can mean "here is/there are ...." We will use this word a lot as a way to present new words, as in *Voilà le livre!* (Here's the book!)

PROCEED WITH CAUTION

All adjectives, even those referring to nationality (*français* [French]; *américain* [American]) are written in lowercase. Also, when speaking the preceding sentences, remember that a final *s* is not pronounced. Even the *s* of *ils* and *elles* is silent unless followed by a vowel, when it is pronounced as a *z*. The formation of the plural is treated in detail later in this hour.

MASTER THE DEFINITE ARTICLES

The definite article is used when referring to something specific or concrete, as in "The man is tall" or "Give me the book that you bought." English has but one form of the definite article "the," whereas French has four: *le, la, l',* and *les.* The use of the definite article in French does not always correspond with English usage; for example, French uses the definite article before abstract nouns, geographic place names, days of the week, titles, parts of the body, and expressions of quantity when talking about prices.

LEARN THE DEFINITE ARTICLES: *LE, LA, L', LES*

Let's look at how the definite article is used in French. In the following examples you will see that …

- *Le* is used before masculine nouns beginning with a consonant.
- *La* is used before feminine nouns beginning with a consonant.
- *L'* is used before any singular noun beginning with a consonant or a silent *h.*
- *Les* (pronounced *lay*) is used before any plural noun.

JUST A MINUTE

You learned in Hour 1 that the letter *h* is always silent in French. That's still true. However, when a word begins with *h* it can be either *aspirated* or *unaspirated,* which refers to whether or not one makes a liaison with the vowel following the *h.* Simply put, an aspirated *h* acts like a consonant and permits no liaison, for example, *le haricot (le-areeko), les haricots (lay-areeko);* if the *h* is unaspirated, you make the liaison, for example, *l'homme (lum), les hommes (lay-zum).* Words beginning with an aspirated *h* are indicated in dictionaries with an asterisk (*).

Carefully note how these rules for the use of the definite articles are applied in the following examples:

- *le garçon* (the boy)
- *la femme* (the woman)
- *l'homme* (the man)
- *l'université* (the university)
- *le hamster: *hamster* (the hamster)
- *la harpe: *harpe* (the harp)
- *les garçons, les femmes, les hommes, les universités, les hamsters, les harpes*

USE THE DEFINITE ARTICLE WITH ABSTRACTIONS

French requires a definite article before abstract nouns such as the following:

- *l'amour* (love)
- *la haine* (hate)
- *le respect* (respect)
- *la liberté* (liberty)
- *les trois vertus* (the three virtues)
- *les problèmes* (problems)

USE THE DEFINITE ARTICLE WITH GEOGRAPHIC NAMES

Use the definite article before names of countries, provinces, regions, continents, rivers, and mountains:

- *la France: La France est belle.* (France is beautiful.)
- *le Portugal: Le Portugal est beau.* (Portugal is beautiful.)
- *les États-Unis* (the United States), pronounced *lay-zay-ta-zu-nee*
- *l'Europe* (Europe)
- *les Alpes* (the Alps)
- *le Nil* (the Nile)
- *la Seine* (the Seine)

Generally, the definite article is not used before the names of cities; for example, *Paris est une belle ville* (Paris is a beautiful city). However, the names of several major cities always include the article:

- *Le Havre* (Le Havre, France)
- *La Havane* (Havana, Cuba)
- *La Haye* (the Hague, the Netherlands)
- *La Rochelle* (La Rochelle, France)
- *La Nouvelle Orléans* (New Orleans, USA)
- *Le Caire* (Cairo, Egypt)

GO TO ▶
A complete discussion of geographic place names and their usage with prepositions (to, from, in, and so forth) follows in Hour 13, "Master the Prepositions."

USE THE DEFINITE ARTICLE WITH DAYS OF THE WEEK

The definite article is used with days of the week when speaking in a general sense or when referring to a routine, as in the following:

GO TO ▶
Starting with Monday and ending with Sunday, the days of the week are *lundi, mardi, mercredi, jeudi, vendredi, samedi,* and *dimanche.* The months and days of the week will be presented in detail in Hour 5, "Express Yourself in the Present Indicative."

- *La classe de français est le lundi.* French class is (every) Monday.
- *Je dîne avec Steve le mardi et le mercredi.* I eat dinner with Paul (every) Tuesday and Wednesday.

The article is omitted when speaking of a particular day:

- *La classe est lundi.* The class is (this particular) Monday.
- *Le meeting est mardi.* The meeting is (this particular) Tuesday.

USE THE DEFINITE ARTICLE WITH TITLES

The definite article is required before titles and proper nouns modified by an adjective; in English, no article is used. The article is omitted before *Monsieur* (Mr.), *Madame* (Mrs.), and *Mademoiselle* (Miss), as in *Voilà Monsieur Dupont* (There's Mr. Dupont). The following list illustrates the use of the definite article with titles:

- *l'empereur Napoléon* (Emperor Napoleon)
- *la princesse Marie-Louise* (Princess Mary-Louise)
- *le professeur Larue* (Professor Larue)
- *le docteur Dupont* (Doctor Dupont)
- *le roi Louis XIV* (King Louis the Fourteenth)
- *le célèbre Shakespeare* (the famous Shakespeare)

The use of the definite article in greetings presents particular problems. However, because you might use these greetings often, simply learn the following conventional phrases and substitute the appropriate name:

- *Bonjour, Madame (Monsieur, Mademoiselle) Dupont.* (Hello, Mrs. [Mister, Miss] Dupont.)
- *Bonjour, Professeur Larue.*
- *Bonjour, Docteur Dupont.*
- *Bonjour, Monsieur le professeur.*
- *Bonjour, Monsieur le docteur.*

FYI The articles *le, la,* and *les* are the same words used for the object pronouns meaning "him," "her," "it," and them: *Voilà le livre! Le voilà!* (There it is!) You will learn about object pronouns in Hour 14, "Free Time."

USE THE DEFINITE ARTICLE IN SPECIAL CASES

The definite article also is used when speaking of the price of a quantity of items and with parts of the body. Here are a few examples:

- *Les tomates coûtent 10 francs le kilo.* (The tomatoes are 10 francs a kilo.)
- *Le lait coûte 15 francs le litre.* (Milk is 15 francs a liter.)
- *Je me lave les mains.* (I wash my hands.)
- *Elle s'est coupé la main.* (She cut her hand.)

LEARN CONTRACTIONS OF THE DEFINITE ARTICLES

Contractions are short ways to combine words. English has many contractions such as "it's" for "it is," "they're" for "they are," and "don't" for "do not"; most often these are used in, spoken language. French also has contractions but they do not use the apostrophe as in English. Instead, French uses contracted forms of some words and, unlike English, you don't have the choice about using the contracted form—when a contraction exists, you must use it.

The following prepositions have required contracted forms when followed by the definite article:

- *à* (meaning "to")

  à + *le* becomes *au* (pronounced o): *au cinéma* (to the movies)

  à + *les* becomes *aux* (pronounced o): *aux monuments* (to the monuments)

- *de* (meaning "from, of")

  de + *le* becomes *du*: *la porte du taxi* (the door of the taxi); *le livre du garçon* (the book of the boy, the boy's book)

  de + *les* becomes *des* (pronounced *day*): *les livres des garçon* (the books of the boys, the boys' books)

MASTER THE INDEFINITE ARTICLES

The indefinite articles in English and French are used to refer to any person or thing. English has two forms: "a" and "an." French also has two forms: *un* for masculine nouns and *une* for feminine nouns. You recall from Hour 1 that *un* and *une* also can mean the number "one":

GO TO ▷
There are some instances in which French dispenses with the article or uses an article different from English. These circumstances will be discussed in Hours 13, "Master the Prepositions," and 18, "At Work."

GO TO ▷
De used to show possession is presented in Hour 11, "Learn to Show Possession."

- *un homme* (a man, one man)
- *une femme* (a woman, one woman; a wife, one wife)
- *un livre* (a book, one book)
- *une table* (a table, one table)

The indefinite article in French is used generally where English would use "a" or "an" with one main exception: When speaking of one's profession, nationality, or title and using the verb *être* (to be), the article is omitted if the noun is not modified by an adjective:

- *Il est américain.* (He's American/an American.)
- *Il est peintre.* (He's a painter.)
- *Elle est étudiante.* (She's a student.)
- *Elle est ambassadrice.* (She's an ambassador.)

However, if the profession or title is modified, the pronoun *ce* is used to mean "he" or "she," and the article follows the verb:

- *C'est un peintre abstrait.* (He/She is an abstract painter.)
- *C'est une bonne étudiante.* (She's a good student.)

FYI The distinction between *il est, elle est,* and *c'est* is discussed in detail in Hour 3, "Actions in the Present Tense." They can be described briefly as follows: *Il est* and *elle est* mean "he is; it is" and "she is; it is" when followed by an adjective, as in *Il est grand* (He is tall). If the profession or title is modified or if the word that follows is a noun, French uses *c'est* where English would use "he/she/it/this is," depending on the context.

LEARN THE PLURAL OF INDEFINITE ARTICLES

Unlike English, French has a plural form of the indefinite article: *des* (pronounced *day*). *Des* is used in French where English might use "some," "any," or "none." Note that in the following two examples *des* is both masculine and feminine:

- The plural of *un homme* is *des hommes* (some men, men).
- The plural of *une femme* is *des femmes* (some women, women).

You see that the nouns also add an *s* to form the plural. However, be careful not to pronounce this final *s* on the nouns; also be sure to make the liaison in *des hommes*.

LEARN THE PARTITIVE ARTICLES

In addition to the plural of the indefinite article (*des*), French also has partitive articles that do not exist in English. As the name implies, the partitive article expresses the idea of having a part of or an uncertain quantity or number of something. It is used when referring not to the whole of something, but to part of it. English expresses this concept in the following ways:

- Using the word "some"
- Omitting the article altogether

The French partitive is formed by combining the preposition *de* (of) with the indefinite articles as follows:

- *de + le* becomes *du*
- *de + les* becomes *des*
- *de + l'* remains *de l'*
- *de + la* remains *de la*

Compare the following sentences to learn the use of the partitive article:

- *Voilà du pain.* (There's some bread/There's bread.)
- *Voilà des oranges.* (There are some oranges.)
- *Ce n'est pas de la musique, c'est du bruit.* (This isn't music, it's noise.)
- *Il mange des bananes et du pain.* (He eats [some] bananas and [some] bread.)

Take a careful look again at the preceding examples; you see that *du* and *de la* are used with nouns that signify things that usually cannot be counted: "bread," "music," and "noise." For example, when we ask for bread we're usually asking for a part of a loaf. If we want the whole loaf, we ask for "a loaf of bread." Bread, music, and noise are examples of noncountable nouns. Oranges, apples, and people are examples of countable nouns. The partitive article is most often used with noncountable nouns. Compare these three sentences:

- *Avec le fromage, je mange du pain.* (With [the] cheese, I eat [some] bread.)
- *J'aime le pain français.* (I like French bread.)
- *J'aime les bons vins français.* (I like [the] good French wines.)
- *Je bois du vin.* (I drink [some] wine.)

GO TO ▶

As is true with all articles, there are common exceptions to the usage of the partitive article. The most common will be discussed in Hours 7, "Describe Your Surroundings," and 8, "Learn to Express Yourself in the Future."

GO TO ▶
The use of the partitive articles is a difficult concept, especially because they don't exist in English. They will be discussed again in Hour 8, before you learn to use the negation.

In the first example, *du* is used to indicate that you are eating "some bread" with the cheese, not all the bread that is available. Thus, you use the partitive article. In the second and third examples, you are stating that you like French bread (all types in general) and that you like good French wines (all good types in general). Thus, you use the definite article. The last example uses the partitive because you can't possibly drink all the wine(s) available; you can drink only the part that's available to you. So again you use the partitive article.

MAKE NOUNS AND ADJECTIVES AGREE IN GENDER

An adjective describes (modifies) the characteristics of a noun: "Big," "small," "pretty," and "American" are adjectives. You will learn five different types of adjectives in upcoming hours; for now, you will learn only about descriptive adjectives, which describe or qualify a noun.

First, take a look at the following table to see how the adjective changes to agree with the noun. Also notice where the adjective is placed relative to the noun (before or after); in the following section, you will learn a few rules about where to place adjectives and how to make them agree.

Agreement of Nouns and Adjectives

Masculine	Feminine	English
un grand homme	une grande femme	great
une femme militaire	un homme militaire	military
un petit garçon	une petite fille	small
un homme travailleur	une femme travailleuse	hardworking
un homme cruel	une femme cruelle	cruel
un enfant destructeur	une enfant destructrice	destructive
un bon livre	une bonne classe	good
un homme naïf	une femme naïve	naïve
un oncle heureux	une tante heureuse	happy
un taureau blanc	une vache blanche	white
un frère fou	une sœur folle	foolish
cher Monsieur	chère Madame	dear

The following are the primary rules for changing the gender of adjectives. Study the rules for a few minutes and then find the example in the preceding list that illustrates each rule.

- Add *e* to the masculine form: *grand* becomes *grande*; *petit* becomes *petite*.
- Change *-eur* to *-euse*: *travailleur* becomes *travailleuse*.
- Change *-teur* to *-trice*: *destructeur* becomes *destructrice*.
- Change *-eux* to *-euse*: *heureux* becomes *heureuse*.
- Change *f* to *v* and add *e*: *neuf* (new) becomes *neuve*.
- If the adjective ends in a vowel + consonant, either double the final consonant and add *e*: *bon* becomes *bonne*, *cruel* becomes *cruelle*; or change *-er* to *-ère*: *cher* becomes *chère*.

No doubt you also have noticed that some of the preceding adjectives (*blanc*, *fou*) have radically different masculine and feminine forms. The following table lists some very common irregular adjectives.

Irregular French Adjectives

Masculine	Feminine	English
blanc	blanche	white
doux	douce	soft
faux	fausse	false
favori	favorite	favorite
fou	folle	foolish
frais	faîche	fresh
franc	franche	frank
gentil	gentille	gentle
long	longue	long
public	publique	public
sec	sèche	dry

KNOW WHERE TO PLACE ADJECTIVES

There are no sure rules for the placement of adjectives in French. Although there are some general guidelines, you should keep in mind that the French often will "misplace" an adjective for emphasis or because, in fact, the adjective has a different meaning if placed before or after the noun.

LEARN ADJECTIVES THAT FOLLOW THE NOUN

GO TO ▶
The rules for placement of adjectives are fully discussed in Hour 7.

The following categories of adjectives generally follow the noun: colors (*une automobile rouge* [a red car]), nationality (*un poète français* [a French poet]), and adjectives of three or more syllables (*un livre intéressant* [an interesting book], *une réponse intelligente* [an intelligent response]).

LEARN ADJECTIVES THAT PRECEDE THE NOUN

These adjectives typically precede the noun: *beau* (handsome), *bon* (good), *gentil* (nice), *long* (long), *nouveau* (new), *joli* (pretty), *mauvais* (bad), *grand* (great), *petit* (small).

JUST A MINUTE

Adjectives dealing with beauty (*beau, joli*), age (*jeune, vieux*), goodness (*bon, mauvais*), and size (*grand, petit*) most often precede the noun. You can remember these categories using the acronym BAGS. Also, most short, common adjectives are placed before the noun; long adjectives, after the noun.

CHANGE PLACEMENT TO CHANGE MEANING

You can change the meaning of certain adjectives depending on where you place them in relation to the noun. These adjectives can have either a literal or a figurative meaning. For example, in English, you can speak of an "old friend," which might mean that she is either old in terms of age (literal meaning) or that she has been your friend for a long time (figurative meaning). When the adjective is placed after the noun in French, it has a literal meaning; when placed before the noun, it has a figurative meaning. The following list shows some common adjectives used literally and figuratively:

- *une histoire ancienne* (literal): an old story
- *un ancien élève* (figurative): a former student
- *un garçon brave* (literal): a brave boy
- *un brave garçon* (figurative): a good boy
- *un ami vieux* (literal): an aged friend
- *un vieil ami* (figurative): a long-time friend
- *un livre cher* (literal): an expensive book
- *cher Claude* (figurative): dear Claude

- *un homme grand* (literal): a tall man
- *un grand homme* (figurative): a great man
- *un homme pauvre* (literal): a poor (not rich) man
- *le pauvre homme!* (figurative): the poor (unfortunate) man!

Notice particularly that "a tall man" is *un homme grand* but "a short man" is *un petit homme*. However, when *grand* describes a place or thing, it usually precedes the noun and means "big" or "large":

- *une grande ville* (a large city)
- *une grande distance* (a great distance)
- *des grands pieds* (big feet)

MODIFY A NOUN WITH A NOUN

In English, nouns often are used to describe other nouns. For example, we have constructions such as "car door," "gas station," "coffee cup," "cotton shirt," and "onion soup." In these examples, the first word of each pair (car, train, coffee, cotton, onion) qualifies or describes the second word. Nevertheless, all the words are nouns, not adjectives.

In general, French does not permit this construction, but instead connects the two nouns using a preposition, which can be *de* (of), *à* (to), or *en* (in). Some general rules to guide you will be presented in Hour 12, "Learn to Link Ideas"; for now you can learn a few common expressions as vocabulary:

- *la porte de la voiture* (the car door)
- *un poste d'essence* (a gas station)
- *une tasse à café* (a coffee cup), but *une tasse de café* (a cup of coffee)
- *une chemise en coton* (a cotton shirt)
- *la soupe à l'oignon* (onion soup)
- *une salade de fruits* (fruit salad)

MAKE NOUNS AND ADJECTIVES PLURAL

Nouns and adjectives form their plurals in the same way, by adding an *s* (which is written but not pronounced): *un grand homme* becomes *des grands hommes*; *une petite femme* becomes *des petites femmes*. There are very few exceptions:

- If the noun or adjective already ends in *s* or *x* there is no change in the plural: *gros* remains *gros* (large); *heureux* remains *heureux* (happy).
- If the noun or adjective ends in *-eau* or *-al*, change to *-aux*: *bateau* becomes *bateaux*, *château* becomes *châteaux*, *cordial* becomes *cordiaux* (friendly).

STRICTLY DEFINED

Careful speech requires that *des* become *de* before a plural adjective, as in *de grands hommes.* However, this rule often is ignored in everyday speech.

LEARN THREE SPECIAL ADJECTIVE FORMS

Three adjectives have special forms (see the following list), and because they are commonly used they should be learned early: *beau* (handsome/pretty), *nouveau* (new), and *vieux* (old, referring to age). Remember that *vieux* is an adjective that changes meaning according to where it is placed (see the preceding list of these adjectives in the section titled "Change Placement to Change Meaning").

- *beau, bel, beaux, belle, belles*
- *nouveau, nouvel, nouveaux, nouvelle, nouvelles*
- *vieux, vieil, vieux, vieille, vieilles*

In addition to their normal masculine and feminine forms, these adjectives include an additional form that is used before a masculine noun beginning with a vowel or before an unaspirated *h.* These special masculine forms are used as follows:

- *un bel arbre* (a pretty tree)
- *un nouvel hôtel* (a new hotel)
- *un vieil ami* (a long-time friend)
- *un bel homme* (a handsome man), but *une belle harpe* (a beautiful harp) (**harpe*)

Now let's move on to learning some new numbers, which are also adjectives in French.

LEARN THE NUMBERS ELEVEN TO SIXTY-NINE

You learned the numbers 0 to 10 in Hour 1. Here are the numbers from 11 to 69 followed by some near-English pronunciation tips to help you get close to the sound. Notice that the numbers 20, 30, and 40 all contain a nasal sound. The *-in* of *vingt* is the same sound you find in the French word for wine: *vin;* the final *-gt* is silent unless followed by a vowel (liaison again) or another number (as in *vingt-deux*) when the *t* (but never the *g*) is pronounced. The *-en* of *trente* and the *-an* of *quarante, cinquante,* and *soixante* are the same nasal sound.

Once you pass 21, 31, 41, 51, and 61 simply add the appropriate number to continue counting from 22 to 29, and so forth. The pronunciation tips in parentheses are near-English equivalents. Consult your dictionary for the IPA pronunciations.

Numbers Eleven Through Sixty-Nine

Numeral	Number	Pronunciation	Numeral	Number	Pronunciation
11	onze	(onz)	30	trente	(trant)
12	douze	(dooz)	31	trente et un	(tran-tay-un)
13	treize	(trehz)	32	trente-deux	(trant-deu)
14	quatorze	(catorz)	40	quarante	(ka-rant)
15	quinze	(canz)	41	quarante et un	(ka-ran-tay-un)
16	seize	(sez)	42	quarante-deux	(ka-rant-deu)
17	dix-sept	(deess-sèt)	50	cinquante	(sank-ant)
18	dix-huit	(deez-ooweet)	51	cinquante et un	(sank-an-tay-un)
19	dix-neuf	(deez-nœf)	60	soixante	(swa-ssant)
20	vingt	(vin)(nasal)	61	soixante et un	(swa-ssan-tay-un)
21	vingt et un	(vin-tay-un)			
22	vingt-deux	(vint-deu)			

FYI The *t* in *vingt* is silent but is pronounced from 21 to 29 (*vint-nœf*). There is no hyphen when writing 21, 31, 41, 51, or 61. Numbers usually are written in numerals except when writing the amount of francs on a check, as in *Vingt-deux francs.* The French equivalent of *-nd, -rd,* and *-th* is *-ième;* for example, *onzième* means "eleventh"; *douzième* means "twelfth"; *treizième* means "thirteenth"; and so forth. These are called ordinal numbers because they are used to order things. The ordinal number for *un/une* is *premier/première.*

HOUR'S UP!

You've now completed your second hour of study. You know all about nouns, pronouns, adjectives and how to make them agree in number and gender. In the next hour, you'll learn how to use the subject pronouns with verbs to create complete sentences. But first, test your knowledge of the current material with this brief quiz.

1. Which of the following words is not masculine?

   a. *père*

   b. *roi*

   c. *fille*

   d. *fils*

2. Which of the following words is not feminine?

   a. *reine*

   b. *frère*

   c. *mère*

   d. *tante*

3. Which of the following endings suggests that a noun is masculine?

   a. *-tion*

   b. *-ière*

   c. *-isme*

   d. *-ette*

4. Which of the following endings suggests that the noun is feminine?

   a. *-er*

   b. *-tion*

   c. *-age*

   d. *-on*

5. Which pair of words correctly completes this sentence: _____ *hommes sont _____.*

   a. *les/américain*

   b. *les/Américains*

   c. *l'/Américain*

   d. *les/américains*

6. Which of the following countries is masculine?

   a. *Canada*

   b. *France*

   c. *Italie*

   d. *Suisse*

7. Select the correct article to complete this sentence: I like oranges:
J'aime _____ *oranges.*

   a. *l'*

   b. *les*

   c. *des*

   d. *de l'*

8. Select the correct article to complete this sentence: French bread is
very good: _____ *pain français est très bon.*

   a. *du*

   b. *la*

   c. *les*

   d. *le*

9. A pretty tree is *un* _____ *arbre.*

   a. *bel*

   b. *belle*

   c. *beau*

   d. *beaux*

10. In which of the following phrases is the adjective probably used in its
literal meaning?

   a. *un livre cher*

   b. *un cher ami*

   c. *un vieil homme*

   d. *un ancien élève*

QUIZ

HOUR 3

Actions in the Present Tense

In this hour, you will learn the two fundamental verbs in French: *avoir* (to have) and *être* (to be). Once you grasp these two verbs, which are used to form many of the tenses you will learn later (the future and the past tenses), you'll have taken a major step toward understanding and speaking French.

During this hour, you will also learn how the French verb system works, how to use the present tense in French in ways that it is not used in English, and how to conjugate 99 percent of all French verbs. That's right, 99 percent! In fact, all but a relatively few verbs in French are "regular" in their conjugation, that is, they follow a pattern, which, once learned, you can use to create the forms of any other verb of the same type. French has three categories or groups of verbs, plus about 30 common irregular verbs.

REVIEW THE FRENCH SUBJECT PRONOUNS

Before you begin learning the new verbs, let's review the subject *pronouns*. You will recall that these pronouns were presented briefly in Hour 2, "Describing Things," so you could see how nouns, adjectives, and pronouns all must agree in number and gender in French. Now it's time to learn how they function in a sentence.

A **pronoun** is a word that takes the place of or represents a noun.

The presentation of subject pronouns always follows a conventional form, as illustrated in the following table.

Comparison of French and English Subject Pronouns

English	Conventional Grammatical Name	French
I	first-person singular	*je* (not capitalized, except at the beginning of a sentence)
you	second-person singular	*tu*
he (also "it")	third-person singular, masculine	*il*
she (also "it")	third-person singular, feminine	*elle*
one	third-person singular, neuter	*on* (a "generic" pronoun that may mean many things, depending on the context in which it is used)
we	first-person plural	*nous*
you	second-person plural	*vous*
they	third-person plural, masculine	*ils*
they	third-person plural, feminine	*elles*

 FYI English is the only major language that capitalizes the first person singular pronoun, I.

DISTINGUISH *TU* AND *VOUS*

There are several very important differences between English and French subject pronouns. First, the French pronoun *tu* is a familiar pronoun. It does mean "you" but is used only when speaking with close friends, members of your family, and pets. Adults also will use the *tu* form with children, teenagers, and young adults, usually up to about the age of 21. This pronoun is always singular.

FYI The verbs *tutoyer* and *vouvoyer* are used to refer to whether you use *tu* or *vous* with someone, as in *Je tutoie ma mère* (I use *tu* with my mother) and *Je vouvoie le professeur de français* (I use *vous* with my French teacher).

The other pronoun meaning "you" is *vous*. This is the formal pronoun and is used when speaking with persons whom you do not know well, or persons who you would address as Mr. or Mrs. in English. When meeting a French person for the first time, you will almost always want to address him or her using *vous*. Using *tu* to address someone you don't know well often will be taken as an insult. Using *vous* with persons you know well can distance you from them, as when, perhaps, you're angry with them and you wish to show your feelings by addressing them as *vous*.

Whereas "you" in English is both singular and plural, *vous* in French can be singular, plural, masculine, or feminine. Read the following sentences to see the four uses of *vous*:

- *Pierre, vous êtes français?*: Peter, you're French? ("you" is singular and masculine)
- *Marie, vous êtes française?*: Mary, you're French? ("you" is singular and feminine)
- *Pierre et Paul, vous êtes français?*: Peter and Paul, you're French? ("you" is plural and masculine)
- *Marie et Suzanne, vous êtes françaises?*: Mary and Susan, you're French? ("you" is plural and feminine)
- *Pierre, Marie, et Suzanne, vous êtes français?*: Peter, Mary, and Susan, you're French? ("you" is plural, referring to a group with at least one male)

In the final example, note a peculiar rule of gender in French: It takes only one male to make a group masculine. Following this convention, the pronoun *ils* is always used when "they" includes at least one male; for example, *Voilà Suzanne, Claudine, Marie, Yvette, et Paul ... ils sont français.* Moreover, notice that the adjective *français* also is in the masculine form. However, if the group is all female, you must use *elles* and the feminine form of the adjective, as in *Voilà Suzanne, Claudine, Marie, et Yvette ... elles sont françaises.*

Like *vous*, the pronoun *nous* can be masculine or feminine. Thus, if *nous* refers to a strictly feminine group, adjectives modifying the pronoun must be in the feminine form, as in *Nous sommes françaises* (We are French [women]).

LEARN HOW TO USE THE PRONOUN *ON*

One other pronoun deserves particular attention because its use often is *idiomatic*: the pronoun *on* (one). Although English has the pronoun "one," it is not often used in everyday speech except to invoke an impersonal tone; for example, "One must not do that in public." In contrast, in French, *on* is very conversational and often used. *On* can have many meanings, as shown by the following examples:

- *On parle français ici.* (We speak French here/French is spoken here/They speak French here.)

- *On s'amuse maintenant?* (Are we having fun now?)

- *On ne doit pas faire ça en public.* (One must not do that in public.)

STRICTLY DEFINED

An **idiomatic** expression, or **idiom**, has meaning only in the context of a particular language; it can rarely be translated exactly into another language. Idioms will be discussed in detail in Hour 20, "Campus Life."

In the first example, you see that *on* can mean "we" or "they" or refer to unspecified persons. In the second example, *on* refers to a group of which you (the speaker) are a part. In the final sentence, *on* functions like the English "one."

The most common use of *on* is the second example. Whereas English uses "we" to refer to a group, you can use *on* in French. *On* is very useful because it is *conjugated* with the third-person singular verb, which often is shorter and easier to remember than the "we" form of the verb.

STRICTLY DEFINED

To **conjugate** a verb means to write or say all forms of the verb in a particular tense (present, future, or past) along with the associated pronouns.

Learn *Avoir* and *Être*

All languages have one or two verbs that serve as the building blocks for constructing all tenses. French has two: *avoir* (to have) and *être* (to be); both *infinitives*. You should write down and practice these two verbs daily, saying them aloud until they become automatic for you. In future hours, you will need these verbs to form all the other tenses.

STRICTLY DEFINED

Verbs are presented in dictionaries using what is called the **infinitive** form. In English, an infinitive is composed of two words: the preposition *to* and the verb; for example, to speak, to walk, to have, to be. French infinitives are one word: *parler* (to speak), *marcher* (to walk). You can't look up most forms of a verb in a dictionary; you must look up the infinitive.

CONJUGATE THE VERB *AVOIR*

The following table shows the conjugation of the verb *avoir* (to have). You should master this verb early because it will be used in many idiomatic expressions, as well as to form a number of past and future tenses, which you will learn shortly.

Present Tense of *Avoir*

French	Near-English	English Meaning
j'ai	*jay*	I have (note: *je* becomes *j'* before a vowel)
tu as	*tu ah*	you have (familiar)
il a	*eel ah*	he has
elle a	*el ah*	she has
on a	*on-na*	we/they have
nous avons	*noo-zavon*	we have (liaison of *s* + *a* = *z*)
vous avez	*voo-zavay*	you have (singular/plural, formal)
ils ont	*eel-zon*	they have (liaison of *s* + *o* = *z*)
elles ont	*el-zon*	they have (liaison of *s* + *o* = *z*)

When pronouncing the forms with *nous, vous, ils,* and *elles,* be sure to make the liaison. (Review the section on liaison in Hour 1, "Saying It Right.") Often in spoken French it is only the liaison, the *z* sound, that indicates plurality. Moreover, you will see when you learn the verb *être* that only the liaison distinguishes the French for "they have" from "they are."

TALK ABOUT AGE WITH *AVOIR*

The verb *avoir* is used in many idiomatic expressions such as when talking about your age. In English we say "I am 35 years old," using the verb "to be." French uses the verb *avoir: J'ai trente-neuf ans* means "I'm 39 [years old]." To ask "How old are you?" you say *Quel âge avez-vous?* (literally: What age do you have?). *Quel* is pronounced *kell.*

GO TO ▶
You will learn the numbers 70 through 100 in Hour 4, "Actions in the Present Tense with Irregular Verbs."

CONJUGATE THE VERB *ÊTRE*

The meaning of the verb *être* is "to be." Notice that the infinitive has a circumflex accent over the first *e,* as does the *vous* form of the verb. Otherwise, the accent does not appear in the conjugation, nor does it affect pronunciation. See the following table.

Present Tense of *Être*

French	Near-English	English
je suis	*je swee*	I am
tu es	*too ay*	you are (*es* almost rhymes with "day")
il est	*eel ay*	he is (*est* almost rhymes with "day")
elle est	*el ay*	she is
on est	*on-nay*	we/they are
nous sommes	*noo sum*	we are (final *s* is silent)
vous êtes	*voo-zett*	you are (make the liaison)
ils sont	*eel son*	they are (*ss* pronounced *s*, silent *t*)
elles sont	*el son*	they are (*ss* pronounced *s*, silent *t*)

Correct pronunciation is vital with both *avoir* and *être*. Remember, final consonants are not pronounced unless followed by a vowel: *s* + *a* sounds are pronounced as *z*; double *s* is pronounced as an *s*, just like in the English word "bass." Practice the following forms, taking care not to pronounce the final *t*:

Être: to be
- *ils sont* (*eel son*)(they are)
- *elles sont* (*el son*)(they are)

Avoir: to have

ils ont (*eel-zon*) (they have)

elles ont (*el-zon*) (they have)

TELL TIME WITH *ÊTRE*

The verb *être* is used in many idioms in French. One such usage is telling time. Where we might use the word "o'clock," French uses the feminine noun *heure* (hour). To say "It is ___ o'clock," you use the verb *être* as follows:

- *Il est une heure.*
- *Il est deux heures.*
- *Il est trois heures.*
- *Il est quatre heures.*
- *Il est cinq heures.*

Notice that once you pass *une heure* you add an *s* to the word *heure*. Noon is *midi*; midnight is *minuit*, as in *Il est midi* and *Il est minuit*, respectively.

English has many ways to state time before and after an hour. For example, 10:30 can be stated as "it's ten thirty" or "it's half-past ten"; 10:45 can be stated as "it's ten forty-five" or "it's a quarter to eleven"; 10:35 can be "it's ten thirty-five" or "it's twenty-five minutes 'til eleven." In French, the time is stated simply as minutes added to the current hour or minutes subtracted from the next hour with the half-hour marking the division point. The word *et* (and) is used to mark the quarter-hour and half-hour; the word *moins* (minus), pronounced *mwoin* is used after the half-hour. Read the following times to see how this works:

10:10	*Il est dix heures dix.* (pronounced *eel ay deez-eur deess*)
10:15	*Il est dix heures et quart.* (pronounced *eel ay deez-eur ay car*)
10:30	*Il est dix heures et demie.* (pronounced *eel ay deez-eur ay demee*)
10:35	*Il est onze heures moins vingt-cinq.* (pronounced *eel ay on-zeur mwoin vin sank*)
10:45	*Il est onze heures moins le quart.* (pronounced *eel ay on-zeur mwoin le car*)
10:50	*Il est onze heures moins dix.* (pronounced *eel ay on-zeur mwoin deess*)
11:00	*Il est onze heures.* (pronounced *eel ay on-zeur*)

The key phrases are *et quart*, meaning "a quarter past" or "fifteen (minutes) after the hour"; *moins le quart* meaning "a quarter 'til" or "fifteen minutes 'til"; and *et demie*, meaning "thirty" or "half-past" the hour. Notice again that usually once you pass the half-hour, you subtract time from the next hour.

JUST A MINUTE

To ask what time it is you say *Quelle heure est-il?* (pronounced *kell eur ay-tee*). You will learn other question words in Hour 5, "Express Yourself in the Present Indicative."

If necessary, you can add the following phrases to indicate A.M. or P.M. time:

- *du matin* (in the morning, A.M.)
- *de l'après-midi* (in the afternoon, P.M.)
- *du soir* (in the evening, P.M.)

French states time in yet another common way. If you are speaking about any kind of schedule (such as a train, plane, or bus schedule) or about the hours of operation of a store or business, French uses military time, calculated on a 24-hour clock. You've probably heard military personnel telling time as "o nine hundred hours" (09:00 equals 9 A.M.) or "seventeen hundred hours" (17:00 equals 5 P.M.). In military time, one o'clock in the A.M. is "o one hundred hours" and the counting continues as if the clock had 24 numbers rather than 12.

This system of telling time is very common in France and is used, even in familiar conversation, any time one wants to be sure to distinguish A.M. time from P.M. time. Thus, in French *une heure* is one o'clock in the morning, *treize heures* is one o'clock in the afternoon, and *dix-sept heures* is 5 P.M. (12:00 + 5:00 = 17:00). To indicate minutes between the hours, simply add the number: 17:15 is *dix-sept heures quinze* (five fifteen P.M.); 21:30 is *vingt et une heure trente* (nine thirty P.M.).

FYI You will see military time used on the door of almost every shop or business to indicate operating hours; for example, *Ouverte de 9h à 12h, 14h à 19h.*

LEARN TO DISTINGUISH *IL EST* AND *C'EST*

The verb *être* is such a common verb that it has many special and exceptional uses; rules that apply to other verbs often don't apply when you use *être*. For instance, the way French expresses "he/she is" and "it is" seems peculiar to speakers of English. You've already learned that *il* and *elle* mean "he/she/it." However, the word *ce*, which often means "this" or "that" also can mean "he/she/it" when used with the verb *être*. Actually, the rules for using *il*, *elle*, or *ce* are quite uncomplicated; but they are so different from English usage that they cause problems for beginners. Here are the rules:

- *Il est/elle est* are followed by an adjective and can mean "he is," "she is," or "it is."
- *C'est* is followed by an article + noun and can mean "he is," "she is," "it is," or "this is."

The key to understanding the rules is to distinguish between an adjective and a noun. The following examples will make the distinction clearer:

- *Pierre est un bel homme français. Il est français et il est beau. C'est un beau Français.* (Peter is a handsome French man. He's French and he's handsome. He's a handsome French man.)

- *Voilà un beau monument français. Il est français et il est beau. C'est un beau monument français.* (There's a pretty French monument. It's French and it's pretty. It's a pretty French monument.)

- *Marie est une belle femme française. Elle est française et elle est belle. C'est une belle Française.* (Mary is a beautiful French woman. She's French and she's beautiful. She's a beautiful French woman.)

- *Voilà une belle voiture française! Elle est française et elle est belle. C'est une belle voiture française.* (There's a beautiful French car! It's French and it's beautiful. It's a beautiful French car.)

In each of these examples the second sentence contains only adjectives (*beau* and *français*), so the subject has to be *il* or *elle*, depending on the gender of the person or thing to which it refers. In the third sentence of each example, an article plus a noun follows the verb *est*. Notice that English uses "he," "she," or "it" in both cases, whereas French uses *il* or *elle* to mean "he/she/it" when there's an adjective, but *c'est* when an article plus a noun follow.

PROCEED WITH CAUTION

C'est often is used in conversation with an adjective; for example, *C'est bon! C'est fantastique! C'est impossible!*

Now that you've reviewed the subject pronouns and learned the verbs *avoir* and *être*, it's time to tackle the French verb system.

UNDERSTAND THE FRENCH VERB SYSTEM

The French verb system developed out of Latin, the language that evolved into the various Romance languages. Over a period of many centuries, the complicated verb endings of Latin were simplified into three primary groups of verbs in French, referred to by their distinctive endings: *-er* verbs, *-ir* verbs, and *-re* verbs. Every infinitive in the French language falls into one of these groups; even the most irregular of verbs, *avoir* and *être*, end in *-ir* and *-re*. Here's the good news: Once you learn how to conjugate one verb in each group, you can conjugate almost every verb in that group (of course, there will always be exceptions).

Tense refers to the time (present, future, past) a particular verb describes. The origin of the word tense is *tempus*, the Latin word for "time." When we say "I am eating," we are describing an action taking place now, in the

GO TO ▶
In Hours 8, "Learn to Express Yourself in the Future," and 9, "Express Yourself in the Past," you will learn how to express yourself in the future and the past tenses.

GO TO ▶
You will learn more about the aspect of verbs (as it becomes necessary to understand past tenses) in Hours 9 and 10. Mood and voice will be discussed in detail when you learn about commands (Hour 5, "Express Yourself in the Present Indicative"), the subjunctive (Hour 6, "Express Yourself in the Present Subjunctive"), and the passive (Hour 21, "Communicating in the Real World").

present time (you will learn present tense in this hour). To refer to actions in the future, you use the future tense: "Tomorrow, we will eat." To refer to actions in the past, you use the past tense: "Yesterday, we ate." Another word used to refer to the "tense" of a verb is "aspect."

In addition to tenses, verbs also have a *mood* and a *voice*. For example, certain forms of the verb can express the particular mood or feeling (for example, doubt, anger, desire) of the speaker. There are three moods: the indicative, used to refer to matters of fact; the subjunctive, used to express hypothesis or possibility; and the imperative, used to give orders or commands. Voice refers to the connection between the verb and its subject—that is, whether or not the subject performs the action of the verb (active voice) or receives the action of the verb (passive voice).

LEARN THE REGULAR PRESENT TENSE CONJUGATION OF *-ER* VERBS

The largest group of verbs in French are the *-er* verbs, also called the "first group" verbs. Ninety-five percent of all French verbs are *-er* verbs. The following table shows the conjugation of three common first group verbs:

Conjugation of *-er* Verbs

parler *(to speak)*	marcher *(to walk)*	chanter *(to sing)*
je **parl**e	je **march**e	je **chant**e
tu **parl**es	tu **march**es	tu **chant**es
il **parl**e	il **march**e	il **chant**e
elle **parl**e	elle **march**e	elle **chant**e
on **parl**e	on **march**e	on **chant**e
nous **parl**ons	nous **march**ons	nous **chant**ons
vous **parl**ez	vous **march**ez	vous **chant**ez
ils **parl**ent	ils **march**ent	ils **chant**ent
elles **parl**ent	elles **march**ent	elles **chant**ent

By reading across the columns, you can see a definite pattern. Each verb form is composed of what is called a *verb stem* and an ending. To create the stem for regular *-er* verbs drop the *-er* from the infinitive: *parler* becomes *parl*; *marcher* becomes *march*; *chanter* becomes *chant*.

To this stem (*parl, march, chant*), add the following endings:

je = -e	*nous = -ons*
tu = -es	*vous = -ez*
il/elle/on = -e	*ils/elles = -ent*

As you conjugate the preceding verbs aloud, remember your phonetics from Hour 1: Final consonants are not pronounced. Thus, *il* and *ils* sound the same; *elle* and *elles* sound the same; and *parle, parles,* and *parlent* all are pronounced alike. If a verb begins with a consonant so that there is no liaison with the preceding *s* of *ils* or *elles,* the only way to distinguish between the singular and the plural in spoken French is by context.

The following table is your first list of French verbs. Practice saying them aloud and writing out the conjugations in your notebook:

Some Common -er French Verbs

acheter (to buy)	*manger** (to eat)
aimer (to like, to love)	*penser* (to think)
arriver (to arrive/to happen)	*regarder* (to watch, look at)
chercher (to look for)	*rêver* (to dream)
danser (to dance)	*skier* (to ski)
demander (to ask for)	*téléphoner à* (to telephone)
détester (to hate)	*travailler* (to work)
donner (to give)	*trouver* (to find)
écouter (to listen to)	*jouer* (to play)
entrer dans (to enter, to go into)	*visiter* (to visit [places])
étudier (to study)	*voyager** (to travel)
lancer* (to throw)	

*The verbs manger, voyager, *and all regular verbs ending in* -ger *have one irregularity in the present tense conjugation:* nous mangeons. *The* e *keeps the* g *soft, like the* g *in the English word "gym."* Lancer *and all regular verbs ending in* -cer, *add a* ç *before the* ons *of the* nous *form:* nous lançons. *The* ç *keeps the soft* s *sound of the infinitive. There is only one irregular* -er *verb,* aller (to go), *which you will learn about in Hour 5.*

JUST A MINUTE

In Hour 5 you will learn all about forming commands (the imperative mood) but for now, you can create a simple command by using the *vous* form of these verbs without the subject pronoun: *Regardez!* (Look!); *Mangez!* (Eat!); *Dansez!* (Danse!)

ASK A QUESTION USING INTONATION

Now that you can create simple sentences stating facts, such as *Je chante et je mange*, you need to know how to ask a simple question. Formulating a question is a bit more complicated than one might imagine, so we will save the more specific details until Hour 5. For now, you will learn two easy ways to ask a question requiring a "yes" or "no" response.

The simplest method to ask a yes/no question is to use intonation; that is, raise the tone of your voice slightly at the end of a sentence. First, practice doing this in English by saying this sentence as a question: You're French? Listen to how your voice rises noticeably at the end of the sentence. Using intonation in this sentence might sound a bit awkward or childlike to your English ear, but this is the most common way to ask a question in conversational French. Now practice the following sentences as questions:

- *Vous êtes français?* (pronounced *voo-zet fran-say*) Are you French?
- *Il est dix heures?* (pronounced *eel-ay diz-eur*) Is it 10 o'clock?
- *Vous avez dix ans?* (pronounced *voo-za-vay deez-an*) Are you 10 years old?
- *Vous aimez?* (pronounced *voo-za-may*) Do you like [it]?

ASK A QUESTION USING *N'EST-CE PAS*

The next most common way to ask a yes/no question is to place the phrase *n'est-ce pas* (pronounced *ness-pah*) at the end of any sentence; for example, *Vous êtes français, n'est-ce pas? Il est midi, n'est-ce pas?* Practice the same sentences given in the preceding using *n'est-ce pas*.

JUST A MINUTE

N'est-ce pas can be a useful response as well as an all-purpose question word. If someone remarks that something is good, *C'est bon!* and you agree, you can just say *N'est-ce pas* to indicate you were just thinking the same thing.

LEARN *-ER* VERBS WITH SPELLING CHANGES

Although most *-er* verbs follow a regular pattern, a very few have spelling irregularities, all of which respond to one general rule of spelling: French does not permit a silent *e* + a single consonant + a silent *e*. For example, you will never see the following combinations of letters in French: *ere, ele, ete*, and so forth.

Each of these examples has a single consonant between two silent (unaccented or unpronounced) *e*'s. To avoid this construction, French either accents one or both of the *e*'s or doubles the consonant: *ère* (era), *elle* (she), *été* (summer). Once you learn this spelling rule, you will easily see why the following verbs have an accent or have a double consonant in the conjugation that is not present in the infinitive. Unfortunately, to know whether you add an accent or double the consonant, you must consult a dictionary or verb-conjugation manual.

- *acheter* (to buy)   *j'achète* but *nous achetons, vous achetez*
- *jeter* (to throw)   *je jette* but *nous jetons, vous jetez*
- *mener* (to lead)   *je mène* but *nous menons, vous menez*

Neither the grave accent nor the double consonant is necessary in the *nous* and *vous* forms of the verb because the vowel following the consonant is either an *o* or the *e* is pronounced (*-ez* is pronounced *ay*): *nous achetons, vous achetez*.

LEARN THE REGULAR PRESENT TENSE CONJUGATION OF *-IR* VERBS

The second group of verbs is composed of those ending in *-ir*. Like the *-er* verbs, these verbs follow a pattern in their conjugation. See the following table:

Conjugation of *-ir* Verbs

finir *(to finish)*	choisir *(to choose)*	punir *(to punish)*
je finis	*je choisis*	*je punis*
tu finis	*tu choisis*	*tu punis*
il finit	*il choisit*	*il punit*
elle finit	*elle choisit*	*elle punit*
on finit	*on choisit*	*on punit*
nous finissons	*nous choisissons*	*nous punissons*
vous finissez	*vous choisissez*	*vous punissez*
ils finissent	*ils choisissent*	*ils punissent*
elles finissent	*elles choisissent*	*elles punissent*

The stem for *-ir* verbs is formed by dropping the *-ir* of the infinitive: *finir* becomes *fin*; *choisir* becomes *chois*; *punir* becomes *pun*.

To these stems (*fin*, *chois*, *pun*), add the following endings:

je = *-is*	*nous* = *-issons*
tu = *-is*	*vous* = *-issez*
il/elle/on = *-it*	*ils/elles* = *-issent*

PROCEED WITH CAUTION

Remember that a final *s* is not pronounced; thus, *finis* and *finit* are pronounced alike (*fee-nee*); *-ss-* is pronounced *s;* thus, *finissons* is pronounced *fee-nee-son* and *finissez* is pronounced *fee-nee-say.* The plural form is pronounced *fee-neess;* the final *-nt* is silent but the double *s* is pronounced because it falls between the two vowels *i* and *e.*

Here is a list of common *-ir* verbs. Practice saying them aloud and writing out the conjugations in your notebook:

Some Common -ir French Verbs

agir (to act)	*nourrir* (to feed or nourish)
bénir (to bless)	*réfléchir* (to reflect)
grandir (to grow [up])	*réussir* (to succeed)
guérir (to cure, heal, or recover)	*rougir* (to blush)
maigrir (to lose weight)	

LEARN IRREGULAR *-IR* VERBS

GO TO ▶
The conjugations of *couvrir* and verbs like it appear at the end of Hour 6.

The *-ir* group of verbs contains the largest number of irregular verbs. You might have expected this as you learned that the more common a verb is, the more likely it will be irregular and there are many common *-ir* verbs; most of the irregular ones will be presented gradually in the upcoming hours. However, the following tables will alert you so that you will not mistakenly conjugate them as regular verbs:

-ir Verbs Conjugated Like -er Verbs

French	English	French	English
couvrir	to cover	*offrir*	to offer
cueillir	to gather	*ouvrir*	to open
découvrir	to discover	*souffrir*	to suffer

The verbs in the following table are completely irregular, but they all follow the same irregular pattern. You can consult the verb charts in Appendix B, "Verb Conjugation Charts," for the conjugations of these verbs.

Irregular -ir Verbs That Follow a Similar Pattern

French	English	French	English
dormir	to sleep	sentir	to feel
mentir	to lie	servir	to serve
partir	to leave	sortir	to go out

The following table lists -ir verbs that are completely irregular and follow no specific pattern. Their conjugations must be memorized.

Completely Irregular -ir Verbs (Must Be Memorized)

French	English	French	English
courir	to run	savoir*	to know how to
devoir	should/ought	tenir	to hold
falloir	to be necessary	valoir	to be worth
mourir	to die	venir	to come
pleuvoir	to rain	voir*	to see
pouvoir*	to be able	vouloir*	to wish or want
recevoir	to receive		

These verbs will be presented in Hour 4, "Actions in the Present Tense with Irregular Verbs."

LEARN THE REGULAR PRESENT TENSE CONJUGATION OF -RE VERBS

The third group of verbs is composed of those ending in -re. Like the -er and -ir verbs, these verbs follow a pattern in their conjugation. The following table gives three examples of regular -er verbs.

Conjugation of Regular -re Verbs

attendre *(to wait [for])*	descendre *(to descend)*	entendre *(to hear)*
j'attends	je descends	j'entends
tu attends	tu descends	tu entends
il attend	il descend	il entend

continues

Conjugation of Regular *-re* Verbs   (continued)

attendre *(to wait [for])*	descendre *(to descend)*	entendre *(to hear)*
elle attend	*elle descend*	*elle entend*
on attend	*on descend*	*on entend*
nous attendons	*nous descendons*	*nous entendons*
vous attendez	*vous descendez*	*vous entendez*
ils attendent	*ils descendent*	*ils entendent*
elles attendent	*elles descendent*	*elles entendent*

The stem for *-re* verbs is formed by dropping the *-re* of the infinitive: *attendre* becomes *attend*; *descendre* becomes *descend*; *entendre* becomes *entend*.

To these stems (*attend, descend, entend*), add the following endings:

je = *-s*	*nous* = *-ons*
tu = *-s*	*vous* = *-ez*
il/elle/on = (nothing)	*ils/elles* = *-ent*

PROCEED WITH CAUTION

Final consonants are not pronounced; so *attend* and *attends* are pronounced the same, and the final *ds* or *s* is silent. In the third-person plural, the final *d* is followed by a vowel and therefore is pronounced; thus, *ils attendent* is pronounced *eel-za-tande*. Also, don't forget to make the liaison between the final *s* of *ils, elles, nous,* and *vous* with the following *a* or *e* of *attendre* and *entendre*.

Some other common regular *-re* verbs are …

- *perdre* (to lose)
- *rendre* (to give back or return something)
- *répondre* (to answer)
- *vendre* (to sell)

Learn Irregular *-re* Verbs

There are two irregular *-re* verbs—*prendre* (to take), *mettre* (to put, to place)—that you can learn now because, although irregular, they follow a pattern. *Prendre* is irregular only in the plural.

prendre *(to take)*

je prends	*nous prenons*
tu prends	*vous prenez*
il prend	*ils prennent*
elle prend	*elles prennent*
on prend	

The following verbs are conjugated like *prendre: apprendre* (to learn), *comprendre* (to understand), and *surprendre* (to surprise).

Mettre has an irregular stem in the singular (*met*), which is regular in the plural.

mettre *(to put, to place)*

je mets	*nous mettons*
tu mets	*vous mettez*
il met	*ils mettent*
elle met	*elles mettent*
on met	

The following verbs are conjugated like mettre: *admettre* (to admit), *commettre* (to commit), and *promettre* (to promise).

FYI There are a few less common verbs in the *-re* group, such as *peindre* (to paint), that follow their own pattern. You can find the conjugations of these verbs in your dictionary if you need them.

GO TO ▶

Three common *-re* verbs are completely irregular—*connaître* (to know), *croire* (to believe), and *faire* (to do); these will be presented in Hour 4.

PRACTICE CONJUGATING REGULAR VERBS

There is no better method for mastering the French verbs than to repeat and write them down in your notebook daily. Take a moment now to see how well you can conjugate the following verbs. Check your work by referring to the verb tables in this hour:

- *chanter* (regular *-er* verb)
- *finir* (regular *-ir* verb)
- *attendre* (regular *-re* verb)
- *avoir* (completely irregular verb)
- *être* (completely irregular verb)

UNDERSTAND PRESENT TENSE USAGE

Now that you've learned how to form the present tense of 99 percent of French verbs, let's talk a bit about how the tense is used. You might think the present tense in any language would be used the same way—to talk about actions in the present. In fact, it's a bit more complicated than that.

For example, English has three forms of the present tense: I speak (simple present), I am speaking (present progressive tense), and I do speak (present emphatic). If you actually are in the process of doing something in the present moment, in English, you naturally use the present progressive, as in "I am eating dinner [now]." When you describe an action that you do habitually or repeatedly, you use the simple present, as in "I eat dinner every night at 7:00 P.M." When you want to emphasize an action in the present, you might respond to the statement "You should eat three good meals a day" with "But I *do* eat three good meals a day!" Here you are using the emphatic mood of the verb in the present tense.

French does not have these forms. *Je parle français* means "I speak French" (habitual action), "I am speaking French" (action in progress), and "I do speak French" (emphatic)—all at once. This difference between French and English explains why you might have heard a French person who is just learning English say something such as "So, we go now?" instead of "So, are we going now?" Because there is no progressive form of the verb in French (as well as in some other languages), the English presents a problem to the foreign learner.

Of course, going from three forms of the present tense in English to one in French also presents many opportunities for confusion. However, don't be tempted to translate phrases such as "is going" or "are eating" using the verb *être* (to be), or to search for the word "do" in your dictionary. Instead, remember that *je mange* means "I eat," "I do eat," and "I am eating."

If it is absolutely necessary to communicate that you are in the process of doing something, use the idiomatic expression *être en train de* followed by an infinitive—literally, "to be in the train of doing something." Here are some examples:

- *Je suis en train de parler.* (I am talking [right now].)
- *Elle est en train de chanter.* (She is singing [at this moment].)
- *Nous sommes en train de manger.* (We are eating [right now].)

The emphatic "do" of English usually is expressed in French by adding the word *mais* (but) to the beginning of the sentence and streessing the verb *parle*, as in *Mais, je PARLE français!*

HOUR'S UP!

Now you know how to conjugate most of the regular verbs in French in the present tense and how to use them to create basic sentences. You've also mastered the two most common irregular verbs, *être* and *avoir*, and how to use them to talk about age and time. Before going on to Hour 4, test your knowledge of this material with the following quiz.

1. True or False: When speaking to someone you don't know well, you should use *tu*.

2. True or False: *On* can mean "we," "they," or "one."

3. True or False: *Savoir* and *connaître* are synonyms.

4. True or False: The French verb system developed out of Latin.

5. How old are you? is:
   a. *Quel âge êtes-vous?*
   b. *Quel âge avez-vous?*

6. What time is it? is:
   a. *Quelle heure est-il?*
   b. *Quelle heure est-elle?*

7. *Il est dix heures et quart.*
   a. 10:45
   b. 10:30
   c. 10:00
   d. 10:15

8. Complete this sentence with the correct pronoun: *Voilà Paul. _____ est français.*
   a. *elle*
   b. *il*
   c. *c'*
   d. *on*

9. Which of the following verbs is not a regular *-ir* verb?

    a. *grandir*

    b. *rougir*

    c. *partir*

    d. *nourrir*

10. Which of the following verbs is not a regular *-re* verb?

    a. *prendre*

    b. *rendre*

    c. *perdre*

    d. *attendre*

HOUR 4

Actions in the Present Tense with Irregular Verbs

Most of this hour is devoted to learning the conjugations of irregular verbs and their usage. At first, it may seem like a daunting task to learn so many verbs in one hour; however, you don't have to memorize them all at one time. Instead, go through the hour saying the material out loud and writing down the conjugations in your notebook. Then, when you need a particular verb or you see it reappear in later hours, come back to this hour and review its forms and usage.

Because all the common irregular verbs are presented during this hour, you will have them conveniently located here for future reference. Verbs are the concrete that holds a language together, so, of course, the more verbs you can memorize now, the better you will be able to construct French in the future!

LEARN THE NUMBERS SEVENTY TO ONE THOUSAND

Before you read the numbers in the following list, review the IPA pronunciation chart in Hour 1, "Saying It Right." There are nasal sounds in all the numbers from 20 to 999.

LESSON PLAN:
In this hour you will learn …

- How to count from 70 to 1,000.
- How to discuss prices.
- How to give telephone numbers.
- How to conjugate irregular verbs.
- How to conjugate irregular -ir verbs.

Numbers from Seventy to One Thousand

70	*soixante-dix*	101	*cent un*
71	*soixante et onze*	110	*cent dix*
72	*soixante-douze*	200	*deux cents*
80	*quatre-vingts*	300	*trois cents*
81	*quatre-vingt-un*	400	*quatre cents*
82	*quatre-vingt-deux*	500	*cinq cents*
90	*quatre-vingt-dix*	600	*six cents*
91	*quatre-vingt-onze*	700	*sept cents*
92	*quatre-vingt-douze*	800	*huit cents*
99	*quatre-vingt-dix-neuf*	900	*neuf cents*
100	*cent*	1,000	*mille*

When you look closely at the spelling of the numbers, you see that 70 is composed of 60 + 10, the numbers 71 to 79 are composed by adding the numbers 11 through 19 to the word *soixante*, 80 is 4 × 20, 90 is 4 × 20 + 10, and 99 is 4 × 20 + 19.

FYI The French numbers from 70 to 99 can be confusing for a non-native speaker; however, if you keep working on them they will become natural. In Belgium and some Francophone parts of Switzerland, the numbers are simplified: 70 is *septante;* 80 is *octante;* 90 is *nonante*.

When saying the numbers, keep the following tips in mind:

- The final *t* of *quatre-vingt* from 80 to 99 is silent. The *t* of *cent* is silent in 101, 108, and 111; otherwise, normal liaison rules apply.
- One hundred and one, one hundred and two, and so forth are *cent un, cent deux*, and so forth. (There is no *et*.)
- There is an *s* in *quatre-vingts* that is silent, but there is no *s* in *quatre-vingt-un*, nor in all the numbers from 82 to 99. The *s* also is dropped when 80 is used as an ordinal, as in *la page quatre-vingt* (page eighty).
- *Mille* is always singular: 2,000 is *deux mille;* 5,000 is *cinq mille*.

Now let's see how numbers are used to talk about the prices of things and to give telephone numbers and addresses.

Use Numbers to Ask About Prices

When talking about the price of something, most often numbers are followed by the word *franc(s)* or by an indicator of size or quantity preceded by the definite article such as *le kilo, le litre,* and *la douzaine* (dozen). To ask how much something costs in familiar language, you ask simply *C'est combien?* (pronounced *say-kon-bee-ein;* literally, "This is how much?"). The response will be something like *C'est trois francs, le kilo, Madame.* (It is/They are three francs per kilogram.)

JUST A MINUTE

French merchants typically address customers using *Madame* or *Monsieur* at the end of a response. English-speaking merchants, however, rarely add "sir" or "madam" to their response. This cultural difference will be discussed in Hour 5, "Express Yourself in the Present Indicative."

Because the franc is divided into 100 centimes, a price also might be given as *trois francs cinquante* (3 francs and 50 centimes) or *cinq francs soixante-dix* (5 francs and 70 centimes). Prices in a store will be written as follows: 3F50, 2F60, 150F, and so forth. France has no sales tax to be added on to a price at the store level. If a sign states that something is 100F, you will pay exactly that at the cash register.

Practice using the numbers in the following everyday sentences:

- *C'est combien, le journal, Monsieur? C'est 4 francs, Monsieur.* (How much is the newspaper? It's 4 francs.)
- *C'est combien, un café, Madame? C'est 6 francs 50, Monsieur.* (How much is a cup of coffee? It's 6 francs 50 centimes.)
- *C'est combien, le billet de train, Monsieur? C'est 400 francs, Monsieur.* (How much is the train ticket? It's 400 francs.)
- *C'est combien, une place de cinéma, Madame? C'est 45 francs, Monsieur.* (How much is the movie ticket? It's 45 francs.)
- *C'est combien, le plat du jour, Monsieur? C'est 125 francs, Monsieur.* (How much is the daily [restaurant] special? It's 125 francs.)

You also will need to use numbers when using the telephone or giving your address. Let's see how these situations differ in English and French.

USE TELEPHONE NUMBERS

Although talking on the telephone is a very advanced skill, you might need to communicate your hotel phone number to someone or get a number from the operator or your hotel clerk in case of an emergency. Since 1996, telephone numbers in France have 10 digits, not 7 as in most U.S. cities. Also, all countries have an international code you must dial when you make a long-distance call across international borders. For France that number is 33; for the USA it is 1. When you call within French borders, you also must dial a city code. The city code for Paris, the center of France, quite naturally is 1.

Next, telephone numbers are written in pairs of numbers separated by a space or period, such as 01.03.45.16.91 or 22 14 56 72 00. When saying the number, you say the digits in pairs, as follows: *zéro un, zéro trois, quarante-cinq, seize, quatre-vingt-onze*. Always use *zéro* (zero) and not the letter *o*, as is often done in English.

PROCEED WITH CAUTION

Certain numbers can cause real confusion on the telephone; for example, all the numbers from 60 to 99. Why? Because you must wait to hear the complete number before you write it down. If, for example, you hear *soixante ...*, you might be tempted to start writing the 6 of 60; however, if you continue to listen, you might hear the rest of the number *-douze,* 71. Be patient, listen to the full number, and then repeat it to the speaker.

You can ask for a telephone number by saying *Le numéro de téléphone de* _____, *s'il vous plaît?* (The telephone number for _____, please?) Always add the *s'il vous plaît* (please); you'll get a much quicker response. Here are some common numbers you might ask for during your first days in France. These are the actual telephone numbers of the services indicated:

- *Le numéro de téléphone de l'hôtel Holiday Inn, s'il vous plaît? C'est le 01.45.84.61.61, Madame.*

- *Le numéro de téléphone de l'Hôpital Croix St Simon, s'il vous plaît? C'est le 01 44 64 16 00, Madame.*

- *Le numéro de téléphone de Air France, s'il vous plaît? C'est le 08 20 82 08 20, Monsieur.*

- *Le numéro de téléphone de l'Ambassade des Etats-Unis d'Amérique, s'il vous plaît? C'est le 08 36 70 14 88, Madame.*

Emergency numbers in France are only two digits, as follows:

- **Police: 17**   (To say "Help!" shout *Au secours!* and stay on the line.)
- **Fire: 18**   (To say "Fire!" shout *Au feu!* and stay on the line.)
- **Ambulance: 15**   (To say "Emergency!" shout *Au secours!* and stay on the line.)
- **Operator: 12**   (Ask if he or she speaks English; operators in major cities often do.)

To reach an international operator within France, call 00.33.12 + your country (1 for the USA).

JUST A MINUTE

You can find the telephone number and address of any business in France using the Internet at www.pagesjaunes.tm.fr. The site is entirely in French but is very intuitive. Just enter the name of the place you are looking for and select RECHERCHER (search).

USE NUMBERS TO GIVE YOUR ADDRESS

In addition to getting or giving a telephone number, you might need to ask for an address of a restaurant or tourist attraction, give an address to a taxi driver, or give someone the address of your hotel. Addresses have a unique format in French. Here is the address of the American Embassy in Paris:

> *Ambassade des Etats-Unis d'Amérique*
> *2, rue St Florentin*
> *75001 Paris*
> *FRANCE*

There are several differences to note. First, the street number usually is separated from the street name by a comma. Next, the postal code precedes the city name; in the preceding example, 75001 is the postal code. Each city has a primary postal number; Paris is 750. The capital city also is divided into *arrondissements* so you can tell from the postal code ending that the United States Embassy is in the (very chic) First Arrondissement (01).

To indicate the preceding address, you say *L'adresse est le deux, rue Saint Florentin*, using the definite article and the cardinal number, 2. If you live at *14, rue Victor Hugo*, you say *J'habite au numéro 14, rue Victor Hugo.*

In the United States there are many words meaning street: road, place, lane, circle, way, boulevard, street, and so forth. Not so in France, where every address falls on one of the following: *boulevard* (*bvd*), *rue* (*r*), *place* (*pl*), or *avenue* (*av*). Examples include *boulevard Saint-Michel, rue Saint-Denis, Place Royale,* and *avenue Victor Hugo*. Of course, there also is the famous *Champs Élysées* where all the expensive shops are located. Named after the Elysian Fields of the Greek gods, *les Champs*, as it is called by Parisians, is in a category by itself.

Now that you've learned the new numbers and how to use them to talk about prices, telephone numbers, and addresses, let's learn some new verbs.

Learn Irregular Present Tense Verbs

All the following verbs are very commonly used in everyday speech. Unless otherwise indicated, each verb has basically the same meaning as its English equivalent. When there is a special use of the verb in French that differs from its equivalent in English, that will be explained and illustrated with an example.

Learn the Verb *Aller*

The verb *aller* not only means "to go," it also is used, with a modifier, to translate many English verbs that indicate that one is going somewhere and how one is going. Generally the verb *aller* is not used, as in English, to state simply that one "is going"; rather, you must indicated either *where* you are going (*je vais à Paris*) or *how* you are going (*je vais en avion*). Here is conjugation of *aller* in the present tense followed by several examples of how it is used.

The Verb *Aller* (To Go)

Person	Singular	Plural
first	*je vais*	*nous allons*
second	*tu vas*	*vous allez*
third, masculine	*il va*	*ils vont*
third, feminine	*elle va*	*elles vont*
third, generic	*on va*	

In the following examples, note the underlined phrases that indicate *how* one is going someplace: by car, on foot, by plane, or by train. Again, the French never use the verb *aller* without indicating where or how they are going; this point is stressed below.

- I am driving to Paris: *Je vais à Paris <u>en voiture.</u>* (Literally, "I am going to Paris by car.")

- I am walking to the hotel: *Je vais <u>à pied</u> à l'hôtel.* (Literally, "I am going by foot to the hotel.")

- I am flying to Paris: *Je vais à Paris <u>en avion.</u>* (Literally, "I am going to Paris by plane.")

- I am going to Nice by train: *Je vais à Nice <u>par le train.</u>* (Just like the English.)

FYI Notice that the preposition *à* (to) contracts with *le* and *les* to form *au* and *aux*. There is no contraction with *à + l'* or *à + la*.

Aller also can be used to form the near future (*le futur proche*), just like in English. If you are going to do something in the very near future, in English you use the verb "to go" followed by an infinitive, as in "I am going to eat" or "I am going to go." In French you can use the same construction: *Je vais manger* (I am going to eat); *Je vais aller* (I am going to go).

Most important, when you use the verb *aller* to mean "to go," you must usually indicate where you are going. For example, in English you might say something like, "I'm tired, so I'm going," meaning you're leaving. In this case, French will always use the verb *partir* (to leave), or the verb *s'en aller* (to go away.) A simple rule for using *aller* is that it must always be followed either by the preposition *à* meaning "to" (*Je vais à Paris*; *Je vais au cinéma*), *en/par* meaning "by" (*Je vais en bus*; *Je vais par train*), or by an infinitive (*Je vais manger*; *Je vais partir*).

LEARN THE VERB *BOIRE*

The verb *boire* may be used in a literal sense, such as "to drink a drink" (*boire une boisson*), or in a figurative sense, such as "to drink in someone's words" (*boire les paroles de quelqu'un*). When used alone, *boire* often has the meaning of "to drink alcohol"; for exammple, *il boit trop* (he drinks too much), *il boit comme un trou* (he drinks like a fish). Here is the present tense of *boire*.

The Verb *Boire* (To Drink)

Person	Singular	Plural
first	*je bois*	*nous buvons*
second	*tu bois*	*vous buvez*
third, masculine	*il boit*	*ils boivent*
third, feminine	*elle boit*	*elles boivent*
third, generic	*on boit*	

"I drink water" is *Je bois de l'eau.* "I am drinking a cup of coffee" is *Je bois un café.* However, the verb *prendre* (to take), presented in Hour 3, "Actions in the Present Tense," is used to mean "to have a drink," as in *Je prends un verre* (I'm drinking a glass [of wine]). The French for "to drink to someone's health" is *boire à la santé de* (someone). The French for "to drink from a bottle" is *boire à même la bouteille.*

LEARN THE VERB *CONNAÎTRE*

Connaître has a circumflex accent on the infinitive and on the third-person singular. Use *connaître* to talk about people, ideas, or things with whom you are familiar (with which you have had personal experience), as in *Je connais Marie* (I know Mary) and *Je connais Paris* (I know Paris).

The Verb *Connaître* (To Know [Someone or Something])

Person	Singular	Plural
first	je connais	nous connaissons
second	tu connais	vous connaissez
third, masculine	il connaît	ils connaissent
third, feminine	elle connaît	elles connaissent
third, generic	on connaît	

Contrast *connaître* with the verb *savoir*, which means "to know how to do something" or "to know a fact," presented in the following section.

LEARN THE VERB *CROIRE*

The verb *croire* has general meaning of "to believe" in all the English senses: "to believe/to think" (*je crois que non*: I think not); "to believe in" (*je crois aux fantômes*: I believe in ghosts): "to believe in God" (*je crois en Dieu*: I believe in God).

The Verb *Croire* (To Believe)

Person	Singular	Plural
first	je crois	nous croyons
second	tu crois	vous croyez
third, masculine	il croit	ils croient
third, feminine	elle croit	elles croient
third, generic	on croit	

Notice that the *i* of *croire* changes to *y* in the first- and second-person plural. "To believe in something" is *croire à;* "to believe in God" is *croire en Dieu*.

LEARN THE VERB *DIRE*

Remember the rule about not pronouncing final consonants. *Dis* and *dit* are pronounced exactly alike. The *t* of *dites* is pronounced because it is followed by the vowel *e*. The single *s* of *disons* and *disent* is pronounced as *z*. The final *-nt* of the plural is, as always, silent.

The Verb *Dire* (To Say, To Tell)

Person	Singular	Plural
first	je dis	nous disons
second	tu dis	vous dites
third, masculine	il dit	ils disent
third, feminine	elle dit	elles disent
third, generic	on dit	

LEARN THE VERB *ÉCRIRE*

From the verb *écrire* comes the noun *une écriture*, "a writing, something written." When you want to express "writing **to**" someone, you must use the preposition *à;* for example, *j'écris **à** ma tante* (I write to my aunt). See the following table.

The Verb *Écrire* (To Write)

Person	Singular	Plural
first	j'écris	nous écrivons
second	tu écris	vous écrivez
third, masculine	il écrit	ils écrivent
third, feminine	elle écrit	elles écrivent
third, generic	on écrit	

"I write a letter" is *j'écris une lettre*. "I write to a person" is *j'écris **à** une personne*. The preposition *à* must be used to indicate "to" when writing to a person.

LEARN THE VERB *FAIRE*

Faire can be used like "to do" in English to indicate something you are doing, as in *je fais un voyage* (I'm making [taking] a trip); *je fais une erreur* (I make a mistake); *je fais ça* (I'm doing that). The following table shows the verb *faire* in the present tense.

The Verb *Faire* (To Make, To Do)

Person	Singular	Plural
first	*je fais*	*nous faisons* (exceptional pronunciation, *feu-zon*)
second	*tu fais*	*vous faites*
third, masculine	*il fait*	*ils font*
third, feminine	*elle fait*	*elles font*
third, generic	*on fait*	

Faire is never used to mean simply "I do" as in these English examples: Do you make errors? Yes, I do (make errors). Do you go to Paris often? Yes, I do (go to Paris often).

In French, you must repeat the entire phrase or simply respond *oui* or *non*, as in *Vous faites une erreur? Oui! Non!*; *Vous allez souvent à Paris? Oui, je vais souvent à Paris.* In short, the verb *faire* is never used without saying what you do or are doing.

FYI The phrases "I do," "he does," "we do," and so forth are the first part of the emphatic mood of the verb. Because French does not have this mood, you must use the entire verb form to indicate that you do or are doing something, as in *Je parle* (I speak, I am speaking, I do speak).

GO TO ▶
Faire also is used in many idioms, particularly when talking about the weather. See Hour 16, "Going Places," to learn about these idioms.

LEARN THE VERB *LIRE*

The verb *lire* may be used literally to mean "to read a book, an article, and so forth" (*Je lis le journal:* I read the newspaper); or, figuratively, as in "to read someone's mind" (*Je lis dans la pensée de mon ami:* I read my friend's mind.)

The Verb *Lire* (To Read)

Person	Singular	Plural
first	je lis	nous lisons
second	tu lis	vous lisez
third, masculine	il lit	ils lisent
third, feminine	elle lit	elles lisent
third, generic	on lit	

LEARN THE VERB *POUVOIR*

Pouvoir often is used with an infinitive to indicate that one can (is physically able to) or may (has permission to) do something. The English distinction between "may I?" and "can I?" does not exist in French, as illustrated here: *Je peux parler français* (I can speak French); *Tu peux lire maintenant* (You may read now).

The Verb *Pouvoir* (To Be Able To, Can)

Person	Singular	Plural
first	je peux	nous pouvons
second	tu peux	vous pouvez
third, masculine	il peut	ils peuvent
third, feminine	elle peut	elles peuvent
third, generic	on peut	

Pouvoir is not used with verbs of sensing such as *entendre* (to listen) or *voir* (to see), unless you mean to communicate that you are physically capable of hearing (you're not deaf) or seeing (you're not blind). The English phrases "I can hear the music" or "I can see the film" are expressed in French by using the verbs for "to hear" (*entendre*) and "to see" (*voir*), as in *j'entends la musique* (I hear [can hear] the music); *je vois le film* (I see [can see] the film).

LEARN THE VERB *SAVOIR*

Contrast *savoir* with the verb *connaître* presented earlier in the hour. *Savoir* means to know how to do something and to know a fact, as in *Je sais parler français* (I know how to speak French); *Il sait lire* (He knows how to read); *Elle sait le numéro* (She knows the number). The following table gives the verb *savoir* in the present tense.

The Verb *Savoir* (To Know How to; To Know a Fact)

Person	Singular	Plural
first	je sais	nous savons
second	tu sais	vous savez
third, masculine	il sait	ils savent
third, feminine	elle sait	elles savent
third, generic	on sait	

LEARN THE VERB *VIVRE*

The verb *vivre* can be used to express the idea of living someplace, as in *Je vis à Paris* (I live in Paris). From this verb comes the noun *la vie* (life). The following table presents the verb *vivre* in the present tense.

The Verb *Vivre* (To Live)

Person	Singular	Plural
first	je vis	nous vivons
second	tu vis	vous vivez
third, masculine	il vit	ils vivent
third, feminine	elle vit	elles vivent
third, generic	on vit	

LEARN THE VERB *VOIR*

Voir means "to see," both literally and figuratively, as in *Je vois le garçon* (I see the boy) or *Ah, je vois* (Oh, I see/I understand). From this verb come several nouns: *la vue* (sight), *la vision* (vision); and, of course, the phrase *déjà vu* (something previously seen or experienced in the past). In the following table, note that *i* changes to *y* in the first- and second-person plural.

The Verb *Voir* (To See/To Understand)

Person	Singular	Plural
first	je vois	nous voyons
second	tu vois	vous voyez
third, masculine	il voit	ils voient
third, feminine	elle voit	elles voient
third, generic	on voit	

LEARN THE VERB *VOULOIR*

You can use *vouloir* followed by an infinitive to say that you want to do something, as in *Je veux lire* (I want to read); *Je veux manger* (I want to eat). The polite form for "I would like (something)" is *je voudrais* + thing; for example, *je voudrais du pain* (I would like some bread); *je voudrais un coca*; and so forth. The following table shows the verb *vouloir* in the present tense.

The Verb *Vouloir* (To Want)

Person	Singular	Plural
first	je veux	nous voulons
second	tu veux	vous voulez
third, masculine	il veut	ils veulent
third, feminine	elle veut	elles veulent
third, generic	on veut	

To express the English construction "I want you to (do something)" involves using special constructions and verb forms (the subjunctive). For now, avoid using *vouloir* except as indicated in the preceding.

LEARN SOME IRREGULAR *-IR* VERBS

In Hour 3, "Actions in the Present Tense," you learned to conjugate regular *-ir* verbs. Now you will learn one subgroup of *-ir* verbs that are irregular but all follow a similar pattern. Note in the following table that the *-ir* verbs use the ending of regular *-re* verbs (s, s, [nothing], ons, ez, ent).

PROCEED WITH CAUTION

Partir means "to leave from a place" and requires the preposition *de*, as in *Je pars de Paris demain*. "To leave something behind" is *laisser*, as in *Je laisse le journal à ma place*. "To leave a place" is *quitter*, with no preposition, as in *Je quitte Paris demain*.

Irregular *-ir* Verbs

dormir (to sleep)	partir (to leave)	sortir (to go out)
je dors	je pars	je sors
tu dors	tu pars	tu sors
il dort	il part	il sort
elle dort	elle part	elle sort

dormir *(to sleep)*	partir *(to leave)*	sortir *(to go out)*
on dort	*on part*	*on sort*
nous dormons	*nous partons*	*nous sortons*
vous dormez	*vous partez*	*vous sortez*
ils dorment	*ils partent*	*ils sortent*
elles dorment	*elles partent*	*elles sortent*

The irregular pattern for these verbs centers on the stem. The stem for the singular is the infinitive minus the final consonant plus -*ir*; thus *par*. The stem for the plural is regular, drop the -*ir* from the infinitive; thus *part*. The endings for this sub-group of verbs are *s*, *s*, *t*, *ons*, *ez*, and *ent*. Other common verbs conjugated the same way are *mentir* (to tell a lie), *sentir* (to feel, to smell), and *servir* (to serve).

HOUR'S UP!

Congratulations! You've successfully completed all of Part 1, "The Basics." You know how to conjugate most French verbs, regular and irregular, in the present tense, and you know how to count and use adjectives and pronouns correctly. In Part 2, "The Present and the Future," you'll learn how to form the future tenses, and you'll learn more ways to describe the world around you. But before you enter the next part, test your mastery of the current material with this quiz.

1. True or False: 80 in France is *octante*.

2. True or False: French phone numbers have seven digits.

3. True or False: Paris is divided into *arrondissements*.

4. *C'est combien?* means:
    a. How old are you?
    b. What time is it?
    c. How much is it?
    d. How are you?

5. To form the near future, you use:
    a. *aller* + infinitive
    b. *savoir* + infinitive
    c. *avoir* + infinitive
    d. *être* + infinitive

QUIZ

6. Complete this sentence logically: *Le matin, je _____ le journal.*

    a. *écris*

    b. *lis*

    c. *lit*

    d. *peux*

7. Complete this sentence logically: *Je _____ au numéro 14, boulevard Foche.*

    a. *vois*

    b. *veux*

    c. *peux*

    d. *vis*

8. Complete this sentence logically: *Je _____ parler français.*

    a. *peux*

    b. *va*

    c. *fais*

    d. *peut*

9. Which verb does not make sense in the following sentence: *Il _____ lire les romans.*

    a. *aime*

    b. *dit*

    c. *peut*

    d. *veut*

10. Which of the following verb forms is not pronounced like the other three?

    a. *parle*

    b. *parle*

    c. *parlez*

    d. *parlent*

PART II

The Present and the Future

HOUR 5

Express Yourself in the Present Indicative

CHAPTER SUMMARY

LESSON PLAN:

In this hour you will learn ...

- How to say the days, months, and seasons.
- How to greet someone.
- How to use *il y a*.
- How to create basic sentences.
- How to ask simple questions.
- How to say no.
- How to give a command.

In this hour you'll work on creating basic sentences and asking questions which require more than a yes or no answer, as well as learn how to say no and tell someone what you want him to do. The hour begins with learning the days of the week and months of the year, how to greet someone for the first time and how to say good-bye; you'll also learn the idiom, *il y a* (approximately: "there is, there are").

LEARN TO SPEAK OF DATES

France uses the same Gregorian calendar used in most of the world: seven days, twelve months, and four seasons. In addition to being accepted today as the international standard for civil use, the Gregorian calendar regulates the ceremonial cycles of the Roman Catholic and Protestant churches. France is 98 percent Roman Catholic. However, as you will see, France's use of the calendar is slightly different from that of the United States.

LEARN THE DAYS OF THE WEEK

The days of the week are all masculine. French calendars present the week starting on Monday and ending with Sunday, rather than starting with Sunday as is typical of calendars in the United States.

There are two words for "day": *le jour* and *la journée*. *Jour* is used in a general sense for "day" and is preceded by a number: 2 *jours*, 3 *jours*, and so forth. *Journée* means "all day (long)" and is rarely preceded by a number, as in *pendant la journée* (during the day); *une bonne journée* (a good day [all day long]).

There are similar words for "all morning long" (*la matinée*) and "all evening long" (*la soirée*). Notice also that *une journée* means "a day"; to say "one day," use *jour*, as in *un jour*. *Une matinée*, as in English, also means "an afternoon theatre performance."

 Often the adjective *toute* is used with these words: *toute la journée, toute la matinée, toute la soirée* (all day/morning/evening long).

The word for "week" is *la semaine*. To do something "during the week" is to do it *en semaine*. The following are the days of the week:

- *lundi*   Monday
- *mardi*   Tuesday
- *mercredi*   Wednesday
- *jeudi*   Thursday
- *vendredi*   Friday
- *samedi*   Saturday
- *dimanche*   Sunday

Note that the days of the week (*les jours de la semaine*) are not capitalized in French. "On Monday," "on Tuesday," and so forth is *lundi* or *mardi*, with no article or preposition, as in *Je travaille lundi*, "I work on Monday." To say "on Mondays," "on Tuesdays," and so forth, use the definite article, as in *Je travaille le lundi et le mardi* (I work on Mondays and Tuesdays). *Samedi* and *dimanche* form *le week-end* or *la fin de la semaine*.

Because *lundi* conventionally is the first day of the week, French counts one week as 8 days and two weeks have 15 days, similar to the British fortnight. For example, *en huit jours* (in a week) counts Monday to Monday; there are eight days. *En quinze jours* is "in two weeks."

 The concept of a weekend (not working on Saturday afternoon or Sunday) was borrowed from the British. *Faire la semaine anglaise* (to do an English week) still has this meaning. French elementary and high school students typically have no classes on Wednesday afternoons, but go to school Saturday mornings.

Other words referring to the days are …

- **Today**   *Aujourd'hui. Aujourd'hui en huit* (a week from today); *le journal d'aujourd'hui* (today's paper).

- **Yesterday**   *Hier. Le journal d'hier* (yesterday's paper).

- **Morning**   *Le matin. Le matin* (in the morning); *la matinée* (all morning long).

- **Tomorrow**   *Demain. Demain (au) matin* (tomorrow morning); *hier (au) matin* (yesterday morning).

- **Afternoon**   *L'après-midi. L'après-midi* (in the afternoon); *tout l'après-midi* (all afteroon).

- **Evening**   *Le soir. Le soir* (in the evening); *hier (au) soir* (yesterday evening); *demain (au) soir* (tomorrow evening); *lundi soir* (Monday evening); *la soirée* (all evening [long]); *les longues soirées d'hiver* (the long days of winter); *Bonne soirée!* (Have a good evening!)

- **The next day**   *Le lendemain. Le lendemain matin* (the next morning).

- **The day before yesterday**   *Avant-hier. La nuit d'avant hier* (the night before last).

- **The day after tomorrow**   *Le jour après demain. Après-demain* (the day after tomorrow); *Je pars après demain.* (I'm leaving the day after tomorrow.)

Notice in the preceding examples that "in the morning," "in the afternoon," and "in the evening" are expressed without using a preposition, as in *Le matin, je bois du café* (In the morning, I drink coffee); *Je lis le journal d'aujourd'hui le soir* (I read today's paper in the evening). The only exception is *dans la matinée* (in [the course of the entire] morning). *Une soirée* also is used as a noun meaning "a party," usually in the evening.

GO TO ▶
You will learn how to use the days of the week to talk about dates and events in Hour 16, "Going Places."

LEARN THE MONTHS

In French, the months have the same roots as their English equivalents; however, be careful of their pronunciation as indicated in the following list:

- *janvier*   January
- *février*   February
- *mars* (pronounced *marse*)   March
- *avril*   April

- *mai* May
- *juin* June
- *juillet* July
- *août* (pronounced *oot*)   August
- *septembre* September
- *octobre* October
- *novembre* November
- *décembre* December

Note that the months of the year are not capitalized. "In the month of" is *au mois de*, as in *au mois de juin* (in the month of June); *au mois d'août* (in the month of August).

There are two words for year: *un an* and *une année*. An and *année* are used like *jour/journée* to indicate one year or the whole year. You have already learned the word *an* in talking about age, as in *J'ai trois ans*. Saying your age will help you remember to use *an* with numbers; but use *année* to refer to the whole year (long), as in *Il neige toute l'année en Suède*. (It snows all year [long] in Sweden).

LEARN THE SEASONS

There are four wonderful seasons in France, listed in the following. Notice that, because each begins with a vowel sound, the preposition *en* is used with *été*, *automne*, and *hiver* to mean "in"; with *printemps*, use *au*:

- *Le printemps*   Spring. *Au printemps* (in the spring).
- *L'été*   Summer. *En été* (in the summer).
- *L'automne*   Autumn. *En automne* (in the autumn).
- *L'hiver*   Winter. *En hiver* (in the winter).

Once you know the days, months, and seasons, you can begin to greet new French friends appropriately. In the following section, you'll learn the most common French greetings and farewells.

LEARN ABOUT GREETINGS AND FAREWELLS

The greetings (Hello! Hi!) and farewells (Good day! So long!) we use when meeting or leaving people are highly conventional. Often they really don't mean anything; rather, they simply indicate that we recognize or don't recognize someone. Think about the English "hello," for example. What does it really mean? Most people don't know and don't need to know. We simply use the word automatically when we encounter someone. Remember this as you learn to say "hello" and "good-bye" in French. Don't translate the greetings; simply learn when to use them.

Also, note that the French are very polite people when first greeting someone. When saying "hello" or "good-bye" to someone you don't know extremely well, you should always append the word *Monsieur* or *Madame* to the greeting or the farewell. These words don't mean "sir" or "madam" in this context, but are used simply as a matter of politeness.

The following are some common forms of greeting:

- *Bonjour, Monsieur/Madame.* Hello. (Typical greeting that can be used all day, from morning until night.)
- *Salut, Paul.* (pronounced *sa-loo*) Hi, Paul. (Familiar greeting.)
- *Bonsoir, Monsieur/Madame.* Good evening. (Used after dark.)

PROCEED WITH CAUTION

The word *âllo* exists in French but is used only when answering the telephone, as in *Âllo, c'est Paul* (Hello, this is Paul [on the line]).

The following are some common farewells:

- *Au revoir, Madame/Monsieur.* Good-bye, good day. (Used at any time of the day or night.)
- *Salut, Paul.* Bye, Paul. (Familiar.)
- *À tout à l'heure, Marie.* See you later, Mary.
- *Ciao, Pierre!* Later, Peter! (An Italian greeting much used by young French.)
- *À bientôt, Suzanne.* See you later, Susan.
- *À demain, Claude.* See you tomorrow, Claude.
- *À la prochaine, Pierre.* See you soon, Peter. (Literally "until our next meeting.")
- *Adieu, mon ami.* So long, my friend. (Usually used only when you don't think you'll see the person again.)
- *Bisous, Maman!* Kisses, Mom! (Very familiar!)

When you greet or say farewell to someone in France, you also typically shake hands. One firm grip and a single, quick shake (not the pumping action of the U.S. kind) will suffice. Typically, rules of politeness require that you extend this courtesy to everyone you are addressing. If, for example, you leave a dinner party with a dozen friends, you quickly shake hands and say *Au revoir* to all 12.

If you know all the persons well, or if you are (more or less) under the age of 25, you also might *faire la bise,* or give a quick cheek-to-cheek kiss to everyone, male and female, as you leave. As a foreigner among a group of native French, you might well be included in this tradition even if you don't know the persons well. It's a charming custom—smile and enjoy it.

PROCEED WITH CAUTION

To kiss someone casually is *donner une bise à* someone, a peck on the cheek as it were. To kiss someone romantically is *embrasser* someone; literally "to embrace someone." The noun for "a kiss" is *un baiser.* Do not use this word as a verb; it has a very vulgar meaning.

The custom of giving a *bise* dates back centuries and is an important moment in parting company with friends and family members. How many times you offer the *bise* (on one cheek, both cheeks, or back and forth three or four times) depends on how well you know someone and where you are in France. The Parisian *bise* typically is done three times (proceed cautiously so as not to knock heads).

LEARN *IL Y A*

In Hour 2, "Describing Things," you encountered the expression *voilà,* the same word used by magicians as they complete a trick and something not seen before suddenly appears. *Voilà* means "there is" or "there are" in the sense of "Look! There's (something)!": *Voilà l'avion* "Look! There's the plane!" It has either a singular or plural meaning depending on whether the noun that follows is singular or plural, as in *Voilà un homme* (There is a man); *Voilà des hommes* (There are some men). *Voici* means "here is/here are" and is used the same way but to indicate something very close to you.

However, if you want to say "there is" in the sense of "There is a fly in my soup" (and not "Look! A fly just appeared in my soup!" *Voilà! Une mouche dans ma soupe!*), you use the idiom *il y a* (pronounced *ee-lee-ah*).

Because this is an idiom, you won't find it listed alphabetically in your dictionary; it's a combination of the words *il* (it), the pronoun *y* (there), and the verb form *a* (third-person singular of *avoir*). A few examples will show you how *il y a* is used and how it differs from *voilà/voici*:

- *Il y a trois personnes dans le taxi.* (There are three people in the taxi.) *Voilà le taxi!* (Look! There's the taxi!)

- *Il y a une mouche dans ma soupe.* (There's a fly in my soup.) *Voilà la mouche!* (Look! There's the fly!)

- *Il y a un film à trois heures.* (There's a movie at 3 o'clock.) *Voici un bon film!* (Look! Here's a good film!)

- *Il y a un bon programme à la télévision mardi soir.* (There's a good program on television Tuesday night.) *Voilà! Un bon programme à la télévision!* (Look! A good program on television!)

In addition to meaning there is/there are, *il y a* is used with *heure*, *jour*, *mois*, and *an* to mean "ago":

- ***il y a une heure***   an hour ago
- ***il y a six heures***   six hours ago
- ***il y a un jour***   a day ago
- ***il y a un mois***   a month ago
- ***il y a un an***   a year ago
- ***il y a deux jours***   two days ago
- ***il y a cinq ans***   five years ago

FYI   "A long time ago" is *il y a longtemps;* however, "a little while ago" is *tout à l'heure.*

Now let's move on to creating basic sentences in French.

CREATE A BASIC SENTENCE

Before you continue, let's pause to review what a sentence is. The most basic sentence is composed of at least a verb, such as Listen! Stop! and Look! But even in these examples, which are commands, there is an understood subject—you: (You) listen! (You) stop! (You) look!

Therefore, to have a complete sentence, you must use at least one verb. In addition, a sentence will have a subject (which you've already learned) and might have an object. Whereas the subject is the person or thing that performs the action of the verb, the object of the verb is the person or thing that receives the action. For example, in the following sentence, *Jean* is the subject of the verb; *lit* is the verb; *journal* is the object of the verb: *Jean lit le journal. Voilà! Une phrase compléte!* (Look! A complete sentence!)

LEARN THE STRUCTURE OF A FRENCH SENTENCE

French sentence structure often is very similar to English. I stress this somewhat obvious point because it is not true for all Romance languages; notably Spanish, which does not use a subject pronoun in all sentences. However, in French you will always have a subject (implied in commands), a verb, and perhaps an object. When a sentence simply makes a statement, it is called a declarative sentence; you are declaring something to be true or false. The structure of a declarative sentence is generally subject, verb, noun object (or adjective/adverb/prepositional phrase).

GO TO ▶
In Hour 14, "Free Time," you will learn how to use pronouns as the objects of verbs.

In the following section you are given three words to use in a sentence. Use a file card to cover the answers that follow, and see if you can compose the sentence from the words given.

Create a French sentence using these words:

1. *je regarder la télévision*

   I watch TV.

   Je regarde la télévision.

2. *nous avoir un ticket*

   We have a ticket.

   Nous avons un ticket.

3. *ils être beau* (*beau* agrees with *ils*)

   They are handsome.

   Ils sont beaux.

4. *elle choisir la robe*

   She chooses the dress.

   Elle choisit la robe.

5. *vous aller à Paris*

   You are going to Paris.

   Vous allez à Paris. (aller + à + place)

6. *on manger la viande*

    We/they eat meat.

    On mange la viande.

7. *Jean voir Suzanne*

    John sees Susan.

    Jean voit Suzanne.

JUST A MINUTE

Did you remember to make the adjective *beau* agree with *ils?* Adjectives always agree with the noun or pronoun they modify, no matter where the adjective is placed in the sentence.

Well done! Now you know how to construct a sentence in French. Now that you understand the difference between the subject of the verb and the object of the verb, let's take a look at when and where objects can be used with verbs in French.

USE TRANSITIVE AND INTRANSITIVE VERBS

Like English, French has verbs that can take an object (called transitive verbs) and verbs that cannot take an object (called intransitive verbs). Some verbs have an object when they mean one thing, and don't have an object when they mean something else. Confusing? Well, yes—perhaps at first—but let's see if we can make the difference clear by using some images and examples.

First, let's consider an image to help you remember the distinction between transitive and intransitive. Think of the word "train" and taking a trip. If you "take a train," you're *transitive*; that is, you're mobile and you can take yourself and your baggage along with you. However, if you don't get on the train, you can't take yourself anywhere; you're *intransitive*.

    On the train = take an object = transitive

    Off the train = can't take an object = intransitive

Now let's look at a couple of examples. In English, we can use the verb "to leave" with or without an object:

1. I am leaving.

2. They are leaving Paris.

3. She leaves the book on the table.

4. Elvis is leaving the stadium.

In sentence 1, "to leave" is used intransitively because it has no object. "I am leaving" is a perfectly good and complete English sentence. In sentences 2, 3, and 4 "to leave" is used transitively because in each case there is an object: Paris, book, stadium.

The verb "to leave" can be used transitively or intransitively depending on its meaning. However, English (like French) has certain verbs that can be only one or the other. For example, "to lie (down)" and "to lay (down)" are famous for confusing even native English speakers. The former is intransitive: I lie down to sleep. The latter is transitive: I lay down my head to sleep.

The following are other examples of intransitive verbs:

- to fall (You can fell a tree but you can't fall something.)
- to go (You can't go something.)
- to die (You can kill something but you can't die something.)

Verbs such as "to walk" can be both: I walk in the rain (intransitive); I walk the dog (transitive). Again, if you can attach an object to the verb, it is transitive; if you can't, it's intransitive.

FYI A good dictionary will indicate, with appropriate abbreviations, if a verb is transitive (v.t.) or intransitive (v.i.).

Because most English verbs can be used transitively or intransitively, native speakers are hardly ever concerned by the distinction. Not true in French! Being able to make the distinction between transitive and intransitive verbs is essential to choosing the right verb to use in French.

To illustrate this point, let's return to the preceding examples and look at the French translations:

1. I am leaving. (*Je pars.*)

2. They are leaving Paris. (*Je quitte Paris.*)

3. She leaves the book on the table. (*Elle laisse le livre sur la table.*)

4. Elvis is leaving the stadium. (*Elvis sort du stade.*)

Immediately you see that French has four different verbs meaning "to leave":

- *partir de*   to leave from (v.i.)
- *quitter*   to leave a place (v.t.)

- *laisser* to leave something (behind) (v.t.)
- *sortir de* to go out of (v.i.)

Partir also can be used to express leaving a place, using the preposition *de* (from): *Je pars de Paris* (I am leaving Paris). In contrast, *sortir de* most often is used to indicate leaving from an interior place such as a room, a car, or a plane:

- *Il sort de la chambre.* (He's leaving the room.)
- *Je sors de la voiture.* (I'm getting out of the car.)
- *Elles sortent de l'avion.* (They are leaving the plane.)

Sortir also means "to go out on a date," as in *Jean sort avec Marie tous les soirs* (John is going out with Mary every night). Fortunately, the list of verbs most often used intransitively is limited to about 15. Here are the principle ones:

Intransitive Verbs

French	English
aller	to go
arriver	to arrive
descendre	to go down
entrer dans	to enter
monter	to go up
mourir	to die
naître	to be born
partir de	to leave from
passer par	to pass by
rester	to stay
retourner à	to return to
sortir de	to go out of
tomber	to fall
venir	to come

The following verbs from this list also can be used transitively but can change meaning:

French	English
descendre	to take something down
monter	to put something up
sortir	to take something out of

For example:

French	English
Je descends la valise.	I take down the suitcase.
Je monte les skis.	I put up the skis.
Il sort le passeport de la valise.	He takes the passport out of the suitcase.

Try to learn these verbs now—you will encounter them again when you learn to form the past tense in Hour 9, "Express Yourself in the Past." Also be sure to learn the prepositions given with certain verbs as if they are part of the verb itself.

LEARN TO ASK QUESTIONS AND GIVE ANSWERS

Answering a question often is easier than asking one, especially when the answer is yes or no (*oui* or *non* in French). Nevertheless, because you already know how to compose a simple sentence (subject, verb, object), you can quite easily change that sentence into a question.

USE *Est-ce que* ... TO ASK A QUESTION

One common way to ask a yes or no question is to place the question phrase *Est-ce que* in front of the sentence. Literally, *Est-ce que* means "Is it that ...?" The phrase functions very similarly to the English words "do" or "does." Compare the following examples:

English	French
You speak French.	*Vous parlez français.*
Do you speak French?	*Est-ce que vous parlez français?*
He eats snails.	*Il mange des escargots.*
Does he eat snails?	*Est-ce qu'il mange des escargots?*

STRICTLY DEFINED

Even where English inverts the subject and verb, French might use e*st-ce que,* as in *Nous allons à la tour Eiffel. Est-ce que nous allons à la tour Eiffel?* (We are going to the Eiffel Tower. Are we going to the Eiffel Tower?)

Without looking at the answers on the right, try making the following statements into questions using *est-ce que*:

Statement	Question
Tu parles français.	*Est-ce que tu parles français?*
Vous parlez anglais.	*Est-ce que vous parlez anglais?*
Il va à Nice.	*Est-ce qu'il va à Nice?*
Elles écrivent une lettre.	*Est-ce qu'elles écrivent une lettre?*

INVERT SUBJECT AND VERB TO ASK A QUESTION

As in English, you can form a question by inverting the subject and verb. However, there are several details to watch for. First, one rarely uses inversion in the first person, except in poetic language. Second, the third-person singular adds *-t-* between the subject and verb if the verb doesn't already end in *t* or *d*. Third, a hyphen connects the verb and subject.

FYI Because there already is a final *t* on all forms of the third person plural (*ils* and *elles* forms), the singular and plural questions of most -er verbs in French sound exactly alike, as in *Parle-t-il?/Parlent-ils?; Mange-t-elle?/Mangent-elles?* You must rely on context to determine whether the sentence is singular or plural in spoken French.

Study the following table to see how inversion works:

Inversion of Subject and Verb to Form a Question

Est-ce que + je	Est-ce que + je	Est-ce que + je
As-tu un livre?	*Es-tu beau?*	*Parles-tu français?*
A-t-il un livre?	*Est-il beau?*	*Parle-t-il français?*
A-t-elle un livre?	*Est-elle belle?*	*Parle-t-elle français?*
A-t-on un livre?	*Est-on beau?*	*Parle-t-on français?*
Avons-nous un livre?	*Sommes-nous beaux?*	*Parlons-nous français?*

continues

Inversion of Subject and Verb to Form a Question   (continued)

Est-ce que + je	Est-ce que + je	Est-ce que + je
Avez-vous un livre?	*Êtes-vous beau?*	*Parlez-vous français?*
Ont-ils un livre?	*Sont-ils beaux?*	*Parlent-ils français?*
Ont-elles un livre?	*Sont-elles belles?*	*Parlent-elles français?*

USE INTONATION TO ASK A QUESTION

You have already learned how to use intonation to ask a question by raising the tone of your voice at the end of the sentence. Practice that method again using the following examples:

- *Tu as un livre?*
- *Elle est belle?*
- *Vous parlez anglais?*

LEARN QUESTION WORDS: *COMMENT? QUOI? PARDON?*

Sometimes, when you don't understand a question the first time it is asked, you must ask the person to repeat it. Here are several ways to do that:

Comment?	What? (familiar language)
Répétez, s'il vous plaît.	Please repeat that. (very polite)
Pardon?	Pardon? (very polite)
Quoi?	Huh? What? (impolite, but used)

LEARN TO SAY NO USING *NE ... PAS*

You also might need to tell someone that you don't do something! There are many ways to do this in French, so we will delay a full explanation of the use of negations until Hour 8, "Learn to Express Yourself in the Future." For now, you will learn the simplest way to make a sentence negative by using ne before the verb and pas after the verb.

The primary English negation requires two words, "do/does" and "not," as in I sing/I do not sing; He goes to Paris/He does not go to Paris; She has time/ She does not have time. However, not all English negations require two words; for example, "He never sings," "He never goes to Paris," and "She has no time." On the other hand, the French negation always uses two words: *ne* paired with a second word that changes depending on the meaning of the negation.

Notice where the two negative words appear in the following sentences and that *ne* becomes *n'* before a vowel:

GO TO ▶
A full explanation of the formation and use of negations appears in Hour 8.

Il chante la chanson.	*Il ne chante pas la chanson.*
Il regarde la photo.	*Il ne regarde pas la photo.*
J'écoute!	*Je n'écoute pas!*
Nous allons au cinéma.	*Nous n'allons pas au cinéma.*
Vous parlez anglais?	*Vous ne parlez pas anglais?*

As you see, the rule for forming a simple negation is using *ne* in front of the verb; *pas* after the verb. To make an infinitive negative, place *ne pas* in front of it, as follows:

Je demande à Jean de ne pas parler. (I ask John not to talk.)

Elle continue à ne pas vouloir sortir avec moi. (She continues not to want to go out with me.)

There are many other negations in French; equivalents of "never," "neither/nor," and "so forth." However, the formation of more complex negations also involves important changes in other parts of the sentence. For the moment, use the preceding examples to guide you in practicing the use of *ne … pas* followed by the definite article (*le, la, les*) and a noun.

LEARN TO FORM COMMANDS

Learning to use commands in spoken French is quite easy. Just omit the subject pronoun of the *tu, nous,* and *vous* forms of the verb as follows:

Forming Commands: The Imperative Mood

Positive	Negative	English
Parle!	*Ne parle pas!*	Speak! Don't Speak!(familiar form)
Parlons!	*Ne parlons pas!*	Let's speak! Let's not speak!
Parlez!	*Ne parlez pas!*	Speak! Don't speak!(formal form and plural)
Finis!	*Ne finis pas!*	Finish! Don't finish!
Finissons!	*Ne finissons pas!*	Let's finish! Let's not finish!

continues

Forming Commands: The Imperative Mood   (continued)

Positive	Negative	English
Finissez!	Ne finissez pas!	Finish! Let's not finish!
Vends!	Ne vends pas!	Sell! Don't sell!
Vendons!	Ne vendons pas!	Let's sell! Let's not sell!
Vendez!	Ne vendez pas!	Sell! Don't sell!

PROCEED WITH CAUTION

The s is dropped on the tu form of a command for all -er verbs. The –ir and -re commands keep the s. Also, the s is retained on the -er commands when followed by a pronoun beginning with a vowel.

Four verbs have special forms of the imperative. You must learn these individually.

Special Forms of the Imperative

avoir	être	savoir	vouloir
Aie!	Sois!	Sache!	Veuille!
Ayons!	Soyons!	Sachons!	Veuillons!
Ayez!	Soyez!	Sachez!	Veuillez!

The imperative of *avoir* is rarely used, but the imperative of *être* is quite common, as in *Sois honnête!* (Be honest!); *Soyons francs!* (Let's be frank!); *Soyez courageux!* (Be brave!)

The Imperative of *vouloir* followed by an infinitive can be used to mean "please," as in these examples:

Veuillez ne pas fumer.	Please don't smoke.
Veuillez ne pas faire de bruit.	Please don't make noise.
Veuillez partir.	Please leave.

In the preceding situations you also could use the imperative of the infinitive and add *s'il vous plaît*:

Ne fumez pas, s'il vous plaît.	Don't smoke, please.
Ne faites pas de bruit, s'il vous plaît.	Don't make noise, please.
Partez, s'il vous plaît.	Leave, please.

HOUR'S UP!

You've come to the end of another hour and mastered much new material. You can now recite the days, months, and seasons, use greetings and fare-wells properly, and form basic sentences and commands. Remember to go back to earlier hours and review the verb forms so you won't forget them. Now review the material from this hour and test your knowledge with the following quiz.

1. Le jour <u>après</u> vendredi, c'est …

   a. mardi

   b. dimanche

   c. lundi

   d. samedi

2. Le jour <u>avant</u> jeudi, c'est …

   a. mardi

   b. mercredi

   c. samedi

   d. lundi

3. Yesterday, today, and tomorrow:

   a. hier, aujourd'hui, demain

   b. demain, le soir, aujourd'hui

   c. hier, demain, aujourd'hui

   d. le matin, le jour, le soir

4. Le mois <u>avant</u> août, c'est …

   a. avril

   b. juin

   c. mai

   d. juin

5. When meeting someone, you might say all but which one of the fol-lowing?

   a. Bonjour!

   b. À demain!

   c. Salut!

   d. Bonsoir!

6. To say "It's 6 o'clock," you would use:

    a. *Voilà 6 heures.*

    b. *Il y a 6 heures.*

    c. *Il est 6 heures.*

    d. *Elle a 6 heures.*

7. Which of the following verbs is not transitive?

    a. *parler*

    b. *marcher*

    c. *chanter*

    d. *tomber*

8. Which of the following verbs is transitive?

    a. *aller*

    b. *mourir*

    c. *quitter*

    d. *venir*

9. Which of the following is a correct negative sentence?

    a. *Il n'écoute pas.*

    b. *Il écoute pas.*

    c. *Il n'écoute.*

    d. *Il ne pas écoute.*

10. Which of the following is not a command form?

    a. *Écoute*

    b. *Écoutent*

    c. *Écoutez*

    d. *Écoutons*

QUIZ

HOUR 6

Express Yourself in the Present Subjunctive

CHAPTER SUMMARY

LESSON PLAN:
In this hour you will learn …

- How to use collective numbers and fractions.
- How to conjugate the verbs *venir* and *tenir.*
- How to use the verb *falloir.*
- How to form the present subjunctive of first-, second-, and third-group verbs.
- How to form the present subjunctive of irregular verbs.
- How to use the subjunctive mood.
- How to conjugate the verbs *couvrir, offrir,* and *ouvrir.*

In this hour, you learn how to express feelings, doubt, and suppositions using the present subjunctive mood. The subjunctive mood, as the name implies, is used to communicate a subjective view of the world, as you, the speaker, perceive it. This mood exists in English but is rarely used; therefore, it will require particular attention on your part to master it. Luckily the forms of the present subjunctive in French often resemble the present indicative; however, there are a number of common irregular verbs whose forms you must memorize. Don't worry, though, you're given some pointers about how to do this in the course of the hour.

MASTER COLLECTIVE NUMBERS AND FRACTIONS

By now you will not be surprised to learn that French has three words for the English word "number." You're not surprised because you just learned in Hour 5, "Express Yourself in the Present Indicative," that there are four words for "to leave" and two words each for "day," "morning," "evening," and "year." Here are three words for "number" and explanations of how they are used:

- *un nombre* A general word used when talking about numbers, such as *les nombres cardinaux* (cardinal numbers: one, two, three, and so forth), *les nombres ordinaux* (ordinal numbers: first, second, … fifth, sixth, and so forth).

- *un numéro*   Used when you are speaking about a collection of numbers such as a telephone number or an address, or a serial number (such as your Social Security number).

- *un chiffre*   Used to designate the figure, number, numeral, or digit(s) that compose *un nombre* or *un numéro*.

FYI In Hours 1, "Saying It Right," 2, "Describing Things," and 4, "Actions in the Present Tense with Irregular Verbs," you learned all the numbers between 0 and 1,000. You should quickly review those numbers as you learn about collective numbers and fractions.

The following table shows some common uses of each word.

Using *Nombre, Numéro,* and *Chiffre*

Nombre	Number
le nombre atomique	atomic number
un (bon) nombre de livres	a (good) number of books
Le Livre des Nombres	The Book of Numbers (Bible)
On est en nombre	We have a quorum
Ils sont au nombre de huit	They are eight in number
les nombres entiers	whole numbers, integral numbers
Numéro	*Number*
J'habite au numéro 15.	I live at number 15 (street number)
la chambre numéro 30	room (number) 30 (hotel room)
priorité numéro 1	first priority
L'Express, numéro 20	L'Express (magazine), issue number 20
Mon numéro de téléphone	my telephone number
un numéro de compte courant	a bank account number
Chiffre	*Figure, Number, Numeral, Digit*
Le nombre 345 a trois chiffres: 3, 4, 5	The number 345 has three digits: 3, 4, 5
les chiffres arabes	Arabic numbers
un nombre de six chiffres	a six-figure number
le chiffre d'affaires	turnover (business term)
un chiffre sur Internet	a (secret) Internet code
un message chiffré	a (secret) coded message

LEARN THE COLLECTIVE NUMBERS

Collective numbers are called *les nombres colletifs*. In the list in this section, those that end in *-aine* usually mean approximately that number; for example, *Il y a une vingtaine de livres sur la table*. (There are about 20 books on the table.) However, when used in commercial situations, such as at the bakery, it means exactly a dozen.

GO TO ▶
"Invariable" means a word does not change form. See Hour 7, "Describe Your Surroundings," for further discussion of this concept.

All these collective numbers are considered to be expressions of quantity and therefore are always followed by the invariable word *de*, meaning "of." Watch out—you can't invent new collective numbers. Only the numbers indicated in the following table are used (and they are used often):

Collective Numbers

Number	Collective Number
8	*une huitaine*
10	*une dizaine*
12	*une douzaine*
15	*une quinzaine*
20	*une vingtaine*
30	*une trentaine*
40	*une quarantaine*
50	*une cinquantaine*
60	*une soixantaine*
100	*une centaine*
1,000	*un millier*
1,000,000	*un million*
1,000,000,000	*un milliard, un billion*

Because often collective numbers are used in conversation, you should practice them out loud (just as you do with the numbers 1 through 1,000) and add a noun, as in: *J'ai une dizaine de valises* (I have about 10 suitcases); *Il y a une huitaine de garçons dans la classe* (There are about eight guys in the class); *Je peux manger une douzaine d'escargots* (I can eat about a dozen snails).

Like collective numbers, fractions in French have some special everyday uses.

LEARN FRACTIONS

You have already learned how to form the ordinal numbers: *premier, deux-ième, troisième, quatrième* (first, second, third, fourth) by adding the ending *-ième*. Except for *premier* (first), this rule works for all numbers with only three exceptions; for example, for the numbers ending in 1 (21, 31, 41, and so on), you say *vingt et unième, trente et unième*, and so forth. In addition, *cinquième* adds a *u* before the ending for pronunciation reasons; *neuvième* changes the *f* of *neuf* to *v* before adding the ending.

Fractions normally are composed using the cardinal numbers as the numerator and the ordinal numbers as the denominator, as follows. Notice that the number in the denominator is spelled with a final *s* that is not pronounced:

- $^7/_8$ *sept huitièmes*
- $^9/_{16}$ *neuf seizièmes*
- $^{19}/_{31}$ *dix-neuf trente et unièmes*

The following fractions have special names. Note that *tiers* is always spelled with a final *s* but that *quart* adds an *s* only with *trois quarts*:

- $^1/_2$ *un demi*
- $^1/_3$ *un tiers*
- $^2/_3$ *deux tiers*
- $^1/_4$ *un quart*
- $^3/_4$ *trois quarts*

To use fractions with whole numbers, just say the whole number and the word *et* (and) followed by the fraction, as in $3^1/_2$ (*trois et demi*); $6^1/_4$ (*six et un quart*); $9^3/_4$ (*neuf et trois quarts*).

STRICTLY DEFINED

Except when using *un demi*, you can leave out the word *et* and just say *six un quart* ($6^1/_2$); *neuf trois quarts* ($9^3/_4$).

Demi is feminine when used with the feminine word *heure*, as in *une heure et demie, six heures et demie*, and so forth. However, when attached to a noun with a hyphen, *demi* usually is invariable:

- *une demi-heure* (half an hour)
- *une demi-bouteille* (half a bottle)

- *une demi-journée* (half a day)
- *la demi-lune* (the half moon)
- *la demi-pension* (half a board)

The noun corresponding to *demi* is *la moitié*, as in *Au dîner, je bois la moitié d'une bouteille de Beaujolais* (At dinner, I drink half a bottle of Beaujolais).

LEARN TO ADD, SUBTRACT, MULTIPY, AND DIVIDE

Now that you know the numbers and fractions you can add, subtract, multiply, and divide them.

To add, use the word *et* (and) and the verb *faire* (not the verb *être*).

Say: 9 *et* 9 *font* 18 (*neuf et neuf font dix-huit*)

To subtract, use the word *moins* (minus) and the verb *faire*.

Say: 20 *moins* 13 *font* 7 (*vingt moins treize font sept*)

To multiply, use the word *fois* (times) and the verb *faire*.

Say: 5 *fois* 6 *font* 30 (*cinq fois six font trente*)

To divide, use the phrase *divisé par* and the verb *faire*.

Say: 21 *divisé par* 7 *fait* 3 (*vingt et un divisé par sept fait trois*)

STRICTLY DEFINED

When you add, subtract, or multiply, use the the third-person plural form of the verb *faire: font*. When you divide, use the third-person singular form: *fait*.

LEARN THE VERBS *VENIR* AND *TENIR*

That's enough arithmetic for a while, so let's learn two new verbs that have unusual stems: *venir* (to come) and *tenir* (to hold). See the following table:

Conjugations of *Venir* and *Tenir*

venir	tenir
je viens	*je tiens*
tu viens	*tu tiens*
il vient	*il tient*
elle vient	*elle tient*

continues

Conjugations of *Venir* and *Tenir* (continued)

venir	tenir
on vient	*on tient*
nous venons	*nous tenons*
vous venez	*vous tenez*
ils viennent	*ils tiennent*
elles viennent	*elles tiennent*

Other verbs conjugated like *venir* are *revenir* (to come back), *retenir* (to hold something back, to detain), and *convenir* (to suit, to fit).

LEARN THE VERB *FALLOIR*

In just a moment you will be learning about the present subjunctive mood in French. The primary verb used with this mood in everyday speech is *falloir* ("to be necessary" or "to be required"). *Falloir* is a defective impersonal verb because it is used only in the third-person singular with a masculine pronoun; thus it's incomplete compared to other verbs.

FYI *Falloir* can be conjugated in any tense or mood except the imperative.

Learn *falloir* as a vocabulary item: *Il faut* (pronounced *eel fo*; It is necessary)

- *Il faut partir.* (It is necessary to leave.)
- *Il faut manger!* (It is necessary to eat!)
- *Faites comme il faut!* (Do [Behave] as required. Behave like you should!)

In just a few minutes, you'll be learning to form and use the present subjunctive mood. You will soon see that the expression *il faut que* (it is necessary that) is often used with the subjunctive.

LEARN ABOUT MOODS

In addition to having tenses, which indicate time, verbs also have moods, just like people. There are four moods: indicative (states a fact), imperative (gives a command), conditional (implies circumstance), and subjunctive (communicates feeling, possibility, or doubt). The subjunctive mood has all but disappeared from English. You will hear it occasionally in very formal speech, such as "The teacher requires that I be on time every day." However, in French the subjunctive is used all the time by educated and uneducated speakers, adults and small children.

In the following minutes, you will learn first how to form the subjunctive without knowing yet how or why it is used. Don't be frustrated. Once you master the forms, usage will be much easier to understand. Most important, do not try to find a special meaning in English for the subjunctive in French. French often uses the subjunctive mood where in English you use the indicative.

GO TO ▶
Before continuing with the subjunctive, go back to Hour 3, "Actions in the Present Tense," and review the conjugations of the three verb groups in the present indicative.

FORM THE PRESENT SUBJUNCTIVE OF *-ER* VERBS

The subjunctive of *-er* verbs looks just like the indicative except in the *nous* and *vous* forms of the verb where an *i* is added to the endings.

Note that the conjugations are all presented using the word *que* (that). As you will soon learn, the subjunctive is almost always preceded by *que* when used in a complete sentence. For now, you should repeat the examples using the word *que* in front of each form.

FYI   *Que* becomes *qu'* before a vowel.

To form the subjunctive of regular *-er* verbs, drop the *-ent* from the third-person plural of the indicative and add the endings *e, es, e, ions, iez,* and *ent.* See the following table:

Present Subjunctive of Regular *-er* Verbs

parler	écouter	téléphoner
Stem: parl	*Stem:* écout	*Stem:* téléphon
que je parle	*que j'écoute*	*que je téléphone*
que tu parles	*que tu écoutes*	*que tu téléphones*
qu'il parle	*que il écoute*	*qu'il téléphone*
qu'elle parle	*qu'elle écoute*	*qu'elle téléphone*
qu'on parle	*qu'on écoute*	*qu'on téléphone*
que nous parlions	*que nous écoutions*	*que nous téléphonions*
que vous parliez	*que vous écoutiez*	*que vous téléphoniez*
qu'ils parlent	*qu'ils écoutent*	*qu'ils téléphonent*
qu'elles parlent	*qu'elles écoutent*	*qu'elles téléphonent*

Notice that of the three conjugations in the preceding table, only the *nous* and *vous* forms of the first-group verbs differ from the present indicative.

You might wonder why the stem for the subjunctive is the third-person verb minus the *-ent* instead of the infinitive minus the *-er*. The reason will become clear when you learn to form the subjunctive of the *-ir* verbs in the next section.

FORM THE PRESENT SUBJUNCTIVE OF REGULAR *-IR* VERBS

To form the present subjunctive of *-ir* verbs, drop the *-ent* from the third-person plural of the indicative and add the endings *-e*, *-es*, *-e*, *-ions*, *-iez*, and *-ent*.

The following table shows three regular *-ir* verbs in the present subjunctive:

Present Subjunctive of Regular *-ir* Verbs

finir *Stem:* finiss	choisir *Stem:* choisiss	rougir *Stem:* rougiss
que je finisse	*que je choisisse*	*que je rougisse*
que tu finisses	*que tu choisisses*	*que tu rougisses*
qu'il finisse	*qu'il choisisse*	*qu'il rougisse*
qu'elle finisse	*qu'elle choisisse*	*qu'elle rougisse*
qu'on finisse	*qu'on choisisse*	*qu'on rougisse*
que nous finissions	*que nous choisissions*	*que nous rougissions*
que vous finissiez	*que vous choisissiez*	*que vous rougissiez*
qu'ils finissent	*qu'ils choisissent*	*qu'ils rougissent*
qu'elles finissent	*qu'elles choisissent*	*qu'elles rougissent*

Now you see why the verb stem for forming the present subjunctive is the third-person plural minus the *-ent*. For *-ir* verbs, you must include the *-iss* as part of the stem.

Be sure to pronounce the double *-ss-* as *s* when it falls between two vowels, and a single *-s-* as *z* when it falls between two vowels, as in *choisisse* (pronounced *swa-zees*); *choisissent* (pronounced *swazees*); and *choisissez* (pronounced *swa-zee-say*).

FORM THE PRESENT SUBJUNCTIVE OF *-RE* VERBS

Forming the present subjunctive of regular *-re* verbs follows the same rules of the first two groups of verbs. The following table shows three regular *-er* verbs in the subjunctive:

Present Subjunctive of Regular *-re* Verbs

vendre	rendre	perdre
Stem: vend	*Stem:* rend	*Stem:* perd
que je vende	*que je rende*	*que je perde*
que tu vendes	*que tu rendes*	*que tu perdes*
qu'il vende	*qu'il rende*	*qu'il perde*
qu'elle vende	*qu'elle rende*	*qu'elle perde*
qu'on vende	*qu'on rende*	*qu'on perde*
que nous vendions	*que nous rendions*	*que nous perdions*
que vous vendiez	*que vous rendiez*	*que vous perdiez*
qu'ils vendent	*qu'ils rendent*	*qu'ils perdent*
qu'elles vendent	*qu'elles rendent*	*qu'elles perdent*

Because the final *d* of *-re* verbs is always followed by a vowel in the present subjunctive, it is always pronounced; in contrast with the present indicative.

In Hours 3 and 4, you learned a number of irregular verbs in the present indicative. If a verb is irregular in the present indicative, it will most likely be irregular in all the other tenses and moods. You simply have to memorize the irregular forms of these verbs.

FORM THE PRESENT SUBJUNCTIVE OF IRREGULAR VERBS

To form the present subjunctive of irregular verbs, use the same endings (*-e, -es, -e, -ions, -iez, -ent*) added to the irregular stem of the verb. You should work on learning two or three of these every day. Come back to this section regularly for review.

The verbs *avoir* and *être* are completely irregular in the subjunctive, as shown in the following table:

Present Subjunctive of *Avoir* and *Être*

avoir	être
que j'aie	*que je sois*
que tu aies	*que tu sois*
qu'il ait	*qu'il soit*
qu'elle ait	*qu'elle soit*
qu'on ait	*qu'on soit*
que nous ayons	*que nous soyons*
que vous ayez	*que vous soyez*
qu'ils aient	*qu'ils soient*
qu'elles aient	*qu'elles soient*

Faire, pouvoir, and *savoir* have irregular stems, as shown in the following table:

Present Subjunctive of *Faire, Pouvoir,* and *Savoir*

faire (*Stem:* fass)	pouvoir (*Stem:* puiss)	savoir (*Stem:* sach)
que je fasse	*que je puisse*	*que je sache*
que tu fasses	*que tu puisses*	*que tu saches*
qu'il fasse	*qu'il puisse*	*qu'ils sache*
qu'elle fasse	*qu'elle puisse*	*qu'elle sache*
qu'on fasse	*qu'on puisse*	*qu'on sache*
que nous fassions	*que nous puissions*	*que nous sachions*
que vous fassiez	*que vous puissiez*	*que vous sachiez*
qu'ils fassent	*qu'ils puissent*	*qu'ils sachent*
qu'elles fassent	*qu'elles puissent*	*qu'elles sachent*

The irregular verbs in the following table use two different stems in the subjunctive:

Present Subjunctive of *Aller, Boire, Prendre,* etc.

aller *(to go)*	boire *(to drink)*	prendre *(to take)*
que j'aille	*que je boive*	*que je prenne*
que tu ailles	*que tu boives*	*que tu prennes*
qu'il aille	*qu'il boive*	*qu'il prenne*

aller *(to go)*	boire *(to drink)*	prendre *(to take)*
qu'elle aille	qu'elle boive	qu'elle prenne
qu'on aille	qu'on boive	qu'on prenne
que nous allions	que nous buvions	que nous prenions
que vous alliez	que vous buviez	que vous preniez
qu'ils aillent	qu'ils boivent	qu'ils prennent
qu'elles aillent	qu'elles boivent	qu'elles prennent
tenir *(to hold)*	venir *(to come)*	voir *(to see)*
que je tienne	que je vienne	que je voie
que tu tiennes	que tu viennes	que tu voies
qu'il tienne	qu'il vienne	qu'il voie
qu'elle tienne	qu'elle vienne	qu'elle voie
que nous tenions	que nous venions	que nous voyions
que vous teniez	que vous veniez	que vous voyiez
qu'ils tiennent	qu'ils viennent	qu'ils voient
qu'elles tiennent	qu'elles viennent	qu'elles voient

vouloir *(to wish, to want)*
que je veuille
que tu veuilles
qu'il veuille
qu'elle veuille
qu'on veuille
que nous voulions
que vous vouliez
qu'ils veuillent
qu'elles veuillent

The following four verbs, although irregular in the present indicative, are regular in the subjunctive: *dire, connaître, écrire, lire*.

- **dire**   *que je dise, que nous disions*
- **connaître**   *que je connaisse, que nous connaissions*
- **écrire**   *que j'écrive, que nous écrivions*
- **lire**   *que je lise, que nous lisions*

Now that you can form the subjunctive of most verbs, let's learn when to use it.

LEARN WHEN TO USE THE SUBJUNCTIVE

The subjunctive in French is used only under certain circumstances, as outlined in the following. To use the subjunctive, each and every one of these conditions must apply. As always, there will be exceptions, which will be presented as the need arises.

The sentence must have …

- Two different subjects.
- A trigger phrase or verb that requires the subjunctive. (These phrases must be memorized; however, most refer to emotions, doubt, or possibility.)
- The word *que*.

The following are some examples:

- ***Je veux que tu ailles à Paris.***   In this case, you use the subjunctive because …
  1. There are two different subjects: *je* and *tu*.
  2. The verb *vouloir* requires the subjunctive.
  3. The word *que* connects the two parts of the sentence.
- ***Je veux aller à Paris.***   Do not use the subjunctive because the sentence has only one subject.
- ***Je vois que vous allez à Paris.***   Do not use the subjunctive because the verb *voir* does not require it.
- ***Je veux partir quand tu arrives.***   Do not use the subjunctive because the word *que* is not in the sentence. (*Quand* means "when.")

Once you understand these basic rules, the only problem is learning the trigger verbs and phrases. Most of them are listed in the following section.

PROCEED WITH CAUTION

The verbs of feeling (*aimer, craindre,* etc.) require the subjunctive when the construction of the sentence meets the requirements given in the preceding explanation. However, when these verbs are followed by an infinitive, the indicative mood is used, as in *J'aime à voir que vous êtes heureux.*

AFTER VERBS OF FEELING

Use the subjunctive after verbs that communicate feelings or emotions:

aimer (to love)	*détester* (to detest)
aimer mieux (to prefer)	*irriter* (to irritate)
craindre (to fear)	*souhaiter* (to wish)
déplorer (to deplore)	*regretter* (to regret)
désirer (to desire)	*vouloir* (to wish, to want)

Examples include the following:

- *Je veux que vous alliez à Paris.* (I want you to go to Paris.)
- *Vous regrettez que j'aille à Paris?* (Do you regret that I am going to Paris?)

FYI Notice that English often uses an infinitive where French uses *que* plus the subjunctive.

Also, use the subjunctive after the following adjectives when used with the verb *être* + *que*. Remember, these are adjectives; therefore, they must agree with the person they modify:

charmé (charmed)	*fâché* (mad, angry)
content (content, happy)	*heureux* (happy)
désolé (sad)	*satisfait* (satisfied, content)
étonné (very surprised)	*surpris* (surprised)

Examples include the following:

- *Je suis désolé que tu n'ailles pas à Paris.* (I'm sad [that] you are going to Paris.)
- *Il est étonné que j'aille à Paris.* (He's surprised [that] I'm going to Paris.)

PROCEED WITH CAUTION

Notice that the word "that" can be left out of the English sentence because often it is understood as being there. However, the word *que* must always be used in French where "that" in English would be used.

AFTER EXPRESSIONS OF DOUBT

Use the subjunctive after expressions of doubt, as in …

- *Douter.*
- After the negation of *croire*, *dire*, *écrire*, *espérer*, *penser*, *savoir*, *trouver*, and *voir*.

Examples include the following:

- *Je doute que vous alliez à Paris.* (I doubt [that] you're going to Paris.)
- *Je ne crois pas qu'ils aillent à Paris.* (I don't believe [that] they are going to Paris.)

AFTER IMPERSONAL EXPRESSIONS

The following verbal impersonal expressions communicate emotions or doubt and are followed by the subjunctive:

- *Il faut que* (it is necessary that)
- *Il est bizarre que* (it is bizarre that)
- *Il est bon que* (it is good that)
- *Il est désirable que* (it is desirable that)
- *Il est douteux que* (it is doubtful that)
- *Il est étrange que* (it is strange that)
- *Il suffit que* (it is sufficient that, it is enough that)
- *Il vaut mieux que* (it is better that)

The following adjectives also require the subjuntive when used with the impersonal expression *il est*; for example, *Il est essentiel que tu sois à l'heure* (It is essential that you be on time): *essentiel* (essential), *étonnant* (astonishing), *extraordinaire* (extraordinary), *faux* (false), *honteux* (shameful), *important* (important), *impossible* (impossible), *juste* (just/right), *injuste* (unjust), *naturel* (natural), *nécessaire* (necessary), *possible* (possible), *préférable* (preferable), *rare* (rare/unusual), *regrettable* (regrettable), *temps* (time), *utile* (useful), *inutile* (useless), and *urgent* (urgent).

Examples include the following:

- *Il faut que nous écrivions une lettre.* (We must write a letter.)
- *Il est important que j'écrive une lettre.* (It's important that I write a letter.)
- *Il est urgent que tu écrives une lettre.* (It's urgent that you write a letter.)

As you can see, the subjunctive is used quite frequently in French. It will take you some time to master the forms and usage; however, you will hear it so often in spoken French that soon you will recognize it easily.

To conclude this hour, let's learn three new irregular -ir verbs: *couvir* (to cover), *offrir* (to offer), and *couvrir* (to open).

GO TO ▶

Additional uses of the subjunctive will be presented in Hours 12, "Learn to Link Ideas," and 16, "Going Places."

LEARN THE VERBS *COUVRIR*, *OFFRIR*, AND *OUVRIR*

The verbs *couvrir*, *offrir*, and *ouvrir* are -ir verbs but use the endings of the -er verbs. Here are their conjugations:

Conjugation of *Couvrir*, *Offrir*, and *Ouvrir*

couvrir	offrir	ouvrir
je couvre	j'offre	j'ouvre
tu couvres	tu offres	tu ouvres
il couvre	il offre	il ouvre
elle couvre	elle offre	elle ouvre
on couvre	on offre	on ouvre
nous couvrons	nous offrons	nous ouvrons
vous couvrez	vous offrez	vous ouvrez
ils couvrent	ils offrent	ils ouvrent
elles couvrent	elles offrent	elles ouvrent

The following verbs are conjugated like *couvrir*: *cueillir* (to gather), *découvrir* (to discover), *souffrir* (to suffer).

HOUR'S UP!

In this hour, you've learned to use collective numbers and fractions and mastered the basics of the use of the present subjunctive mood. Because the subjunctive requires that you learn new forms of verbs as well as when to use these forms, it is very important that you return to this hour regularly and practice using the examples provided. Every day, you should also commit to mastering a new verb in the subjunctive mood. Now test your knowledge of the material in this hour by taking the following quiz.

QUIZ

1. Which word correctly completes this sentence: *J'habite au* _____ *15, boulevard Charles de Gaulle.*

    a. *numéro*

    b. *chiffre*

    c. *nombre*

    d. *adresse*

2. Which word correctly completes this sentence: *Ils sont au* _____ *de huit.*

    a. *numéro*

    b. *chiffre*

    c. *nombre*

    d. *adresse*

3. Which of the following numbers does not have a collective form?

    a. 10

    b. 20

    c. 70

    d. 100

4. Which of the following verbs is followed by the subjunctive in a subordinate clause?

    a. *venir*

    b. *courir*

    c. *falloir*

    d. *faire*

5. Which of the following verb forms is in the subjunctive mood?

    a. *parliez*

    b. *choisis*

    c. *rend*

    d. *ai*

6. Which of the following verb forms is not in the subjunctive mood?

    a. *perde*

    b. *aient*

    c. *soit*

    d. *fait*

7. Which of the following verbs is followed by the subjunctive mood in a subordinate clause?

    a. *faire*

    b. *voir*

    c. *aimer*

    d. *aller*

8. Which of the following verbs is not followed by the subjunctive mood in a subordinate clause?

    a. *détester que*

    b. *penser que*

    c. *être étonné que*

    d. *être surpris que*

9. The subjunctive mood does not indicate …

    a. doubt

    b. certainty

    c. emotion

    d. supposition

10. Which of the following verbs is followed by the subjunctive mood in a subordinate clause?

    a. *dire que*

    b. *raconter que*

    c. *observer que*

    d. *vouloir que*

QUIZ

HOUR 7

Describe Your Surroundings

CHAPTER SUMMARY

LESSON PLAN:
In this hour you will learn ...

- How to use past participles as adjectives.
- How to use multiple adjectives in descriptions.
- How to use demonstrative adjectives.
- How to use the indefinite adjectives.
- How to compare things.
- How to form and use adverbs.

In this hour you will focus on learning about adjectives and adverbs. First you'll learn some new ways to form and use adjectives, including how to use more than one adjective to modify a noun. You'll also learn the demonstrative adjectives, *ce, cette,* and *ces,* meaning "this," "that," "these," and "those," and several indefinite adjectives, such as "some," "each," and "every."

Next, you'll learn how to compare things and how to form and use adverbs. An adverb is a word that modifies a verb (ad + verb = added to the verb). As in English, French adverbs have special forms and certain places they can and can't be placed in a sentence.

LEARN MORE ABOUT ADJECTIVES

In Hour 2, "Describing Things," you learned some adjectives and how to make them agree in number and gender with the noun they modify. Let's review this before we continue.

REVIEW THE AGREEMENT AND PLACEMENT OF ADJECTIVES

Adjectives are words, and sometimes phrases, that modify nouns. In French they agree in number (singular or plural) and gender (masculine or feminine) with the noun. The largest group of adjectives is composed of descriptive adjectives because they describe a noun. Demonstrative adjectives clarify to which person, place, or thing you're referring. In English, "this," "that," "these," and "those" are demonstrative adjectives; for example, "this book";

GO TO ▶
There are two other types of adjectives: interrogative adjectives, presented in Hour 8, "Learn to Express Yourself in the Future," and possessive adjectives, presented in Hour 11, "Learn to Show Possession."

"that book." Indefinite adjectives refer to people, places, or things in general such as "some," "each," and "several"; for example, "some places," "each place," and "several places." You will learn about several types of adjectives during this hour.

USE MULTIPLE ADJECTIVES IN DESCRIPTIONS

In Hour 2 you learned that adjectives can come before or after a noun. To review, the following table shows the primary adjectives that precede nouns.

Adjectives That Normally Precede the Noun

French	English	Forms and Usage
beau	handsome	*beau, bel, beaux, belle*; also can mean "beautiful," "good-looking," "lovely," as in *un bel homme, une belle femme* (a handsome man, a pretty woman)
bon	good	*bon, bonne*; also can mean "nice," "correct," as in *un bon garçon, la bonne réponse* (a nice boy, the correct answer)
gentil	nice	*gentil, gentille*; also can mean "pretty, pleasing," as in *un gentil enfant; C'est gentil, Madame; Elle est gentille; Sois gentil* (a pretty child; That's kind of you; She's nice; Be nice)
grand	great	*grand, grande*; means "large" or "great" when used in front of the noun; means "tall" when used after the noun, as in *un grand homme, un homme grand* (a great man, a tall man)
jeune	young	*jeune, jeune*
joli	pretty	*joli, jolie*; also can be used ironically, as in *Ce n'est pas joli joli!* (That's not pretty! That's a poor show!)
long	long	*long, longue*; also can mean "drawn out, lengthy, protracted," as in *une longue histoire, un long hiver* (a long-winded story, a protracted winter)
mauvais	bad	*mauvais, mauvaise*; also can mean "evil, wicked," incorrect, wrong, as in *une mauvaise personne, la mauvaise réponse, la mauvaise rue* (an evil person, the incorrect response, the wrong street)
nouveau	new	*nouveau, nouvel, nouveaux, nouvelle*; also can mean "new" in the sense of "fresh, rising" or "another," as in *un nouveau livre, la nouvelle génération, le nouvel an* (a fresh new book, the rising generation, the New Year)
petit	small	*petit, petite*; also can mean "short, little, light," as in *un petit homme, un petit hôtel, la petite industrie* (a short man, a little hotel, light industry)
vieux	old (aged)	*vieux, vieil, vieux, vieille*

The categories of adjectives shown in the following table generally follow the noun:

Adjectives That Follow the Noun

Category	French	English
Colors	Les couleurs *(fem.)*	
	blanc, blanche	white
	bleu, bleue	blue
	brun, brune	brown
	gris, grise	gray
	rouge, rouge	red
	jaune, jaune	yellow
	marron, marron	(chestnut) brown
	noir, noire	black
	orange, orange	orange
	rose, rose	pink
	vert, verte	green
	violet, violette	violet
Form	La forme	
	rond, ronde	round
	oval, ovale	oval
	carré, carrée	square
	rectangulaire	rectangular
Nationality	La nationalité	
	allemand, allemande	German
	américain, américaine	American
	canadien, canadienne	Canadian
	chinois, chinoise	Chinese
	espagnol, espagnole	Spanish
	français, française	French
	italien, italienne	Italian
	japonais, japonaise	Japanese
	portugais, portugaise	Portuguese
	russe, russe	Russian
Adjectives of Three or More Syllables		
	compliqué, compliquée	complicated
	fantastique, fantastique	fantastic

continues

Adjectives That Follow the Noun   (continued)

Category	French	English
Adjectives of Three or More Syllables		
	difficile, difficile	difficult
	facile, facile	easy
	formidable, formidable	fantastic
	important,importante	important
	incroyable, incroyable	unbelievable
	intelligent, intelligente	intelligent
	intéressant, intéressante	interesting
	merveilleux, merveilleuse	marvelous

PROCEED WITH CAUTION

Note that the spellings of nationalities are lowercase. Adjectives are never capitalized in French; for example, *un monument parisien* (a Parisian monument), *la capitale américaine* (the American capital).

You may also recall that certain adjectives change meaning if placed before a noun (literal meaning) or after the noun (figurative meaning). Review the following adjectives:

- *une histoire ancienne* (literal): an old story
- *un ancien élève* (figurative): a former student
- *un garçon brave* (literal): a brave boy
- *un brave garçon* (figurative): a good boy
- *un ami vieux* (literal): a aged friend
- *un vieil ami* (figurative): an longtime friend
- *un livre cher* (literal): an expensive book
- *cher Claude* (figurative): dear Claude
- *un homme grand* (literal): a tall man
- *un grand homme* (figurative): a great man
- *un homme pauvre* (literal): a poor (not rich) man
- *Le pauvre homme!* (figurative): The poor (unfortunate) man!

Now that you know where adjectives normally are placed you can create phrases that use more than one adjective. When using multiple adjectives, each one takes its habitual place and agrees with the noun; for example, *une jolie femme française* (a beautiful French woman), *un bel homme russe* (a handsome Russian man), *une nouvelle voiture blanche* (a new white car).

When two adjectives precede or follow the noun, normally they are connected with the word *et* (and); for example, *une grande et belle fleur* (a big and pretty flower), *un petit et gentil garçon* (a small, nice boy), *une question difficile et intéressante* (a difficult and interesting question), *une robe verte et noire* (a green and black dress).

FYI The adjective *jeune* (young) is used inseparably with the word *fille* to mean "young girl," as in *une jeune fille.* A young man is *un jeune homme.* However, "the young men/people" is *les jeunes gens.*

In addition to the adjectives in the preceding table, you can create many new adjectives from the verbs you've learned so far. To do this, use the past participle of the verb as an adjective.

Use Past Participles as Adjectives

You will learn how to use *past participles* to form the past tenses in Hour 9, "Express Yourself in the Past"; for now you can use them as adjectives. Unlike English, in which many past participles are irregular, the vast majority of past participles in French are formed regularly.

STRICTLY DEFINED

The **past participle** is the form of the infinitive used to create past tenses. The final word in each of these sentences is a past participle: I have *fallen.* I have *spoken.* I have *written.* Past participles also can be used as adjectives in English; for example, "a fallen soldier" or "the spoken and written word." Most past participles in English end in *-ed;* for example, finished, painted, opened, and closed.

To form the past participles of regular French verbs, do the following:

- For regular *-er* verbs, drop the *-er* from the infinitive and add *é: Parler* becomes *parlé, chanter* becomes *chanté,* and *détester* becomes *détesté.*

- For regular *-ir* verbs, drop the *-ir* from the infinitive and add *i: Finir* becomes *fini; choisir* becomes *choisi.*

- For regular *-re* verbs, drop the *-re* from the infinitive and add *u: Entendre* becomes *entendu; perdre* becomes *perdu.*

PROCEED WITH CAUTION

Only regular verbs form their past participles following these rules. Irregular verbs often have irregular past participles. You will learn these in Hour 9.

Be careful—some past participles aren't used as adjectives because they don't make sense as adjectives. For example, how might you use *téléphoné* (telephoned) as an adjective? You probably wouldn't. Common sense will guide you in deciding which past participles should or should not be used as adjectives.

Here are a few examples of past participles commonly used as adjectives in French:

- *aimé* (beloved)   *un ami aimé* (a beloved friend)
- *attendu* (awaited)   *la réponse attendue* (the awaited [expected] answer)
- *détesté* (hated)   *un homme détesté* (a hated man)
- *fini* (finished)   *un travail fini* (finished work)
- *guéri* (healed)   *l'homme guéri* (the healed man)
- *perdu* (lost)   *un enfant perdu* (a lost child)
- *posé* (asked)   *la question posée* (the question asked)
- *puni* (punished)   *l'enfant puni* (the punished child)
- *réussi* (successful)   *un plan réussi* (a successful plan)
- *trouvé* (found)   *un objet trouvé* (a found object)

In the preceding examples, notice that often where a past participle is used as an adjective in French, English would use a phrase. Compare the following sentences to see the difference in usage:

- *Ce n'est pas la réponse attendue.* (That is not the answer [that I] expected.)
- *Ce n'est pas la question posée.* (That is not the question [I] asked.)

Earlier in this hour, we mentioned that there are various types of adjectives. Now that you're familiar with descriptive adjectives, let's look at two other types: demonstrative and indefinite adjectives.

MASTER DEMONSTRATIVE ADJECTIVES

The demonstrative adjectives are *ce, cet, cette* (this, that, these, and those.) Notice that French as a special form of the masculine singular form—*cet*—which is used before masculine singular nouns beginning with a vowel. The plural of *ce, cet,* and *cette* is *ces.* See the following list for examples:

- *Ce monsieur est gentil.* (This/That man is nice.)
- *Cet homme est grand.* (This/That man is tall.)
- *Cette femme est vieille.* (This/That woman is old.)
- *Ces hommes et ces femmes sont beaux.* (These/Those men and women are good-looking.)

PROCEED WITH CAUTION

There is only one plural form for the demonstrative adjectives: *ces.*

As you see, the demonstrative adjectives mean "this" or "that," "these" or "those," according to the context of the sentence. Often these adjectives are used along with a visual indication with the hand or finger to demonstrate their meaning. If the context does not make the distinction clear, add *-ci* (here) or *-là* (there) to the noun as follows:

- *Ce monsieur-ci est gentil.* (This man [here] is nice.)
- *Cet homme-là est grand.* (That man [there] is tall.)
- *Cette femme-ci est vieille.* (This woman [here] is old.)
- *Ces hommes-ci et ces femmes-là sont beaux.* (These men and those women are good-looking.)

LEARN THE INDEFINITE ADJECTIVES

Some adjectives do not fall into the groups of descriptive or demonstrative adjectives. Therefore, they are referred to as indefinite adjectives. The following table lists the principal indefinite adjectives:

Indefinite Adjectives

French	English	Usage
autre	another	*Voilà un autre problème.* (There is another problem.)
d'autres	some (others)	*Cet adjectif a d'autres sens.* (This adjective has some other meanings.) *D'autres* has the meaning of the partitive "some."
certain	certain, some	*Certains hommes sont grands, et certains hommes sont petits.* (Some men are tall, some men are short.) Use *certain* instead of *des* ("some" is the plural of *un/une*) when referring to particular things.

continues

Indefinite Adjectives (continued)

French	English	Usage
chaque	each	*Chaque étudiant a un examen.* (Each student has an exam.) *Chaque* is invariable; thus, it's always singular.
différents	different	*Ils habitent des maisons différentes.* (They live in different houses.)
divers	diverse	*Elles ont des opinions diverses.* (They have diverse opinions.)
maint	many, many a	*Maint auteur* (many an author); *maintes fois* (many times).
même	same	*le même problème* (the same problem) *les mêmes problèmes* (the same problems)
plusieurs	several	*J'ai plusieurs amis français.* (I have several French friends.)
quelconque	any, whatsoever	*un job quelconque* (any [old] job [whatsoever])
quelque	a little	*Cet homme a quelque talent.* (This man has a little [some but not much] talent.)
quelques	some, a few	*Je veux quelques jours de vacances.* (I want some/a few vacation days.)
tel	such, such as, like	*Tel père, tel fils.* (Like father, like son.) *Une telle femme.* (Such a woman.)

Notice in the preceding examples that not all these adjectives have four forms. Use the following table to learn the forms. Where you see a blank, the adjective is not used in that form.

Masculine Singular	Masculine Plural	Feminine Singular	Feminine Plural
autre	*autres*	*autre*	*autres*
	d'autres		*d'autres*
certain	*certains*	*certaine*	*certaines*
chaque		*chaque*	
	différents		*différentes*
divers	*divers*	*diverse*	*diverses*
maint	*maints*	*mainte*	*maintes*
même	*mêmes*	*même*	*mêmes*
	plusieurs		*plusieurs*
quelconque	*quelconques*	*quelconque*	*quelconques*
quelque	*quelques*	*quelque*	*quelques*
tel	*tels*	*telle*	*telles*

One other adjective belongs in this group of indefinite adjectives: *tout*. However, it has uses that require special attention. The adjective *tout* means "all, each," or "the whole (of)." It has four forms: *tout, tous, toute,* and *toutes*.

GO TO ▶
Tout, used as a pronoun, is found in Hour 11, "Learn to Show Possession."

- *Tout homme est libre.* (Every man is free.)
- *Toute question a une réponse.* (Every [each] question has a response.)
- *Tous ces jeunes hommes sont français.* (All these young men are French.)
- *Toutes les réponses sont fausses.* (All the answers are false.)

Once you master the form and placement of adjectives you can compare things.

LEARN TO COMPARE THINGS

Like English, French has comparative constructions (something is bigger or better than something else) and superlative constructions (something is the biggest or the best). Many English comparisons are formed by adding *-er* to the adjective—for example, "bigger than," "smaller than," or "greener than." French has no such endings for adjectives. Instead, with only a few exceptions, which I'll present shortly, French uses the words *plus* (more), *moins* (less), and *aussi* (equal to) to form comparisons. The following sections explain in detail how these words are used.

USE THE COMPARATIVE

As you form comparatives, remember to make the adjectives agree with the nouns they modify.

To compare two or more people or things, do the following:

- Use *plus* + adjective + *que* to say "more … than."
- Use *moins* + adjective + *que* to say "less … than."
- Use *aussi* + adjective + *que* to say "as … as."

Examples include the following:

- *Jean est plus grand que Suzanne.* (John is taller than Susan.)
- *Suzanne est moins grande que Jean.* (Susan is shorter than John.)
- *Jean et Suzanne sont aussi qrands que Pierre.* (John and Susan are as tall as Peter.)

The comparative in English usually adds *-er* to the adjective (taller, bigger, smaller, and so forth) where French uses the constructions *plus ... que, moins ... que,* and *aussi ... que.* However, as in English, certain adjectives have special comparative forms in French, as shown in the following:

good, better: *bon, meilleur*

bad, worse: *mauvais, pire*

GO TO ▶
The comparison of nouns is presented in Hour 12, "Learn to Link Ideas."

Thus:

- *Ce livre-ci est meilleur que ce livre-là.* (This book is better than that book.)
- *Ce prix est meilleur que l'autre prix.* (This price is better than the other price.)
- *Le remède est pire que le mal.* (The remedy is worse than the illness.)
- *Certains problèmes sont pires que d'autres problèmes.* (Some problems are worse than other problems.)

USE THE SUPERLATIVE

The superlative is used to indicate that something is the best, worse, or most. To form the superlative in English, you place the article "the" in front of the adjective and usually add *-est* to it; for example, the largest, the brightest, and the highest. French also uses the definite articles (*le, la, les*), followed by *plus* or *moins* + adjective.

PROCEED WITH CAUTION

Aussi obviously is not used in the superlative because things can't be equally best, biggest, and so forth.

The main rule to remember as you form the superlative is that adjectives maintain their normal places. That is, adjectives placed in front of the noun will be placed in front of the noun in the superlative. Those placed after the noun will be placed after the noun in the superlative. Before you continue, review the rules for the placement and agreement of adjectives in the preceding.

To form the superlative in French, follow these models:

- *Jean est le plus intelligent.* (John is the most intelligent.)
- *Suzanne est la plus grande.* (Susan is the tallest.)

- *Paul est le moins grand.* (Paul is the shortest [least tall].)
- *Pierre et Suzanne sont les plus intéressants.* (Peter and Susan are the most interesting.)

To translate the English words "in" or "of," always use a form of *de* (*du, de l',
de la, des*) as follows:

- *Jean est le plus intelligent des étudiants.* (John is the most intelligent of the students.)
- *Suzanne est la grande du groupe.* (Susan is the tallest in the group.)
- *Paul est le moins grand de la classe.* (Paul is the shortest [boy] in the class.)
- *Pierre et Suzanne sont les plus intéressants de tous les participants.* (Peter and Susan are the most interesting of all the participants.)

When using a noun in the comparative, adjectives that follow the noun normally follow the noun in the comparison. For example:

- *Paul est l'étudiant le plus intéressant de la classe.* (Paul is the most interesting student in the class.)
- *Yvette est la femme la plus grande du groupe.* (Yvette is the tallest woman in the group.)
- *La France a les trains les plus rapides du monde.* (France has the fastest trains in the world.)

In contrast to adjectives, adverbs modify verbs, adjectives, or other adverbs.

LEARN TO FORM AND USE ADVERBS

Adverbs in English typically can be identified by their characteristic ending,
-ly, as in loudly, shortly, interestingly, and so forth. However, there are many
common adverbs that don't follow this pattern; for example, here, there,
often, never, far, and so forth. Consider the following examples:

- **I sing badly.** The adverb "badly" tells how you sing.
- **I saw him yesterday.** The adverb "yesterday" tells when you saw him.
- **He is here.** The adverb "here" tells where he is.
- **The basketball players are very tall.** The adverb "very" indicates the degree of tallness of the players.
- **I speak French quite well.** The adverb "quite" indicates the degree to which you speak French well.

> An **adverb** modifies a verb and answers the questions "how," "how much of," "when," or "where" an action occurs. Adverbs can modify adjectives (very hot) and other adverbs (very badly) and answer the question "how much."

Adverbs are used the same way in French as they are in English; however, their formation and placement in the sentences differs from that of English.

How to Form Adverbs

To form adverbs regularly in French, add -*ment* to the feminine singular of an adjective. The following table shows some common examples:

Some Common French Adverbs

French Adjective	French Adverb	English Adverb
brave	bravement	bravely
calme	calmement	calmly
douce	doucement	sweetly, nicely
fausse	faussement	falsely
franche	franchement	frankly
froide	froidement	coldly
grande	grandement	largely
heureuse	heureusement	happily
honnête	honnêtement	honestly
naïve	naïvement	naïvely
énorme	énormément	enormously
profonde	profondément	profoundly
précise	précisément	precisely

> There are many exceptions to the general rule of forming adverbs in French. Consult your dictionary each time you form a new adverb.

Notice that the last three examples change the final *e* of the feminine form to *é*.

Of course, there are many adverbs that are not formed directly from adjectives. The following table lists the most common ones. Remember that adverbs are invariable; thus, they don't agree with nouns, verbs, and so forth.

More Common Adverbs

English	French	English	French
above	*dessus*	later	*plus tard*
always	*toujours*	much, a lot	*beaucoup*
badly	*mal*	now	*maintenant*
behind	*derrière*	often	*souvent*
below	*dessous*	outside	*dehors*
early	*tôt*	over there	*là-bas*
enough	*assez*	sometimes	*quelquefois*
enough, also	*aussi*	soon	*bientôt*
everywhere	*partout*	then	*ensuite, puis, alors, donc*
far	*loin*	there	*là*
fast	*vite; rapidement*	today	*aujourd'hui*
few	*peu*	tomorrow	*demain*
here	*ici*	too	*trop*
in front of	*devant*	very	*très*
inside	*dedans*	well	*bien*
in the back	*au fond*	yesterday	*hier*
late	*tard*		

The placement of adverbs in French differs significantly from English usage.

WHERE TO PLACE ADVERBS

Because the word "adverb" really means "added to the verb," you can remember that French adverbs normally follow (are added to) the conjugated verb. In the following examples, note that the English adverb moves around in the sentence. Generally this is not true in French:

- *Il chante bien à l'église.* (He sings well at church.)
- *Elle parle bien français.* (She speaks French well.)
- *Vous mangez trop le dimanche?* (Are you eating too much on Sundays?)
- *Je vais toujours parler français en classe.* (I am always going to speak French in class.)

Again, as you see in the preceding, the normal place of the adverb is after the conjugated verb. This rule will become particularly useful when you learn the compound tenses of the past, so it is important to learn it now.

FYI As in English, adverbs of time or place such as often, today, tomorrow, here, there, and so forth (*souvent, aujourd'hui, demain, ici, demain*) can be placed either at the beginning or the end of a sentence, as in *Demain, je vais à Paris* (Tomorrow, I am going to Paris); *Ici, on parle français* (French is spoken here).

In addition to adverbs that indicate how or when one does something, there are adverbs that indicate the quantity of something.

HOW TO USE ADVERBS OF QUANTITY

Adverbs of quantity merit special attention for one reason: They are always followed by the invariable preposition *de*. The following table shows the primary adverbs of quantity and examples of the use of each. Note in all cases that the word for "of" is *de*:

Common Adverbs of Quantity

French	English	Examples
assez de	enough of	*assez de voitures*
autant de	as many, as much	*autant de temps* (*que* means "as")
beaucoup de	lots of, many	*beaucoup de viande*
combien de	how many	*combien de kilos?*
moins de	fewer, les	*moins de problèmes*
peu de	a litte of, few	*peu de problèmes*
plus de	more	*plus d'argent* (*que* means "than")
tant de	enough of, sufficient	*tant de bonheur*
trop de	too much of	*trop de vin*
un bon nombre de	a good number of	*un bon nombre d'enfants*
un sac de	a sack of	*un sac de bananes*
un tas de	a pile of	*un tas de papiers*
une boîte de	a box of	*une boîte de cigares*
une bouteille de	a bottle of	*une bouteille de bière*
une douzaine de	a dozen of	*une douzaine d'oeufs*
une quantité de	a quantity of	*une quantité de gens*
une centaine de	about a hundred of	*une centaine de taxis*

USE ADVERBS TO COMPARE THINGS

The comparison of adverbs follows the same rules used for the comparison of adjectives. Because adverbs are invariable, the article used in the superlative is always masculine singular, *le*.

Comparative:

- *Il chante aussi souvent que Paul.*   (He sings as often as Paul.)
- *Il chante plus souvent que Paul.*   (He sings more often than Paul.)
- *Il chante moins souvent que Paul.*   (He sings less often than Paul.)

Superlative:

- *Elle parle le plus clairement de tous.*   (She speaks the clearest of all.)
- *Ils parlent le plus clairement de tous.*   (They speak the clearest of all.)
- *Les Français parlent le plus vite.*   (The French speak the fastest.)
- *Les Texans parlent le moins vite.*   (Texans speak the slowest.)

HOUR'S UP!

That's the end of another hour! You may feel that time is going by quickly, but you are also trying to master a lot of material, so keep to your schedule of working on new structures while reviewing the old ones on a daily basis. Before going on to the final hour of Part 2, "The Present and the Future," review the demonstrative and indefinite adjectives, the comparative and superlative, and the formation of adverbs; then test your knowledge with the following quiz.

QUIZ

1. Which of the following adjectives normally precedes the noun?

   a. *bon*

   b. *brun*

   c. *rond*

   d. *français*

2. Which of the following adjectives normally follows the noun?

   a. *beau*

   b. *jeune*

   c. *noir*

   d. *petit*

3. Which type of adjective normally does not follow the noun?

   a. colors

   b. forms

   c. long adjectives

   d. size

4. True or False: *Un vieil ami* means "a longtime friend."

5. True or False: *Un livre cher* means "a beloved book."

6. To say "larger than," you would use …

   a. *meilleur*

   b. *pire*

   c. *plus grand que*

   d. *aussi grand que*

7. To say "the worst," you would use …

   a. *le pire*

   b. *le meilleur*

   c. *le plus beau*

   d. *le moins beau*

8. Complete the following sentence with the correct form of *tout*: _____ *les étudiantes sont intelligentes.*

   a. Tous

   b. Toutes

   c. Toute

   d. Tout

9. Which word correctly completes the sentence? *Il y a un très _____ arbre dans le jardin.*

   a. *bel*

   b. *beau*

   c. *belle*

   d. *beaux*

10. In which of the following phrases are the adjectives placed correctly?

    a. *une maison blanche et grande*

    b. *une grande maison blanche*

    c. *une petite rouge maison*

    d. *un intelligent homme français*

QUIZ

HOUR 8

Learn to Express Yourself in the Future

LESSON PLAN:

In this hour you will learn ...

- How to use partitive articles in new situations.
- How to use the interrogative adjective *quel*.
- How to form the negation.
- How to form a negative question.
- How to express yourself in the future tense.
- How to form and use the present conditional mood.

Mastering the forms and use of the subjunctive will continue to be a goal over the next few hours, so we will continue to review its usage as we introduce new tenses. However, the new tense for this hour is the future, and the new mood you will learn is the conditional. The future tense and the present conditional mood are relatively easy to form and use in French. You've already learned how to use the near future by using the verb *aller* plus an infinitive. You may want to review quickly that construction in Hour 4, "Actions in the Present Tense with Irregular Verbs," before you continue into this hour.

LEARN THE INTERROGATIVE ADJECTIVES

Interrogative means "question," so when used to modify a noun, interrogative adjectives ask a question. For example, in English you might ask: "What color do you prefer? What book are you reading?" The word "what" is an adjective that announces a question. French uses *quel* in the same way. There are four forms of this word: *quel*, *quels*, *quelle*, and *quelles*.

To form a question using *quel*, remember that, as with all adjectives, it must agree in number and gender with the noun. For now, you can use the question phrase *est-ce que* to complete the question. Here are some examples of the use of *quel*:

- *Quel livre est-ce que vous lisez?* (What book are you reading?)

- *Quelle couleur est-ce qu'elle préfère?* (What color does she prefer?)
- *Quels fromages est-ce que tu veux?* (What cheeses do you want?)
- *Quelles boissons est-ce qu'ils boivent?* (What drinks do they drink?)

Quel also can be used as an exclamation meaning "What a …!" When used in this way, it does not ask a question; rather, it indicates surprise, agreement, or distaste, for example: *Quel homme!* (What a man!) *Euh, quel mauvais vin.* (Ugh, what bad wine.)

LEARN MORE ABOUT PARTITIVE ARTICLES

In Hour 2, "Describing Things," you learned about the partitive articles *du, de l' de la,* and *des,* which do not exist in English. The partitive article is used in special ways with the negation, so before we learn to form negative sentences, let's review the use of the partitive articles.

First, think about the meaning of the word "partitive": "part of." In English when we say "I'll have some bread," we're really saying "I'll have some of the bread that is available." We're not asking for all the bread. The French translation is *Je prends du pain.* You remember that *du* is a contraction of *de + le,* so you can think of the *du* as meaning "some of the."

Here's another example: *Je prends de la viande.* I'll have (I'll take) some meat. In this sentence, again, you are indicating you want "some of the" meat that is available.

Now compare the preceding two sentences with the following:

Je prends le pain. Je prends la viande.

You must imagine a context in which these two sentences would make sense; perhaps in a bakery or in a restaurant. In the first instance you're standing in front of a counter, eyeing all the luscious French croissants, pastries, and such. But your eye catches a large, fresh load of French bread. You make your decision and tell the baker *Je prends le pain, s'il vous plaît, Monsieur.* In this case, you do want the whole loaf of bread, not just part of it. Thus, you don't use the partitive.

For the second example, *Je prends la viande,* you might be in a restaurant that offers vegetarian items (more and more common in France today) as well as meat dishes. Perhaps the waiter (*le monsieur*) offers you several choices, including the meat dish. Again you make your choice: *Je prends la viande, s'il vous plaît, Monsieur.* (I'll have the meat [dish, all of it], please.)

The following table has a few more examples to work on. Cover the French translations on the right and see whether or not you can use the partitive.

Use of the Partitive Articles: *du, de l', de la, des*

English	French
I drink water.	*Je bois de l'eau.*
The water is fresh.	*L'eau est fraîche.*
I'll have (some) wine, please.	*Je prends du vin, s'il vous plaît.*
She adores the wine.	*Elle adore le vin.*
Wine is good!	*Le vin est bon!*
The wine is good!	*Le vin est bon!*
I like (the) bread and (the) desserts!	*J'aime le pain et les desserts!*
He wants butter with his bread.	*Il veut du beurre avec son* (butter is *le beurre*) *pain.*

Notice that in the two sentences "Wine is good," and "The wine is good," the definite article *le* is used. That's because, as you learned in Hour 2, the definite article is used when speaking of something in general terms and to mean "the" in English.

As you proceed into learning about the negative, keep the use of the partitive in mind because the partitive articles behave differently in negative sentences.

LEARN TO FORM THE NEGATION

In English the negation is formed using a negative word such as "no," "not," or "never." However, the structure of an English sentence also changes when you make it negative; for example, "I speak French" versus "I do not speak French." Notice that English adds the word "do" to complete the negative construction. You'd never just say "I not speak French."

French also requires two words in every negation. In correct, standard French, the essential negative word is *ne*. The basic rule for forming the negation is to place *ne* before the conjugated verb and a second negative word, such as *pas*, after the conjugated verb.

PROCEED WITH CAUTION

In complete disregard for this standard rule, spoken French often omits the *ne*, even though it is the primary sign of the negation. This is true perhaps because the spoken language moves so quickly over the little word *ne*, as in *Je sais pas!* (I don't know!) *Je veux pas!* (I don't want [any]!) However, it's best to learn the correct forms from the beginning.

The following are a few examples of standard negative sentences:

Ils n'ont pas l'heure. (They don't have the time [of day].)

Je ne prends pas l'avion. (I'm not taking the plane.)

Nous ne sommes pas américains. (We're not American.)

Elle n'achète pas le vin. (She's not buying the wine.)

Je ne parle pas français. (I don't speak French.)

Note that like *je* and *que*, *ne* becomes *n'* before a vowel.

Once you learn the basic placement of the negation you can use a whole range of French negative words, always paired with the word *ne*.

MASTER THE MOST COMMON NEGATIONS

The following list gives you the most common negations and an example of their usage. The ellipses mark the position of the verbs, which are preceded by *ne* and followed by the second words of each negation:

- *ne … personne* (no one, not anyone)
  Il n'aime personne. (He likes no one. He doesn't like anyone.)

- *ne … plus* (no longer, no more)
  Je ne parle plus! (I'm not speaking any longer.)

- *ne … guère* (hardly)
  Je ne suis guère fatigué. (I'm hardly tired.)

- *ne … point* (not at all)
  Il n'écrit point. (He doesn't write at all. [restricted to literary usage])

- *ne … que* (only)
  Elle ne parle que français. (She speaks only French.)

- *ne … rien* (nothing, not anything)
  Je ne vois rien. (I see nothing. I don't see anything.)

- *ne … jamais* (never)
  Ils ne boivent jamais le vin. (They never drink the wine.)

- *ne ... pas encore* (not yet)
  Il ne va pas encore parler. (He's not going to speak yet.)
- *ne ... ni ... ni* (neither [either]/nor [or])
  Nous ne voulons ni manger ni boire. (We don't want [either] to eat or to drink.)
- *ni ... ni ... ne* (neither [either]/nor [or])
  Ni Paul ni Suzanne ne parlent français. (Neither Paul nor Susan speak French.)

STRICTLY DEFINED

Most of the negative words in this list are considered adverbs; thus, they are invariable. *Ne ... que* and *ne ... ni ... ni* technically are conjunctions, but they are used the same way as adverbs in most cases.

Notice that *ne ... ni ... ni* can be reversed to become *ni ... ni ... ne* when you use it to make it mean "neither/nor." You can use a noun, a pronoun, or a verb form, usually an infinitive, after *ni*.

Most important, when reviewing the preceding negations note that the *ne* always forms part of the negation. This usage might seem to be a double negative, such as "I don't see nothing," in English; however, obviously this is not the case in French. All French negatives are technically (by English rules, of course) double negatives because they all are composed of two negative words.

Use the following English examples to see if you can compose the French equivalents:

- I am not French. (*Je ne suis pas français.*)
- He does not drink. (*Il ne boit pas.*)
- She never speaks English. (*Elle ne parle jamais anglais.*)
- We are not yet in Paris. (*Nous ne sommes pas encore à Paris.*)
- They don't want anything. (*Ils ne veulent rien.*)
- There is no one here. (*Il n'y a personne ici.*)

Several of the preceding negative expressions also can be used by themselves when responding to a question with a negative answer. In these cases you omit the *ne*, which is understood, and simply use the second part of the negation, as in the following examples:

GO TO ▶
You will learn where to place these negations in compound tenses in Hour 9, "Express Yourself in the Past."

- *Vous êtes fatigué? Non, pas moi.* (No, not me.)
- *Tu manges de la viande? Non, jamais.* (No, never.)
- *Qui* (who) *est là? Personne.* (No one.)
- *Que* (what) *veux-tu? Rien.* (Nothing.)

In the first part of this hour you reviewed the partitive articles. Review them again because these articles behave differently after a negation.

LEARN TO USE THE PARTITIVE *DE* AFTER NEGATIONS

After most negations in French, the partitive articles (*du, de l', de la, des*) and the indefinite articles *un/une* change to *de*, which is invariable after a negation. This is a simple rule, but you will need to practice it because there is no equivalent in English.

Look at the following sentences; then we'll talk again about the rule:

- *J'ai **un** livre. Je n'ai pas **de** livre.*
- *Je bois **du** vin. Je ne bois pas **de** vin.*
- *Il a **de la** patience. Il n'a plus **de** patience.*
- *Nous prenons **du** beurre. Nous ne prenons pas **de** beurre.*
- *Vous avez **des** problèmes? Vous n'avez pas **de** problèmes.*

The one exception to this rule is with the negation of the verb *être*. After this verb, the partitive and indefinite articles remain in their usual form; for example, *Je suis un bon étudiant. Je ne suis pas un bon étudiant. C'est un homme brave. Ce n'est pas un homme brave. C'est du vin blanc. Ce n'est pas du vin blanc.*

As you might suspect, there are some exceptions to the general rule for using the negations. The first one you learned in the preceding involves the verb *être*, after which the partitive articles do not change to *de*. Let's look at some other common exceptions.

LEARN THE MOST COMMON EXCEPTIONS

The following negations can be used in special ways that do not follow the rule of *ne* + verb + negative word.

PERSONNE, RIEN

The word *personne* can be used as the subject of a sentence to mean "no one." *Rien* also can be used as the subject of a sentence and also uses *ne* in front of the verb. When used in this way, *personne* and *rien* are negative pronouns (because they are used as the subject of the sentence) and are conjugated with the third-person singular of the verb. Consider the following examples:

- **ne ... personne**   *Personne ne parle.* (No one is speaking.) *Personne ne répond?* (No one is answering?) (Notice that you still must use *ne* in front of the verb.)

- **ne ... rien**   *Rien ne change dans la vie.* (Nothing changes in life.)

NE ... QUE

The negation *ne ... que* does not require the partitive articles to change to *de*. The reason for this exception is that *ne ... que* is not considered to be a true negative adverb, but rather a conjunction. However, usually it has the meaning of the adverb *seulement* (only), as in the following examples:

- *Il n'a que 3 frères. Il a seulement 3 frères.* (He has only 3 brothers. He has only 3 brothers.)

- *Il n'y a que 3 étudiants dans la classe.* (There are only 3 students in the class.)

- *Je ne prends que des photos en couleur.* (I only take color photographs.)

AUCUN/AUCUNE, NUL/NULLE

These words are negative adjectives meaning "no" or "any," as in the English sentences "No man is an island" or "I don't have any time (I have no time)." Because they are adjectives, *aucun* and *nul* agree in number and gender with the nouns they modify, but they are always singular because of their negative meaning. *Nul* is more literary and is rarely heard in conversation.

 FYI   *Aucun* can be used in the plural before nouns that have no singular form in French; however, this is rare.

Here are a couple of examples:

- *Aucun étudiant ne travaille suffisamment.* (No student works enough.)
- *Je n'ai aucune idée.* (I have no idea.)
- *Nous ne connaissons nulle femme plus belle que Suzanne.* (We know [of] no woman more beautiful than Susan.)

Aucun also can be used alone to mean "none," as in *Avez-vous une bonne idée? Non, aucune.* (Do you have a good idea? No, none [not a one]). *Nul* is not used alone. *Aucun,* followed by the preposition *de* and a singular verb, also can serve as a pronoun, as in *Aucun de mes amis ne vient ce soir.* (None of my friends are coming tonight.)

Jamais

Jamais often is placed at the beginning of a sentence to insist upon the idea of never, ever doing something; for example, *Jamais je ne fais ça.* (Never do I do that.) Note that *jamais,* when used without *ne,* means "ever," as in *Si jamais vous venez à Paris, allez visiter la Tour Eiffel.* (If ever you come to Paris, go visit the Eiffel Tour.)

Negation of the Infinitive

To negate an infinitive, place both parts of the negation in front of the infinitive, as follows:

- *Je préfère <u>ne pas</u> partir.* (I prefer not to leave.)
- *Veuillez <u>ne pas</u> fumer.* (Please don't smoke.)
- *Paul espère <u>ne pas</u> manquer le train.* (Paul hopes not to miss the train.)
- *Nous avons peur de <u>ne pas</u> réussir dans cette classe.* (We are afraid of not succeeding in this class.)

The Negation with *Savoir, Pourvoir, Cesser,* and *Oser*

These four verbs (to know how to, to be able, to stop, to dare) often are used in the negative without the word *pas.* This use simply sounds more elegant to the French ear. However, it is perfectly fine to include *pas.* Most often you will hear this usage in certain commonly repeated sentences, such as the following:

Je ne saurais vous le dire. (I wouldn't know how to tell you.)

Je n'ose entrer. (I dare not enter.)

Now quickly go back over the forms and placement of the negative before you learn how to form a negative question.

LEARN TO FORM A NEGATIVE QUESTION

In a question, normally *ne* is placed in front of the verb; *pas* is placed after the subject. Here are some examples:

- *Allez-vous au musée?*   *N'allez-vous pas au musée?*
- *A-t-il l'heure?*   *N'a-t-il pas l'heure?*
- *Parlez-vous anglais?*   *Ne parlez-vous pas anglais?*
- *Prennent-ils le train demain?*   *Ne prennent-ils pas le train demain?*

RESPOND TO A NEGATIVE QUESTION WITH *SI*

You might recognize the word *si* as Spanish for "yes." It also is a French word used to respond affirmatively to a negative question and is very useful in avoiding confusion. For example, in English, if someone asks you "Are you not going to the movies?" you're in a fix. If you say simply "Yes," you might be understood as saying "Yes, I'm not going to the movies" or "Yes (on the contrary), I am going to the movies." French avoids this possible confusion by using *si*, as shown in the following:

- *Vous n'allez pas au cinéma? Oui!* (Yes, I'm not going.)
- *Vous n'allez pas au cinéma? Non!* (No, I'm not going.)

However …

- *Vous n'allez pas au cinéma? Si!* (Oh, but yes, I'm going!)

Once you've learned all the negative adverbs you can use more than one in a single sentence. Typically in English, using two negatives in one sentence creates a double negative, which generally is bad grammar; however, it's perfectly acceptable in French.

USE MULTIPLE NEGATIONS

Here are some examples of the use of multiple negatives in a single sentence:

GO TO ▸
Before continuing with this section you might want to review how to form questions in French by looking back at Hour 5, "Express Yourself in the Present Indicative."

- *Je n'ai **plus rien** dit*. I said nothing more.
- *Il **ne** dit **jamais rien** d'intéressant*. He never says anything of interest.
- *Il n'apprend **jamais rien**.* He never learns anything.
- *Il n'y a **plus guère que** les professeurs qui comprennent le latin aujour-d'hui*. It's only just professors who understand Latin nowadays.

At this point you've learned just about all there is to know about the negation in French. (There are a few other things to learn, such as the infamous *pleonastic ne*, but these are matters for an advanced grammar lesson.) Let's move on to learning the future tense.

STRICTLY DEFINED

Pleonastic means "redundant," using more words than necessary to express an idea. French uses the pleonastic *ne* in careful speech after certain verbs, verbal expressions, and comparisons. It has no significant meaning and does not indicate a negation.

LEARN TO EXPRESS YOURSELF IN THE FUTURE TENSE

The future tense is used almost exactly in French as it is used in English; with one exception, which you will learn easily. In Hour 4 you learned how to form the near future using the verb *aller*. Now you will learn how to form and use the future tense itself.

REVIEW THE IMMEDIATE FUTURE

Before you attack the future, let's review the near future with *aller*, as it is often used in conversation. *Aller* is used to form the near future (*le futur proche*), just like in English. If you are going to do something in the very near future, in English you use the verb "to go" followed by an infinitive, as in "I am going to eat"; "I am going to go." In French you can use the same construction, as in *Je vais manger* (I am going to eat). *Je vais aller* (I am going to go). Review the conjugation of *aller* in Hour 4.

MASTER THE FUTURE TENSE OF REGULAR VERBS

The future tense in French—unlike in English—is a simple tense; that is, it is composed of a single word, whereas English uses the word "will" plus the verb, as in "I will go," "I will walk," and so forth. Therefore, the English future tense is called a *compound tense*, for it is composed of two forms that are combined, or compounded, to form the future.

The French future is much simpler. First, let's see how to form the simple future tense. All regular verbs, whether *-er*, *-ir*, or *-re*, form their future in the following manner:

1. The future stem is the entire infinitive of the verb; for *-re* verbs, drop the final *e* before adding the endings.

2. To the stem, add the following endings:

je:	*-ai*		*nous:*	*-ons*
tu:	*-as*		*vous:*	*-ez*
il:	*-a*		*ils:*	*-ont*
elle:	*-a*		*elles:*	*-ont*
on:	*-a*			

When you look carefully at the future tense endings, you will see that they come from the verb *avoir*, except for the *nous* and *vous* endings, which are the endings characteristic of these persons.

Review the verb *avoir* quickly now:

Person	Singular	Plural
first	*j'ai*	*nous avons*
second	*tu as*	*vous avez*
third, masculine	*il a*	*ils ont*
third, feminine	*elle a*	*elles ont*
third, generic	*on a*	

Now you see why learning the conjugation of *avoir* is so important. As you learn more tenses you'll notice many of the verb endings are based on the forms of the verb *avoir*.

The following table shows three regular verbs conjugated in the future. You can use them as models to create the future of any regular verb. Even many of the irregular verbs you learned in Hour 2 (such as *écrire*, *boire*, *prendre*, and *mettre*) are regular in the future tense.

The Future Tense of Regular Verbs

parler	finir	perdre
je parlerai	je finirai	je perdrai
tu parleras	tu finiras	tu perdras
il parlera	il finira	il perdra
elle parlera	elle finira	elle perdra
on parlera	on finira	on perdra
nous parlerons	nous finirons	nous perdrons
vous parlerez	vous finirez	vous perdrez
ils parleront	ils finiront	ils perdront
elles parleront	elles finiront	elles perdront

MASTER THE FUTURE TENSE OF IRREGULAR VERBS

A small number of verbs have irregular stems in the future tense. However, the endings are always regular; so in the following table only the first and second persons are shown:

Future Tense of Irregular Verbs

Verb	Stem	First Person	Second Person	Translation
aller	ir	j'irai	tu iras	I/you will go
avoir	aur	j'aurai	tu auras	I/you will have
courir	courr	je courrai	tu courras	I/you will run
être	ser	je serai	tu seras	I/you will be
faire	fer	je ferai	tu feras	I/you will do, will make
mourir	mourr	je mourrai	tu mourras	I/you will die
pouvoir	pourr	je pourrai	tu pourras	I/you will be able(to)
savoir	saur	je saurai	tu sauras	I/you will know
venir	viendr	je viendrai	tu viendras	I/you will come
voir	verr	je verrai	tu verras	I/you will see
vouloir	voudr	je voudrai	tu voudras	I/you will want (to)
Verb	Stem	Third Person		Translation
falloir	faudr	il faudra		it will be necessary
valoir	vaudr	il vaudra mieux		it will be better

As stated before, the future tense is used in French just as in English with one easy exception that, although different from English usage, is quite logical. Here's the exception: When you use the future with the conjunction *quand* (when), you use the future tense in both parts of the sentence. To understand the logic of this rule, let's look at the English sentence using the future tense and the word "when":

I will telephone Paul when he arrives.

Notice that after the word "when," the verb is in the present tense—but this not logical. All the action described in the sentence, including Paul's arrival, will take place in the future. Therefore, French uses the future in both parts of the sentence—*C'est logique!*

Look at this example of the difference in usage of the future in English and French:

I will telephone Paul when he arrives. *Je téléphonerai à Paul quand il arrivera.* (Literally: I will telephone [to] Paul when he will arrive.)

A simple formula to remember this rule is …

future + *quand* + future

In addition to the conjunction *quand*, the following conjunctions also invoke the rule: *lorsque* (synonym for *quand*), *dès que, aussitôt que* (both meaning, as soon as), *tant que* (as long as) and *après que* (after). Here are several examples:

- *Je verrai Paul dès qu'il arrivera.* (I will see Paul as soon as he arrives.)
- *Nous irons à Paris aussitôt que nous aurons les billets.* (We will go to Paris as soon as we have the tickets.)
- *Dès qu'elles arriveront, nous dirons bonjour!* (As soon as they arrive, we will say hello!)

Once you've mastered the forms and use of the future you can easily form a new mood: the conditional.

LEARN THE PRESENT CONDITIONAL MOOD

As the name implies, the conditional mood is used to express a relationship between actions, one of which is dependant upon another; for example, "I would go with you, but I don't have enough money yet." English uses the

GO TO ▶
There is another form of the future, called the *futur antérieur,* which translates the English "will have done (something)." This tense has special uses, which will be presented in Hour 17, "Eating Out."

verb form "would" to express the conditional mood in a compound construction, as in "would go," "would talk," and so forth.

MASTER THE FORMS OF THE PRESENT CONDITIONAL

French has a simple conditional form. To form the conditional of all regular verbs, use the future stem and add the following endings:

Person	Singular	Ending	Plural	Ending
first	je	-ais	nous	-ions
second	tu	-ais	vous	-iez
third, masculine	il	-ait	ils	-aient
third, feminine	elle	-ait	elles	-aient
third, generic	on	-ait		

You can use the following conjugations as models to form the conditional of any verb in French:

The Present Conditional Mood

parler *Stem:* parl	aller *Stem:* ir	être *Stem:* ser
je parlerais	j'irais	je serais
tu parlerais	tu irais	tu serais
il parlerait	il irait	il serait
elle parlerait	elle irait	elle serait
on parlerait	on irait	on serait
nous parlerions	nous irions	nous serions
vous parleriez	vous iriez	vous seriez
ils parleraient	ils iraient	ils seraient
elles parleraient	elles iraient	elles seraient

The translations of the first person of the preceding verbs in the conditional are "I would talk," "I would go," and "I would be." As you can see, the future and the conditional are closely related in form. In fact, grammarians often call the conditional "the future in the past" because it is used to describe actions that would happen if something else happened.

Now that you can form the conditional mood, when do you use it?

LEARN TO USE THE PRESENT CONDITIONAL

The conditional most often is used in English in conjunction with past tenses and the word "if"; for example, "If I **had** the money, I **would go** to France to live." In this example, going to France to live is conditional upon having enough money. In Hour 10, "Use the Correct Past Tense," you will learn the past tenses and come back to the conditional mood to learn how it is used in this instance. For now, you can use the conditional without the word "if" (*si*) to express doubt or to express wishes and desires in polite terms.

STRICTLY DEFINED

Note that *si* can mean either "yes" or "if," but the context will always make the meaning clear.

The following are some examples of the conditional mood used in these senses:

- *Tu aurais encore faim?* (Would you still be hungry? Is it possible that you are still hungry?) (expressing doubt)
- *J'aimerais voyager mais je suis pauvre.* (I would like to travel but I'm poor.) (statement of condition)
- *Je voudrais un verre de vin, s'il vous plaît.* (I would like a glass of wine, please.) (politeness)

You might be asking yourself why you should avoid the conditional mood in its most common usage. To answer that question, let's talk a bit about what is called *concordance* of tenses.

LEARN ABOUT CONCORDANCE OF TENSES

As is true of all languages, French has several patterns for the use of tenses. These patterns are referred to as "concordance" (agreement) of tenses. To better understand the term, first consider some examples in English.

Without looking at the answers in the next paragraph, complete the following sentences using a form of the verb "to go" in English:

If I have enough money next month, I _____ to Paris.

If I had enough money, I _____ to Paris.

If I had saved enough money last year, I _____ to Paris.

Did you answer "will/shall go," "would go," and "would have gone," respectively? Why? In simple terms, the answer is concordance of tenses. Consider quickly the following rules for concordance of tenses with "if," which speakers of French must learn to determine the correct tense to use in English:

- When the "if" clause is in the present tense, the resulting clause is in the future tense.
- When the "if" clause is in the past tense, the resulting clause is in the present conditional.
- When the "if" clause is in the past perfect, the resulting clause is in the past conditional.

Of course, as a speaker of English, you don't stop each time you use the word "if" to consider these rules of concordance. They come automatically and naturally to your ear.

However, as you learn French, you must learn which tenses are used together and when. Mastering these rules will take some time and, using this text, you will proceed one step at a time. Because you've not yet learned all the tenses you need, you should wait before trying to construct more complex sentences using the conditional mood. In the following hours you will be introduced to all the various rules governing the use of tenses. Be patient—everything will come together at the right time.

HOUR'S UP!

Bien fait! Well done! You've just completed Part 2, "The Present and the Future," and you've mastered the negation and two new tenses, the future and the conditional. In Part 3, "The Past," you're going to learn all about how to form and use the past tenses. So, you're well on your way to being able to say almost anything in French, in the past, present, and future. Before taking up the past tenses, review the material in this hour and test your knowledge with the following quiz.

1. "He likes no one" is …
   a. *Il n'aime plus.*
   b. *Il n'aime personne.*
   c. *Il n'aime pas.*
   d. *Il n'aime rien.*

2. "He doesn't like anything" is …

    a. *Il n'aime plus.*

    b. *Il n'aime personne.*

    c. *Il n'aime pas.*

    d. *Il n'aime rien.*

3. *Je ne bois jamais de vin* means:

    a. I never drink wine.

    b. I always drink wine.

    c. I hardly drink wine.

    d. I drink only wine.

4. The negative of *J'ai des amis* is …

    a. *Je n'ai pas amis.*

    b. *Je n'ai pas des amis.*

    c. *Je n'ai pas d'amis.*

    d. *Je n'ai pas un ami.*

5. The negative of *J'aime le vin* is …

    a. *Je n'aime pas le vin.*

    b. *Je n'aime pas de vin.*

    c. *Je n'aime pas vin.*

    d. *Je n'aime pas du vin.*

6. What is the negative form of the following question: *Partez-vous demain?*

    a. *Ne partez-vous demain?*

    b. *Ne partez-vous pas demain?*

    c. *Ne partez pas vous demain?*

    d. *Ne pas partez-vous demain?*

7. Which of the following is not a correct use of the negation?

    a. *Il ne dit plus rien.*

    b. *Il n'apprend jamais rien.*

    c. *Il ne veut jamais rien.*

    d. *Il ne veut pas plus rien.*

QUIZ

8. Which of the following phrases is in the future tense?

    a. *il part*

    b. *il finira*

    c. *ils parlent*

    d. *ils perdent*

9. Which of the following sentences means "I will see"?

    a. *Je vois.*

    b. *Je viendrai.*

    c. *Je verrai.*

    d. *Je voudrai.*

10. Which of the following phrases is in the conditional mood?

    a. *il sera*

    b. *il pourra*

    c. *je saurai*

    d. *j'irais*

PART III

The Past

HOUR 9

Express Yourself in the Past

LESSON PLAN:

In this hour you will learn ...

- How to form the *passé composé*.
- How to use the past tense in the negative.
- How to use the verbs *courir*, *devoir*, *mourir*, and *recevoir*.

In this hour, you'll learn hot to form and use the most common past tense in the French, the *passé composé*. This tense is widely used in conversation and, once you've mastered it, you'll be prepared to form almost any other tense in French.

There is also more on negation because the negative phrases you learned in Hour 8, "Learn to Express Yourself in the Future," have special rules of placement when used with compound tenses like the *passé composé*.

Finally, you will continue to add some new verbs to your vocabulary as you master the verbs *courir* (to run), *devoir* (to have to), *mourir* (to die), and *recevoir* (to receive). These four verbs are irregular *-ir* verbs.

EXPRESSING ACTION VS. MOVEMENT

Before learning the formation of the *passé composé*, you must understand a couple of basic distinctions the French intuitively make between verbs that express an action and verbs that express a movement.

In Hour 5, "Express Yourself in the Present Indicative," you learned the distinction between transitive and intransitive verbs. At that time we defined transitive verbs as those that can take an object, as in "I hit the ball" ("to hit" is transitive) and intransitive verbs as those that can't take an object, as in "I fell" ("to fall" is intransitive). You also learned that this distinction is not a major concern of native speakers of English. You probably never stop to think whether a verb can take an object

GO TO ▶
Before proceeding, you should go back to Hour 5 and review the section on transitive and intransitive verbs, "Use Transitive and Intransitive Verbs."

except, as mentioned before, with several annoying verbs such as "to lie" (intransitive) and "to lay" (transitive).

However, understanding this distinction is vital to using the correct verb in French; because you cannot count on your ear to guide you, you must learn which common verbs are transitive and which are intransitive. Again, they are not the same as in English, so you cannot rely on that knowledge, either.

When we get to the formation of the past tense, you'll see more clearly why you must understand transitive versus intransitive. Here's a hint: Each group is conjugated with a different helping verb in the past tense.

THE DIFFERENCE BETWEEN ACTION AND MOVEMENT

To help you better understand transitive versus intransitive, let's talk a moment about the difference between an action and a movement. At first glance you might say that an action involves a movement, and if you make a movement, you've performed an action—so what's up? You'd be right, of course. Before continuing, let's assign a definition to each of these words to clearly separate their meanings:

- **Action**   The doing of something.
- **Movement**   Moving from one point to another point.

Using these definitions, the following verbs you've learned are verbs of action: *travailler* (to work), *marcher* (to walk), *manger* (to eat), *voyager* (to travel), *écrire* (to write), *boire* (to drink), *faire* (to do), and *lire* (to read). Notice that these verbs do not indicate that you are starting at one place and ending up at another place—that's movement. Instead, these verbs simply describe an action, the act of doing something. Are you wondering why *voyager* (to travel) is an action verb? That's because this verb is not used to describe traveling "to" someplace; it only states that you are already someplace and that you traveling "around" there. Thus, it describes the action of traveling, but not the movement of traveling. More on that in a moment.

Again, using the preceding definitions, the following verbs you've learned are verbs of movement: *aller à* (to go to), *partir de* (to leave from), *sortir de* (to go out of), *venir de* (to come from), and *entrer dans* (to enter into). Think about the meanings and uses of these verbs for a moment. If you say you're leaving (from) someplace, you're describing a movement. For example, notice that *partir* is not the verb to express the idea of leaving something behind (like a book on the table); rather, it means "to leave (a city, town, or other place)."

Also notice that each of these verbs has a preposition associated with it; for example, *aller à, entrer dans,* and so forth. That's because often when you express movement, you also express where you are moving to. As we proceed, be sure to learn the prepositions associated with each verb, when given.

THE THIRTEEN VERBS OF MOVEMENT

Now that you understand action versus movement, here's some good news: There are only a limited number of verbs that express movement in French. In fact there are only 13 basic verbs of movement. When you learn these verbs you can remember that all the other thousands of verbs in French are verbs of action. The following table lists them.

The Thirteen Verbs of Movement

Verb	English
aller à	to go (to)
venir de	to come (from)
partir de	to leave (from)
arriver à	to arrive (at)
sortir de	to go out (of)
entrer dans	to enter (in, into)
monter à	to go up (to)
descendre de	to come down (from), to descend
mourir	to die
naître	to be born
tomber	to fall
retourner à	to return to
rester à	to remain in, to stay in/at

Alright, you've read the list and you're no doubt wondering, "How can the verbs *mourir* (to die), *naître* (to be born), and *rester* (to stay) be verbs of movement?" Well, you can think of the act of dying or being born as a movement from one state of being to another! As for *rester*, you might consider that as no movement at all.

It is essential at this point to learn this list of verbs because shortly you will see that verbs of action and verbs of movement are conjugated with different helping verbs in French.

GO TO ▶
Before continuing, go back to Hour 3, "Actions in the Present Tense," and review the present tenses of *avoir* and *être*.

TWO HELPING VERBS: *AVOIR* AND *ÊTRE*

What is a helping verb? In English, we use a helping verb whenever we form compound tenses; that is, tenses composed of at least two words; for example, "I have written"; "I had left." The helping verb here, also known as an auxiliary verb, is "to have." Except for the progressive tenses (I am walking, I was walking, and so forth) English compound tenses are always formed using some form of the verb "to have." On the other hand, in French there are two helping verbs: *Avoir* is used with verbs of action; *être* is used with verbs of movement.

Now let's proceed to the formation of the past tense, after which we'll discuss its usage.

FORM THE *PASSÉ COMPOSÉ*

To form the *passé composé*, conjugate the appropriate helping verb in the present tense and add the past participle. (You learned how to form and use past participles as adjectives in Hour 7, "Describe Your Surroundings.") When a verb has an irregular past participle, I'll give that to you as you learn the verb.

Here's a quick review of how to form the past participle of regular verbs:

- For regular *-er* verbs, drop the *-er* from the infinitive and add *é*: *Parler* becomes *parlé*, *chanter* becomes *chanté*, and *détester* becomes *détesté*.
- For regular *-ir* verbs, drop the *-ir* from the infinitive and add *i*: *Finir* becomes *fini*, and *choisir* becomes *choisi*.
- For regular *-re* verbs, drop the *-re* from the infinitive and add *u*: *Entendre* becomes *entendu*, and *perdre* becomes *perdu*.

Because verbs of action are conjugated with *avoir* and verbs of movement are conjugated with *être*, we'll look at each group of verbs individually.

LEARN THE PAST TENSE WITH *AVOIR*

The following table shows the conjugations of three regular verbs of action in the *passé composé*. Note carefully the translations of the *passé composé*. English has three past tenses, all of which are translated by the *passé composé* in French.

STRICTLY DEFINED

Remember that all three present tenses in English (I speak, I am speaking, I do speak) are translated in French by the simple present: *Je parle.* (See Hour 3.)

Regular Verbs in the *Passé Composé*

French	English
j'ai parlé	I spoke, I have spoken, I did speak
tu as parlé	you spoke, you have spoken, you did speak
il a parlé	he spoke, he has spoken, he did speak
elle a parlé	she spoke, she has spoken, she did speak
on a parlé	one spoke, one has spoken, one did speak
nous avons parlé	we spoke, we have spoken, we did speak
vous avez parlé	you spoke, you have spoken, you did speak
ils ont parlé	they spoke, they have spoken, they did speak
elles ont parlé	they spoke, they have spoken, they did speak
j'ai fini	I finished, I have finished, I did finish
tu as fini	you finished, you have finished, you did finish
il a fini	he finished, he has finished, he did finished
elle a fini	she finished, she has finished, she did finish
on a fini	one finished, one has finished, one did finish
nous avons fini	we finished, we have finished, we did finish
vous avez fini	you finished, you have finished, you did finish
ils ont fini	they finished, they have finished, they did finish
elles ont fini	they finished, they have finished, they did finish
j'ai perdu	I lost, I have lost, I did lose
tu as perdu	you lost, you have lost, you did lose
il a perdu	he lost, he has lost, he did lose
elle a perdu	she lost, she has lost, she did lose
on a perdu	one lost, one has lost, one did lose
nous avons perdu	we lost, we have lost, we did lose
vous avez perdu	you lost, you have lost, you did lose
ils ont perdu	they lost, they have lost, they did lose
elles ont perdu	they lost, they have lost, they did lose

The following table is a list of the irregular past participles of the verbs you've learned so far. To use these verbs in the past tense, simply conjugate the verb *avoir* in the present tense and add the past participle.

Part Tense of Irregular Verbs

French	Past Participle	Example	English Equivalent
avoir	*eu*	*j'ai eu*	I had, I have had
boire	*bu*	*j'ai bu*	I drank
connaître	*connu*	*j'ai connu*	I knew
croire	*cru*	*j'ai cru*	I believed
dormir	*dormi*	*j'ai dormi*	I slept
écrire	*écrit*	*j'ai écrit*	I wrote
faire	*fait*	*j'ai fait*	I did, I made
falloir	*fallu*	*il a fallu*	It was necessary
être	*été*	*j'ai été*	I was, I have been
lire	*lu*	*j'ai lu*	I read
mettre	*mis*	*j'ai mis*	I put
pouvoir	*pu*	*j'ai pu*	I was able, I could
prendre	*pris*	*j'ai pris*	I took
savoir	*su*	*j'ai su*	I knew, found out
suivre	*suivi*	*j'ai suivi*	I followed
tenir	*tenu*	*j'ai tenu*	I held
vivre	*vécu*	*j'ai vécu*	I lived
voir	*vu*	*j'ai vu*	I saw
vouloir	*voulu*	*j'ai voulu*	I wanted (to)

FYI The verb *savoir* (to know how to) has a special meaning in the *passé composé*: to discover, to find out. For example, *Un jour il a su la vérité.* (One day, he discovered [knew] the truth.)

Remember that the verb *falloir* is used only in the third-person singular and means "it is necessary." It is always followed by a noun, an infinitive, or the subjunctive, as in *Il me faut de l'eau* (I need some water), *Il lui a fallu partir* (He had to leave), *Il a fallu que je parte* (It was necessary that I leave [subjunctive]).

Both the verb *avoir* and the verb *être* are conjugated with *avoir* in the *passé composé*.

Don't confuse *connaître* and *savoir*. *Connaître* is used to express the idea of knowing a person or a place; *savoir* has the sense of knowing how (to do something). Compare these two sentences:

- *Je connais bien Paris.* (I know Paris well.)
- *Je sais parler français.* (I know how to speak French.)

Finally, remember that all the preceding examples can be translated into English using the past, the present perfect, or the past emphatic. For example:

- *J'ai écrit une lettre.* (I wrote a letter. I have written a letter. I did write a letter.)
- *J'ai lu le journal.* (I read the paper. I have read the paper. I did read the paper.)
- *J'ai pris le train.* (I took the train. I have taken the train. I did take the train.)

Once you see the pattern of the *passé composé*, you can form the past tense of any verb. As you learn new verbs in your reading and studying, write the past participle beside the infinitive and learn it at the same time you learn the present tense.

The rules for forming the past tense of verbs of action are the same ones used to form the past tense of verbs of movement. However, there are some additional rules involving the agreement of the past participles.

LEARN THE PAST TENSE WITH *ÊTRE*

Earlier in this hour we took some time to discuss the difference between verbs of action and verbs of movement. Now it will become clearer why we needed to make that distinction: All verbs of movement are conjugated with *être* in the *passé composé*.

FYI You'll soon learn that verbs of movement will use *être* as the helping verb when forming any compound tense. However, once you've mastered the *passé composé*, the rest will be easy.

The following are the two rules for forming the *passé composé* of verbs of movement:

- Conjugate *être* in the present tense and add the past participle of the verb.
- Make the past participle agree in number and gender with the subject of the sentence.

This last rule is very important, as you will soon learn. Because just as if it were an adjective, the past participle agrees with the subject of the sentence (at times you will add an *e*, an *es*, or an *s* to the past participle).

PROCEED WITH CAUTION

 As you've learned, adding *e* or *es* after a consonant will make that consonant pronounced.

Let's look at two verbs of movement in the *passé composé*:

Verbs Conjugated with *Être* in the *Passé Composé*

Person	aller	to go
first	*je suis allé(e)*	I went, I have gone, I did go
second	*tu es allé(e)*	you went, have gone, did go
	vous êtes allé(e)(s)(es)	you went, have gone, did go
third	*il est allé*	he went, has gone, did go
	elle est allée	she went, has gone, did go
	on est allé	one went, has gone, did go
	nous sommes allés(es)	we went, have gone, did go
	ils sont allés	they went, have gone, did go
	elles sont allées	they went, have gone, did go
Person	partir	to leave
first	*je suis parti(e)*	I left, have left, did leave
second	*tu es parti(e)*	you left, have left, did leave
	vous êtes parti(e)(s)(es)	you left, have left, did leave
third	*il est parti*	he left, has left, did leave
	elle est partie	she left, has left, did leave
	on est parti	one left, has left, did leave
	nous sommes partis(es)	we left, have left, did leave
	ils sont partis	they left, have left, did leave
	elles sont parties	they left, have left, did leave

There are two very important points to notice in forming the *passé composé* of verbs of movement, discussed in the following section.

THE PAST PARTICIPLE AGREES WITH THE SUBJECT

First, notice in the preceding table that there are indications in parentheses of the possibilities for agreement. As an example, Suzanne would write *Je suis allée à Paris* (I went to Paris) with an *e* in the past participle, agreeing with a feminine subject *je*. Paul would write *Je suis allé à Paris*, without a final *e*, agreeing with the masculine subject *je*.

Because the *vous* form of the verb can be masculine singular, masculine plural, feminine singular, or feminine plural, there are four possibilities for agreement. Fortunately, the final additional *e*, *s*, or *es* does not often affect pronunciation. As you've learned, final consonants usually are silent in French. The one exception is the verb *mourir*, whose past participle is *mort*. Therefore, when an *e* is added, the final *t* is pronounced as follows:

> *Il est mort.* (eel ay mor)
>
> *Elle est morte.* (el ay mort)
>
> *Elles sont mortes.* (el son mort)

GO TO ▶

In Hour 14, "Free Time," you will learn the agreement rule for past participles of verbs conjugated with *avoir*. Until that hour, we'll use nouns only as objects of these verbs.

TRANSLATION INTO ENGLISH USES "TO HAVE"

Second, even though these verbs are conjugated with *être*, their translation into English uses the one English helping verb "to have." Do not confuse the translation of these verbs in the past tense. You might be tempted to translate *je suis allé* as "I am going"—be careful! This is the past tense: I went, I have gone, I did go.

PROCEED WITH CAUTION

Mourir, naître: French does not distinguish between the statements "he died/he is dead"; "he was born/he is born." Both are expressed in French, respectively, as: *Il est mort. Il est né.*

To help you learn the past tenses of the verbs of movement, the following is a list of the verbs again, followed by their past participles:

Past Participles of Verbs of Movement

Verb	Past Participle	Verb	Past Participle
aller à	allé	descendre de	descendu
venir de	venu	mourir	mort
partir de	parti	naître	né
arriver à	arrivé	tomber	tombé
sortir de	sorti	retourner à	retourné
entrer dans	entré	rester à	resté
monter à	monté		

PROCEED WITH CAUTION

The verbs *sortir, descendre,* and *monter* can be used transitively, but their meaning changes as follows: to take out, to take down, to put up. When transitive, these verbs are conjugated with *avoir* in compound tenses, as in *J'ai sorti mon stylo.* (I took out my pen.) *J'ai descendu ma valise.* (I took down my suitcase.)

USE THE PAST TENSES IN THE NEGATIVE

In Hour 8 you learned the principal negations and how to place them in a sentence. When using a negation with compound tenses (such as the *passé composé*), observe the same rules used for the placement of the negation in noncompound tenses, as follows:

1. Place *ne* in front of the conjugated verb.

2. Place the negative adverb after the conjugated verb.

Study the following examples to see where the negative words are placed with the *passé composé*:

J'ai compris la question. Je n'ai pas compris la question.

Tu as lu le magazine. Tu n'as pas lu le magazine.

Elle a fini le travail. Elle n'a pas fini le travail.

Vous avez pris le train. Vous n'avez pas pris le train.

Ils sont allés à Rome. Ils ne sont pas allés à Rome.

Elles sont parties à 3 heures. Elles ne sont pas parties à 3 heures.

Vous avez acheté des robes. Vous n'avez pas acheté de robes.

To make the preceding sentences into negative questions, simply invert the subject and verb and connect the two with a hyphen. The negative adverb then follows the subject.

GO TO ▶
Note in the last example that *des* changes to *de* after the negation. Review this rule, presented in Hour 8.

Remember from Hour 5, when you learned to form questions, that the first person rarely uses inversion to create a question. Instead of inversion, use the question phrase *est-ce que* with the first person, as in the following examples:

Je n'ai pas compris la question. Est-ce que je n'ai pas compris la question?

Tu n'as pas lu le magazine. N'as-tu pas lu le magazine?

Elle n'a pas fini le travail. N'a-t-elle pas fini le travail?

Vous n'avez pas pris le train. N'avez-vous pas pris le train?

Ils ne sont pas allés à Rome. Ne sont-ils pas allés à Rome?

Elles ne sont pas parties à 3 heures. Ne sont-elles pas parties à 3 heures?

Vous n'avez pas acheté de robes. N'avez-vous pas acheté de robes?

Of course, you can use *est-ce que* with all persons and thus avoid having to invert the subject and verb and add the negative adverbs. However, you should practice saying these sentences aloud so you hear the negative and the question. Because this construction often is used in conversation, you will want to be able to recognize it when you hear it.

Practice making the following five sentences into questions using inversion. Cover the responses on the right and see how well you do:

- *Vous n'avez pas l'heure.*   *N'avez-vous pas l'heure?*
  (Don't you have the time [of day]?)

- *Il n'est pas encore parti.*   *N'est-il pas encore parti?*
  (Hasn't he left yet?)

- *Vous n'avez pas vu Paul.*   *N'avez-vous pas vu Paul?*
  (Haven't you seen Paul?)

- *Elle n'a rien dit.*   *N'a-t-elle rien dit?*
  (Didn't she say anything?)

- *Il n'est jamais tombé.*   *N'est-il jamais tombé?*
  (Didn't he ever fall?)

Once you see the pattern—*ne* in front of the conjugated verb and the negative adverb after the conjugated verb—you can make any sentence negative, whether a declarative or an interrogative sentence. There is only one exception: the negation *ne ... personne*.

USE *NE ... PERSONNE* WITH COMPOUND TENSES

Ne ... personne, meaning "no one," has a special place in compound tenses. *Personne* comes after the past participle. Here are a few examples:

- *Je n'ai vu personne.* (I saw no one.)
- *Il n'a cru personne.* (He believed no one.)
- *Nous n'avons écrit à personne.* (We wrote to no one.)

Now that you understand how to form the *passé composé* and generally what it means, let's talk briefly about when and how it is used.

LEARN WHEN TO USE THE *PASSÉ COMPOSÉ*

The *passé composé* is one of the two most common of the past tenses used in conversation. It is used, much as in English, to describe an action or event, or series of actions and events, that have been performed and completed in the past.

The other common past, called the *imperfect,* will be presented in the next hour. This tense is used primarily to describe actions or events that began and continued in the past. A few examples in English will alert you to the distinction at this point. In Hour 10, "Use the Correct Past Tense," you'll learn in more detail when to use which tense.

First, compare these two examples and think about how the verb tenses indicate the duration of time involved in performing each action.

- Yesterday I watched TV and then I called my friends on the phone.
- Yesterday while I was watching TV, I called my friends on the phone.

In the first sentence, you performed one action (watched TV); then performed a second action (called your friends). The sequence of events is apparent: First you watched TV; then you called your friends. The tense you would use in French would be the *passé composé*. Again, the *passé composé* is used to describe an action or event, or series of actions and events, that have been performed and completed in the past.

In the second example, you do not indicate which action took place first. The sequence of actions is not clear and not important. In fact, the two actions might have taken place simultaneously. You are simply telling the listener what you were doing in the past. The tenses used here in French would be the *imperfect*.

For now, all you really need to know is that there are two past tenses in French. You will learn how to form the imperfect tense in Hour 10.

Sometimes the distinction between the *passé composé* and the imperfect will be crystal clear. At other times, selection of one tense or the other can communicate subtle differences in meaning. In the following hours you will learn techniques to master these differences. Again, be patient; listen to native speakers and note when and how they use the tenses in everyday situations.

Let's take a break from the past tenses, and learn four new verbs in the present tense.

LEARN MORE IRREGULAR *-IR* VERBS

At the end of Hour 6, "Express Yourself in the Present Subjunctive," you learned the irregular *-ir* verbs *couvrir* (to cover), *offrir* (to offer), and *ouvrir* (to open). In this section we'll discuss some new verbs that have similar irregular conjugations in the present tense.

LEARN THE VERBS *COURIR* AND *DEVOIR*

The Verbs *Courir* and *Devoir*

Person	courir *(to run)*	devoir *(to have to, should, ought to)*
first	*je cours*	*je dois*
second	*tu cours*	*tu dois*
third, masculine	*il court*	*il doit*
third, feminine	*elle court*	*elle doit*
third, generic	*on court*	*on doit*
first	*nous courons*	*nous devons*
second	*vous courez*	*vous devez*
third, masculine	*ils courent*	*ils doivent*
third, feminine	*elles courent*	*elles doivent*
Past participle	*couru*	*dû, due*

Devoir is most often used followed by an infinitive to indicate that one should or ought to do something; for example, *Tu dois honorer tes parents* (You should honor your parents); *Je dois partir maintenant* (I should [ought to] leave now). *Devoir* also can be used to express the English idea of "must" in the sense of "it's likely that"; for example, *Tu dois avoir faim* (You must be hungry).

GO TO ▶
Other idiomatic uses of *devoir* will be presented in Hour 19, "Going Shopping."

LEARN THE VERBS *MOURIR* AND *RECEVOIR*

Mourir (to die) and *recevoir* (to receive) have distinctive changes in the stem of the verb in the present tense. See the following two lists:

mourir (to die)

> *je meurs*
>
> *tu meurs*
>
> *il meurt*
>
> *elle meurt*
>
> *on meurt*
>
> *nous mourons*
>
> *vous mourez*
>
> *ils meurent*
>
> *elles meurent*
>
> Past participle: *mort* (conjugated with *être*)

recevoir (to receive)

> *je reçois*
>
> *tu reçois*
>
> *il reçoit*
>
> *elle reçoit*
>
> *on reçoit*
>
> *nous recevons*
>
> *vous recevez*
>
> *ils reçoivent*
>
> *elles reçoivent*
>
> Past participle: *reçu*

Note that the *ç* appears before the letter *o* to keep the soft *s* sound of the *c*. In the *nous* and *vous* forms of the verb, the *c* is followed by the vowel *e* and therefore is already soft.

HOUR'S UP!

Now you know all about forming one of the past tenses in French. In the next hour, you'll learn more about pronouns. Keep up the good work! Now review the material in this hour and confirm your mastery by taking this short quiz.

1. Which of the following words is not a past participle?

   a. *chanté*

   b. *fini*

   c. *perdu*

   d. *parler*

2. Complete the sentence with *savoir* or *connaître*: Je _____ parler italien.

   a. *sais*

   b. *connais*

3. Complete the sentence with *savoir* or *connaître*: Il _____ mon père.

   a. *sait*

   b. *connaît*

4. Which of the following verbs is not conjugated with *être* in the *passé composé?*

   a. *naître*

   b. *finir*

   c. *partir*

   d. *sortir*

5. Which of the following verbs is conjugated with *avoir* in the *passé composé?*

   a. *savoir*

   b. *descendre*

   c. *entrer*

   d. *arriver*

6. True or False: Past participles of verbs conjugated with *être* agree with the subject.

7. *Je suis allé* does not mean:

    a. I went

    b. I did go

    c. I have gone

    d. I am going

8. Which of the following verbs is not a verb of movement in French?

    a. *venir*

    b. *marcher*

    c. *monter*

    d. *tomber*

9. True or False: Verbs of movement are conjugated with *être* in compound tenses.

10. True or False: Verbs of action are conjugated with *avoir* in compound tenses.

HOUR 10

Use the Correct Past Tense

CHAPTER SUMMARY

LESSON PLAN:
In this hour you'll learn …

- How to describe completed actions using the *passé composé.*
- How to form the imperfect tense.
- How to use the imperfect tense in descriptions of past actions.
- How to use the imperfect tense to describe habitual actions.
- How to use the imperfect tense in conjunction with the present conditional mood.

Mastering the French past tenses is somewhat tricky because they don't always correspond to English and there are no sure rules for learning when to use them. Native speakers develop a sense of when to use the imperfect or when to use *passé composé* based on what sounds right. Of course, a non-native speaker can't do this. You'll have to depend on learning a few general rules and then listening and reading the language to become more proficient in distinguishing one tense from the other. And because the use of the past tenses requires some work, all of this hour is devoted to learning and reviewing these tenses.

DESCRIBE COMPLETED ACTIONS: *PASSÉ COMPOSÉ*

Remember that there are three possible English translations of the *passé composé*, for example:

J'ai étudié le français can be translated as "I studied French," "I have studied French," or "I did study French."

Compare these translations of the *passé composé* with the three translations you've learned for the present tense:

J'étudie le français can be translated as "I study French," "I am studying French," or "I do study French."

You might have noticed that when you are speaking of an action taking place in the present time, you use the present tense in French, no matter the tense in English. When you think about the *passé composé*, keep this same idea in mind: When you are speaking about an action that took place and was completed in the past, use the *passé composé*. You won't always be right—but most of the time you will.

The following three guidelines are rules of thumb for when to use the *passé composé*. When you get to the rules for the use of the imperfect tense, come back to this section and compare the use of the two tenses.

WHEN ONE EVENT LOGICALLY FOLLOWS ANOTHER IN TIME

Use the *passé composé* when describing a series of actions whose sequence is important to the narrative; that is, when one event logically follows another in a past time, for example:

> *J'ai vu une belle chemise, puis j'ai demandé le prix, et ensuite, j'ai acheté la chemise.* (I saw a pretty shirt, I asked the price, and then I bought the shirt.)

The order of events is important here. First you saw the shirt, then you asked for its price, then you bought it. Here the *passé composé* insists on the importance of the sequence of events.

WHEN THE ACTION HAS A SPECIFIC DURATION IN TIME

When the action described in the past has a specific duration in time, use the *passé composé*; that is, when the action has clearly ended, usually within a measurable period of time; for example:

> *Je suis resté deux jours à Paris.* (I stayed two days in Paris.) The action is completed and was a measurable duration in the past (two days).

WHEN ENGLISH USES THE PAST OR PRESENT PERFECT

When English would use the past or present perfect, use the *passé composé* in French. Although translation is not a sure way to determine which tense to use, almost always use the *passé composé* in French when you'd use the present perfect in English; for example, "I have written," "I have eaten," and "I have gone." See the following example:

> *J'ai lu le livre, j'ai appris le français, et j'ai acheté un billet d'avion pour aller à Paris.* (I have read the book, I have learned French, and I have bought an airplane ticket in order to go to Paris.)

Now that you've learned to form and use the *passé composé*, it's time to learn how to form and use the other common past tense, the imperfect.

LEARN THE IMPERFECT TENSE

First, some excellent news: The formation of the imperfect is absolutely regular for every verb in the French language (with one exception, of course). Forming the imperfect is a two-step process.

The first step is to drop the *-ons* from the first person plural of the present tense, the *nous* form of the verb:

- *nous parlons: parl*
- *nous finissons: finiss*
- *nous choisissons: choisiss*
- *nous perdons: perd*
- *nous avons: av*
- *nous mangeons: mange*
- *nous allons: all*
- *nous écrivons: écriv*

PROCEED WITH CAUTION

Note that for *-ir* verbs you drop only the *-ons* from the verb; not the entire *-issons* ending.

Next, add the following endings to the stem:

Person	Singular	Ending	Plural	Ending
first	-je	-ais	-nous	-ions
second	-tu	-ais	-vous	-iez
third, masculine	-il	-ait	-ils	-aient
third, feminine	-elle	-ait	-elles	-aient
third, generic	-on	-ait		

Note that the endings for forming the imperfect are the same endings used to form the present conditional mood, which you learned in Hour 8, "Learn to Express Yourself in the Future." The stem of the conditional is the same stem used to form the future tense.

There is only one exception to this rule of formation: the verb *être*. Because the first-person plural of *être* does not end in *-ons* (*nous sommes*), it has a special imperfect stem: *ét*. Here is the entire conjugation of *être* in the imperfect.

Person	Singular	Plural
first	j'étais	nous étions
second	tu étais	vous étiez
third, masculine	il était	ils étaient
third, feminine	elle était	elles étaient
third, generic	on était	

GO TO ▶
Before you proceed, you might want to review the present tense conjugations of the irregular verbs by going back to Hour 4, "Actions in the Present Tense with Irregular Verbs."

Use the following table to practice the formation of the imperfect for some of the regular and irregular verbs you've learned so far. Note that even verbs that are irregular in the present tense are regular in the imperfect. All of the verbs in the table are irregular in the present tense, except for *choisir* (to choose) and *perdre* (to lose).

Conjugation of the Imperfect Tense

Infinitive	English	Imperfect Stem	First-Person Singular
aller	to go	all	j'allais
boire	to drink	buv	je buvais
choisir	to choose	choisiss	je choisissais
connaître	to know	connaiss	je connaissais
croire	to believe	croy	je croyais
dire	to say	dis	je disais
écrire	to write	écriv	j'écrivais
faire	to do	fais	je faisais
lire	to read	lis	je lisais
perdre	to lose	perd	je perdais
pouvoir	to be able	pouv	je pouvais
savoir	to know	sav	je savais
vivre	to live	viv	je vivais
voir	to see	voy	je voyais
vouloir	to want	voul	je voulais

As you work on conjugating the imperfect, you will note that in the first- and second-person plural (*nous*, *vous*) of many verbs there is only one letter different between the present and the imperfect: the letter *i*. Compare the following examples:

Nous allons. (We go.)   *Nous allions.* (We went.)

Nous finissons. (We finish.)   *Nous finissions.* (We finished.)

For the verbs *voir* and *croire*, which have a *y* at the end of the imperfect stem, pronounce the *y* as an *i* so that you actually have two *i* sounds in the word, as in *nous voyions, vous voyiez, nous croyions, vous croyiez*.

As you see, the imperfect is one of the easier tenses to form in French because the forms are very regular. Of course, you must know the present tense of the verb to find the correct imperfect ending, so now might be a good time to go back to Hours 3, "Actions in the Present Tense," and 4 and review the present tense of regular and irregular verbs.

Although the formation of the imperfect is relatively simple, its usage is somewhat problematic. Let's talk about several ways it is used in French; then we'll go back and compare the use of the imperfect with the use of the *passé composé*.

USE THE IMPERFECT TENSE WITH DESCRIPTIONS

Obviously, the imperfect is a past tense, and you've noticed in the preceding examples that it has been translated just like the *passé composé: je parlais* (I spoke), *je lisais* (I read), and so forth.

This translation shows that you can't count on your English to tell you when to use the imperfect, or the *passé composé*. Instead, you must have some guidelines for the use of each tense. Before proceeding, go back to the section in this hour that discusses the use of the *passé composé*, "Describe Completed Actions: *Passé Composé*." Then compare those uses with the following explanation of the use of the imperfect.

Use the imperfect in the following circumstances:

- When you describe the scene or setting in which actions took place in the past
- When you describe actions that took place in the past and have no precise ending time in the past

- When you describe habitual or repeated actions in the past
- When you describe an ongoing action within the course of which another single action is completed (the latter will be in the *passé composé!*)
- When you use the word *si* (if) in conjunction with the conditional mood to indicate a condition

Let's explore each of these uses.

Describe the Setting in the Past

Typically when you begin to tell a story, you start by setting the stage, describing the scene in which the action takes place. You might think of such descriptions as background information for your story. The French call this *le décor*. In setting the scene or background, you might talk about what the weather was like, what has happening around you, or what time of day it was. These are all bits of information that occur in no particular sequence and simply describe the setting in the past.

As an example, you might start your story something like this: "It was raining that night; it was close to 9 o'clock. There was not much traffic in the street, it was cold, and I was thinking about going to see a movie." You could reorder the events described in these sentences without changing their meanings. For example, perhaps you prefer mentioning first that you were thinking about going to the movies, and then you proceed to describe the weather and the traffic. In any arrangement of your sentences, all you hope to communicate is what was happening around you in general terms. In French, you would use the imperfect to describe this *décor*:

> *Il pleuvait, il était presque 9 heures. Il n'y avait pas de circulation dans les rues, il faisait froid, et je pensais aller voir un film.*

Once the scene is set, you probably would continue to tell the listener what you did. Perhaps you decided to telephone your friend Susan and invite her to go with you. You went to the ATM to get some money and then you went to the cinema. Note that these actions would be recounted in a logical sequence to tell what you did first, second, and third. For example, you didn't go to the cinema, go to the bank, and then call your friend. Because this is a sequence of actions whose order is logically important, you'd use the *passé composé* to continue your narrative:

Alors, j'ai téléphoné à Suzanne et je l'ai invitée à m'accompagner au cinéma. Ensuite, je suis allé au DAB pour chercher de l'argent, et puis je suis allé au cinéma.

STRICTLY DEFINED

Distributeur automatique de billets (DAB) is an automatic bill distributor, or ATM.

This use of the imperfect to set the scene is very common. Often you will start your story with a series of general sentences setting the scene in the imperfect and then move into using the *passé composé* to recount the action or events that followed.

DESCRIBE PAST ACTIONS WITH NO DEFINITE END

The second most common use of the imperfect is to describe an action or a state of being that has no definite end in the past. For example, in talking about your vacation when you were young, you might say, "When I was young, I loved to go to the beach." This is a broad statement about your general preference at an unspecified time in the past. In French you would use the imperfect to communicate this idea of an event or preference with no definite end:

Quand j'étais jeune, j'aimais aller à la plage.

Here are several more examples of this usage:

- *Quand il pleuvait, je portais mon parapluie.* (When it rained, I carried my umbrella.)
- *Elle lisait le journal tous les matins.* (She read the paper every morning.)
- *Il sortait avec Yvette pendant longtemps.* (He went out with Yvette for a long time.)
- *Nous n'étions pas du tout heureux du voyage.* (We weren't at all happy with the trip.)

In each preceding example there is no reference to the end time of the action taking place. Often in English we use expressions like "used to" or "often" to communicate this idea of indefinite time. For example, you might translate the preceding sentences as follows: When it would rain, I used to carry my umbrella; or she used to/often read the paper every morning; and so forth. Therefore, one hint for using the imperfect in French in this sense is this: When you would use "often" or "used to" in English, use the imperfect in French.

Try these examples:

- When I was young, I used to speak French: *Quand j'étais jeune, je parlais français.*
- As a baby, he (often) cried a lot: *Comme bébé, il pleurait beaucoup.*
- When I was a child, I used to want to be rich: *Quand j'étais enfant, je voulais être riche.*

DESCRIBE HABITUAL ACTIONS

The imperfect is also used to describe habitual, repeated actions in the past.

- *Suzanne étudiait beaucoup au lycée.* (Susan studied a lot in high school.)
- *Dans ma famille, nous dînions toujours à 8 heures.* (In my family, we always had dinner at 8 o'clock.)
- *Comme enfant, j'étais espiègle.* (As a child, I was [always] mischievous.)
- *Les adolescents des années 70 buvaient trop.* (Teenagers in the '70s drank too much.)

Following this guideline, you'll notice that often when you talk about historical events, you'll use the imperfect if the events occurred repeatedly.

USE THE IMPERFECT IN CONJUNCTION WITH THE *PASSÉ COMPOSÉ*

When, in the course of an ongoing action, another single action occurs, you can indicate this by using the imperfect and the *passé composé*. For example, while you were reading the paper (ongoing action), the telephone rang (single action). This is one of the most common uses of the imperfect. Study the following examples:

- *Je lisais le journal quand le téléphone a sonné.* (I was reading the paper when the phone rang.)
- *Elle parlait au téléphone quand Paul est arrivé.* (She was talking on the phone when Paul arrived.)
- *Il neigeait quand je suis arrivé à New York.* (It was snowing when I arrived in New York.)

Contrast these examples with this one: *Néron jouait au violon pendant que Rome brûlait.* (Nero played the violin while Rome burned.) Here the two actions are ongoing and taking place at the same time. Use the imperfect in both clauses.

USE THE IMPERFECT + CONDITIONAL TO SAY "WHAT IF"

In Hour 8 you learned the present conditional mood. Let's review quickly what you've already learned about the conditional mood. First it is used to express politeness, just as in English. Rather than saying "I want something," you say in polite speech, "I would like something," as follows: *Je voudrais un verre de vin, s'il vous plaît* (I would like a glass of wine, please).

Second, you've learned that the conditional mood, as the name implies, is used to express that the completion of one action is conditional (dependent) on another action, as in *J'aimerais voyager mais je suis pauvre* ("I would like to travel but I'm poor" [statement of condition]).

The third way to use the conditional is with the word *si*, when *si* means "if": *Si elle avait plus d'argent, elle irait à Londres.* (If she had more money, she would go to London.)

PROCEED WITH CAUTION

In English, "if" often is used to mean whether: I don't know if/whether he is going or not. The same is true of the French word *si*. However, the conditional is used with *si* only when *si* means "if," and never when it means "whether."

You did not learn this use of the conditional in Hour 8 because you'd not yet learned the tense with which it is used in sentences using *si*. Now you know that tense—it's the imperfect.

Now you will be able to form complete conditional sentences; following are a few examples. As you study them, notice that the verb in the *si* clause is in the imperfect in all cases; the verb in the main clause is in the present conditional mood:

- *Si j'**avais** assez d'argent, j'**irais** à Paris.* (If I **had** enough money, I **would go** to Paris.)

- *Je **comprendrais** les Français, si je **savais** parler français.* (I **would understand** the French if I **knew** how to speak French.)

- *Il **lirait** le journal, s'il **avait** plus de temps.* (He **would read** the paper if he **had** more time.)
- *Nous **inviterions** Marie à dîner, si elle **était** libre.* (We **would invite** Mary to dinner if she **were** free.)
- *Si vous **étudiiez** beaucoup, vous **apprendriez** beaucoup.* (If you **studied** a lot, you **would learn** a lot.)
- *Tu **pourrais** partir, si tu **voulais**.* (You **would be able** to [could] leave if you **wanted** to.)

PROCEED WITH CAUTION

Note that *si* becomes *s'* before *il* and *ils,* but stays *si* before *elle* and *elles,* as in *s'il, s'ils, si elle, si elles.*

As you look closely at these examples, you will see that a pattern arises as follows:

si + imperfect + conditional

This is the basic rule for creating conditional statements. It's important to master this rule because it does not reflect common English usage. While it is not "proper" English, you can say "If you would just ask me, I would go out with you." As you see in this example, English permits the use of the conditional mood in the same clause with the word "if"; this is not so in French. As a general rule, the word *si* is never followed directly by either the future tense or the conditional mood.

Do you recall our discussions of "concordances of tenses" at the end of Hour 8? We talked about how all languages have tenses that are used together and tenses that are never used together. The concordance of the future and the conditional in French is not the same as in English.

The rules of concordance of the future and conditional are so important that they merit repetition here. In future hours, you will learn other rules of concordance, so work hard to master these two now.

RULE ONE

The first rule is as follows:

si + present (or sometimes *passé composé*) + future or imperative or present

Examples:

> *Si j'ai assez d'argent, j'achèterai une nouvelle voiture.* (If I have enough money, I will buy a new car.)
>
> *Si je suis fatigué, je dors.* (If I'm tired, I sleep.)
>
> *Si vous avez assez d'argent, achetez une nouvelle voiture.* (If you have enough money, buy a new car.)

Note that the only tenses used in the *si* clause in these examples is either the present or *passé composé*. In the main clause, use the present, the future, or the imperative, whichever is appropriate to express your meaning.

RULE TWO

The second rule is as follows:

si + imperfect + present conditional

Examples:

> *S'il avait le temps, il irait à Rome.* (If he had enough time, he would go to Rome.)
>
> *Si vous aimiez les escargots, vous les mangeriez.* (If you liked snails, you would eat them.)
>
> *Si je savais la réponse correcte, je répondrais à la question.* (If I knew the correct answer, I would respond to the question.)

Note that the only tense used in the *si* clause in these examples is the imperfect. When you use the imperfect in the *si* clause, you'll always use the present conditional in the main clause. Once you've mastered these two rules, the use of the conditional will become much easier.

In addition to learning the rules, you'll soon discover that some verbs are almost always used in the *passé composé* and others are almost always used in the imperfect. Let's look at some of the more common verbs in these groups.

LEARN VERBS COMMONLY USED IN THE IMPERFECT

Because the imperfect is used to describe actions or events in the past without a definite end, you will find it logical that verbs that express a state of mind or a state of being quite often are used in the imperfect.

Here's a short list of these verbs:

avoir	*penser*
croire	*pouvoir*
espérer	*savoir*
être	*vouloir*
faire	

In fact, some of these verbs have a slightly different nuance when used in one tense or the other:

- *il pouvait* (he could) *il a pu* (he was able)
- *il savait* (he knew) *il a su* (he discovered)
- *il voulait* (he wanted) *il a voulu* (he insisted upon)

For now, just be aware of this nuance. As you become more proficient in the language, you can come back to this hour and work on making the distinctions when appropriate. (You also will want to come back to this hour when you learn the remaining French tenses in Hour 17, "Eating Out.")

Of course, you will always be using the past tenses and the conditional within a context. You won't be composing a bunch of unrelated sentences when you talk. To help you create the appropriate context for using the past tenses, let's consider some helping words to link everything together.

FORMULATE DESCRIPTIONS USING THE IMPERFECT

Once again, the imperfect is used to create the *décor* surrounding your story or conversation. Thus, there are expressions of time and place that often are used in conjunction with the imperfect. The following table lists the most useful ones.

Expressions Often Used with the Imperfect

French	English
souvent	often
toujours	always
pendant longtemps	for a long time
chaque jour, chaque semaine, etc.	each day, each week
tous les jours, tous les ans, etc.	every day, every year
le lundi, le samedi, and so forth	every Monday, every Saturday

French	English
d'habitude	usually
chaque fois	each time
pendant	while

Two idiomatic expressions also are always used in the imperfect when in the past:

- *Être en train de* (to be in the midst of) is used to convey that you are doing something right at this moment; for example, *Je suis en train d'apprendre le français.* (I'm [right in the midst] of learning French.) The past tense of this expression is always the imperfect: *J'étais en train d'apprendre le français.* (I was [right in the midst] of learning French.)

- *Venir de* is used to express the idea in English of just having done something; for example, *Elle vient de partir.* (She is just [now] leaving.) The past tense of this expression is always the imperfect: *Elle venait de partir.* (She has just [now] left.)

Before we end this hour, let's see how well you've mastered the difference between the use of the *passé composé* and the use of the imperfect. Here are eight sentences. Cover the answers that follow and see if you can select the right tense to use in each case. A brief explanation of the correct answers follows the exercise.

1. The baby was born yesterday.
2. I was 19 when Mr. Reagan was president.
3. When we were in Paris, we visited the Louvre every Sunday.
4. I watched that film every day when I was young.
5. We never saw the Eiffel Tower.
6. Aunt Mary died when she was 80.
7. Paul left yesterday. I was very sad.
8. I returned to Paris when I was 30.

The following are the translations using the correct tense:

1. *Le bébé est né hier.*
2. *J'avais 19 ans quand Monsieur Reagan était président.*
3. *Quand nous étions à Paris, nous visitions le Louvre tous les dimanches.*
4. *Je regardais ce film chaque jour quand j'étais jeune.*

5. *Nous n'avons jamais vu la Tour Eiffel.*

6. *Tante Marie est morte quand elle avait 80 ans.*

7. *Paul est parti hier. J'étais très triste.*

8. *Je suis retourné à Paris quand j'avais 30 ans.*

Explanation:

1. The verb *naître* is almost always in the *passé composé* because births happen only once. Of course, the word "renaissance" comes from the French *re-naître* (rebirth), but usually our physical birth is a one-time event, as are all actions in *passé composé*.

2. This sentence is a general statement of historical events. Mr. Reagan was president for an unspecified period of time while you were nineteen. There is no sequence of events or chronological relationship between to two events; thus imperfect.

3. Here again, you are setting a scene and making a general statement that the whole time you were in Paris, every Sunday, habitually, you went to the Louvre. (Entry to French museums often is free on Sundays.) General description + habitual action becomes imperfect.

4. Habitually, *chaque jour* (every day), you watched the same movie; thus, imperfect is used.

5. Here the *passé composé* is used just as in English to express a simple fact in the past, as in "We've never seen" or "We never saw." This is not a description; thus, *passé composé* is used.

6. Death, like birth, is a one-time event; thus, *mourir* is almost always used in the *passé composé*. Aunt Mary was 80 when she died, and *avoir* most often is used in the imperfect (always when speaking of age).

7. Simple statement that Paul has left—not that he was leaving or used to leave; the action is completed in the past; thus *passé composé*. However, you were sad and still might be saddened by his leaving. The imperfect describes your state of mind, especially when talking about emotions that often are ongoing; thus imperfect.

8. The first verb, *suis retourné*, is in the *passé composé* because it is a one-time, completed action. The second verb gives the subject's age, which is simply a description, and thus imperfect is used.

Hour's Up!

Bravo! You've mastered some very difficult material this hour. Learning when to use the *passé composé* and when to use the imperfect takes some time and effort, so continue to review the general rules for usage given in this hour. Also, try to read French either on the Internet or in French publications at your local library, paying attention to how these two tenses are used by native speakers. Review the materials in this hour again, and then test your level of mastery with the following quiz.

1. Which of the following verbs is in the imperfect?

    a. *avait*

    b. *irait*

    c. *aura*

    d. *serait*

2. Which of the following verbs is not in the imperfect?

    a. *était*

    b. *viendra*

    c. *perdait*

    d. *allait*

3. True or False: *Être* is the only verb in French with an irregular stem in the imperfect.

4. True or False: The imperfect is used to describe the setting of a story in the past.

5. True or False: The *passé composé* is used to describe habitual actions.

6. Complete the following sentence with the correct verb form: *Si j'_____ assez d'argent, j'irais à Paris.*

    a. *ai eu*

    b. *ai*

    c. *avais*

    d. *aurai*

7. Complete the following sentence with the correct verb form: *S'il avait plus de temps, il _____ le journal le matin.*

    a. *lit*

    b. *lira*

    c. *lisait*

    d. *lirait*

8. Complete the following sentence with the correct verb form: *Si j'ai assez d'argent, j'_____ de nouvelles chaussures.*

    a. *achètent*

    b. *achèterai*

    c. *achèterais*

    d. *ai acheté*

9. Complete the following sentence with the correct verb form: *S'il _____ le temps, il irait à Rome.*

    a. *a*

    b. *aura*

    c. *avait*

    d. *aurait*

10. Which adverbial expression would least likely be used in conjunction with the imperfect?

    a. *demain*

    b. *souvent*

    c. *d'habitude*

    d. *toujours*

HOUR 11

Learn to Show Possession

In this hour you'll take a short break from verbs and learn much more about pronouns and adjectives, particularly those that indicate possession. You'll also learn about two special groups of pronouns called demonstrative pronouns (they "demonstrate" something) and tonic pronouns, also called "stressed" pronouns because they are used to emphasize, or stress, a statement.

USE *DE* TO SHOW POSSESSION

As stated above, French does not use the apostrophe to indicate possession as in the English "Paul's book." This is a very important distinction for two reasons. First, the apostrophe is used in French, but only to indicate required contractions such as *s'il*, *j'ai*, and *d'autres*. You will remember that French has no optional uses of the apostrophe. In contrast, English permits one to say either "I'm going to the store" or "I am going to the store"; you can choose whichever form you prefer. Usually contractions are used in conversation and are avoided in formal writing. This is not true of French. Every time the word *je* is followed by a vowel, you must contract it to *j'*.

Second, the use of the English apostrophe to show possession often causes even native speakers to pause. For example, often mistakes are made when we have to indicate both plurality and possession in English, as in these examples: the girl's dress, the girl's dresses, the girls' dresses. Also there is some discussion among grammarians about whether objects can possess something, as in "the book's title." Of course, in everyday speech this is common usage, but it doesn't sound as elegant as "the title of the book."

LESSON PLAN:

In this hour you will learn ...

- How to use *de* to show possession.
- How to use possessive adjectives.
- How to use possessive pronouns.
- How to use demonstrative pronouns.
- How to use the pronoun *tout*.
- How to use the tonic pronouns.

GO TO ▶

Review in Hour 2, "Describing Things," the required contraction when *de* is followed by the definite articles: *de + le* becomes *du; de + les* becomes *des.*

As you learn about how to indicate possession in French, just forget completely about the apostrophe. You'll see that the French possession is much simpler than the English. French has a very regular formation of the possessive using the preposition *de,* meaning "of," plus the definite articles (*le, la, les*), as shown in the following:

noun + *de* (*du, de la, de l', des*) + possessor

Consider the following examples:

- Paul's book: *le livre de Paul*
- The book's title: *le titre du livre*
- The woman's hat: *le chapeau de la femme*
- The man's coat: *le manteau de l'homme*
- The women's dresses: *les robes des femmes*
- The girl's dress: *la robe de la jeune fille*
- The girl's dresses: *les robes de la jeune fille*
- The girls' dresses: *les robes des jeunes filles*

This is the only way to indicate possession in French when both words are nouns. Note that the order of the words is reversed from the English when the apostrophe is used; however, English also has the same construction as French.

Consider these examples:

- The car door/the door of the car: *la porte de la voiture*
- The tree leaves/the leaves of the tree: *les feuilles de l'arbre*
- The book's title/the title of the book: *le titre du livre*
- The men's car/the car of the men: *la voiture des hommes*
- The men's cars/the cars of the men: *les voitures des hommes*

Now try a few examples on your own. Cover the translations on the right and see if you can create the French equivalent. Remember to start with the second word of the English expression, use the correct form of *de,* and end with the first word of the English expression. In other words, reverse the order of the English expression.

- The hotel's address: *l'adresse de l'hôtel*
- Yves's phone number: *le numéro de téléphone d'Yves*
- The professor's book: *le livre du professeur*
- Mary's friend: *l'ami de Marie*

- The United States' president: *le président des États-Unis*
- The president of France: *le président de France*
- The airplane door: *la porte de l'avion*

Notice particularly that English often uses two nouns together to indicate possession without using an apostrophe, as in "the airplane door," whereas French typically uses the same construction for all possessions, as in *la porte de l'avion* (the door of the airplane).

Here are some other common expressions using the noun + *de* + noun construction:

- The subway entrance: *la bouche du métro* (literally: the mouth of the metro)
- The flight number: *le numéro du vol*
- The movie times: *les heures du film* (the times of the movie)
- The shop owner: *le patron de la boutique*
- The passport number: *le numéro du passeport*

Of course not every English construction will be translated this way into French. Here are some everyday words that don't translate using the noun + *de* + noun construction. Instead, there is a particular word or phrase to translate the concept. Generally you will recognize similar words as vocabulary items and you should add them to your personal vocabulary list:

GO TO ▶
You learned about nouns modifying nouns in Hour 2.

- The ticket window: *le guichet*
- The exit door: *la sortie*
- The entry door: *l'entrée*
- The information sign: *le panneau*
- The bus station: *la gare routière*
- The checkout counter: *la caisse* (literally: the cashier)

When English uses one noun to modify another noun, rather than to show possession, French most often uses only *de* to connect the two words.

Here is a list of some more common examples:

- A bank employee: *un employé de banque*
- The bus stop: *l'arrêt d'autobus*
- A movie star: *une vedette de cinéma*
- The house key: *une clé de maison*

- A house robe: *une robe de chambre*
- A race car: *une voiture de course*
- The French class: *la classe de français*
- The tourist agency: *l'agence de tourisme*

Note the logic of these constructions: *un employé de banque* means simply "a bank employee." If you want to refer to the employees of the Bank of France, you'd say *les employés de la Banque de France*.

FYI The preposition *en* sometimes replaces *de* to indicate what an object is made of, as in *un sac de cuir* (a leather bag); *un sac en cuir* (bag made of leather).

Of course, there are exceptions to all the preceding rules, but they are few in number:

- Household expenses: *les frais du ménage or de ménage*
- The automobile club: *le club automobile*
- A student (ID) card: *une carte étudiante*
- Tourist class: *la classe touriste*

Now let's look at some of the other ways to indicate possession, first using adjectives; then pronouns.

LEARN POSSESSIVE ADJECTIVES

In English, when you say, "This is my book," "my" is a possessive adjective because it modifies the word "book" and shows possession. French also has possessive adjectives and, because they are adjectives, they agree in number and gender with the nouns they modify.

This rule is very important because it is quite different from English. Possessive adjectives in English agree in number and gender with the person who possesses the object. Let's look at a few examples:

- This is Susan's book. It is **her** book.
- This is Paul's book. It is **his** book.
- This is Mary and Peter's book. This is **their** book.
- These are Mary's and Peter's books. These are **their** books.

Of course you've learned well that adjectives in French agree in number and gender with the noun they modify. So before we look at all the forms of the possessive adjectives, let's translate the four sentences in the preceding list into French:

- This is Susan's book. It is her book.

  C'est le livre de Suzanne. C'est son livre.
- This is Paul's book. It is his book.

  C'est le livre de Paul. C'est son livre.
- This is Mary and Peter's book. This is their book.

  C'est le livre de Marie et de Paul. C'est leur livre.
- These are Mary's and Peter's books. These are their books.
- *Ce sont les livres de Marie et de Paul. Ce sont leurs livres.*

Immediately you noticed in the first two sentences that the word *son* means both "his" and "hers" in French. It does not agree with the owner (Susan or Paul), but rather with the word *livre*, which is masculine.

In the second two sentences, *leur* means "their," but it agrees in the plural with the *livres*; thus, *leur livre* (their book) and *leurs livres* (their books). Again, the rule is that adjectives agree in number and gender with the nouns they modify.

The following table lists all the possessive adjectives.

Possessive Adjectives

French	Gender/Number	English
mon	masculine singular (used before any word beginning with a vowel)	my
ma	feminine singular	my
mes	masculine/feminine plural	my
ton	masculine singular (used before any word beginning with a vowel)	your
ta	feminine singular	your
tes	masculine/feminine plural	your
son	masculine singular (used before any word beginning with a vowel)	his/her
sa	feminine singular	his/her
ses	masculine/feminine plural	his/her
notre	masculine/feminine singular	our
nos	masculine/feminine plural	our
votre	masculine/feminine singular	your
vos	masculine/feminine plural	your
leur	masculine/feminine singular	their
leurs	masculine/feminine plural	their

The following are some examples of possessive adjectives:

- *mon père:* my father
- *ma mère:* my mother
- *mes parents:* my parents (masculine/feminine plural)
- *ton oncle:* your uncle
- *ta tante:* your aunt
- *tes cousins, tes cousines:* your cousins (masculine/feminine plural)
- *son frère:* his, her brother
- *sa soeur:* his, her sister
- *ses cousins, ses cousines:* his, her cousins (masculine/feminine plural)
- *notre grand-père:* our grandfather
- *notre grand-mère:* our grandmother
- *nos grands-parents:* our grandparents (masculine/feminine plural)
- *votre grand-père:* your grandfather
- *votre grand-mère:* your grandmother
- *vos grands-parents:* your grandparents (masculine/feminine plural)
- *leur cousin, leur cousine:* their cousin (masculine/feminine)
- *leurs oncles, leurs tantes:* their uncles, their aunts (masculine/feminine)

Note particularly that although *mon, ton,* and *son* are the masculine possessive adjectives, they also are used before any word (noun, adjective, and so forth) beginning with a vowel, as follows:

mon automobile (feminine)	but	*ma nouvelle automobile*
ton amie (feminine)	but	*ta bonne amie*
son énorme maison (feminine)	but	*sa maison*
son autre soeur (feminine)	but	*sa soeur*

Usually *mon/ma/mes, ton/ta/tes, notre/nos,* and *votre/vos* will not cause you problems as long as you remember that they agree with the nouns they modify. However, *son/sa/ses* and *leur/leurs* often cause problems for speakers of English because of the plural forms. *Ses* is used before a plural noun to mean "his/her"; *leur/leurs* mean "their" and are used before a singular or a plural noun, respectively. Let's work a bit on these forms, and then we'll review the usage with all the forms.

SON, SA, AND SES

Son, sa, and *ses* all mean "his" or "her." Confusion arises most often for English speakers in the plural because, of course, English has no equivalent plural form of "his" or "her"; no "his-es" or "hers-es," as it were. However, because these are adjectives, French has forms for them to agree with all possible cases. Let's try the simple translation examples shown in the following table to work on these forms.

Use of *son/sa/ses*

English	French	Noun	Gender/Number
his house	sa maison	maison	feminine, singular
his hotel	son hôtel	hôtel	masculine, singular
her house	sa maison	maison	feminine, singular
his houses	ses maisons	maisons	feminine, plural

Note that "his house" and "her house" are *sa maison*, and "his hotel" and "her hotel" are *son hôtel* because *maison* is feminine, and *hôtel* is masculine. Context most often will clarify the meaning in French. Also, *ses* is both masculine and feminine, as well as plural, as in *ses maisons* (his/her houses).

LEUR AND LEURS

Both *leur* and *leurs* mean "their," as in *leur ticket* (their ticket [singular]); *leurs tickets* (their tickets [plural]). Let's use the same examples as the preceding to illustrate the use of *leur* and *leurs*:

Use of *leur* and *leurs*

English	French	Noun	Gender/Number
their house	leur maison	maison	feminine, singular
their hotel	leur hôtel	hôtel	masculine, singular
their houses	leurs maisons	maisons	feminine, plural
their hotels	leurs hôtels	hôtels	masculine, plural

Now try translating some phrases yourself by using the following words, which have the same spelling and meaning in French and English (such words are called "cognates"). Cover the answers on the right and translate the English phrase in the middle column, paying particular attention to the gender and number of the English nouns.

GO TO ▶
See the "Use the Tonic Pronouns" section toward the end of this hour to learn how to distinguish between the meanings of "his" and "hers" when the context does not make the distinction clear.

PROCEED WITH CAUTION

Remember that the masculine forms *mon/ton/son* are used before any word beginning with a vowel, whether the word is masculine or feminine.

French Cognate	English Cognate	French Translation
un train	my train	*mon train*
une table	our table	*notre table*
une institution	their institutions	*leurs institutions*
une orange	his orange	*son orange*

In addition to possessive adjectives, French has pronouns that indicate possession.

LEARN POSSESSIVE PRONOUNS

As adjectives agree in number and gender with the nouns they modify, pronouns agree with the nouns they replace. The possessive pronouns in English are mine, his, hers, ours, yours, and theirs. They agree in gender and number with the possessor. In contrast, French possessive pronouns agree in number and gender with the person or object possessed, as shown in the following table.

Possessive Pronouns

French	Gender/Number	English
le mien	masculine singular	mine
les miens	masculine plural	mine
la mienne	feminine singular	mine
les miennes	feminine plural	mine
le tien	masculine singular	yours
les tiens	masculine plural	yours
la tienne	feminine singular	yours
les tiennes	feminine plural	yours
le sien	masculine singular	his/hers
les siens	masculine plural	his/hers
la sienne	feminine singular	his/hers
les siennes	feminine plural	his/hers
le nôtre	masculine singular	ours
la nôtre	feminine singular	ours

French	Gender/Number	English
les nôtres	masculine/feminine plural	ours
le vôtre	masculine singular	yours
la vôtre	feminine singular	yours
les vôtres	masculine/feminine plural	yours
le leur	masculine singular	theirs
la leur	feminine singular	theirs
les leurs	masculine/feminine plural	theirs

Note that *la leur* is feminine singular, but there is no *e* on *la leur*. Also, *le nôtre* and *le vôtre* and their forms have a circumflex accent that makes the ô sound as an open *o*.

The plural forms of *le nôtre* and *le vôtre* are *les nôtres* and *les vôtres*. The plural forms of the possessive adjectives *notre* and *votre* (our, your) are *nos* and *vos*, as in *nos livres* (our books), *vos livres* (your books), *les nôtres* (ours), and *les vôtres* (yours).

Before you proceed, note that the definite article is an integral part of the possessive pronouns. By paying attention to the article of the object you are replacing, you can get a clue about which form of the pronoun to use. Also, because the article is part of the pronoun, it follows the rules of contraction you've learned previously, as in the following examples:

*Je préfère mon pays **au** vôtre.* (I prefer my country to yours.)

*Je n'ai plus de beurre. Est-ce que je peux avoir un peu **du** tien?* (I don't have any butter. May I have a little of yours?)

Study the following examples to see how the possessive pronouns are used:

- *C'est mon livre.*   *C'est le mien.* (It's mine.)
- *C'est ma voiture.*   *C'est la mienne.* (It's mine.)
- *C'est son adresse.*   *C'est la sienne.* (It's his/hers.)
- *C'est ton amie.*   *C'est la tienne.* (He/She is yours.)
- *Voilà notre hôtel.*   *Voilà la nôtre.* (There's ours.)
- *C'est votre chambre.*   *C'est la vôtre.* (This is yours.)
- *Ce sont vos clés.*   *Ce sont les vôtres.* (These are yours.)
- *C'est leur taxi.*   *C'est le leur.* (It's theirs.)
- *Ce sont leurs livres.*   *Ce sont les leurs.* (They are theirs.)

FYI In the preceding list *adresse* and *amie* are feminine but they begin with a vowel; thus *son adresse* and *ton amie*. Therefore, the pronouns used to replace them are also feminine, as in *la sienne* and *la tienne*, respectively.

LEARN DEMONSTRATIVE PRONOUNS

In Hour 7, "Describe Your Surroundings," you learned the demonstrative pronouns, meaning "this," "that," "these," and "those": *ce, cet, cette, ces*. You also learned that "demonstrative" means "to demonstrate, to point out, to show." For example, to say "this book and that book," you say, *ce livre-ci et ce livre-là*. The demonstrative pronouns work much the same way as other pronouns. They agree in number and gender with the person or object to which you are referring.

There are three types of demonstrative pronouns in French. We'll look at each type individually in the following sections.

CELUI, CEUX, CELLE, AND CELLES

First, notice that there are four forms of this demonstrative pronoun: masculine singular, masculine plural, feminine singular, and feminine plural. These pronouns can mean either "this one/that one" or "these/those"; so to distinguish between these possible meanings, they are usually modified with the adverbs *-ci* (indicating this one, these) or *-là* (indicating that one, those); for example, *Voilà deux voitures. Celle-ci est rouge, celle-là est verte.* (There are two cars. This one [here] is red, that one [there] is green.)

PROCEED WITH CAUTION

Remember these are pronouns; thus the adjectives (*rouge, vert*) that modify them agree in number and gender.

Here are a few examples of the use of these pronouns to help you distinguish between two choices:

Quelle chemise préférez-vous, Monsieur? Celle-ci ou celle-là? (Which shirt do you prefer, sir? This one or that one?)

Vous cherchez un bon vin, Madame? Eh bien, celui-ci est meilleur que celui-là. (You're looking for a good wine, mad'am? Well, this one is better than that one.)

Il y a deux trains en provenance de Paris aujourd'hui. Celui-ci arrive à midi, celui-là arrive à 14 heures. (There are two trains arriving from Paris today. This one arrives at noon, that one arrives at 2:00 P.M.)

CECI, CELA

Ceci (this) and *cela* (that) are used as the subject of a sentence. *Cela* often is replaced by *ça* in conversation.

Paul veut partir demain matin, mais cela (ça) me semble ridicule. (Paul wants to leave tomorrow morning, but that seems silly to me.)

Ceci est évident: Paul va partir demain matin. (This is evident: Paul is going to leave tomorrow morning.)

CE (C')

You've already learned the pronoun *ce* in Hour 3, "Actions in the Present Tense." Usually it means "this" or "that" when used with the verb *être*, but it also can mean "he," "she," or "they" before a noun modified by an article or an adjective:

- *Qui est-ce? C'est ma soeur.*
  (Who is this? This is, it is, she is my sister.)
- *Quelle ville est-ce? C'est Paris!*
  (What city is this? It's Paris!)
- *J'aime bien Suzanne. C'est une femme très sympa.*
  (I really like Susan. She's a very nice woman.)
- *Connais-tu Marie? C'est une jeune artiste française.*
  (Do you know Mary? She's a young French artist.)
- *Voilà Jean et Jacques. Ce sont mes cousins.*
  (There are John and Jack. They are my cousins.)

PROCEED WITH CAUTION

The pronouns *il, ils, elle,* and *elles* can be used instead of *ce* when referring to persons; however, this usage is very restricted and should be avoided. **C'est une jeune artiste française** is always preferable to **Elle** *est une jeune artiste française.*

C'est is always used before proper nouns:

Qui est cet homme? C'est Paul Martin. (Who is this man? It's Paul Martin.)

Now you know almost all the types of adjectives in French and almost all the pronouns. There are only three other types of pronouns to learn: the pronoun *tout* (meaning all, every); the tonic pronouns used for emphasis or clarity; and the pronouns used as objects of verbs (me, to me, you, to you, and so forth). This last group, the object pronouns, is presented in Hour 14, "Free Time." They are a bit tricky, so you'll learn them all at once.

Let's complete this hour by learning about *tout* and the tonic pronouns.

LEARN THE PRONOUN *TOUT*

Tout can be an adjective, an adverb, or a pronoun. As an adjective or pronoun, it has four forms: *tout, tous, toute,* and *toutes,* so that it can agree with the word it modifies (when used as an adjective) or the word it replaces (when used as a pronoun). First let's learn to use *tout* as an adjective. As an adjective, *tout* and *toute* (used with an article) have the same meaning as *chaque* (each). Consider the following examples:

Tout étudiant doit faire ses devoirs. (Each [every] student must do his/her homework.)

Toute ville a sa propre histoire. (Each [every] town has its own history.)

PROCEED WITH CAUTION

In English we can say either "all of the men" or "all the men." However, when using *tout* to mean "all," don't translate the English word "of" into French. In French "all of the men" is *tous les hommes;* "all of the cheeses" is *tous les fromages;* and so forth.

When used in either the singular or plural, *tout* has the meaning of "all," "the whole," or "the entire." When used as an adjective, of course, *tout* agrees in number and gender with the noun it modifies and the definite article (*le, la, les*) is used. *Tout* and *tous* (as adjectives) are pronounced alike (*tou*); *toute* and *toute* are pronounced *tout,* the final *t* being pronounced because in precedes the voiceless *e.* The following list illustrates how *tout* is used as an adjective:

- *Il mange tout le croissant.* (He eats all [of] the croissant.) (*Tout* is pronounced *tou.*)

- *Toute la ville fête le 14 juillet.*
  (The entire town celebrates July 14th.
  Or: All [of] the town celebrates July 14th.)

- *Tous les hommes aiment le football.* (All men like soccer.) (*Tous* is pronounced *tou.*)

- *Toutes vos excuses sont ridicules.*
  (All [of] your excuses are silly.)

- *Toute ma famille part en vacances.*
  (All [of] my family is leaving on vacation.)

- *Je reste à Paris toute l'année.*
  (I'm staying in Paris the whole [all of, the entire] year.)

- *Tout le monde aime le pain français.*
  (All the world [everyone] loves French bread.)

FYI *Tout le monde* always means "everyone." Literally, it translates as "all the world." It is singular and can be used any time you'd say "everyone" or "everybody" in English, as in *Tout le monde part* (Everyone is leaving); *Au revoir, tout le monde!* (Good-bye, everyone!) "Anyone" is *personne,* as in *Je ne vois personne ici* (I don't see anyone here).

PROCEED WITH CAUTION

As adjectives, *tout* and *tous* are pronounced the same: *tou.* As pronouns, *tout* also is pronounced *tou,* but *tous* is pronounced *tousse;* the final *s* is voiced. However, remember to make the liaison with *tout* when followed by a vowel or mute *h,* as in *tout homme* (tou-tum); *tout étudiant* (tou-tay-tu-dee-an).

When *tout* is used as a pronoun, it has the same forms as the adjective *tout* (*tout, tous, toute,* and *toutes*) and means "everything" or "all." It agrees in number and gender with the word it replaces or represents. The following are examples:

- *Je comprends tout.* (I understand everything.)

- *L'argent n'est pas tout.* (Money isn't everything.)

- *Tout est bien qui finit bien.* (All's well that ends well.)

- *Ses amis sont tous très gentils.* (His/her friends are all very nice.) (*Tous* is pronounced *tousse.*)

- *Leurs amies sont toutes très gentilles.* (Their [female] friends are all very nice.)

To say "all that," *tout* is followed by the relative pronouns *ce qui* or *ce que*, depending on the use in sentence. You will learn about this usage in Hour 12, "Learn to Link Ideas," but here are two preview examples:

- *Je comprends tout ce que vous dites.* (I understand all that you say.) (object: *ce que*)
- *Tout ce qui est bon, est français.* (All that is good, is French.) (subject: *ce qui*)

Finally, here are some vocabulary items using the word *tout* that you can add to your notebook lists:

- *Pas du tout!* (not at all!)
- *Tout seul/toute seule* (all alone)
- *Tout droit* (straight ahead, bolt upright)
- *Tous à la fois* (all [everyone] together)
- *Tout le monde* (everyone, everybody)
- *Tout au bout* (at the very end)
- *Tout à fait!* (Exactly! Quite [right]!)
- *C'est tout comme chez nous!* (It's just like home.)

TOUT AS ADVERB

Tout also can be used as an adverb to modify an adjective. When used in this way, it means "really" or "quite." As you've learned, adverbs generally are invariable; that is, they don't agree with any other parts of speech. However, when used as an adverb, *tout* becomes *toute* or *toutes* in front of a feminine adjective beginning with a consonant or an aspirated *h*. Here are a few examples:

- *Ils sont tout seuls.* (They are quite alone.)
- *Elles sont toutes seules.* (They [fem.] are quite alone.)
- *Elle est toute jeune.* (She's quite young.)
- *Une tout autre personne.* (An entirely different person.)

The final group of pronouns you'll learn this hour are the tonic pronouns.

USE THE TONIC PRONOUNS

"Tonic," in grammatical terms, means "stressed" or "accentuated." Thus, tonic pronouns are used to accentuate, and often to clarify, the meaning of other pronouns. The tonic pronouns are also used as objects of prepositions. Let's first look at the forms of the tonic pronouns and then consider each use individually.

Forms of the Tonic Pronouns

moi	*nous*
toi	*vous*
lui	*eux*
elle	*elles*
soi	

Note that we did not give a translation yet for these pronouns. That's because their meanings are varied when translated into English, as you will see shortly. The tonic pronouns must be understood first in the context of their usage in French.

FYI *Soi* usually means "one's self" but is so rarely used in conversation that it is not treated in the examples that follow.

ADD STRESS TO A STATEMENT

Tonic pronouns can be used to add stress to a statement, as in the following examples:

- **Moi,** *je ne veux pas partir!* ([As for] me, I don't want to leave.)
- *Il est bête,* **lui!** (He's stupid, that guy.)

WITH THE VERB *ÊTRE*

Use a tonic pronoun with the verb *être* to mean "it is I, he, and so forth," as in the following:

- *C'est moi.* (It's I. [Familiar English: It's me.])
- *C'est lui.* (It's he. [Familiar English: It's him.])
- *C'est elle.* (It's she. [Familiar English: It's her.])

- *C'est nous.* (It's we. [Familiar English: It's us.])
- *C'est vous.* (It's you.)

In the plural, *c'est* becomes *ce sont:*

- *Ce sont eux.* (It's they. [Familiar English: It's them.])
- *Ce sont elles.* (It's they. [Familiar English: It's them.])

IN COMPARISONS

Use tonic pronouns in comparisons to mean "I, you, he, she, and so forth," as in the following:

- *Il est plus grand que moi.* (He is taller than I.
  [Familiar English: … than me.])
- *Elle est plus intelligente que lui.* (She is more intelligent that he.
  [Familiar English: … than him.])
- *Nous sommes plus heureux qu'eux.* (We are happier than they.
  [Familiar English: … than them.])
- *Ils sont plus petits que nous.* (They are shorter then we.
  [Familiar English: … than us.])

Notice that proper English uses the subject pronouns (I, he, she, and so forth) in comparisons, whereas proper French uses the tonic pronouns.

WHEN A COMPOUND SUBJECT CONTAINS BOTH A NOUN AND A PRONOUN

Use a tonic pronoun when the subject of a sentence contains two pronouns or a noun and a pronoun. This usage differs radically from the English. It is very bad English grammar to say "Susan and me are going to the movies." However, in French the tonic (also called *disjunctive*) pronouns are used, as in the following:

- *Suzanne et **moi** allons au Louvre.* (Susan and I are going to the Louvre.)
- *Paul et **lui** arrivent à midi.* (He and Paul are arriving at noon.)
- ***Vous** et votre famille êtes très sympathiques.* (You and your family are very nice.) Note: This *vous* is the tonic pronoun; it just looks like the subject pronoun *vous*. *Vous* (you) + *votre famille* (your family) = *vous* (you/plural); thus, the verb is the second-person plural, *vous êtes.*
- ***Eux** et **moi** sommes contents d'être ici.* (They and I are happy to be here.) Note: *Eux* (they) + *moi* (I) = *nous* (we); thus, the verb is in the first-person plural, *nous sommes.*

AFTER A PREPOSITION

Use a tonic pronoun after a preposition. Some of these prepositions are presented here for the first time. Write them in your vocabulary list; then see Hour 13, "Master the Prepositions," for a complete treatment of prepositions.

- *Tu veux sortir **avec** moi?* (Do you want to go out <u>with</u> me?)
- *Il fait la cuisine **pour** elle.* (He does the cooking <u>for</u> her.)
- *Vous pouvez partir **sans** eux.* (You can leave <u>without</u> them.)
- *Est-ce que je peux rester **chez** vous?* (Can I stay <u>at</u> your house?)
- ***Après** vous!* (<u>After</u> you!)
- *Passez **devant** moi, s'il vous plaît.* (Pass <u>in front of</u> me, please.) (***Devant*** most often refers to being <u>physically</u> in front of something or someone; compare with ***avant*** in the following example.)
- *Tous les matins il arrive **avant** nous.* (Every morning he arrives <u>before</u> us.) (***Avant*** most often refers to things or persons being <u>chronologically</u> in front of something; compare with ***devant*** in the previous example.)

STRICTLY DEFINED

Chez is a preposition with numerous meanings determined by context. *Chez Jules* can mean "at Jules's home," "at a business named after Jules," or "in a body of work (music, literature) composed or written by Jules."

WITH POSSESSIVE ADJECTIVES

A tonic pronoun is used with the possessive adjectives to distinguish clearly between the masculine and feminine forms, as in the following examples:

- *C'est son livre **à elle**.* (It's <u>her</u> book.)
- *C'est son livre **à lui**.* (It's <u>his</u> book.)
- *C'est sa maison **à elle**.* (This is <u>her</u> house.)
- *C'est sa maison **à lui**.* (This is <u>his</u> house.)
- *Ce sont leurs billets **à eux**.* (These are <u>their</u> tickets. [the men's tickets, or a group of men and women])
- *Ce sont leurs billets **à elles**.* (These are <u>their</u> [the women's] tickets.)

WITH CERTAIN IDIOMATIC EXPRESSIONS

GO TO ▶
Tonic pronouns also are used with a large group of verbs called *pronominal,* or *reflexive,* verbs. You will learn about these verbs in Hour 18, "At Work."

Some verbs in French use the tonic pronouns instead of an object pronoun. These expressions are very limited but very commonly used, so you might just learn them as vocabulary. In Hour 14 you will learn the pronouns that are most often used as the object of a verb, such as in the sentences "I hit the ball/I hit it" and "I talk to Paul/I talk to him." You will see that these pronouns are not the tonic pronouns used in the following idiomatic expressions:

penser à: to think about someone

- *Je pense à toi.* (I think about **you.**)
- *Elle pense à moi.* (She thinks about **me.**)
- *Nous pensons à eux.* (We think about **them.**)

faire attention à: to pay attention to someone

- *Faites attention à moi.* (Pay attention to **me.**)
- *Elle ne fait pas attention à nous.* (She is not paying attention to **us.**)

tenir à: to value someone

- *Elle tient à moi parce que je parle français.* (She values **me** because I speak French.)

être à: to belong to

- *Cette voiture est à moi.* (This car is **mine.**)
- *Ces tickets sont à eux.* (These are **their** tickets.)

WHEN A PRONOUN IS USED BY ITSELF

Qui est là? (Who's there?)

Moi! ([It is] I!)

Qui cherches-tu? (Who are you looking for?)

Eux! (Them!)

Qui fait ce bruit? (Who's making that noise?)

Elle! (She [is]!)

Now that you know both the tonic pronouns and how to use *tout,* add the following expressions to your vocabulary list:

- *nous tous* (all of us)
- *vous tous* (all of you)

- *eux tous* (all of them [masculine])
- *elles toutes* (all of them [feminine])

Hour's Up!

You're making great progress! You'll complete Part 3, "The Past," in the next hour as you learn how to link together many of the expressions you've learned so far. Now quickly review the material in this hour and check your knowledge with the following quiz.

1. True or False: French possessive adjectives agree in number and gender with the possessor of the object.

2. Choose the correct pronoun to complete the sentence: *C'est la maison de Pierre et de Suzanne. C'est _____ maison.*

    a. *sa*

    b. *son*

    c. *leur*

    d. *leurs*

3. Choose the correct pronoun to complete the sentence: *C'est l'oncle de Claudine. C'est _____ oncle.*

    a. *sa*

    b. *son*

    c. *leur*

    d. *ses*

4. Choose the correct pronoun to complete the sentence: *C'est ma voiture. C'est _____.*

    a. *le mien*

    b. *mon*

    c. *la mienne*

    d. *ma*

5. Choose the correct pronoun to complete the sentence: *C'est la voiture de Paul. C'est _____.*

    a. *les leurs*

    b. *la leur*

    c. *la sienne*

    d. *le sien*

QUIZ

6. Choose the correct pronoun to complete the sentence: *Quelle chemise préfères-tu? Je préfère* _____.

    a. *celui-ci*

    b. *celui-là*

    c. *ceux-ci*

    d. *celle-là*

7. Choose the correct pronoun to complete the sentence: *Qui est ce monsieur?* _____ *Monsieur Dupont.*

    a. *Il est*

    b. *Ces*

    c. *C'est*

    d. *Celui-ci est*

8. Choose the correct form of *tout* to complete the sentence: *Ils restent à Paris* _____ *l'année.*

    a. *tout*

    b. *toute*

    c. *tous*

    d. *toute de*

9. Choose the correct pronoun to complete the sentence: *Suzanne et* _____ *allons au cinéma ce soir.*

    a. *moi*

    b. *je*

    c. *tu*

    d. *il*

10. Choose the correct pronoun to complete the sentence: *C'est la maison de Claude et de Francine. C'est à* _____.

    a. *lui*

    b. *elle*

    d. *elles*

    d. *eux*

QUIZ

HOUR 12

Learn to Link Ideas

CHAPTER SUMMARY

LESSON PLAN:
In this hour you will learn ...

- How to use the relative pronouns *qui* and *que*.
- How to use some new conjunctions with the subjunctive.
- How to use impersonal expressions.
- How to compare nouns.
- How to use linking words.

In this hour, you will continue to learn how to link ideas and sentences together through the use of pronouns (many of which you've already learned) and conjunctions. The conjunctions you'll learn in this hour are those that are followed by the present subjunctive mood, so you should go back to Hour 6, "Express Yourself in the Present Subjunctive," and review the forms and use of the subjunctive.

MASTER RELATIVE PRONOUNS

As the term implies, *relative pronouns* replace a noun and show a relationship between two ideas or clauses (parts) of a sentence. For example, in the following sentence there are two clauses, or parts: "I think that he is leaving in a minute." If you remove the word "that," you'd have two complete sentences: "I think. He is leaving in a minute." The word "that" shows the relationship between "I think" and "he is leaving in a minute." The word "that" in English is a relative pronoun.

Before continuing, let's review some of the ways that pronouns (and nouns, for that matter) can be used in a sentence. You'll remember that a pronoun can be used as the subject of a sentence; that is, it tells you who or what performs the action of the verb, as in "He hits the ball." In this example, "he" is a subject pronoun.

A pronoun also can be used as the object of the verb. That is, it tells you who or what receives the action of the verb; for example, "He hits it." In this example, "it" is an object pronoun—the object of the verb "to hit."

A pronoun also can be used as the object of a preposition; that is, it tells you to what or to whom the preposition is referring. Some of the prepositions you've learned so far are *à* (to), *de* (of, from), *avec* (with), *sur* (on), *dans* (in), *chez* (at the home of, and so forth), *pour* (for), *après* (after), *devant* (physically in front of, before), *avant* (before, referring to time), and *sans* (without). When you learned the tonic pronouns in Hour 11, "Learn to Show Possession," you learned to use them with prepositions such as *chez moi* (at my home), *après vous* (after you), and so forth.

Because relative pronouns are, obviously, pronouns, remember that they will be used in the same way as other pronouns.

QUI, QUE

Qui is used as the subject of the verb and can mean "who," "what," and "that." *Qui* refers to persons, animals, or things. *Que* is used as the object of the verb and can mean "what," "that," and "which." Like *qui*, *que* refers to persons, animals, or things.

You will quickly see that both *qui* and *que* can mean many things in English, so the only sure way to determine which pronoun to use is to consider its function in the sentence. Take a look at these examples; then we'll explain the use of each pronoun:

- *C'est Paul **qui** parle français le mieux.* (It's Paul **who** speaks French best.)
- *Je vois une peinture **qui** est belle.* (I see a painting **that** is pretty.)
- *J'ai un chien **qui** est méchant.* (I have a dog **that** is mean.)
- *Marie est la femme **que** j'aime.* (Mary is the woman **whom** I love.)
- *Voilà l'homme **que** nous avons vu au Louvre.* (There's the man **that** we saw at the Louvre.)
- *Avez-vous un chien **que** vous aimez?* (Do you have a dog **that** you love?)
- *J'ai une chemise blanche **que** je porte tous les dimanches.* (I have a white shirt **that** I wear every Sunday.)

FYI In ordinary conversation, you'd probably leave out the relative pronoun and simply say *Je vois une belle peinture,* or *J'ai un chien méchant,* and so forth.

No doubt you noticed that *qui* and *que* often have the same meaning in English: "who" or "that." This means you must determine how *qui* or *que* is used in the sentence before you can select the correct word.

To determine the function of the relative pronouns, look back at the preceding examples, and you'll see that *qui* is always followed by a verb form (*qui parle, qui est*). *Que* is always followed by a subject and a verb form (*que j'aime, que nous avons, que vous aimez, que je porte*). Therefore, *qui* is used as the subject of the verb; *que* is used as the object of the verb.

You also might have noticed that relative pronouns can be omitted in English, as in "the man I saw" or "the man that I saw." Not so in French. You must use the relative pronouns in French; there is no exception to this rule.

Use this rule (don't translate the English) to see if you can complete the following sentences with the correct pronoun. Use a file card to cover the answers following the sentences, fill in the correct word (*qui* or *que*), and then explain why you chose the pronoun:

1. *C'est Paul _____ parle espagnol le mieux.*

   qui: subject of the verb *parle* (who speaks)

   It's Paul who speaks Spanish best.

2. *Je préférerais _____ tu viennes avec nous.*

   que: object of the verb *venais* (that you came with us)

   I would prefer that you come with us.

3. *Mesdames et Messieurs, la table Louis XIV _____ est devant vous est à vendre.*

   qui: subject of the verb *est* (that is before you)

   Ladies and gentlemen, the Louis XIV table that is before you is for sale.

4. *J'habite la maison _____ est à côté de la vôtre.*

   qui: subject of the verb *est* (that is beside yours)

   I live in the house that is next to yours.

PROCEED WITH CAUTION

Some of the English translations given here might seem awkward and overly correct; however, they are used to illustrate the parallels between the French and English constructions where possible. The French sentences are quite natural.

These sentences give you examples of the many English translations possible for *qui* and *que*. Of course, in some cases in English you could leave out "that" altogether without changing the meaning of the sentence. However, remember that if you can use the word "that" in English, you must use *que* or *qui* in French. French never permits this construction: *Le roman vous lisez est bon;* instead, *Le roman **que** vous lisez est bon.*

In addition to serving as the subject of a verb, *qui* also can serve as the object of a preposition. We'll explore this usage in more detail later when we discuss the object pronouns in Hour 14, "Free Time"; for now, here are a few examples:

- *Est-ce l'homme à qui j'ai parlé?* (Is this the man to whom I spoke?)
- *Avec qui sortez-vous maintenant?* (With whom are you going out now? Who are you dating now?)
- *De qui parlez-vous?* (Of whom are you speaking?)
- *En qui est-ce que je peux avoir confiance?* (In whom can I place my confidence? [Who can I trust?])

PROCEED WITH CAUTION

Note that in these sentences, *qui* refers to a person only when he or she is the object of a preposition. When referring to things, the object of a preposition is *lequel*. See the explanation of *lequel, laquelle,* and so forth later in this hour.

Of course, in everyday English you might say "Is this the man I spoke to?" or "Who are you going out with now?" ending your sentence with a preposition. However, this usage generally is considered faulty. Be careful to never do this in French, even in familiar speech.

FYI Even proper English occasionally permits a preposition at the end of a sentence; for example, "What is this book about?" French simply does not permit this construction. To translate this sentence, say *Quel est le sujet de ce livre?* (What is the subject of this book?)

CE QUI, CE QUE

If you'll look once more at the preceding examples, you'll notice that whenever you use a pronoun, there is a noun close by that tells you what the pronoun means. In the sentence "It's Paul who speaks French best," we know immediately that "who" refers to Paul. The noun to which a pronoun refers most often precedes that pronoun so that we know what it means. This noun, which identifies the pronoun, is called an *antecedent*.

STRICTLY DEFINED

An **antecedent** is a word, phrase, or clause to which a pronoun refers.

In French, whenever you want to replace a phrase with a pronoun, or if there is no antecedent for *qui* or *que*, or it is uncertain, use *ce qui* if you need a subject pronoun, or *ce que* if you need an object pronoun. (Notice that *ce qui* and *ce que* often have the meaning of "what" [or sometimes "that which"] in English.)

Here are a few examples:

- *Il n'a pas dit ce qu'il veut faire.* (He didn't say what he wanted to do.) The antecedent of *que* is the whole phrase *il n'a pas dit*; use *ce que*.

- *Dites-moi ce que vous avez fait à Paris.* (Tell me what you did in Paris.) There is no clear antecedent for *que*; use *ce que*.

PROCEED WITH CAUTION

Que always contracts to *qu'* before a vowel; *qui* never contracts.

Either *ce qui* or *ce que* is used in the following four sentences; see whether you can place them correctly. Hint: If you see a subject followed by a verb, you'll use *ce que*; if not, use *ce qui*:

1. *Je ne comprends pas _____ il a dit.*
   I don't understand what he said.

2. *C'est exactement _____ je cherche.*
   That's exactly what I'm looking for.

3. *J'adore tout _____ est français.*
   I love everything (that is) French.

4. *Elle ne comprend pas _____ est arrivé.*
   She doesn't understand what happened.

Did you get the following answers?

1. *ce qu'*
2. *ce que*
3. *ce qui*
4. *ce qui*

Well done! You've got it. Did you miss one or more? Don't despair—just go back and read the preceding explanation again.

Now let's move on to the other relative pronouns.

LEQUEL, LESQUELS, LAQUELLE, AND LESQUELLES

If you look closely at the relative pronouns *lequel, lesquels, laquelle,* and *lesquelles,* you'll see that each is a combination of two words you've already mastered: the definite article (*le, la,* and *les*) and the interrogative adjective *quel,* which you learned in Hour 8, "Learn to Express Yourself in the Future."

Lequel (and its forms) is used as the object of a preposition, other than *de,* when referring to things. In fact, under certain conditions *lequel* and so forth can be used as the object of a preposition to refer to persons; but because *qui* is almost always correct, stick with *qui* for persons and use *lequel* for things. There are two notable exceptions: Use *lequel* after the prepositions *entre* (between) and *parmi* (among) to refer to persons or things.

Lequel most often can be translated as "which," as in the following examples:

- *Le cahier **dans lequel** j'ai écrit votre adresse est dans mon sac.* (The notebook in **which** I wrote your address is in my bag.)
- *La valise **dans laquelle** j'ai mis mon passeport est perdue.* (The suitcase in **which** I placed my passport is lost.)

When *lequel* and so forth are preceded by the prepositions *à* or *de,* the forms contract following the rules of contraction you learned in Hour 2, "Describing Things." You should be able to recognize these forms when you hear or see them, but often they can be avoided.

- *auquel* to which (masculine singular)
- *auxquels* to which (masculine plural)
- *auxquelles* to which (feminine plural)
- *duquel* of/from which (masculine singular)
- *desquels* of/from which (masculine plural)
- *desquelles* of/from which (feminine plural)

DONT

Dont is a contraction of the preposition *de* + the relative pronoun *qui* or *lequel* and so forth; thus, it means "of whom, of which." You can almost always use *de qui* for persons or *duquel* and so forth for things instead of using *dont,* but because *dont* is a contraction—thus short and to the point—it is quite commonly used both in conversation and writing.

The following are some examples of the use of *dont.* Remember that it is a contraction only of *de* + *qui* or *de* + *lequel* and so forth. Notice also that the examples contain formal English translations so that you can see the parallel between the French and English constructions. In familiar English you often might end the sentence with a preposition:

- *Voilà le problème dont (duquel) je parlais (parler de).* (There's the problem of which I was speaking.)

- *Le monsieur dont (de qui) je parlais vient d'arriver.* (The man of whom I was speaking just arrived.)

- *Je n'arrive pas à trouver l'adresse dont (de laquelle) j'ai besoin.* (I can't find the address that I need. [Literally: of which I have need.] *Avoir besoin de* means "to have need of.")

STRICTLY DEFINED

Many French prepositions end in *de,* as in *à côté de* (beside); *près de* (near). These prepositions cannot be replaced by *dont.*

Dont also is used to translate the word "whose," as in the following examples. Note that the construction of the French sentence differs significantly from the English:

- *C'est le garçon dont je connais le père.* (This is the boy whose father I know.)

- *C'est elle, la jeune fille dont le frère est mort dans un accident de voiture?* (Is she the girl whose brother died in a car accident?)

Although the French word order does not follow the English, note that the usual order of a French sentence (subject, verb, object) is maintained after *dont:*

Le professeur dont vous connaissez la femme est mon ami. (The professor whose wife you know is my friend.) *dont + vous* (subject) *+ connaissez* (verb) *+ la femme* (object)

FYI As with *qui* and *que,* there is the form *ce dont,* used when there is no clear antecedent for *dont,* as in *C'est ce dont j'ai besoin.* (This is what [that which] I need.)

Où

You've already learned the word *où,* meaning "where." *Où* also is used as a relative pronoun to replace prepositions indicating a place; for instance, *à* (at), *sur* (on), *dans* (in), *sous* (under), and so forth; plus a relative pronoun, as in the following examples:

- *La table où (sur laquelle) j'ai laissé mes affaires …* (The table where [on which] I left my things …)
- *Le sac où (dans lequel) j'ai mis mon stylo …* (The bag where [in which] I put my pen …)

AGREEMENT OF THE RELATIVE PRONOUN

GO TO ▶
See Hour 9, "Express Yourself in the Past," for a discussion of the agreement of past participles of verbs conjugated with *être*.

Remember that pronouns agree in number and gender with the nouns they replace. When using the relative pronoun *qui*, you must make the verb agree with it. If there are adjectives modifying *qui*, they also will agree in number and gender. If the verb is in the *passé composé* and conjugated with *être*, the past participle will agree with *qui*.

- *C'est elle qui est partie.* (It is she who has left.)
- *C'est moi qui suis le plus content.* (It is I who is the happiest.)

TOUT CE QUI, TOUT CE QUE

To say "everything that" in French, use *tout ce qui* as the subject of the verb and *tout ce que* as the object of the verb, as follows:

- *Tout ce qui est bon, est français.* (Everything [that is] good, is French.)
- *Tout ce que je sais, je l'ai appris à l'école maternelle.* (Everything [that] I know I learned in kindergarten.)

Now let's move on to talk about another group of linking words: conjunctions.

LEARN MORE ABOUT CONJUNCTIONS

Conjunctions are words that link two or more words or clauses. Up to this point, you've learned some conjunctions as vocabulary items, but now you need to get them organized into groups because, in French, different conjunctions behave in different ways. The most important point to learn is that some conjunctions trigger the use of the subjunctive mood; others do not. To help you learn which are which, the most common ones are listed in the following two tables.

Common Conjunctions That Do Not Trigger the Subjunctive

French	English	French	English
alors que	when, even though	*où*	where
après que	after	*parce que*	because
car	because	*pendant que*	while
et	and	*puisque*	since
lorsque	when	*quand*	when
mais	but	*tandis que*	while

PROCEED WITH CAUTION

Note that *après que* takes the indicative, whereas *avant que* takes the subjunctive.

Common Conjunctions That Trigger the Subjunctive

French	English	French	English
à condition que	on condition that	*de peur que*	for fear that
à moins que	unless	*jusqu'à ce que*	until
afin que	in order that	*pourvu que*	provided that
avant que	before	*pour que*	in order that
bien que	although	*quoique*	although
sans que	without	*de crainte que*	for fear that

Perhaps the first thing you noticed in reviewing the two preceding tables is that, with very few exceptions, French conjunctions end with *que*. This is a very important characteristic to note because soon you will learn that most of these conjunctions have corresponding prepositions—and prepositions never end with *que*.

The conjunctions that do not trigger the use of the subjunctive are used just as they are used in English. You should write them in your notebook and learn a couple each day. By linking your sentences together with conjunctions, you'll sound much more like a native speaker.

The conjunctions that trigger the use of the subjunctive (shown in the preceding table) deserve a bit more attention now.

In Hour 6 you learned three rules for the use of the subjunctive, shown in the following list. There are several exceptions to these rules, which will be pointed out as the need arises.

1. You must have two different subjects in the sentence, connected by a conjunction.
2. You must have the word *que*.
3. You must have a phrase that triggers the subjunctive.

As you've already noted, all the conjunctions in the table that do trigger the subjunctive end with *que*. Whenever you use these conjunctions in a sentence with two different subjects, they must be followed by the subjunctive. Here are several examples:

- *J'ouvre la porte **afin qu'**ils **puissent** entrer.* (I am opening the door so that they can enter.)
- *Nous partons demain **sans qu'**ils le **sachent**.* (We are leaving tomorrow without their knowing it.)
- *Je dois parler avec Paul **avant qu'**il (ne) **parte**.* (I must speak with Paul before he leaves.)
- *La mère de Paul travaille **pour qu'**il **puisse** faire des études.* (Paul's mother works so that he can go to school; literally, "do his studies.")
- *Je regarde souvent la télé **avant que** mes parents (ne) **rentrent**.* (I often watch TV before my parents get home.)

FYI The *ne* after *avant que* is the pleonastic *ne* discussed in Hour 8.

Note that whenever you have the same subject in both clauses of a sentence, French replaces the conjunction with a preposition plus an infinitive or a noun. This construction will be covered fully in Hour 16, "Going Places."

LEARN MORE IMPERSONAL EXPRESSIONS AND VERBS

Sometimes you can link ideas by using what are called *impersonal expressions*. In proper English we try to avoid beginning a sentence with an impersonal pronoun (such as "it is said," or "they say") or an impersonal expression (such as "it is necessary that"). Proper English prefers the use of a noun or a definite pronoun: "The critic said" is preferable to "It is said"; "You must go" is preferable to "it is necessary that you go."

In contrast, French often uses impersonal pronouns and expressions to high-light or emphasize what is coming next. For example, in English we might say "your work is good," highlighting "work" first and then describing its quality. In French it's quite common to insist first on the adjective and then on the noun, as in *Il est bon, votre travail.* (It is good, your work.) Such constructions are very frequent in conversational French. The following table is a very good list of the most common impersonal expressions, all of which are followed by the subjunctive.

Impersonal Expressions Followed by the Subjunctive

French	English
Il est bizarre que	It is bizarre that
Il est bon que	It is good that
Il est désirable que	It is desirable that
Il est douteux que	It is doubtful that
Il est essentiel que	It is essential that
Il est étonnant que	It is surprising that
Il est étrange que	It is strange that
Il est extraordinaire que	It is extraordinary that
Il est faux que	It is false that
Il est important que	It is important that
Il est impossible que	It is impossible that
Il est injuste que	It is unjust that
Il est inutile que	It is useless that
Il est juste que	It is just (fair) that
Il est malheureux que	It is unfortunate that
Il est naturel que	It is natural that
Il est nécessaire que	It is necessary that
Il est possible que	It is possible that
Il est préférable que	It is preferable that
Il est rare que	It is rare that
Il est regrettable que	It is unfortunate that
Il est temps que	It is time that
Il est urgent que	It is urgent that
Il est utile que	It is useful that

The following table lists impersonal expressions that are followed by the indicative.

Impersonal Expressions Followed by the Indicative

French	English
Il est sûr que	It is sure that
Il est certain que	It is certain that
Il est clair que	It is clear that
Il est évident que	It is evident that

GO TO ▶
Impersonal verbs describing the weather are presented in Hour 16.

Generally, when an impersonal expression communicates certainty, it is followed by the indicative. When communicating doubt or emotion, the expression is followed by the subjunctive.

In addition to the impersonal expressions presented above, French has a number of very common impersonal verbs. An impersonal verb is one that uses only the third-person singular form of the verb. In English we have similar verbs, but much fewer than in French; for example, "it is raining" ("to rain" is used here impersonally). You've already learned several impersonal verbs without knowing it. When you learned to tell time, you learned *Il est trois heures.* (It is three o'clock.) This is an example of an impersonal use of the verb *être. Il y a* (there is, there are) is an example of an impersonal use of the verb *avoir*.

Here is a list of the other most common impersonal verbs in French:

- *Il faut que* … (it is necessary that) + subjunctive
- *Il faut que je parte.* (I have to go.)
- *Il se peut que* … (it is possible that) + subjunctive
- *Il se peut qu'il vienne.* (He may come.)
- *Cela se peut.* (That may be.)
- *Il vaut mieux que* … (it is better that) + subjunctive
- *Il vaut mieux que vous restiez.* (You'd better stay.)
- *Il s'agit de* … (it is a question of) + infinitive, noun, or pronoun
- *Il s'agit de mon père.* (It's about my father.)
- *Il s'agit de lui.* (It's about him.)
- *Il s'agit de savoir la réponse.* (It's a question of knowing the answer.)

- *il arrive que ...* (it happens that) + subjunctive

- *Il est arrivé un accident à Claude.* (Claude had an accident.) (Literally: An accident happened to Claude.)

- *il convient que ...* (it is fitting/proper that) + subjunctive

- *Il convient que vous alliez à New York.* (You should go to New York.)

LEARN TO USE LINKING WORDS

Now let's quickly review some ways to connect ideas, words, and phrases to create more complex sentences.

Use relative pronouns:

- *Une personne qui parle bien français sera plus heureuse à Paris.* (A person who speaks French well will be happier in Paris.)

- *J'aime bien l'hôtel où nous nous logeons.* (I like the hotel where we are staying.)

- *Est-ce le train que vous prenez?* (Is this the train that you are taking?)

Use conjunctions:

- *Je voudrais savoir quand tu partiras.* (I'd like to know when you're leaving.)

- *Il veut rester encore un jour, mais il ne peut pas.* (He wants to stay another day, but he can't.)

- *Je ne bois pas de lait parce que j'ai des allergies.* (I don't drink milk because I have allergies.)

- *Je prendrai un café pendant que nous attendons le bus.* (I'll have a cup of coffee while we wait for the bus.)

- *Parlez lentement, s'il vous plaît, pour que je puisse comprendre.* (Please speak slowly so that I can understand you.)

Use impersonal verbs or expressions:

- *Il est bon que tu portes ton passeport sur toi.* (It's good that you carry your passport with you.)

- *Il est urgent que vous téléphoniez à vos parents.* (It's urgent that you call your parents.)

- *Il faut que tu ailles immédiatement à l'hôpital.* (You must go to the hospital immediately.)

To complete this hour, let's discuss further the comparative that you learned earlier.

LEARN TO COMPARE NOUNS

In Hour 7, "Describe Your Surroundings," you learned to compare adjectives and adverbs using sentences of the following sort:

- *Il est plus grand que moi.* (He is taller than I.)
- *Elle parle mieux que vous.* (She speaks better than you.)

You also can use the comparative with nouns; for example, "I have more courage than you"; "He has fewer problems than I." The comparison of nouns uses the following forms:

- *autant de* + noun   as many as, as much as
- *plus de* + noun   more than
- *moins de* + noun   less than

Note that the invariable *de* precedes the noun in these cases.

- *Il a **autant de** travail **que** moi.* (He has as much work as I [have].)
- *J'ai **plus d**'argent **que** lui.* (I have more money than he [has].)
- *Vous avez **moins de** temps **que** nous.* (You have less time than we [have].)
- *Il avait **moins de** cent francs dans son porte-feuille.* (He had less than a hundred francs in his wallet.)

HOUR'S UP!

Now you've successfully completed the first three parts of your 24 hours. Part 4, "Leisure Time," is devoted to learning structures and vocabulary to talk about things you do outside work. You'll master some new grammatical structures and learn vocabulary so you can talk about your free time, where you live, and your travels. Take a few moments before entering Part 4 to review the material in Part 3, "The Past," and complete the following quiz. We'll see you soon for some leisure time!

QUIZ

1. Choose the correct pronoun to complete the sentence: *C'est Paul _____ parle français le mieux.*

    a. *que*

    b. *qui*

    c. *dont*

    d. *duquel*

2. Choose the correct pronoun to complete the sentence: *Voilà l'homme _____ nous avons vu.*

    a. *qui*

    b. *dont*

    c. *que*

    d. *où*

3. Choose the correct pronoun to complete the sentence: *J'ai un chien _____ est méchant.*

    a. *qui*

    b. *celui-ci*

    c. *que*

    d. *lequel*

4. Choose the correct pronoun to complete the sentence: *De _____ parlez-vous?*

    a. *quel*

    b. *dont*

    c. *que*

    d. *qui*

5. Choose the correct pronoun to complete the sentence: *Dites-moi _____ vous voulez faire.*

    a. *que*

    b. *dont*

    c. *ce que*

    d. *ce qui*

6. Which of the following conjunctions is followed by the subjunctive mood?

    a. *bien que*

    b. *quand*

    c. *parce que*

    d. *où*

7. Which of the following conjunctions is not followed by the subjunctive mood?

    a. *avant que*

    b. *lorsque*

    c. *sans que*

    d. *pour que*

8. Choose the correct verb form to complete the sentence: *Il est douteux qu'il _____.*

    a. *venait*

    b. *viennent*

    c. *vient*

    d. *vienne*

9. Choose the correct verb form to complete the sentence: *Il est sûr qu'il _____ à Rome la semaine prochaine.*

    a. *vas*

    b. *aille*

    c. *va*

    d. *vais*

10. Choose the correct word to complete the sentence: *Il a _____ travail que moi.*

    a. *autant de*

    b. *autant*

    c. *plus*

    d. *le plus*

QUIZ

PART IV
Leisure Time

HOUR 13

Master the Prepositions

LESSON PLAN:

In this hour you will learn ...

- How to use prepositions of place.
- How to use prepositions of time.
- How to use prepositions after verbs.

This hour is devoted entirely to one of the more interesting of grammatical elements, the preposition.

What is a preposition? The answer to this question is not easy. The dictionary definition often calls prepositions "relation words" that connect nouns or pronouns to some other element of the sentence. That's pretty vague as a definition, but it's as close as one can get. Actually, you might find it easier to not think in terms of definition, but rather to learn prepositions as vocabulary items. This hour will provide you with many examples.

One important characteristic of prepositions is that they are invariable. As with adverbs, there is never a question of agreement. A second characteristic of prepositions is that they can be classed logically by their functional use. Here are the three main categories of prepositions, including French examples and their English equivalents:

- Prepositions of place: *sur* (on)
- Prepositions of time: *pendant* (during)
- Prepositions with special meanings: *selon* (according to)

Because prepositions are classed by their function, some prepositions may fall into one or more category. For example, the preposition "on" in English can be used to show placement (the book is on the table) or to indicate time (he arrived on time). Therefore, problems arise when the meaning of the French preposition does not correspond with English usage. Using the English preposition "on," the difference can be illustrated by comparing these two sentences:

*Le livre est **sur** la table.* (The book is **on** the table.)

*Il est arrivé **à** l'heure.* (He arrived **on** time.)

Whereas "on" in English can be both a preposition of place and time, French has two different prepositions: *sur* (preposition of place) and *à* (preposition of time). Additionally, some French prepositions fall into several categories; for example, *à* also can be a preposition of place in certain instances: *J'habite à la campagne* (I live in the country).

To help you choose the right preposition, they've been arranged into categories for you.

Now let's take a look at the various types of prepositions.

Use Prepositions of Place

The following table lists the most common prepositions of place. Use these prepositions to indicate where you are in relation to something or someone else:

Prepositions of Place

French	English
à côté de	next to, beside
à la hauteur de	abreast of, level with
à	to, at, in (with places or place names)
après	after
avec	with
chez	at the home/office of, among
contre	against
dans	in, inside of
de côté	sideways
de	from
derrière	in back of, behind
devant	in front of
du côté de	from (indicating a direction)
en dehors de	outside of

French	English
en face de	facing, across from
en	in, on, to (countries, regions, and so forth)
entre	between
hors de	outside of (in a physical sense)
loin de	far from (in a physical sense)
par	by, through
parmi	among
près de	near, close to
sous	under
sur	on (in a physical sense)

PROCEED WITH CAUTION

Note that some French prepositions, as in English, are composed of two or more words, as in *à côté de* (beside). Others are a single word, as in *devant* (in front of).

Several of these prepositions require particular attention because they are not always used in the same way as their English equivalents. In the following commentary, we've given examples to illustrate these special uses.

à (to, at, in)

- *au soleil* (in the sun)

Chez (at the home/office of, among)

- *Je vais chez moi.* (I'm going home.)
- *J'ai acheté mon bracelet chez Cartier.* (I bought my bracelet at Cartier.)
- *Il y a beaucoup de violence chez Shakespeare.* (There's a lot of violence in Shakespeare's work.)

Contre (against)

- *échanger une chose contre une autre* (to exchange one thing for another)

Dans (in, on, out of); compare with use of *en* in the following:

- *La lettre est dans l'enveloppe.* (The letter is in the envelope.)
- *dans la lune* (on the moon)
- *Il est dans l'avion. Elle est dans le train.* (He's in/on the plane. She's in/on the train.)

FYI With the verb *prendre* (to take), *dans* means "out of": *J'ai pris un stylo dans ma poche* (I took a pen out of my pocket).

When the name of a country is modified, *dans* is used instead of *en* or *au*, for example:

- *J'ai voyagé dans toute l'Europe.* (I have traveled **in** [throughout] all of Europe.)

For the prepositions used with geographical place names, see the explanation later in this hour.

Entre/parmi (between/among)

The clear English distinction of "between" (*entre*) and "among" (*parmi*) is not as clear in French, as illustrated in the following list:

- *Nous sommes entre amis.* (We are **among** friends.)
- *plusieurs d'entre nous* (several **of** us, some of those **among** us)
- *Ils sont d'accord, entre eux.* (They are in agreement **among** themselves.)

Par (by, for, through)

- *par exemple* (**by/for** example)
- *Il est entré par la porte.* (He entered **by/through** the door.)
- *Pour arriver en France, je suis passé par la Belgique.* (In order to get to France, I went **through** Belgium.)

PROCEED WITH CAUTION

Compare *par* (for) with *depuis* (for, since) later in this hour.

Sous (under)

- *sous la pluie* (**in** the rain)
- *sous les tropiques* (**in** the Tropics)
- *sous terre* (**underground**)
- *sous clef* (**under** lock and key)
- *sous l'équateur* (**at** the equator)
- *sous trois jours* (**within** three days)
- *sous Louis XIV* (**in** the reign of Louis XIV)
- *sous peu* (**before** long)

Sur (in, over, by, after, for, out of)

- *Ma tante est **sur** la photo.* (My aunt is **in** the photograph.)
- *Un pont **sur** une rivière.* (A bridge **over** a river.)
- *La clef est **sur** la porte.* (The key is **in** the door.)
- *Page **sur** page.* (Page **after** page.)
- *10 mètres **sur** 5 mètres.* (10 meters **by** 5 meters.)
- *Les trains **sur** Paris.* (The trains **for** Paris.)
- *5 **sur** 10.* (5 **out of** 10.)

Prepositions of place are used in special ways with geographical place names.

GEOGRAPHY

In English we use the prepositions "in," "at," "to," and "from" with all geographical place names: "I'm going to France," "I'm in Paris," "I'm from the United States," and so forth. Determining the preposition to use in French is a bit more problematic because different prepositions are used depending on the type of place to which or from which you're traveling, and the gender of the place. Thus, before we talk about which preposition to use with place names, you need to know how to determine the gender of nouns.

Here are the rules for determining the gender of place names:

- **Cities**   Cities are always considered masculine unless they are preceded by a feminine article that is part of the name of the city, such as *La Nouvelle-Orléans* (New Orleans). See the examples in the following table.
- **Continents, countries, mountain ranges, rivers, and regions**   If the place name ends in *e*, it is feminine; if not, it's masculine. Note particularly that the definite article is used with these place names. There are some exceptions given at the end of the following table.

Geographical Place Names

English	French Feminine
Africa	*l'Afrique*
Asia	*l'Asie*
Australia	*l'Australie*

continues

Geographical Place Names   **(continued)**

English	French Feminine
Europe	l'Europe
Latin America	l'Amérique latine
North America	l'Amérique du Nord
South America	l'Amérique du Sud
Brittany (region of France)	la Bretagne
Champagne (region of France)	la Champagne
Loire River	la Loire
Seine River	la Seine
Austria	l'Autriche
China	la Chine
Colombia	la Colombie
Egypt	l'Égypte
England	l'Angleterre
Finland	la Finlande
France	la France
Germany	l'Allemagne
Great Britain	la Grande-Bretagne
Greece	la Grèce
Holland	la Hollande
India	l'Inde
Ireland	l'Irlande
Italy	l'Italie
Ivory Coast	la Côte d'Ivoire
Jamaica	la Jamaïque
Libya	la Libye
New Zealand	la Nouvelle-Zélande
North Korea	la Corée du Nord
Norway	la Norvège
Poland	la Pologne
Russia	la Russie
Scotland	l'Écosse
South Korea	la Corée du Sud
Spain	l'Espagne
Sweden	la Suède
Switzerland	la Suisse

English	French Feminine
Turkey	la Turquie
Ukraine	l'Ukraine
United Arab Republic	la République Arabe Unie
United Kingdom	le Royaume-Uni
Alps	les Alpes
Andes	les Andes
Rocky Mountains	les Montagnes Rocheuses

English	French Masculine
Jura Mountains	le Jura
Mississippi River	le Mississippi
Canada	le Canada
Chili	le Chili
Costa Rica	le Costa Rica
Denmark	le Danemark
El Salvador	le Salvador
Iran	l'Iran
Iraq	l'Iraq
Japan	le Japon
Kenya	le Kenya
Kuwait	le Koweït
Lebanon	le Liban
Luxembourg	le Luxembourg
Morocco	le Maroc
Peru	le Pérou
Portugal	le Portugal
The Netherlands	les Pays-Bas
Togo	le Togo
United States	les États-Unis
Vatican (state)	le Vatican
Vietnam	le Viêt Nam

English Exceptions	French Masculine Exceptions
Mexico	masculine: le Mexique
Antarctica	masculine: l'Antarctique
Israel	no article: Israël; en Israël (in Israel)

PROCEED WITH CAUTION

Use *en* to mean "in" or "to" with feminine countries unless the country is modified by an adjective, in which case use *dans* (in), as in *dans toute la France* (in all of France).

PREPOSITIONS FOR GEOGRAPHIC PLACES

Once you know the gender of a place name, you can determine which preposition to use with it, as shown in the following sections.

FEMININE COUNTRY (OR MASCULINE COUNTRY BEGINNING WITH A VOWEL)

en (in, to) + country

de (from) + country

Examples include the following:

- *en France, en Espagne, en Italie,* and so forth
- *de France, d'Espagne, d'Italie,* and so forth
- *Je vais en France.* (I'm going to France.)
- *Il vit en Iran.* (He lives in Iran.)
- *Je viens de France.* (I'm coming from France.)

MASCULINE COUNTRY

au, aux (in) + country

du, des (from) + country

Examples include the following:

- *du Maroc, des États-Unis, du Portugal*
- *Je vais au Portugal.* (I'm going to Portugal.)
- *Elle habite au Portugal.* (She lives in Portugal.)
- *Je vais aux États-Unis.* (I'm going to the United States.)
- *J'arrive des États-Unis.* (I'm arriving from the United States.)
- *Je suis du Maroc.* (I'm from Morocco.)

Islands typically are not preceded by an article, as is the case with countries. Use the prepositions *à* (to) and *de* (from), as shown in the following:

- *à Cuba* (to Cuba)
- *de Cuba* (from Cuba)
- *à Tahiti* (to Tahiti)
- *de Tahiti* (from Tahiti)
- *à Hawaï* (to Hawaii)
- *d'Hawaï* (from Hawaii)

FRENCH NAMES FOR CITIES

In most cases, French uses the same city names as are used in English: *Rome* (Rome), *New York* (New York), *Berlin* (Berlin), and so forth. There are a few exceptions, of which the most notable are given in the following table.

Exceptions to French/English City Names

French	English
Athènes	Athens
Barcelone	Barcelona
Berne	Bern
Bruxelles	Brussels
Copenhague	Copenhagen
Genève	Geneva
Jérusalem	Jerusalem
La Havane	Havana
La Haye	The Hague
La Nouvelle-Orléans	New Orleans
Le Caire	Cairo
Lisbonne	Lisbon
Londres	London
Montréal	Montreal
Moscou	Moscow
Pékin	Beijing
Québec	Quebec City
Venise	Venice
Vienne	Vienna

PROCEED WITH CAUTION

Note that the definite article used with feminine cities (*la*) is capitalized when preceded by *à* or *de*, as in *à La Havane, de la Haye,* and *à La Nouvelle-Orléans.*

To say "to" or "from" a city, use the prepositions *à* and *de,* making the necessary contractions, as shown here:

- *Nous allons à Londres et au Caire.* (We're going to London and Cairo.)
- *Elles arrivent de Genève et de La Havane.* (They are arriving from Geneva and Havana.)

USE PREPOSITIONS OF TIME

As is true with prepositions of place, prepositions of time may be used in French different from their English equivalents. After the list of the most common prepositions of time, I've provided some examples of how they are used in special instances.

Prepositions of Time

French	English
à	to, at, in
après	after
avant	before
dans	in
de	from, of, about
depuis	since, for
durant	during, while
en	in, on, to
entre	between
environ	approximately
pendant	during, while
pour	for
près de	near
vers	toward
prêt de	on the verge of

Notice that some of the prepositions of place you learned earlier also are prepositions of time; for example, *dans, à,* and *de.* In addition, French has several prepositions meaning "for" (*depuis*, *pendant*, and *pour*) and each is used in specific instances, which I will explain shortly. You will also notice that both *dans* and *en* are used with time expressions to mean "in"; however, these prepositions are not interchangeable.

Let's look at some of the special uses of these prepositions of time.

à (at, on, in, by)

- *Elle peut faire deux choses à la fois.* (She can do two things **at** a time.)
- *Elles sont arrivées à huit heures.* (They arrived **at** 8 o'clock.)
- *Il est arrivé à l'heure.* (He arrived **on** time.)
- *Nous sommes arrivés juste à temps pour voir nos amis.* (We arrived just **in** time to see our friends.)
- *à son heure* (**in** his/her own good time)
- *au printemps* (**in** springtime [See *en* used with other seasons later in this section.])
- *Je suis payé à l'heure.* (I'm paid **by** the hour.)

De (from, of, in)

- *Je travaille de 8 heures à 17 heures.* (I work **from** 8 o'clock to 5 o'clock.)
- *de temps en temps* (**from** time to time)
- *un quart d'heure* (a quarter [**of** an] hour)
- *à huit heures du matin* (at 8 o'clock **in** the morning)
- *de l'après-midi, du soir* (**in** the afternoon, **in** the evening)

Depuis (since, for, from)

Depuis requires the present tense in French, whereas English uses the past progressive tense.

- *J'habite Paris depuis trois ans.* (I <u>have been living</u> in Paris **for** three years.)
- *Nous <u>sommes</u> ici depuis une semaine.* (We'<u>ve been</u> here **for** a week.)
- *J'<u>attends</u> votre arrivée depuis hier.* (I <u>have been awaiting</u> your arrival **since** yesterday.)
- *depuis le matin jusqu'au soir* (**from** morning until night)

PROCEED WITH CAUTION

Don't confuse *par* (for) with *depuis* (for, since) in time constructions.

En (in, on, at)

En is used in a number of fixed expressions concerning time:

- *en avance* (**in** advance, early)
- *en retard* (late)
- *en même temps* (**at** the same time)
- *chaque chose en son temps* (all **in** good time)
- *en vacances* (**on** vacation)

En also is used with an expression of time to indicate the amount of time necessary to complete an action. Compare the use of *dans*, shown in the following:

- *La population a doublé en dix ans.* (The population has doubled **in** [a period of] 10 years.)
- *Je peux finir en vingt minutes.* (I can finish [with]**in** [a period of] 20 minutes.)

En is used with months, years, and seasons, with the exception of *au printemps* (in springtime), as shown here:

- *en avril* (in April)
- *en juin* (in June)
- *en 2001* (in 2001)
- *en 1789* (in 1789)
- *en hiver* (in winter)
- *en été* (in summer)
- *en automne* (in autumn)

Dans (in)

When followed by an expression of time, *dans* means "at the end of the time indicated)," as illustrated here:

- *J'arrive dans 5 minutes.* (I'll be there **in** 5 minutes [5 minutes from now].)
- *Dans une minute!* (**In** a minute [from now]!)

Pendant (during, in, for)

- *pendant l'hiver* (**during**, in winter)
- *Reste avec moi **pendant** quelques minutes, s'il te plaît.* (Stay with me **for** a few minutes, please.)
- *J'ai travaillé en France **pendant** un mois.* (I worked in France **for** a month.)

Both *pendant* and *pour* mean "for." Compare their uses in the following examples:

Pour (for, in order to)

- *J'irai au Portugal **pour** huit jours.* (I will go to Portugal **for** a week.)
- ***pour** toujours* (forever)
- ***pour** le moment* (for the moment)
- *Nous serons ici **pour** deux jours.* (We will be here for two days.)
- ***Pour** bien comprendre le français, il faut étudier.* (**In order to** understand French well, you must study.)

FYI But: *par exemple* (for example).

Note that *pour* is much less often used to mean "for" with time expressions than *pendant*. *Pendant* has the meaning of extended time; *pour* most often is used with a verb in the future tense. Because *pendant* can almost always be used where *pour* is used, when in doubt, use *pendant* to say "for" or "during."

Pour followed by an infinitive usually means "in order to," as in *Pour trouver son numéro de téléphone, cherchez dans l'annuaire.* (In order to find his telephone number, look in the telephone book.)

PREPOSITIONS WITH SPECIAL MEANINGS

A number of prepositions don't fall neatly into the categories of time and place. Here is a fairly complete list of the special prepositions:

- *d'après* (according to)
- *environ* (approximately)
- *quant à* (as for, regarding)
- *sans* (without)

- *selon* (according to)
- *envers* (toward)
- *à travers* (across)
- *d'après la Bible* (according to the Bible)
- *environ trois mille* (about three thousand)
- *sans argent, sans problème* (without money, without problems [no article; followed by a singular noun])
- *quant à moi* (as for me)
- *Il a coupé à travers bois* (He cut across the woods)
- *selon mes parents* (according to my parents)

FYI "As for" also can be translated as *en ce qui concerne;* for example, *En ce qui concerne la politique américaine ....* (As for [concerning] American politics ....)

LEARN SOME SPECIAL USES OF PREPOSITIONS

The following is a list of some other special uses of prepositions to show possession, to modify nouns and pronouns, and to indicate means or manner of transportation.

- To show possession: *la voiture de Paul* (Paul's car)
- To modify nouns with nouns: *une robe de soie* (a silk dress)
- To modify: *quelque chose* (something), *rien* (nothing), *quelqu'un* (someone), and *personne* (no one): *quelque chose **d'**intéressant* (something interesting); *rien **de** nouveau* (nothing new), and so forth
- To indicate a manner of transportation when used with verbs of movement such as *aller: par le train* (by train), *à pied* (on foot), *en avion* (by plane), *par avion* (by airmail), *à vélo* (by bike), *en voiture* (by car), and *à cheval* (on horseback)

To this point you've learned about prepositions that are followed by nouns or pronouns. Now we will discuss the rather large number of verbs that require a preposition when followed by an infinitive.

MASTER THE VERB + PREPOSITION

In Hour 2, "Describing Things," you learned that an infinitive in English is expressed using the word "to," as in "to run," "to walk," and so forth. French infinitives are a single word such as *courir, marcher,* and so forth. Many French verbs require a preposition, usually either *à* or *de,* when followed by an infinitive; other verbs don't require a preposition at all.

Here are a few examples to show you how the construction works:

- *J'apprends à parler français.* (I'm learning to speak French.)
- *Nous inviterons les Dupont à dîner chez nous.* (We'll invite the Duponts to eat dinner at our house.)
- *Je commence à comprendre la grammaire française.* (I'm starting to understand French grammar.)
- *J'essaye d'étudier un peu chaque jour.* (I try to study a little bit each day.)
- *Il refuse de répondre.* (He refuses to answer.)
- *J'aime parler français.* (I love to speak French.)

There is no rhyme or reason for which preposition is used with which verb. You simply must learn them through usage and repetition. The tables on the next few pages illustrate some of the most common of these verbs. Because you can't learn all of them at once, go slowly—learn a few each day. Most important, be aware of the need for a preposition in French where you don't necessarily have one in English. When in doubt, review these tables to verify the correct preposition.

PROCEED WITH CAUTION

Do not confuse the construction verb + preposition + infinitive with the construction verb + preposition + noun. Compare *Il apprend à parler français* (He is learning to speak French) with *Le professeur apprend le français aux élèves* (The professor is teaching French to the students).

Verbs That Take *à* + Infinitive

French	English
aider à	to help
apprendre à	to learn how to
arriver à	to manage/succeed in
avoir à	to have to/be obliged to
chercher à	to look for
commencer à	to begin (to)

continues

Verbs That Take *à* + Infinitive (continued)

French	English
consentir à	to consent (to)
continuer à	to continue (to)
décider (qqn.) à	to persuade (someone) to
encourager à	to encourage
enseigner à	to teach
hésiter à	to hesitate to
inviter à	to invite (someone) to
parvenir à	to succeed
persister à	to persist (in)
recommencer à	to begin again
renoncer à	to give up
résister à	to resist
réussir à	to succeed at/in
servir à	to serve to
songer à	to dream (of, about) (but *Je songe à toi*)
tarder à	to delay/be late
tenir à	to hold (someone) to/insist on
venir à	to happen to

Verbs That Take *de* + Infinitive

French	English
accepter de	to accept, agree to
s'agir de	to be a question of
avoir peur de	to be afraid of
cesser de	to stop, cease
choisir de	to choose
conseiller de	to advise
continuer de	to continue
convenir de	to agree to
craindre de	to fear
décider de	to decide
empêcher de	to prevent, keep from
essayer de	to try

French	English
féliciter de	to congratulate
finir de	to finish
gronder de	to scold
manquer de	to neglect, fail to
mériter de	to deserve
offrir de	to offer
oublier de	to forget
permettre de	to allow
persuader de	to persuade
prier de	to beg
promettre de	to promise
proposer de	to suggest
refuser de	to refuse
regretter de	to regret, be sorry
remercier de	to thank
rêver de	to dream
tâcher de	to try

Verbs That Take No Preposition + Infinitive

French	English
adorer	to adore
aimer	to love
aller	to go
compter	to count (on)
désirer	to desire
espérer	to hope
penser	to think
pouvoir	to be able
vouloir	to want, to wish

HOUR'S UP!

Bon travail! Good work! You've successfully completed another hour and are well into the second half of your studies. There are only 11 more hours to go, so keep to your schedule, review earlier material regularly, and keep your notebook up to date. Now, before you begin Hour 14, "Free Time," test your mastery of the prepositions by taking this quiz. *À bientôt!*

1. Complete the sentence with the correct preposition: *Je vais _____ moi.*
    a. *chez*
    b. *dans*
    c. *en*
    d. *avant*

2. Complete the sentence with the correct preposition: *Mes clés sont _____ mon sac.*
    a. *chez*
    b. *dans*
    c. *en*
    d. *de*

3. Complete the sentence with the correct preposition: *Nous sommes _____ amis.*
    a. *contre*
    b. *par*
    c. *entre*
    d. *avec*

4. To say "5 out of 10," you say:
    a. *cinq à dix*
    b. *cinq sur dix*
    c. *cinq hors dix*
    d. *cinq dans dix*

5. Which of the following countries uses *en* to mean "to"?
    a. *le Portugal*
    b. *le Japon*
    c. *Le Pérou*
    d. *l'Italie*

6. Which of the following countries uses *au* to mean "to"?

    a. *le Chili*

    b. *la France*

    c. *la Norvège*

    d. *la Russie*

7. The preposition used with most islands to mean "in" or "to" is …

    a. *dans*

    b. *en*

    c. *à*

    d. *chez*

8. Which of the following seasons uses *au* instead of *en* to mean "in"?

    a. *hiver*

    b. *été*

    c. *printemps*

    d. *automne*

9. Complete the sentence with the correct preposition: *Je commence _____ comprendre le français.*

    a. *à*

    b. *de*

    c. *en*

    d. *pour*

10. Complete the sentence with the correct preposition: *J'ai décidé _____ faire ce travail.*

    a. *à*

    b. *en*

    c. *de*

    d. *pour*

QUIZ

HOUR 14
Free Time

CHAPTER SUMMARY

LESSON PLAN:

In this hour you will learn ...

- How to use pronouns with verbs to avoid repetition.
- How to use object pronouns with commands and infinitives.
- How to use vocabulary to talk about your leisure time.

There remain only a few grammatical elements to learn: how to use object pronouns with verbs, how to form a few special verb tenses, how to use the passive voice, and how to use a special group of verbs called *pronominal* verbs. However, these few structures use elements of grammar you've already mastered, so they will come easily to you.

USE PRONOUNS TO AVOID REPETITION

As you've already discovered, one of the primary reasons to use a pronoun is to avoid repetition while increasing clarity of expression. For example, the following series of sentences is both weighty and repetitive: "I saw Paul at the store. I said hello to Paul, talked to Paul a moment, and then I invited Paul to dinner. Paul said he would come. I told Paul good-bye."

Wherever possible, we'd prefer to omit the proper noun, Paul, and replace it with a pronoun: "I saw Paul at the store, talked to him a moment, and then invited him to dinner. He said he would come, so I told him good-bye." Through the use of pronouns, we shorten the sentences and make them clearer.

The pronouns used in this English example are called subject pronouns (I, he, and so forth, which you've already learned in French), and personal object pronouns (him, to him, and so forth). The latter are called "personal object" pronouns because in most cases they refer to persons and are used as the object of a verb.

As a quick review of what you've learned so far, let's recall the other types of pronouns:

- **Subject pronouns**   Used as the subject of a sentence; for example, *je, tu, il, elle, on, nous, vous, ils, elles*. (See Hour 2, "Describing Things.")

- **Possessive pronouns**   Used to show possession; for example, *le mien, le tien, le sien, le nôtre, le vôtre, le leur*, and their forms. (See Hour 11, "Learn to Show Possession.")

- **Demonstrative pronouns**   Used to demonstrate or point out something; for example, *celui, celle, ceux, celles*. (See Hour 11.)

- **Tonic pronouns**   Used as objects of prepositions, as a means to add emphasis, or as the subject of a sentence when one or more of the subjects is a pronoun; for example, *moi, toi, lui, elle, soi, nous, vous, eux, elles*. (See Hours 11 and 13, "Master the Prepositions.")

- **Relative pronouns**   Used to show relationships between clauses in a sentence; for example, *qui, que, lequel* (and its forms), *dont, celui* (and its forms), *où*. (See Hour 13.)

To this list you'll now add the object pronouns—pronouns used to replace the object of a verb.

FYI   The object of a verb can be identified by asking the following questions: Who? What? To whom? To what? Consider the following example: "He gives it to her." What does he give? To whom does he give it? The answers are "it" and "to her," both of which are objects of the verb "gives."

DISTINGUISH BETWEEN DIRECT AND INDIRECT OBJECTS

There are two kinds of personal object pronouns in French and English: direct object pronouns and indirect object pronouns. A simple distinction between the two is that direct objects are linked directly to the verb, and indirect objects are linked indirectly to the verb with a preposition.

Here are two English examples to illustrate the distinction:

- "He offered a ticket to his friend."

  What did he offer? He offered a ticket, the direct object, which is linked directly to the verb, without a preposition.

  To whom did he offer the ticket? He offered it to his friend, the indirect object, which is linked indirectly to the verb by the preposition "to."

- "I sent a letter to my mother."

    What did I send? I sent a letter, the direct object, which is linked directly to the verb, without a preposition.

    To whom did I send it? I sent it to my mother, the indirect object, which is linked indirectly to the verb by the preposition "to."

Notice that English uses the preposition "to" in most cases before an indirect object. However, in addition to *à* (to), French uses several prepositions, which will be discussed shortly.

Also, English might leave out the preposition altogether: "He offered Mary a gift." "I sent Mom a letter." In these cases, English always places the indirect object (Mary, Mom) before the direct object (a gift, a letter). This structure does not exist in French. When you have an indirect object in French, it will always, without exception, be linked to the verb using a preposition.

PROCEED WITH CAUTION

The ability to distinguish between direct and indirect objects is essential to speaking correct French. However, try not to translate these pronouns. Instead, focus on learning how the pronoun is used in the French sentence.

GO TO ▶
Two other indirect object pronouns, *y* and *en*, are presented in Hour 18, "At Work," because they have special uses and meanings. The object pronoun *se* (himself, herself, themselves) is used with reflexive verbs and is also presented in Hour 18.

MASTER THE OBJECT PRONOUNS

The following table illustrates the direct and indirect object pronouns in French. Notice that several of these pronouns can be either a direct or indirect object. Following the table, you are given some direction on how to use the pronouns properly.

Direct and Indirect Object Pronouns

Direct Object	English	Indirect Object	English
me/m'	me	*me/m'*	to me
te/t'	you	*te/t'*	to you
le/l'	him, it (masculine)	*lui*	to him
la/l'	her, it (feminine)	*lui*	to her
nous	us	*nous*	to us
vous	you	*vous*	to you
les	them (masculine)	*leur*	to them
les	them (feminine)	*leur*	to them

Before proceeding, take a moment to reflect on the following points:

- You've seen all these words used in different contexts: *le*, *la*, and *les*, which also are definite articles (the); *lui*, *nous*, and *vous*, which also are tonic pronouns (him, us, you); and *leur*, which also is a possessive adjective (their) and is used to form the possessive pronoun *le leur* (theirs). Thus, there are only these two new pronouns to learn: *me* and *te*.

- Like *je* and *que*, the object pronouns *me*, *te*, *le*, and *la* are contracted (*m'*, *t'*, *l'*, *l'*) before a vowel. This is required.

- *Nous* and *vous* can serve as both direct object pronouns and indirect object pronouns: *nous* (us, to us), *vous* (you, to you).

- As mentioned, sometimes English omits the preposition "to" before an indirect object, as in "I gave them the money." Never count on this structure to help you in French. (See the list of verbs that take direct and indirect objects toward the end of this hour.)

- Whereas English most often uses the preposition "to" before the indirect object, the French indirect object is a single word: *me* (to me) or *lui* (to him, to her).

FYI You remember from Hour 2 that French infinitives also are only one word: *parler* (to talk), *finir* (to finish), and so forth. Additionally, some multiple word prepositions in English are single words in French—and vice versa—as in *devant* (in front of) and *à côté de* (beside).

Note that the standard order of a French sentence when using nouns is as follows:

subject + verb + direct object + indirect object

Here are a few examples to illustrate the use of the personal object pronouns. As you read them, note the placement of the pronouns—before the conjugated verb. (We'll talk more about placement of the pronouns in the next section.) Also, because *me*, *te*, *nous*, and *vous* can be either direct or indirect pronouns, their function in the following sentences is indicated with the abbreviations "d.o." for direct object and "i.o." for indirect object.

- *Je donne les tickets à Suzanne. Je les lui donne.* (I give the tickets to Susan. I give them to her.)

- *Je donne les tickets à Paul. Je les lui donne.* (I give the tickets to Paul. I give them to him.)

Note: *lui* can mean either "to him" or "to her." Context must clarify the meaning.

- *Il parle à notre groupe. Il nous parle.* (*nous* is an i.o. because the verb is *parler à* [someone], to speak **to** someone) (He is speaking to our group. He is speaking to us.)

- *Ils me voient tous les dimanches.* (*me* is a d.o. because the verb *voir* someone, to see someone) (They see me every Sunday.)

- *Maman m'envoie des bonbons à Noël.* (*m'* is an i.o. because the verb is *envoyer* [something] *à* [someone], to send something **to** someone) (Mom sends me candies for Christmas.)

- *Nous voyons votre groupe tous les matins au café. Nous vous voyons tous les matins au café.* (*vous* is a d.o. because the verb is *voir* someone, "to see someone") (We see your group every morning in the café. We see you every morning in the café.)

- *J'envoie la lettre à mes parents ce matin. Je la leur envoie ce matin.* (I am sending the letter to my parents this morning. I am sending it to them this morning.)

Notice that the direct object pronouns (*me, te, le, la, les, nous, vous*) replace the direct object nouns; the indirect object pronouns (*me, te, nous, vous, lui, leur*) replace the indirect object nouns and the preposition *à*.

LEARN TO PLACE OBJECT PRONOUNS

Object pronouns, except when used in commands, follow an unchangeable order and precede the verb. See the following table for examples.

Object Pronoun Order

Subject		First		Second		Third		
je								
tu								
il								
elle	+	me	+	le	+	lui	+	verb
on		te		la		leur		
nous		nous		les				
vous		vous						
ils								
elles								

PROCEED WITH CAUTION

When following commands, object pronouns have a different set order. See the "Use Object Pronouns with Commands" section later in this hour.

As in English, you will never use two direct pronoun objects or two indirect pronoun objects in the same clause or a sentence. When you have more than one pronoun in a sentence, they are placed following a set order. See the following table for the normal patterns for placing two different pronouns in a sentence.

Patterns for Placing Two Different Pronouns

Indirect Object Precedes Direct Object		
me		
te	+	*le*
nous		*la*
vous		*les*

Direct Object Precedes Indirect Object		
le		
la	+	*lui*
les		*leur*

Practice choosing the correct pronouns and placing them correctly by replacing the underlined words in the following sentences with pronouns. The answers are given under each question. Do not translate the sentences into English first; instead, look to see whether the preposition *à* is before the noun. If it is, the noun is an indirect object and will be replaced by *lui, leur*. If there is no preposition preceding the noun, it's a direct object and you will use *le, la, les*, no matter what the English translation would be. Following these sentences you are given several lists of verbs and the prepositions that follow them.

- *Je regarde la télévision. (regarder: to look at)*
  Je la regarde. (I look at it.)
- *J'écoute la radio. (écouter: to listen to)*
  Je l'écoute. (I listen to it.)
- *Nous cherchons nos amis. (chercher: to look for)*
  Nous les cherchons. (We are looking for them.)

- *J'ai dit <<bonjour>> à Pierre.* (*dire à:* to say to [someone])

  Je lui ai dit <<bonjour>>. (I said hello to him.)

- *Il envoie les lettres à ses amies.* (envoyer à: to send to)

  Il les leur envoie. (He is sending them to them.)

- *Ils répondent à leurs parents.* (*répondre à:* to answer)

  Ils leur répondent. (They answer their parents.)

- *Ils obéissent à leurs parents.* (*obéir à:* to obey)

  Ils leur obéissent. (They obey their parents.)

FYI In French typography, << >> are used for quotation marks.

Did you get them all? Perhaps you had to think a minute about the first three sentences because the English translations have a preposition before the nouns. Nevertheless, the French does not include that preposition; thus, in French these are direct objects.

Did you have trouble with the last two sentences? If yes, perhaps that's because the English sentences don't have a preposition before the noun objects. However, again because the French constructions contain the preposition *à*, these verbs (*répondre à, obéir à*) are followed by indirect objects.

FRENCH VERBS WHOSE ENGLISH EQUIVALENTS USE A PREPOSITION

Obviously, you can't always count on the English verb to correspond with the French. Some verbs that take direct objects in English take indirect objects in French—and vice versa. The following is a list of French verbs whose English equivalents use a preposition before a noun; however, the French verb does not use a preposition.

- *attendre* (to wait **for** someone or something): *J'attends le bus et mon ami.*
- *chercher* (to look **for** someone or something): *Je cherche mon livre et mes amis.*
- *demander à* (to ask someone **for** something): *Il demande une voiture à son père.* (However, to ask a question is *poser une question.*)
- *écouter* (to listen **to** someone or something): *J'écoute Paul et la radio.*
- *payer* (to pay **for** something): *Je paie le dîner.*
- *regarder* (to look **at** someone or something): *Je regarde Philippe et la télé.*

FRENCH VERBS WHOSE ENGLISH EQUIVALENTS DO NOT USE A PREPOSITION

The following is a list of verbs that use the preposition *à* (to) before a noun in French, but not in English. Be careful with these verbs because your English sentence will have a direct object where the French will have an indirect object; for example, "I obey my parents" is *J'obéis à mes parents.*

- *assister à* (to attend something—meeting, class, and so forth)
- *conseiller à* (to advise)
- *convenir à* (to please, to be suitable for)
- *défendre à* (to forbid)
- *déplaire à* (to displease)
- *désobéir à* (to disobey)
- *goûter à* (to taste something)
- *interdire à* (to forbid someone [from doing something])
- *manquer à* (to miss someone)
- *nuire à* (to harm)
- *obéir à* (to obey someone)
- *ordonner à* (to order)
- *permettre à* (to permit)
- *plaire à* (to please someone)
- *promettre à* (to promise [something to someone])
- *réfléchir à* (to consider, reflect upon)
- *répondre à* (to answer someone or something [to answer a question])
- *résister à* (to resist [something])
- *ressembler à* (to resemble [something/someone])
- *réussir à* (to pass something [such as a test])
- *se fier à* (to trust [someone])
- *songer à* (to dream/think of)
- *survivre à* (to survive)
- *téléphoner à* (to telephone [someone])

Here are a few examples of how these verbs are used:

- *Je lui défends de fumer.* (I forbid him to smoke.)
- *Je ne lui permets pas de sortir.* (I don't let him go outside.)

- *La France me plaît beaucoup. Elle lui plaît, aussi.* (France pleases me a lot. It pleases her, also.)

STRICTLY DEFINED

Actually, *plaire à* often is used to replace *j'aime* (I like), as in *La France me plaît* (I like France); *Ce voyage lui plaît* (He likes this trip); *Le pain français vous plaît?* (Do you like French bread?)

EQUIVALENT FRENCH AND ENGLISH VERBS THAT USE THE SAME PREPOSITIONS

The following is a list of verbs that use the same prepositions in French and English; for example, "I speak **to** my mother" is *Je parle à ma mère:*

- *dire à* (to say [something] to someone), as in *Je dis bonjour au professeur.*

- *envoyer à* (to send [something] to someone), as in *J'envoie la lettre à ma mère.*

- *donner à* (to give [something] to someone), as in *Je donne les clefs à Yannick.*

- *parler à* (to speak to someone), as in *Je parle à Paul.*

- *être à* (to belong to), as in *Ces livres sont à moi.*

- *faire attention à* (to pay attention to), as in *Elle ne fait pas attention à la route* (She's not watching where she's going).

EQUIVALENT FRENCH AND ENGLISH VERBS THAT USE DIFFERENT PREPOSITIONS

The following are verbs that use different prepositions in French and English; for example, the English preposition might be "at" or "with," but the French preposition is **à:**

- *sourir à* (to smile **at** someone), as in *Je souris à mon amie.*

- *serrer la main à* (to shake hands **with** [someone]) as in *Je serre la main à Paul.*

- *penser à* (to think **of/about**) as in *Je pense à toi.*

- *emprunter (something) à* (to borrow [something] **from** someone/something) as in *J'emprunte deux livres à la bibliothèque* (I borrow two books from the library).

Because the verbs in the preceding lists are quite commonly used in conversation, you should begin learning them along with the prepositions associated with each.

Three common verbs should be learned as exceptions:

- *entrer **dans*** (to enter [**into**] some place), as in *J'entre dans le cinéma.*
- *parler français* (to speak French), as in *Je parle français.* (When followed by the name of a language, there is no article and no preposition. Compare: *Je parle **au** pilote.* [I am speaking to the pilot.])
- *jouer **de*** (to play an instrument), as in *Je joue **de** la guitare.* (But, *jouer **à*** [to play a game], as in *Je joue **au** poker.*)

FYI Remember that verbs that take a direct object are called transitive verbs and are conjugated with *avoir* in compound tenses. See Hours 5, "Express Yourself in the Present Indicative," and 9, "Express Yourself in the Past."

LEARN AGREEMENT OF PAST PARTICIPLES WITH OBJECT PRONOUNS

You might have noticed that to this point we've primarily chosen examples that use personal object pronouns in sentences using the present tense. There's a very good reason for that: The past participles of verbs conjugated with *avoir* agree in number and gender with a preceding personal direct object pronoun. That might seem like a complicated rule, but it can be easily mastered if you keep a couple of things in mind:

- You already know that past participles can be used as adjectives, and therefore agree with the noun they modify; for example, *des enfants perdus* (see Hour 7, "Describe Your Surroundings").
- You already know that the past participles of verbs conjugated with *être* agree with the subject; for example, *Elle est partie, nous sommes partis,* and so forth (see Hour 9).

So, there is a new element of the rule for agreement given in the preceding: The direct object must precede the past participle for the agreement to take place.

Consider the following examples to see how this rule is applied:

- *J'ai **vu** Suzanne au supermarché. Je l'ai **vue** au supermarché.*
- *J'ai **envoyé** la lettre à mon ami. Je l'ai **envoyée** à mon ami.*
- *Nous avons **regardé** la télévision. Nous l'avons **regardée.***
- *Elle a beaucoup **aimé** la France. Elle l'a beaucoup **aimée.***
- *As-tu **acheté** la chemise verte? L'as-tu **achetée?***
- *Avez-vous **vu** Paul et Claudine? Les avez-vous **vus?***
- *Yves et Annick, est-ce que je vous ai **vus** au concert hier soir?*

In each of the preceding examples in which the direct object (*le, la, les, vous*) comes before the past participle, the past participle agrees with it. This rule helps to identify the gender of the direct object when it is not clear from context. For example, in the sentence *il m'a regardée de loin* (he looked at me from afar), it is clear that that *me* (*m'*) refers to a feminine person. Remember that the verb *regarder* does not take a preposition before a noun, as in *regarder une personne* (to look **at** a person).

Now compare the following sentences with the preceding ones. Each of the following sentences contains an indirect object; therefore, no agreement is made.

- *Voilà <u>Claudine!</u> Je <u>lui</u> ai **parlé** ce matin.*
- *J'ai envoyé la lettre <u>à mes amis.</u> Je **leur** ai envoyé une lettre.*
- *<u>Christine,</u> vous êtes toujours là? Mais, je **vous** ai dit de partir.* (*dire **à:** vous* is an indirect object)
- *Allez-vous téléphoner à vos parents ce soir? Non, je leur ai déjà téléphoné ce matin.*

Now of course you can see why it is very important to distinguish between direct and indirect objects. To make the correct agreement of the past participles for verbs conjugated with *avoir*, you have to know if the object you are using is direct (thus agreement of the past participle) or indirect (thus no agreement of the past participle).

To review: Direct objects are linked directly to the verb without a preposition. Indirect objects are linked to the verb with the preposition *à* (sometimes with other prepositions). Personal object pronouns are placed in front of the conjugated verb. Past participles of verbs conjugated with *avoir* agree in number and gender with a preceding personal pronoun direct object. That's the whole story on the personal object pronouns. Well, almost—there are two exceptions!

Learn Exceptional Placement of Object Pronouns

Don't panic yet—the exceptions to the placement of object pronouns are very easy. The two exceptions to the normal order and placement of object pronouns are commands and infinitives.

USE OBJECT PRONOUNS WITH COMMANDS

The same personal object pronouns you learned in the preceding are used in affirmative commands, except that *me* becomes *moi*. The pronouns are placed in the following order:

verb → direct object → indirect object

GO TO ▶
Reflexive verbs, also called pronominal verbs (see Hour 18), have an additional form, *toi,* used in the imperative.

Note that hyphens connect the verb and the object pronouns in affirmative commands.

Study these examples of the verb-d.o.-i.o. formula:

- *Donnez-le-moi!* (Give it to me!)
- *Obéissez-leur!* (Obey them!)
- *Achetez-les-nous!* (Buy them for us!)
- *Dites-moi bonjour!* (Tell me hello!)
- *Envoyez-les-leur!* (Send them to them!)

However, when you form a negative command, the pronouns take their normal order, as follows:

- *Ne me le donnez pas!* (Don't give it to me!)
- *Ne leur obéissez pas!* (Don't obey them!)
- *Ne nous les achetez pas!* (Don't buy them for us!)
- *Ne me le dites pas!* (Don't tell me that!)
- *Ne les lui envoyez pas!* (Don't send them to her/him!)

USE OBJECT PRONOUNS WITH INFINITIVES

In Hour 4, "Actions in the Present Tense with Irregular Verbs," you learned the verb *pouvoir* (to be able to) and that some verbs can be followed by an infinitive. These verbs are called *modal* verbs because often they are used in conjunction with an infinitive to indicate a mood; "may," "might," "must," "can," "would," and "should" are modal auxiliary verbs in English.

When these verbs are followed by an infinitive and have an object pronoun, that pronoun is always the object of the infinitive, not of the modal verb. Therefore, the object pronoun precedes the infinitive, not the modal verb.

The common modal verbs in French are *devoir, pouvoir, vouloir, savoir,* and *falloir.*

Note the placement of the object pronouns in the following sentences:

- *Nous devons **lui** parler immédiatement.* (We must talk to him immediately.)
- *Il sait **le** faire.* (He knows how to do it.)
- *Vous voulez **me** voir?* (Do you want to see me?)
- *Il faut **lui** envoyer ces documents.* (It is necessary to/We must send these documents to him.)

Cover the translations on the right and try translating the following sentences:

I want to give it to him.	*Je veux le lui donner.*
You can do it!	*Vous pouvez le faire!*
She must speak to us soon.	*Elle doit nous parler bientôt.*

Now that you've mastered these new structures, you can learn some vocabulary to talk about your leisure time. The next section gives you a number of words to add to your vocabulary notebook.

LEARN VOCABULARY TO TALK ABOUT YOUR LEISURE TIME

The vocabulary in these lists will help you talk about things you might do during your leisure time such as games, sports, and hobbies.

Nouns of Sports, Relaxation, and Pastimes

English	French
baseball	*le base-ball*
basketball	*le basket-ball*
bicycle	*une bicyclette, un vélo*
board game	*un jeu de société*
book	*un livre*
bookstore	*une librairie*
cinema	*le cinéma*
club	*un club*

continues

Nouns of Sports, Relaxation, and Pastimes   (continued)

English	French
computer	*un ordinateur*
concert	*un concert*
cycling	*le cyclisme*
dance (ball)	*une soirée (dansante)*
deck of cards	*un jeu de cartes*
fishing	*faire de la pêche*
football	*le football américain*
game	*un jeu*
golf	*le golf*
hike	*une randonnée*
hiker	*un randonneur, une randonneuse (à pied)*
leisure activities	*les loisirs (m.)*
leisure time	*le temps libre*
library	*la bibliothèque*
magazine	*un magazine*
mountain bike	*un V.T.T. (vélo à tout terrain)*
mountaineering	*l'alpinisme (m.)*
museum	*un musée*
music	*la musique*
musical instrument	*un instrument de musique*
newspaper	*un journal*
race	*un concours*
reading	*la lecture*
skiing	*le ski*
soccer	*le football*
sport	*un sport*
stadium	*un stade*
swimming pool	*une piscine*
television	*la télévision*
tennis	*le tennis*
theatre	*le théâtre*
toy	*un jouet*

Verbs of Sports, Relaxation, and Pastimes

English	French
to be relaxed	être détendu(e)
to bike	faire du vélo
to dine out	aller au restaurant
to do nothing	ne rien faire (Je ne fais rien.)
to draw	dessiner
to go for a drive	faire une promenade en voiture
to go for a jog	faire du jogging
to go for a walk	faire une promenade
to go to the beach	aller à la plage
to paint	peindre
to picnic	faire un pique-nique
to play cards	jouer aux cartes
to play the guitar	jouer de la guitare
to read	lire
to swim	nager
to take a nap	faire un petit somme
to tell	raconter une histoire
to travel	voyager
to visit (a person)	aller voir une personne
to visit (a place)	visiter un monument, une ville
to watch	regarder
to win	gagner

HOUR'S UP!

Félicitations! Congratulations! You've successfully completed another hour by mastering the use of pronouns and learning some new vocabulary to talk about your leisure activities. In the next hour, you'll learn several new pronouns as well as vocabulary to talk about things you do around the house. Keep up the good work! But before continuing, review the material in this hour and test your knowledge with the following quiz.

1. True or False: The direct object pronoun can be identified by asking "who?" or "what?" performs the action of the verb.

2. True or False: The indirect object pronoun can be identified by asking "to whom?" or "to what?" the action of the verb was done.

3. True or False: A noun used as indirect object in French is always preceded by a preposition.

4. Select the correct translation for the following sentence: "I give it to him."

   a. *Je vous la donne.*

   b. *Je les leur donne.*

   c. *Je te le donne.*

   d. *Je le lui donne.*

5. Which sentence correctly replaces the words underlined in the following sentence: *J'envoie la carte postale à ma mère.*

   a. *Je la leur envoie.*

   b. *Je la lui envoie.*

   c. *Je le lui envoie.*

   d. *Je les lui envoie.*

6. Which of the following verbs is an intransitive verb (cannot take an object)?

   a. *chercher*

   b. *écouter*

   c. *dire*

   d. *partir*

7. Which of the following verbs is a transitive verb (can take an object)?

   a. *aller*

   b. *venir*

   c. *regarder*

   d. *tomber*

8. Which of the following verbs does not take the preposition *à* before a noun object in French?

   a. *regarder*

   b. *plaire*

   c. *défendre*

   d. *répondre*

9. Complete the following sentence with the correct prepostion: *Je souris* _____ *Paul*.

    a. *au*

    b. *de*

    c. *à*

    d. *avec*

10. True or False: The past participles of verbs conjugated with *avoir* agree in number and gender with a preceding personal direct object pronoun.

HOUR 15
Around the House

CHAPTER SUMMARY

LESSON PLAN:

In this hour, you will learn …

- How to use the interrogative pronouns.
- How to use tonic pronouns to ask questions.
- How to form and use the present participle.
- How to talk about where you live.

Y ou've learned all the pronouns; now you'll use them to ask questions. You'll also learn the last form of the verb, the present participle. Present participles always end in -*ing* in English and in -*ant* in French. They can be used as adjectives and to express an action taking place simultaneously with the main verb of the sentence.

USE PRONOUNS TO ASK QUESTIONS

The interrogative pronouns meaning "who," "whom," or "what" are *qui* for persons and *que* for things. In addition to these short forms, there also are long forms of the interrogative pronouns. Study the following table; then I'll talk about the use of each pronoun.

The following are some examples of how the interrogative pronouns are used. Again, try not to translate these pronouns. Instead, work on identifying their use as subjects or objects of the verbs.

- *Qui sait la réponse?* (**Who** knows the answer?)
- *Qui est-ce qui parle français ici?* (**Who** speaks French here?)
- *Qu'est-ce qui est arrivé?* (**What** happened?)
- *Qui cherches-tu?* (**Who** are you looking for?)
- *Qu'est-ce que tu cherches?* (**What** are you looking for?)
- *Que dites-vous?* (**What** are you saying?)
- *Qu'est-ce que vous dites?* (**What** are you saying?)

- *À qui* parles-tu? (**To whom** are you speaking?)
- *À quoi* pensez-vous? (**What** are you thinking **about?**)
- *Avec qui* sortez-vous? (**Who** are you going out **with?**)
- *Avec quoi* est-ce que tu écris? (**What** are you writing **with?**)

Short Forms of the Interrogative Pronouns

	Referring to Persons	Referring to Things
Subject of verb	qui	qu'est-ce qui
Object of verb	qui	que
Object of preposition	qui	quoi

Long Forms of the Interrogative Pronouns

	Referring to Persons	Referring to Things
Subject of verb	qui est-ce qui	qu'est-ce qui
Object of verb	qui est-ce que	qu'est-ce que

LEARN THE INTERROGATIVE PRONOUNS

Now let's talk about the pronouns used in each of these examples. Refer to the preceding list as you go through the following explanations.

QUI/QUI EST-CE QUI

Both *qui* and *qui est-ce qui* are used as the subject of a sentence and refer to persons. *Qui est-ce qui* is used in conversation, but rarely written.

Qui sait la réponse? (Who knows the answer?)

Qui est-ce qui parle français ici? (Who speaks French here?)

QU'EST-CE QUI

Qu'est-ce qui is used as the subject of a sentence and refers to things. It generally means "what." It has no short form.

Qu'est-ce qui est arrivé? (What happened?)

QUI/QUI EST-CE QUE

Qui and *qui est-ce que* are used as the object of a verb and refer to persons. Notice when the short form is used, the subject and verb are inverted, as in *Qui aimez-vous?* (Who do you love?); *Qui vois-tu?* (Who do you see?)

Qui cherches-tu? (Who[m] are you looking for?)

Qui est-ce que tu cherches? (Who are you looking for?)

QUE/QU'EST-CE QUE

Que and *qu'est-ce que* are used as the object of the verb and refer to things. Notice that when the short form is used, the subject and verb are inverted, as in *Que penses-tu?* (What do you think?); *Que voulez-vous?* (What do you want?)

Que dites-vous? (What are you saying?)

Qu'est-ce que vous dites? (What are you saying?)

À QUI/À QUOI/AVEC QUI/AVEC QUOI

Qui is used as the object of a preposition and refers to persons; *quoi* is used as the object of a preposition and refers to things.

À qui parles-tu? (To whom are you speaking?)

À quoi pensez-vous? (What are you thinking about?)

Avec qui sortez-vous? (Who are you going out with?)

Avec quoi est-ce que tu écris? (What are you writing with?)

FYI Notice that you can use either inversion or the question phrase *est-ce que* without inversion in these cases: *Avec qui veux-tu parler? Avec qui est-ce que tu veux parler?* (With whom do you wish to speak?)

Another way to understand the use of these pronouns is to look at their constructions analytically. In each of the long forms, the first *qui* or *que* tells you if you are referring to a person or a thing (*qui* refers to a person; *que* refers to a thing). The second *qui* or *que* tells you if you are using the pronoun as a subject (*qui*) or an object (*que*) of the verb. Here is a visual representation of how the pronouns are used:

- Referring to person   Used as subject
  qui   *est-ce* **qui**
- Referring to person   Used as object
  qui   *est-ce* **que**
- Referring to thing   Used as subject
  qu' (*que*)   *est-ce* **qui**
- Referring to thing   Used as object
  qu'(*que*)   *est-ce* **que**

FYI If the English sentence begins with "who," use *qui;* if it begins with "what," use *que.*

For practice, try translating the following questions, first using the short form of the interrogative pronouns and then using the long form.

Short Form:

- Who are you?   *Qui es-tu?/Qui êtes-vous?*
- What are you doing?   *Que fais-tu?/Que faites-vous?*
- Who(m) are they looking for? *Qui cherchent-ils?*
- What is she looking for?   *Que cherche-t-elle?*
- Who is he thinking about? *À qui pense-il?*
- With whom is she dancing? *Avec qui danse-t-elle?*

Long Form:

- What are you doing?   *Qu'est-ce que tu fais?*
- Who(m) are you looking for? *Qui est-ce que tu cherches?*
- What is she looking for?   *Qu'est-ce qu'elle cherche?*
- Who did that?   *Qui est-ce qui a fait ça?*

LEQUEL/LAQUELLE/LESQUELS/LESQUELLES

The pronoun *lequel* and its forms were presented in Hour 12, "Learn to Link Ideas," as relative pronouns. However, they also are used as interrogative pronouns, most often meaning "which one" or "which ones." As an interrogative pronoun, *lequel* replaces a noun that has been previously mentioned and agrees in gender with that noun. If you'd say "which ones" (plural) in English, use the plural forms *lesquels* or *lesquelles*, depending on the gender of the noun replaced.

Lequel and its forms can be used as the subject or object of a verb and as the object of a preposition, such as *de* or *à*, as in the following list. When preceded by *de* or *à* they contract, following the rules of contraction you've learned: *duquel*, *desquels*, *auquel*, and *auxquels*.

- *Voilà les noms de deux hôtels à Paris; lequel préfères-tu?* (Here are the names of two Paris hotels; which one do you prefer?)

- *Il y a deux routes devant nous; laquelle prenons-nous?* (There are two roads before us; which one do we take?)

- *Vous avez le choix entre les journaux ou les magazines; lesquels voulez-vous?* (You have a choice between the newspapers and the magazines; which ones do you want?)

- *Entre les carottes et les pommes de terre, lesquelles sont meilleures pour la santé?* (Between carrots and potatoes, which [ones] are more healthful?)

USE SINGLE PRONOUNS TO ASK QUESTIONS

In conversation especially, many pronouns can be used alone to ask or to clarify a question. Here is a list of some common short questions using a single pronoun:

Il est parti. (He's left.)

Qui? (Who?)

Paul. (Paul.)

Je ne t'aime plus. (I don't love you anymore!)

Quoi? (What?)

J'ai dit que je ne t'aime plus! (I said I don't love you anymore!)

Je viens de voir un nouveau film. (I just saw a new film.)

Lequel? (Which one?)

Celui de Spielberg. (Spielberg's.)

Qui parle français ici? Vous, Monsieur? (Who here speaks French? You, sir?)

Oui, Madame, je parle français. (Yes, ma'am, I speak French.)

Vous êtes le coupable! (You're the guilty one!)

Qui? Moi? (Who? Me?)

Oui! Vous! (Yes, you!)

PROCEED WITH CAUTION

These mini-dialogs are very conversational. For example, used alone, the pronoun *quoi* can be quite impolite. Use *Pardon?* instead.

Use Common Question Words

In addition to pronouns, there are numerous common question words that can be used alone or in combination with other words. Add these question words to your vocabulary notebook:

- *Quand?*   When?
- *Où?*   Where?
- *D'où?*   From where? (*Vous êtes d'où?* [You're from where?])
- *Comment?*   How? (Also *Pardon?*)
- *Combien?*   How many? How much?
- *Combien de* (+ noun)   How many of ...? How much of ...?
- *Pourquoi?*   Why? (Or, *Pourquoi pas?* [Why not?])
- *À quelle heure?*   At what time? (When?)

STRICTLY DEFINED

In conversation, much liberty is taken with standard French word order. For example, one hears *Tu viens d'où?* (You're from where?) instead of *D'où viens-tu?* (From where do you come?), which would be more standard.

Study these common questions to practice the preceding list of words:

Je pars bientôt. (I'm leaving soon.)

À quelle heure? (When? At what time?)

À onze heures. (At 11 o'clock.)

J'ai trouvé mon portefeuille. (I found my wallet.)

Où? (Where?)

Dans mon sac. (In my purse.)

Qu'est-ce que vous prenez, Monsieur? (What will you have, sir?)

Comment? (Pardon? Excuse me, what did you say?)

J'ai dit, qu'est-ce que vous prenez, Monsieur? (I said, what will you have, sir?)

Je vais dormir. (I'm going to sleep.)

Pourquoi? (Why?)

Parce que je suis fatigué. (Because I'm tired.)

Now let's talk about the last verb form you'll need to learn: the present participle.

LEARN THE PRESENT PARTICIPLE

In English present participles end in *-ing* (as in singing, speaking, running, jumping, and so forth) and are used in a variety of ways. Present participles form verb tenses (he is singing), nouns (his singing was beautiful), and adjectives (this book is interesting).

 FYI Despite the name, present participles are not always linked to the present. In contrast, past participles are closely linked to past events (see Hour 7, "Describe Your Surroundings").

However, the use of the present participle in French rarely follows English usage, so you must be careful. First, you'll learn how to form the present participle in French and then how to use it. To form the present participle of most verbs, drop the *-ons* from the first-person plural of the verb and add *-ant,* as shown in the following table.

Forming the Present Participle

First-Person Plural	Present Participle	English Present Participle
parlons	*parlant*	speaking
finissons	*finissant*	finishing
vendons	*vendant*	selling
disons	*disant*	saying
dormons	*dormant*	sleeping

There are three common exceptions that must be learned as vocabulary, as shown in the following table.

Exceptions to Forming the Present Participle

Infinitive	Present Participle	English Present Participle
avoir	ayant	having
être	étant	being
savoir	sachant	knowing

PROCEED WITH CAUTION

The present participle is not used to create verb tenses in French, as in *Je marche* (I am walking); *Il chante* (He is singing). Use the French present tense to translate the English present progressive or use the idiom *venir de* (see Hour 3, "Actions in the Present Tense").

There are three primary uses of the present participle in conversational French:

- As an adjective
- To replace a relative clause
- With the preposition *en* to mean "upon doing something" or "while doing something"

PRESENT PARTICIPLES AS ADJECTIVES

When a present participle is used as an adjective, it agrees with the noun it modifies in gender and number, as shown in the following table.

Using Present Participles as Adjectives

Present Participle	As an Adjective	English
charmant	des femmes charmantes	charming/delightful women
intéressant	des livres intéressants	interesting books
fatiguant	des voyages fatiguants	tiring trips
obéissant	des chiens obéissants	mindful (obeying) dogs

Be careful to distinguish between the English use of the present participle as an adjective and as a verb form in the present progressive:

- She is singing: *Elle chante*.
- She is charming: *Elle est charmante*.

- The stage set is turning: *La scène tourne*.
- A turning stage set: *une scène tournante*.

PRESENT PARTICIPLE REPLACES A RELATIVE CLAUSE

When replacing a relative clause, the present participle is invariable:

GO TO ▶
Review relative clauses and the relative pronouns presented in Hour 12.

- *Les passagers **qui arrivent** des États-Unis doivent passer par la douane.*
  *Les passagers **arrivant** des États-Unis doivent passer par la douane.* (Passengers **arriving** from the United States must pass through customs.)

- *Les passagers **qui ont** leur passeport peuvent continuer tout droit.*
  *Les passagers **ayant** leur passeport peuvent continuer tout droit.* (Passengers **having** a passport may continue straight ahead.)

En + Present Participle

The only preposition used with the present participle is *en*. When used with *en*, the present participle indicates either how something is being done or that something is being done at the same time (or close in time) as something else. This use is quite similar to the English use of the *gerund*, as you can see when comparing the following examples.

STRICTLY DEFINED

A **gerund** is a verbal noun; that is, a noun ending in *-ing* (French: *-ant*) that has all the uses of a noun while retaining certain characteristics of a verb, including the ability to take an object. The French for "gerund" is *un gérondif*.

How something is being done:

- *Il est sorti du métro **en courant.*** (He ran out of the metro. [Literally: He exited the metro by running.])
- *Ils ont quitté le concert **en chantant.*** (They left the concert singing.)

Simultaneous events:

- ***En arrivant** à Paris, nous avons trouvé un très bel hôtel.* (Upon arriving in Paris, we found a very pretty hotel.)
- ***En sortant** du métro, il est tombé.* ([While] coming out of the metro, he fell.)
- ***En allant** au théâtre, j'ai vu mes amis.* ([While I was] going to the theatre, I saw my friends.)

FYI When the described action has happened immediately before the action of the main verb, omit *en;* for example, *Arrivant à Paris, j'ai perdu mon sac.* ([Just after] arriving in Paris, I lost my purse.)

Try your hand at using the present participle with *en* by combining the following pairs of sentences into one. Replace the underlined word with *en* + present participle:

1. <u>*Il est sorti*</u> *du cinéma. Il est tombé.*

   En sortant *du cinéma, il est tombé.*

2. <u>*Ils dansaient.*</u> *Ils sont partis de la soirée.*

   Ils sont partis de la soirée **en dansant.**

3. <u>*Nous sommes arrivés*</u> *en France. Nous étions fatigués.*

   En arrivant *en France, nous étions fatigués.*

PRESENT VS. PAST PARTICIPLE

You've learned that the present participle is not used to form verb tenses, whereas the past participle is used to form the past tense (the *passé composé*). However, you now see that both participles can be used as adjectives; for example:

- *les temps passés* (the past tenses)
- *les mots prononcés* (the words spoken)
- *l'enfant perdu* (the lost child)
- *une soirée dansante* (a dance, dance party)
- *un vol fatiguant* (a tiring [plane] flight)
- *un homme gênant* (an annoying man)

When used as adjectives, participles agree in number and gender with the nouns they modify.

PRESENT PARTICIPLE VS. INFINITIVE

You've learned that *en* is the only preposition that precedes the present participle in French. So how do you express English phrases such as "after leaving," "before going," and so forth, where the preposition is not *en?* Use the infinitive.

After all prepositions except *en*, French uses the infinitive to translate the English present participle. However, there are very few prepositions that can logically be used in this way. Here are some examples:

- *sans penser* (without thinking)

- *avant de partir* (before leaving)

- *pour comprendre* (in order to understand)

- *après être arrivé* (after arriving)

- *après avoir étudié* (after studying)

Note that when followed by an infinitive, *avant* becomes *avant de*, as in *avant d'arriver*. When followed by a noun or pronoun, use *avant*, as in *avant moi* (before me); *avant demain* (before tomorrow).

GO TO ▶
Après (after) is followed by the past infinitive. See Hour 19, "Going Shopping," for a complete treatment of the past infinitive.

LEARN VOCABULARY TO TALK ABOUT WHERE YOU LIVE

Before you begin learning the vocabulary to talk about where you live, let's talk a bit about differences between French and American homes. First, many French citizens live in apartments because the population is largely urban. Houses tend to be built out of concrete block covered with stucco; apartment buildings often are constructed of a material called *béton* or *béton armé* (reinforced concrete).

Windows usually are covered by shutters on the outside that are closed against the weather in winter and against the long days of sun in the spring and summer. France is quite far north, with Paris on the same longitude as Montreal, Canada; so protection against cold and sun makes interior home life more pleasant.

Few homes have what might be called a front yard or a back yard in the United States. If there is a yard, it is referred to as *le jardin* (the garden). Older homes—both in the city and the country—tend to be surrounded by high, concrete-block fences (*des murs, des clôtures*), often dating back centuries.

Here are some vocabulary words you can use to describe your home and things you might do there.

General Things Around the House

English	French	English	French
apartment	un appartement	house	la maison
apartment house	un immeuble	kitchen	la cuisine
balcony	le balcon	lawn	la pelouse
basement	le sous-sol	on the third (etc.) floor	au troisième étage
bathroom (in a home)	la salle de bains	one-story house	une maison sans étage
bathroom (public)	les toilettes	room	une pièce
bedroom	la chambre	stairs	l'escalier (m.)
ceiling	le plafond	story; first floor	l'étage; à l'étage (m.)
cellar	la cave	terrace	la terrasse
closet	le placard, une armoire	two-story house	une maison avec étage
dining room	la salle à manger	upstairs	à l'étage
door	la porte	wall	le mur
first floor	le rez-de-chaussée	water closet	les cabinets, le petit coin
garage	le garage	window	la fenêtre

Furnishings (*Les Meubles*) Around the House

English	French	English	French
armchair	un fauteuil	plant	la plante
carpet	la moquette	rug	le tapis
chair	la chaise	vase (flower vase)	un vase (un vase à fleurs)
lamp	la lampe	vase of flowers	un vase de fleurs
mirror	le miroir		

PROCEED WITH CAUTION

Le vase means "the vase," but *la vase* means "the mud."

Around the Bedroom (*La Chambre*)

English	French	English	French
alarm clock	un réveil	mattress	le matelas
bed	le lit	pillow	un oreiller
blanket	une couverture	sheet	un drap
dresser	le bureau		

Around the Bathroom (*La Salle de Bain*)

English	French
bathrobe	*un peignoir*
bathtub	*la baignoire*
bidet	*le bidet*
brush	*une brosse*
comb	*un peigne*
hair dryer	*un sèche-cheveux*
razor	*un rasoir*
shower	*la douche*
sink	*le lavabo*
soap	*le savon*
toilet tissue	*le papier hygiénique, le p.h.*
toothbrush	*une brosse à dents*
toothpaste	*la pâte dentifrice*
towel	*un drap de bain, une serviette*

STRICTLY DEFINED

Note that in the kitchen, "sink" is *un évier;* in the bathroom, "sink" is *un lavabo.*

Around the Kitchen (*La Cuisine*)

English	French
bowl	*un bol*
coffee cup	*une tasse à café*
counter top	*le comptoir*
cup	*un tasse*
dishwasher	*une lave-vaisselle*
double boiler	*un bain-marie*
dryer	*le séchoir*
fork	*une fourchette*
fridge	*le frigo*
glass	*un verre*
household appliances	*l'électroménager* (m.)
knife	*un couteau*
microwave oven	*un four à micro-ondes*

continues

Around the Kitchen (*La Cuisine*) (continued)

English	French
napkin	une serviette
oven	le four
plate	une assiette
saucer	une soucoupe
sink	un évier
soup bowl	une assiette creuse
spoon	une cuillère
stove(top)	une cuisinière
table cloth	une nappe
washing machine	une machine à laver

Den/Living Room (*Le Living, La Salle de Séjour*)

English	French
bar	le bar
camcorder	un caméscope
coffee table	une table de salon
computer	un ordinateur
couch, sofa	un sofa
stereo	une stéréo
telephone	le téléphone
television	une télévision, la télé
VCR	un magnétoscope

Miscellaneous Things Around the House

English	French
around	autour de
avenue	une avenue
boulevard	le boulevard
brick; made of brick	la brique; en brique
building	un bâtiment
clean	propre
comfortable	confortable (used with furniture, as in *chaise confortable*)

English	French
comfortable	à l'aise, bien (used to describe persons, as in être bien dans une chaise confortable)
countryside	la campagne
dirty	sale
expensive	cher
far from	loin de
flower	une fleur
lane, place, circle, etc.	une rue
metal, made of metal	le métal; en métal
modern	moderne
neighborhood	le quartier, le voisinage
outside	à l'extérieur, dehors
quiet	calme
rent	le loyer
street	une rue
town	une ville
tree	un arbre
useful	utile
wood; wooden	le bois; en bois

Verbs Around the House

English	French
to answer the phone	répondre au téléphone
to buy	acheter
to clean the house	faire le ménage
to do errands	faire les courses
to do the dishes	faire la vaisselle
to dust	épousseter
to fix a meal	préparer un repas
to go to bed	aller au lit, dormir
to go to the bathroom	no real equivalent; use: aller prendre un bain; aller aux cabinets, etc.
to lease, to rent	louer
to listen to	écouter (la radio, etc.)

continues

Verbs Around the House   (continued)

English	French
to sell	*vendre*
to shop	*faire du shopping*
to take a bath	*prendre un bain*
to take a shower	*prendre une douche*
to watch	*regarder (la télé, etc.)*

Enjoy yourself as you learn to talk about your home surroundings, and get ready for Hour 16, "Going Places," where you'll learn to talk about your travels away from home.

Hour's Up!

Fantastique! Fantastic! You're progressing wonderfully, keeping to your schedule and mastering the new material before continuing to the next hour. Stay with this method because you need to have a firm control of new structures before you learn the new ones. Remember to read the examples aloud and write down the vocabulary in your notebook. Now review the interrogative pronouns and the use of the present participle and test your knowledge with the following quiz.

1. Choose the correct pronoun to complete the sentence: _____ *sait la réponse?* (Who?)

   a. *que*

   b. *qui*

   c. *qu'est-ce que*

   d. *quoi*

2. Choose the correct pronoun to complete the sentence: _____ *cherches-tu?* (What?)

   a. *que*

   b. *quoi*

   c. *est-ce que*

   d. *à qui*

3. Choose the correct pronoun to complete the sentence: *Avec _____ sors-tu?* (Whom?)

   a. *quoi*

   b. *que*

   c. *qui*

   d. *qu'est-ce que*

4. Choose the correct pronoun to complete the sentence: _____ *est arrivé?* (What?)

   a. *quoi*

   b. *qu'est-ce que*

   c. *que*

   d. *qu'est-ce qui*

5. Which of the following is not a question word?

   a. *parce que*

   b. *quand*

   c. *où*

   d. *comment*

6. What is the correct translation of the following sentence: I am going to France.

   a. *J'allais en France.*

   b. *Je suis allé en France.*

   c. *Je vais en France.*

   d. *Allant en France.*

7. Which word or phrase best completes the following sentence: _____ *en France, elles étaient fatiguées.*

   a. *Arriver*

   b. *En arrivant*

   c. *Arrivistes*

   d. *Arrivent*

8. What is the correct translation of the following phrase: the lost child.

    a. *l'enfant perdu*

    b. *l'enfant perdant*

    c. *l'enfant perd*

    d. *l'enfant à perdre*

9. Which of the following prepositions cannot be used to complete this sentence: *Il est parti _____ pleurer* (to cry).

    a. *sans*

    b. *avant de*

    c. *pour*

    d. *en*

10. French homes often are surrounded by what?

    a. *un étage*

    b. *une rue*

    c. *des murs*

    d. *un jardin*

HOUR 16
Going Places

CHAPTER SUMMARY

LESSON PLAN:

In this hour you will learn ...

- How to talk about time, dates, and weather.
- How to use the subjunctive.
- How to use vocabulary to talk about your travels.

At the end of this hour you'll be able to talk about your travels, where you want to go, how you want to go, and what you want to do. However, first you'll learn how to talk about the time, dates, and weather; then you'll review the subjunctive to keep it fresh on your mind. You'll conclude the hour by learning some useful tips about traveling in France and some vocabulary to talk about your travels.

TALK ABOUT TIME, DATES, AND WEATHER

France has a temperate climate and is made up of four broad climatic zones. The northwest has cool summers and cold, humid winters (*Le Havre*) along the English Channel (*La Manche*). The northeast region, in the areas around Alsace-Lorraine bordering the Jura Mountains and the Alps (Strasbourg), has mild summers and cold winters. The central northern regions around Paris and Lille can have very cold winters and hot summers. The southern, or Mediterranean regions (Marseille and Nice), generally have mild winters and very hot summers.

Because France has so much coastline, its weather is very unpredictable and can change suddenly. Springtime comes to Paris in late April. Summers in Paris can range from very hot, in the upper 80s (31 to 33° Celsius) to quite chilly and rainy. (France and all of Europe use the Celsius degree scale.)

FYI To convert degrees Fahrenheit to degrees Celsius (Centigrade) use this formula: $C° = (F° - 32) ÷ 1.8$. To convert degrees Celsius (Centigrade) to degrees Fahrenheit use this formula: $F° = (C° × 1.8) + 32$.

France is approximately the size of Texas (551 100 km², or 180,000 sq. miles). Politically, it is divided into 95 departments, to which 8 overseas departments and territories are added. A *préfet* administers a council, which governs each *département*. The population of France is approximately 58 million, of whom 10 million live in the Parisian region (*Île de France*).

LEARN EXPRESSIONS WITH TIME

In Hour 3, "Actions in the Present Tense," you learned to tell time using the verb *être* and the word *heure* (hour). You will recall that generally the French add minutes to the hour up to the half hour and then subtract minutes from the next hour beginning at the half hour. For example, 10:20 is *Il est **dix** heures vingt*; 10:40 is *Il est **onze** heures moins vingt*. Let's review this construction now.

FYI Daylight saving time in France and throughout the European Union begins on the last Sunday of March at 2:00 A.M. and ends on the last Sunday of October at 3:00 A.M.

Use the expression *il est* to say the following:

- 10:10   *Il est dix heures dix.*
- 10:15   *Il est dix heures et quart.*
- 10:30   *Il est dix heures et demie.*
- 10:35   *Il est onze heures moins vingt-cinq.*
- 10:45   *Il est onze heures moins le quart.*
- 10:50   *Il est onze heures moins dix.*
- 11:00   *Il est onze heures.*

GO TO ▶ Review the interrogative adjectives in Hour 8, "Learn to Express Yourself in the Future."

For clarity, you can add the following phrases to indicate A.M. or P.M. time:

- *du matin* (in the morning, A.M.)
- *de l'après-midi* (in the afternoon, P.M.)
- *du soir* (in the evening, P.M.)

Because you know the interrogative adjective *quelle*, now you can add this question to your vocabulary: *Quelle heure est-il?* (What time is it?)

LEARN ABOUT DATES

Remember that the definite article is used with days of the week when speaking in a general sense or when referring to a repeated day, as in *La classe de français est le lundi*. (French class is [every] Monday.) The article is omitted when speaking of a particular day, as in *La classe est lundi*. (The class is [this particular] Monday.) Using the days of the week, the months, and the adverbs of time you've learned (*aujourd'hui*, *demain*, *hier*, and so forth), now you can talk about dates.

GO TO ▶
In Hour 5, "Express Yourself in the Present Indicative," you learned the days of the week. Review that material before proceeding.

The following are some useful questions and answers:

What is the date today?

- *Quelle est la date aujourd'hui?*
- *Quel jour sommes-nous aujourd'hui?*
- *Quel jour est-ce aujourd'hui?*

What is the date tomorrow?

- *Quelle est la date demain?*

What was the date yesterday?

- *Quelle était la date hier?*

Today is the tenth.

- *Nous sommes le dix.*
- *C'est aujourd'hui le dix.*

Today is the fifth.

- *Nous sommes le cinq.*
- *C'est aujourd'hui le cinq.*

In a week

- *dans une semaine*
- *dans huit jours*

Next Monday

- *lundi prochain*

In two weeks

- *dans deux semaines*
- *dans quinze jours*

To give the full date (day, month, year), orally or in writing, use the following order:

- *Aujourd'hui c'est le lundi 15 février, 2001.*
- *Hier c'était le dimanche 14 février, 2001.*
- *Demain sera le mardi 16 février, 2001.*

To say that you were born in a particular year, use the preposition *en:*

- *Je suis né en 1950.*
- *Elle est née en 1962.*

TALK ABOUT THE WEATHER

When talking about the weather, French uses either the impersonal expression *il fait* (and not the verb *être*) or an impersonal verb that describes the weather. See the following table.

PROCEED WITH CAUTION

Be very careful to choose the correct verb—you can easily embarrass yourself (*faire une gaffe*) by choosing the wrong one, as in *il a chaud* (he is hot); *il fait chaud* (the weather is hot). (Note: *il est chaud* has a sexual connotation and should be avoided.)

Expression to Describe the Weather

French	English	French	English
Il pleut.	It's raining.	*Il fait chaud.*	It's hot.
Il neige.	It's snowing.	*Il fait froid.*	It's cold.
Il tonne.	It's thundering.	*Il fait de l'orage.*	It's storming.
Il gèle.	It's icing.	*Il fait du vent.*	It's windy.
Il grêle.	It's hailing.	*Il fait mauvais.*	It's bad weather.
Il fait frais.	It's mild.	*Il fait sec.*	It's dry.
Il fait beau.	It's pretty.	*Il fait du soleil.*	It's sunny.

USE *DEPUIS* + PRESENT TENSE

Now for a particular problem involving how to say "How long?" "For how long?" and "Since when?" in French. The question word used in all these sentences is *depuis*, which can mean either "since" or "for" in English. The French equivalents for these questions are ...

- *depuis combien de temps?* means "how long?"

- *depuis quand?* means "since when?" ("since what time" and so forth)

When the action in the sentence is still going on in the present, French uses the present tense with *depuis*, where English uses the past tense and the preposition "for." For example, compare these two sentences: *J'habite Paris depuis trois ans.* I <u>have lived</u> in Paris for three years. Note that the French verb is in the present tense while the English verb is in the past tense.

Look at the following examples and note particularly the differences between the French and English verb tenses:

- *Depuis combien de temps habitez-vous Paris?* (present)

  How long have you been living in Paris? (present perfect)

- *J'habite Paris depuis trois ans.* (present)

  I have been living in Paris for three years. (past)

  I've lived in Paris for three years. (present perfect)

- *Depuis quand est-il malade?* (present tense)

  How long (since when) has he been sick? (present perfect)

- *Il est malade depuis la semaine dernière.* (present)

  He's been sick since last week. (present perfect)

  He's been sick for a week. (present perfect)

However, if the action is completed in the past you use the *passé composé* and *pendant*, as follows:

- *J'ai travaillé en France pendant trois ans.* (I worked in France for [during] three years [the action is completed, that is, you no longer work in France].)

- *Combien de temps avez-vous étudié le français? Je l'ai étudié pendant cinq ans.* (How long did you study French? I studied it for [during] five years [the action is completed, you no longer are studying French].)

FYI To say "I had been doing [something]," use the imperfect; for example, *J'habitais la France depuis trois ans, quand j'ai vu Monsieur Mitterand pour la première fois.* (I had been living in France for three years when I saw Mr. Mitterand for the first time.)

Often *depuis* and *pendant* are used when meeting someone in questions such as "How long have you been here?" "How long have your studied French?" and so forth. Try composing and then answering the four following sentences by covering the answers that immediately follow:

- How long have you been in France?

  Depuis combien de temps êtes-vous en France?

- I've been here since Monday.

  Je suis ici depuis lundi.

- I've been here (for) a week.

  Je suis ici depuis une semaine.

- How long have you been learning French?

  Depuis quand étudiez-vous le français?

STRICTLY DEFINED

When referring to a future event you can use *pour* instead of *pendant,* but *pendant* is equally correct, as in *J'espère aller à Cuba pour [pendant] un mois.* (I hope to go to Cuba for a month.)

LEARN MORE ABOUT THE SUBJUNCTIVE

In Hours 6, "Express Yourself in the Present Subjunctive," and 12, "Learn to Link Ideas," you explored the subjunctive mood; let's review it to keep this very common mood fresh in your mind. The following table shows a fairly complete list of the words and expressions that must be followed by the subjunctive when you have two different subjects in a sentence. You should not try to memorize all these phrases at one time; rather, come back to the table regularly and consult it when the need arises. When you see the note "in the negative or interrog.," that means the verb is followed by the subjunctive if it is in the negative or interrogative form, for example:

*Je pense qu'il **vient**. Je ne pense pas qu'il **vienne**.* (neg.)

*Vous pensez qu'il **vient**. Pensez-vous qu'il **vienne**?* (interrog.)

FYI Used in a negative and interrogative construction, these verbs take the indicative: *Ne savez-vous pas qu'il vient?*

Words and Phrases That Require the Subjunctive

French	English
à moins que	unless
afin que	in order that
agacer	to upset
aimer	to love
aimer mieux	to like
attendre	to await
avant que	before
bien aise (être ___ que ...)	to be at ease
*bien que**	although
bizarre que (Il est/C'est ___ que)	bizarre
bon (Il est/C'est ___ que)	good
ce n'est pas que	it's only that
charmé (être ___ que ...)	charmed
commander	to order
consentir à ce que	to consent to
content (être ___ que ...)	content
craindre	to fear
croire (in the negative or interrogative)	to believe
de crainte que	for fear that
de peur que	for fear that
défendre	to prohibit
demander	to ask that
déplorer	to deplore
désirable (Il est/C'est ___ que)	desirable
désirer	to desire
désolé (être ___ que ...)	sorry that
détester	to hate
dire (in the negative or interrogative)	to say
dommage (Il est/C'est ___ que ...)	sorry
douter	to doubt
douteux (Il est/C'est ___ que)	doubtful

continues

Words and Phrases That Require the Subjunctive (continued)

French	English
écrire (in the negative or interrogative)	to write
en attendant que	awaiting
enchanté (être ___ que …)	enchanted
ennuyer	to bore
espérer (in the negative or interrogative)	to hope
essentiel (Il est ___ que)	essential
étonnant (Il est/C'est ___ que)	astonishing
étonné (être ___ que …)	astonished
s'étonner	to astonish
étrange (Il est/C'est ___ que)	strange
exiger	to demand
extraordinaire (Il est/C'est ___ que)	extraordinary
fâché (être ___ que …)	mad
Il faut que	necessary that
faux (Il est/C'est ___ que)	false; untrue
heureux (être ___ que …)	happy
heureux (Il est ___ que)	fortunate
honteux (Il est ___ que)	shameful
important (Il est/C'est ___ que)	important
impossible (Il est/C'est ___ que)	impossible
injuste (Il est/C'est ___ que)	unjust
trouver injuste que	unjust
inutile (Il est/C'est ___ que)	useless
irriter	to irritate
jusqu'à ce que*	until
juste (Il est/C'est ___ que)	just, fair
trouver juste que	just
loin que	far from
malheureux (Il est ___ que)	unhappy
mauvais = trouver mauvais que	bad
mériter	to merit
naturel (Il est/C'est ___ que)	natural
trouver naturel que	natural
ne pas douter*	not to doubt
ne pas tolérer	not to tolerate
ne pas pouvoir	not to be able

French	English
nécessaire (Il est/C'est ___ que)	necessary
nier*	to deny
non que	not that
ordonner	to order
où … que	wherever … that
penser (in the negative or interrogative)	to think
permettre	to permit
peut = Il se peut que	it's possible that
possible (Il est/C'est ___ que)	possible
pour que	in order that
pourvu que*	provided that
préférable (Il est/C'est ___ que)	preferable
préférer	to prefer
prendre garde	to be careful
qui que	whoever
quoi que	whatever
quoique*	although
rare (Il est/C'est ___ que)	rare
regrettable (Il est/C'est ___ que)	regrettable
regretter	to regret
sans que	without
satisfait (être ___ que …)	satisfied
savoir (in the negative or interrogative)	to know
souffrir	to suffer, to tolerate
souhaiter	to wish
Il suffit que	it is sufficient that
surpris (être ___ que …)	surprised
temps (Il est ___ que)	time
trouver (in the negative or interrogative)	to find
trouver bon	to find to be good
trouver injuste	to find to be unjust
trouver juste	to find to be just
trouver mauvais	to find to be bad
trouver naturel	to find to be natural
urgent (Il est ___ que)	urgent
utile (Il est/C'est ___ que)	useful

continues

Words and Phrases That Require the Subjunctive (continued)

French	English
Il vaut mieux que	it is better that
voir (in the negative or interrogative)	to see
vouloir	to wish, to want

* *Conjunction*

Sometimes the subjunctive can be overwhelming for a non-native speaker, but there is good news: Often it can be avoided entirely. In future hours you will learn some tricks to avoid the subjunctive. However, because you can't always do that, do try to learn a few new constructions each day.

LEARN VOCABULARY TO TALK ABOUT YOUR TRAVELS

Before attacking the vocabulary list at the end of this hour, you'll certainly be interested in knowing more about traveling in France. Here is some general information about such matters as passports, emergency services, currency, and driving in France. When traveling, you should also pay attention to national and religious holidays, which can result in changes in the schedules of trains and prices of lodging.

PASSPORTS AND VISAS

For citizens of the European Union (EU) member countries entering France, a valid passport or identity card is sufficient. Visitors from outside the EU must have a valid passport to enter the country. Visitors from some countries will need a visa, so you should check with your national embassy for this information.

FYI Parents of minors traveling alone must provide written authorization for the child to leave his or her territory.

Visa information is available from regional French Consulates or the French Embassy in the United States at www.france-consulat.org/visas.html. If you lose your passport in France you can get a three-month temporary passport from the nearest U.S. consulate. The U.S. consulate in Paris is located at 2, rue St-Florentin, 75001; phone: 42 96 12 02 or 42 61 80 75. Other cities with U.S. consulates are Bordeaux, Lyon, Marseille, and Strasbourg. It is mandatory in France to carry some proof of identification at all times.

DRIVING IN FRANCE

Once you're in France—if you're fearless—you might want to drive. U.S. citizens must carry a valid driver's license, issued in the United States, to drive in France. The minimum age for drivers is 18; proof of insurance coverage is necessary. Some important rules of the road are as follows:

- Seat belts are mandatory in both the front and back seats throughout France, including cities.

- Children under 10 must ride in the vehicle's rear seat (*le siège arrière*).

- At an intersection (*un carrefour*), the driver (*le conducteur*) to the right (*à droite*) has the right-of-way (*la priorité*) over drivers approaching from the left (*à gauche*). (Exceptions: You are in a traffic circle [*un rond point*] or are otherwise instructed by signs [*un panneau de signalisation*]).

- Driving while intoxicated carries severe penalties (*une amende*), and speed limits (*la limite de vitesse*) are strictly enforced.

- Traffic police on the highway (*l'autoroute*) are *les gendarmes*; cops are, familiarly, *les flics*.

FYI The city speed limit is 60 km (37 miles) per hour or as posted. The speed limit on toll highways is 130 km (81 miles) per hour, on no-toll highways 110 km (68 miles) per hour, and 90 km (56 miles) per hour on other roads.

MAJOR NATIONAL HOLIDAYS IN FRANCE

Don't forget that France, like the United States, has a number of nationally observed holidays. Religious holidays are *les jours fériés*, a day off from work is called *un jour de congé*, and "vacation" is always plural (a great idea!) in French: *les vacances*. Most government offices and many museums, restaurants, and so forth will be closed on national holidays.

- New Year's Day   January 1
- Easter   (date changes)
- Labor Day   May 1
- Victory in Europe Day   May 8 (Armistice Day)
- Ascension   (date changes)
- Pentecost   (date changes)
- National Holiday   July 14 (Bastille Day)
- Assumption Day   (date changes)

- All Saints Day   November 1
- Armistice Day   November 11
- Christmas Day   December 25

In addition to *fêter* (celebrating) *un anniversaire* (one's birthday), many French also celebrate the Saint's Day (*la fête*) for whom they are named. These dates appear on many French calendars.

MONEY MATTERS

By the end of a long day of museum-hopping, you'll probably need some funds. The French like to be paid in *francs français* (FF), and foreign currency is rarely accepted except in large hotels where you will pay a premium to have your cash converted to FF. When without cash, use a major credit card.

FF come in the following bills:

500F/200F/100F/50F/20F (The 20F bill is fast disappearing.)

French coins are available as follows:

20F/10F/5F/2F/1F

50 centimes/20 centimes/10 centimes/5 centimes

As of January, 1999, France has become a member of the Monetary Union. The Euro now is France's currency and the national currency units, including the French franc, are subunits of the Euro. The Euro is divided into 100 cents.

Most major international banks have offices in Paris. Banks are open weekdays, 9 A.M. to 4:30 P.M. Banks are closed Sundays, holidays, and the afternoon before holidays. They also are closed Saturdays in Paris and Mondays in the provinces. ATMs are readily available and much used.

EMERGENCY PHONE NUMBERS

In case of emergency, help is only two numbers away. Throughout France, emergency numbers are as follows:

Telephone information:	12
SAMU (24-hour ambulance):	15
Police:	17
Fire:	18

PROCEED WITH CAUTION

Before you blow up your hairdryer and have to use one of the preceding emergency numbers, prepare for differences in electrical current by purchasing a converter before leaving home.

BUSINESS TRAVEL DIVISION

Perhaps you're going to travel to France for business. If so, before you leave, you might want to contact one of the French offices that offers assistance to business travelers. The French Government Tourist Office contains a business travel division offering advisory services for companies wishing to organize conferences, conventions, seminars, exhibitions, incentives, or product launches; contact French Government Tourist Office, 610 Fifth Avenue, New York, NY 10020.

TRAVEL VOCABULARY

Once you arrive in France you will probably travel by train or car. The train station is *la gare*. If you plan to rent a car, it's best to arrange that before leaving home. When you arrive at the airport, look for signs saying *location de voitures*. The Paris subway system (*le métro*) is excellent and you can get a free map at any ticket counter. Here's some more vocabulary you can use to talk about going places.

Nouns for Going Places

English	French
airplane	*un avion*
airport	*un aéroport*
ATM	*un DAB*
backpack	*un sac à dos*
baggage	*le bagage*
bench	*un banc*
bill (hotel)	*la note*
bill (restaurant)	*une addition*
boat	*le bateau*
border	*la frontière*
bus	*un autobus, le bus*
bus (interurban)	*le car*

continues

Nouns for Going Places (continued)

English	French
car	*une voiture*
change	*la monnaie*
companion (travel companion)	*le compagnon (de voyage)*
complaint	*une réclamation*
corner (of the street)	*le coin (de la rue)*
counter (ticket counter)	*le guichet*
credit card	*une carte de crédit (carte bleue)*
customs	*la douane*
double bed	*un grand lit*
elevator	*un ascenseur*
ferry	*le ferry, la navette*
foreigner	*un étranger, une étrangère*
friendly	*amical, sympa*
full (no vacancy)	*complet*
guide	*le guide*
hostel	*une auberge*
hotel	*un hôtel*
hotel desk	*la réception*
hotel (telephone) operator	*le/la standardiste*
locker	*le casier*
long-distance call	*un appel interurbain*
luggage	*les bagages*
maid, housekeeper	*la femme de chambre*
misunderstanding	*une méprise*
money	*l'argent (m.)*
museum	*un musée*
newspaper	*le journal*
no smoking	*défense de fumer*
noisy	*bruyant*
post office	*la poste*
quiet	*calme*
room	*la chambre*
schedule (train, plane, etc.)	*un horaire*
safe (for valuables)	*le coffre-fort*
seat	*la place*

English	French
stairs	l'escalier (m.)
steward	le steward
stewardess	une hôtesse de l'air
street	la rue
subway	le métro
suitcase	une valise
ticket (movie, etc.)	un ticket
ticket (train, plane, etc.)	un billet
tip (included in bill)	le service
tip (left on table)	le pourboire
tip included	service compris
tip not included	service non compris
tourist	un/une touriste
train	le train
train (bullet train)	le T.G.V. (train à grande vitesse)
unfriendly	inamical, désagréable
vacant	libre

Verbs of Travel

English	French
to arrive	arriver
to be lost	être perdu
to carry	porter
to check out	partir
to exchange money	changer de l'argent
to help	aider
to knock	frapper
to leave	partir
to meet	rencontrer
to pack one's bags	plier bagage
to pay	payer
to pay the bill (hotel)	régler la note
to pay the bill (meal)	payer l'addition
to take (train, plane, etc.)	prendre (l'autobus, l'avion, etc.)
to tip	laisser un pourboire

continues

Verbs of Travel   (continued)

English	French
to travel	*voyager*
to travel to; go to (a place)	*aller* (*à* + city; *en/au* + country)
to turn	*tourner*
to wait for	*attendre*

Directions	
north, to the north	*le nord, au nord*
east, to the east	*l'est, à l'est*
south, to the south	*le sud, au sud*
west, to the west	*l'ouest, à l'ouest*

QUIZ

HOUR'S UP!

Hourra! Hurrah! You've come to the end of another hour! You've mastered telling time and talking about your travels, as well as how to use the subjunctive correctly. This is the end of Part 4, "Leisure Time." In Part 5 you'll be "stepping out" into the real world of school and work. To conclude this Part, review the material and test you mastery of it with the following quiz. And then, *bon voyage!* Have a good trip!

1. How does one say "What time is it?"

   a. *Quelle heure est-il?*

   b. *Qu'est-ce que c'est l'heure?*

   c. *Elle est quelle heure?*

   d. *Vous avez l'heure?*

2. Which of the following does not translated the question "What is the date?"

   a. *Quelle est la date?*

   b. *Quel jour sommes-nous?*

   c. *Sommes-nous le dix?*

   d. *Quel jour est-ce?*

3. Complete the following sentence with the correct preposition: *Je suis né* _____ *1980.*

    a. *au*

    b. *en*

    c. *dans*

    d. *à*

4. Which of the following sentences does not refer to weather?

    a. *Il neige.*

    b. *Il pleut.*

    c. *Il fait beau.*

    d. *Il est beau.*

5. Complete the following sentence with the correct form of the verb: *Je/J'* _____ *à Paris depuis hier.*

    a. *étais*

    b. *ai été*

    c. *suis*

    d. *serai*

6. Complete the following sentence with the correct preposition: *Il étudie le français* _____ *trois ans.*

    a. *depuis*

    b. *avec*

    c. *en*

    d. *par*

7. Complete the following sentence with the correct preposition: *J'ai travaillé en France* _____ *trois ans.*

    a. *par*

    b. *pendant*

    c. *sur*

    d. *dans*

8. Which of the following expressions is not followed by the subjunctive mood?

   a. *je suis désolé que*

   b. *il est important que*

   c. *il est bon que*

   d. *il est sûr que*

9. The French National Holiday is celebrated on what day?

   a. December 25

   b. July 4

   c. July 14

   d. November 1

10. To enter France as a U.S. citizen, you must have which of the following?

   a. a passport

   b. driver's license

   c. visa

   d. a and c

QUIZ

PART V
Stepping Out

HOUR 17
Eating Out

CHAPTER SUMMARY

LESSON PLAN:

In this hour you'll learn …

- How to express yourself in past time.
- How to use the *futur antérieur.*
- How to use the past conditional.
- How to use the *plus-que-parfait.*
- How to use the past subjunctive.
- How to use vocabulary to discuss meals.

In this hour, all remaining verb tenses are presented except for one, the *passé simple*, which is used only in writing and will be presented in Hour 24, "Understanding Formal Writing in French." These new tenses are all "compound tenses," that is, they are formed using one of the auxiliary verbs (*avoir* or *être*) plus the past particle of the main verb. Therefore, you've already learned all the verb forms you'll need to create the new tenses; you'll just have to practice combining the forms in new ways.

Because you will be using the future tense and the imperfect tense to form new compound tenses in this hour, you might want to go back and review formation of these tenses in Hours 8, "Learn to Express Yourself in the Future," and 9, "Express Yourself in the Past."

EXPRESS YOURSELF IN PAST TIME

Before learning the four new tenses presented in this hour, let's review the rules for the use of *passé composé* and imperfect, which you learned in Hours 9 and 10, "Use the Correct Past Tense."

Use the *passé composé* …

- To describe an action or event performed and completed in the past.
- To describe a series of actions or events performed and completed in the past.

Use the imperfect …

- To describe the scene or setting in which actions take place in the past.
- To describe actions that take place in the past and have no precise ending in the past.
- To describe habitual or repeated actions in the past.
- To form a conditional sentence using *si* (if) in conjunction with the conditional mood.

Review the earlier hours and keep these rules in mind as you learn the new tenses.

MASTER THE *FUTUR ANTÉRIEUR*

The *future antérieur*, called the "future perfect" in English, is composed of the future of the appropriate auxiliary verb (*être* or *avoir*), plus the past participle of the verb and can be translated as "will have" + past participle:

- *Je serai sorti.* (I will have gone out.)
- *Il aura chanté.* (He will have sung.)
- *Elles seront parties.* (They will have left.)

The future perfect is used to indicate that an action in the future will be completed before another action in the future. This tense most often is used after the following conjunctions:

- *tant que* (as long as)
- *dès que, aussitôt que* (as soon as)
- *quand* (when)
- *lorsque* (when)
- *après que* (after)

GO TO ▶
Review the use of these conjunctions in Hour 8.

Often the distinction between the use of the future and the future perfect is one of precision of language. For example, in the following sentences, either tense might be used depending on the intent of the speaker:

J'enverrai cette lettre à mes parents quand je finirai/j'aurai fini de l'écrire. (I will send this letter to my parents when I finish/have finished writing it.)

However, sometimes the distinction is important to the meaning of the sentence, as illustrated by these two examples:

- *Quand ils arriveront demain, j'aurai fini mon travail.* When they arrive tomorrow, I will have finished my work.
- *Quand ils arriveront demain, je finirai ce travail.* When they arrive tomorrow, I will finish this work.

Note, however, that the future or the future perfect must be used in French where the present or present perfect is used in English.

 FYI The future perfect is used in conversation and formal writing. In familiar writing, it is sometimes (although not properly) replaced by the past tense, as in *J'ai fini dans dix minutes.* (I will have finished in ten minutes.)

LEARN THE *PLUS-QUE-PARFAIT*

The *plus-que-parfait* is called the pluperfect tense in English. It is used to express that an action took place in the past before another action in the past. To form the pluperfect in French, conjugate the appropriate auxiliary verb in the imperfect and add the past participle of the verb, as follows:

- *Il avait parlé.* (He had spoken.)
- *Elle était partie.* (She had left.)
- *Nous avions voyagé.* (We had traveled.)
- *Ils étaient tombés.* (They had fallen.)

Generally the *plus-que-parfact* can be translated as "had" + past participle, as shown in the following. In each of these examples, the verb in the pluperfect indicates that that action was completed before the action of the other verb:

- *Il a remarqué que j'avais oublié son nom.* (He noticed that I had forgotten his name.)
- *Quand j'ai fini mon travail, il était déjà parti.* (When I [had] finished my work, he had already left.)

FYI Notice that French uses the *passé composé* after *quand* if the main clause uses the pluperfect.

LEARN THE PAST CONDITIONAL

In Hour 8 you also learned the present conditional mood: *Il chanterait.* (He would sing.) The present conditional is formed by adding the following endings to the future stem of the verb: *ais, ais, ait, ions, iez,* and *aient.* The past conditional is formed by conjugating the appropriate auxiliary verb in the present conditional and adding the past participle. It can be translated as "would have" + past participle, as shown in the following:

- *Il aurait chanté.* (He would have sung.)
- *Elles seraient parties.* (They would have left.)
- *Nous aurions parlé.* (We would have spoken.)

You've already learned that the present conditional is used with *si* (meaning "if," not "whether") in conjunction with the imperfect to form a conditional sentence, as shown here:

Si j'avais plus d'argent, j'irais en France. (If I had more money, I would go to France.) (*si* + imperfect, present conditional)

The past conditional is used in conjunction with the pluperfect to form a conditional sentence referring to past events:

- *Si j'avais eu plus d'argent, je serais allé en France.* (If I had had more money, I would have gone to France.)
- *S'il avait compris la question, il nous aurait donné la réponse correcte.* (If he had understood the question, he would have given us the correct answer.)
- *Elle n'aurait pas pris le train si elle avait su qu'il était si cher.* (She would not have taken the train if she had known that it was so expensive.)

Thus, the rules for using the present conditional and the past conditional with *si* are as follows:

Si + imperfect creates a present conditional sentence.

Si + pluperfect creates a past conditional sentence.

LEARN THE PAST SUBJUNCTIVE

The past subjunctive is primarily a literary tense, but you might hear it in conversations among careful speakers of French. Most often it is replaced, in familiar conversations, with the present subjunctive, even though the meaning of the verb logically would call for a past tense.

 French also has an imperfect and a pluperfect subjective; however, these tenses are rarely used except by professors (and politicians!) and in affected speech.

To form the past subjunctive, conjugate the appropriate auxiliary verb in the present subjunctive and add the past participle, as follows:

- *que je sois allé* (that I went)
- *qu'il ait parlé* (that he spoke)
- *que nous soyons sortis* (that we left)

The past subjunctive is properly used in the following examples:

- *Je regrette qu'elle n'ait pas pu venir.* (I'm sorry she **was not able** to come.)
- *Le professeur a voulu que nous **ayons fini** l'examen avant midi.* (The professor wanted us to have finished the test before noon.)

Those are all the new structures for this hour; now let's work on some vocabulary to talk about meals and eating out.

LEARN VOCABULARY TO TALK ABOUT MEALS

Before working on the following vocabulary, let's talk a minute about meals in general in France. First of all, the evening family meal (*le dîner*) is traditional but usually lighter than in the United States. The main meal of the day often is lunch (*le déjeuner*), which lasts from noon until 2:00 P.M. Breakfast (*le petit déjeuner*) also is light, typically a large bowl (*un bol*, not *une tasse*) of coffee; and bread, butter, and jam. Coffee is served in cafés in a small cup (*une demi-tasse*), unless you order *un double* (a "double" coffee), in which case you'll get a standard-sized cup. However, the traditional way of drinking coffee at home for breakfast is in a bowl.

Dining out (*aller au restraunt*) is a favorite pastime, and France is known for its fine cuisine (*la cuisine*) and great chefs (*le chef*). Restaurants must post their menus (*la carte*) at the door so you can check prices and offerings before entering. The best choice often is *le plat du jour* (the specialty of the day), which will have a *prix fixe* (fixed price). You also can *commander* (order) *à la carte*, making your selections from the choices available. For *la bonne chère* (a fine meal), one begins with an *apéritif* (a light drink to spark the appetite); then an *hors-d'œuvre* followed by *l'entrée*.

The *entrée* is not the main course but rather a soup or some other choice to enter into the meal. The *entrée* is followed by *le plat de résistance* (the main dish), which could be either *une viande* (beef or pork), *la volaille* (poultry) or *un poisson* (fish). Then one might have *une salade* with a real French dressing (*la vinaigrette*) composed of olive oil, spicy mustard, and fresh herbs. The salad is followed by *le dessert*, then *un café*, and finally perhaps *un digestif* (after-dinner cognac). Many French then will smoke *une cigarette* (a cigarette), as smoking is still permitted almost everywhere in France. Often the first person to begin smoking will offer a cigarette to others at the table.

Le fast-food (fast food) and American food chains have come to France; chains such as MacDonald's (*le Macdo*), Kentucky Fried Chicken, and Baskin-Robbins are available in most large cities. There is even a Macdo on the *Champs-Elysées*. Despite resistance by their elders, the younger set has generally embraced fast food.

Here's some vocabulary to talk about eating at home and dining out. Given the French love of fine dining, it's interesting to note that there is no real equivalent phrase for the English "to dine out"; the French say simply *Nous allons au restaurant* (We're going to a restaurant).

Eating In and Eating Out

Meals	Les repas *(m.)*
breakfast	*le petit-déjeuner*
dinner	*le dîner*
lunch	*le déjeuner*
snack	*le casse-croûte*
supper	*le souper*
Setting the Table	Mettre la table
bottle of	*une bouteille de* (invariable *de*)
bowl	*un bol*
coffee cup	*une tasse à café*
coffee pot	*une cafetière*
condiments	*les condiments* (m.)
cup	*une tasse*
cup of coffee	*une tasse de café*
dish	*un plat*
fork	*une fourchette*
glass	*un verre*
ketchup	*la sauce tomate*
knife	*un couteau*
pepper	*le poivre*
pitcher, carafe	*une carafe*
place mat	*un set de table*
plate	*une assiette*

Setting the Table	Mettre la table
salad oil	l'huile (f.)
salt	le sel
saucer	une soucoupe
serving spoon	une grande cuillère
soup bowl	une assiette creuse
spoon	une cuillère
teapot	une théière

Meat	La viande
beef	le bœuf
chicken	le poulet
duck	le canard
goose	l'oie (f.)
ham	le jambon
lamb	l'agneau (m.)
lamb chop	la côte d'agneau
pork	le porc
pork chop	la côte de porc
poultry	la volaille
quail	la caille
rabbit	le lapin
sausage	la saucisse
snails	les escargots (m.)
turkey	la dinde
veal	le veau
venison	le venaison

Fish	Le poisson
cod	la morue
crab	le crabe
eel	l'anguille (f.)
langoustine	la langoustine
lobster	le *homard
mackerel	le maquereau
perch	la perche
salmon	le saumon
scallops	les coquilles Saint-Jacques (f.)

continues

Eating In and Eating Out (continued)

Fish	Le poisson
seafood	*les fruits de mer*
seafood platter	*une assiette de crustacés*
shark	*le requin*
shellfish	*les crustacés* (m.)
shrimp	*la crevette*
squid	*l'encornet* (m.)
trout	*la truite*
tuna	*le thon*
whiting	*le merlan*
Bread	Le pain
croissant	*un croissant*
rolls	*les petits pains*
rye bread	*le pain de seigle*
white bread	*le pain*
Fruits	Les fruits
apple	*une pomme*
apricot	*un abricot*
banana	*une banane*
blackberry	*la mûre*
black currant	*le cassis*
cherry	*la cerise*
cranberry	*la canneberge*
grape	*un raisin*
grapefruit	*le pamplemousse*
kiwi	*le kiwi*
lemon	*le citron*
lime	*le citron vert*
mango	*la mangue*
melon	*un melon*
orange	*une orange*
peach	*une pêche*
pear	*une poire*
pineapple	*l'ananas* (m.)
plum	*une prune*
raisin	*un raisin sec*

Fruits	Les fruits
raspberry	*la framboise*
red currant	*la groseille*
strawberry	*la fraise*

Vegetables and Spices	Les légumes and les épices
basil	*le basilic*
broccoli	*le brocoli*
Brussels sprouts	*les choux de Bruxelles*
cabbage	*le chou*
carrot	*une carotte*
cauliflower	*le chou-fleur*
fennel	*le fenouil*
eggplant	*l'aubergine* (f.)
garlic	*l'ail* (m.)
green beans	*les *haricots verts* (m.)
herbs	*les fines herbes* (f.)
onion	*un oignon*
parsley	*le persil*
peas	*les petits pois* (m.)
potato	*une pomme de terre*
rosemary	*le romarin*
sugar	*le sucre*
thyme	*le thym*
turnip	*le navet*
watercress	*le cresson*

Drinks	Les boissons
apple (orange, pineapple, etc.) juice	*un jus de pomme (d'orange, d'ananas, etc.)*
beer	*une bière*
bottle (of)	*une bouteille de*
brandy	*le cognac*
cappuccino	*un cappuccino*
carton (of)	*une brique de*
chamomile	*une camomille*
champagne	*le champagne*
Coca-Cola	*un coca*
coffee	*le café*
coffee with milk	*un café crème*

continues

Eating In and Eating Out (continued)

Drinks	Les boissons
decaffeinated coffee	*un déca*
draught beer	*une pression*
expresso	*un espresso; un café*
fruit juice	*un jus de fruit*
gin	*le gin*
hot chocolate	*un chocolat chaud*
instant coffee	*un nescafé*
lemonade	*une limonade*
mineral water	*l'eau minérale* (f.)
orangeade	*une orangeade*
Pepsi	*un pepsi*
red wine	*le vin rouge*
rum	*le rhum*
straw (drinking)	*une paille*
tea	*le thé*
tea-bag	*un sachet de thé*
tisane	*une tisane*
vodka	*la vodka*
water (some water)	*l'eau (de l'eau)*
whisky	*le whisky*
white wine	*le vin blanc*
wine	*le vin*
Dairy Products	Les produits laitiers
butter	*le beurre*
cheese	*le fromage*
cream	*la crème*
half-fat (milk, etc.)	*demi-écrémé (lait demi-écrémé)*
margarine	*la margarine*
milk	*le lait*
sour cream	*la crème fraîche*
whole milk	*le lait entier*
yogurt	*le yaourt*
Miscellaneous	Divers
egg	*un oeuf*
fats	*les matières grasses* (f.)
flour	*la farine*

Miscellaneous	Divers
ice cube, with ice	*un glaçon, avec glaçons*
jam	*la confiture*
liver (goose) pâte	*le pâté de foie gras*
mustard	*la moutarde*
noodles	*les nouilles (f.)*
nuts	*les noix (f.)*
olive oil	*l'huile d'olive*
olives	*les olives*
pasta	*les pâtes (f.)*
spaghetti	*les spaghettis (m.)*
vinegar	*le vinaigre*

At the Restaurant	Au restaurant
ashtray	*un cendrier*
chair	*une chaise*
crepes	*les crêpes (m.)*
dessert	*le dessert*
first course	*l'entrée (f.)*
fries (potatoes)	*les frites*
ice cream	*la glace*
ice cream, chocolate	*la glace au chocolat*
ice cream, vanilla	*la glace à la vanille*
main course	*le plat de résistance*
maitre d'	*le maître d'hôtel*
menu	*la carte*
napkin	*une serviette*
pastry	*les pâtisseries (f.)*
place setting	*le couvert*
receipt	*un reçu*
salad	*la salade*
sandwich	*un sandwich*
sandwich with cheese	*un sandwich au fromage*
sandwich with ham	*un sandwich au jambon*
sauce	*la sauce*
service charge, tip	*le service*
starter	*le hors-d'œuvre*
table	*la table*

continues

Eating In and Eating Out (continued)

At the Restaurant	Au restaurant
tip (in addition to service charge)	le pourboire
waiter	le serveur
waitress	la serveuse
wine steward	le sommelier

QUIZ

HOUR'S UP!

Superbe! Superb! Again, you've done well. This has been a particularly fun hour because you were able to use many of the structures you've learned in past hours to create new structures. Also, talking about food is always enjoyable! In the next hour you'll learn about reflexive verbs and how to talk about the workplace. So, before you go on, review the structures in this hour and test your knowledge with the following quiz.

1. Which form of the verb best completes the following sentence: *Je vous donnerai ce livre quand _____ de le lire.*

   a. *je finirai*

   b. *j'aurai fini*

   c. *j'ai fini*

   d. *je finis*

2. Which form of the verb best completes the following sentence: *Dès qu'il _____ son travail, il partira.*

   a. *finirait*

   b. *finit*

   c. *aura fini*

   d. *a fini*

3. Which form of the verb best completes the following sentence: *Si j' _____ plus d'argent, je serais allé en France.*

   a. *aurais*

   b. *avais*

   c. *ai eu*

   d. *avais eu*

4. Which form of the verb best completes the following sentence: *Elle n'aurait pas pris le train si elle* _____ *qu'il était si cher.*

   a. *avait su*

   b. *savait*

   c. *a su*

   d. *sait*

5. *Qu'il ait parlé* is an example of what?

   a. *passé composé*

   b. past subjunctive

   c. present subjunctive

   d. present indicative

6. *Que je sois parti* is an example of what?

   a. *passé composé*

   b. past subjunctive

   c. present subjunctive

   d. present indicative

7. To order items individually from the menu is:

   a. *commander sur le menu*

   b. *commander à la carte*

   c. *demander la carte*

   d. *demander un repas*

8. Of the following items, which one is ordered first?

   a. *une salade*

   b. *un digestif*

   c. *un hors-d'oeuvre*

   d. *une entrée*

9. The main course is called what?

   a. *l'apéritif*

   b. *l'entrée*

   c. *la salade*

   d. *le plat de résistance*

10. Which of the following is not a meat dish?

    a. *l'aubergine*

    b. *l'oie*

    c. *le canard*

    d. *le boeuf*

HOUR 18
At Work

CHAPTER SUMMARY

LESSON PLAN:

In this hour you will learn …

- How to describe your daily routine.
- How to use reflexive verbs.
- Vocabulary to talk about the work and the workplace.
- How to use the pronouns *y* and *en*.

When describing daily routines French, uses a special group of verbs called pronominal (because they have a pronoun associated with them) or reflexive (because the action of the verb reflects back on the subject) verbs. In this hour you'll learn how to conjugate the reflexive verbs and use them in some idiomatic expressions. You'll also learn two new pronouns: *y* (there) and *en* (of them). Finally, you'll learn about the French workplace and some vocabulary to discuss what you do professionally.

DESCRIBE YOUR DAILY ROUTINE

Most of us have a daily routine, particularly in the morning. We get up, eat breakfast, shower, shave, brush teeth and hair, and so forth. Most of the verbs used in French to describe these routines are called reflexive verbs. Some examples of common reflexive verbs in English include "to talk to oneself," "to hurt oneself," and so forth. French has a vast number of such verbs; often they are used where English would not use a reflexive verb.

To understand how reflexive verbs work, let's begin with their conjugation and then talk about how they are used.

LEARN THE PRESENT TENSE OF REFLEXIVE VERBS

The following two tables show the conjugations of two reflexive verbs. Notice that each person of the verb has an object pronoun associated with it.

Conjugation of Reflexive Verbs: Present Tense

Person	se lever *(to get up)*	se coucher *(to go to bed)*
first	*je me lève*	*je me couche*
second	*tu te lèves*	*tu te couches*
third	*il se lève*	*il se couche*
	elle se lève	*elle se couche*
	on se lève	*on se couche*
	nous nous levons	*nous nous couchons*
	vous vous levez	*vous vous couchez*
	ils se lèvent	*ils se couchent*
	elles se lèvent	*elles se couchent*

Note that the English translation could be "I get myself up"; however, you'd probably not say "I put myself to bed." The English equivalent of most French reflexive verbs is not a reflexive verb, as shown here:

- *Je me lève.* (I get up.)
- *Je me couche.* (I go to bed.)

When used in the plural, some reflexive verbs also can communicate the English sense of doing something "to each other." In this case the verbs have a reciprocal function, as in the following examples:

- *se parler: Ils se parlent.* (They talk to each other.)
- *se disputer: Elles se disputent.* (They are arguing with each other.)

In the first example, *ils se parlent* also can mean that they are individually talking to themselves; that is, each person is talking to him- or herself. If there is a need to clarify, you can add *l'un(e)avec l'autre* (one with the other) or *entre eux.*

- *Ils se disputent l'un avec l'autre.* (They are arguing with each other.)
- *Ils se parlent entre eux.* (They are talking among themselves.)

FYI Reflexive or pronominal verbs are listed in a dictionary alphabetically by the main verb; thus, *s'accoutumer* is listed under *accoutumer; se tromper,* under *tromper;* and so forth.

The following table lists some of the most common reflexive verbs followed by the English equivalent.

Common Reflexive Verbs

French	English	French	English
s'abriter	to shelter (oneself)	s'habiller	to dress
s'accoutumer à	to get used to	s'habituer à	to get used to
s'adresser à	to address oneself to someone	se hâter	to hurry
		s'imaginer	to imagine
s'affoler	to get upset	s'intéresser à	to be interested in
s'en aller	to go away	s'inquiéter	to worry
s'allonger	to stretch out	se jouer de	to make fun of
s'amuser	to have fun	se laver	to wash
s'appeler	to call oneself	se lever	to get up
s'approcher	to approach	se méfier de	to watch out for
s'arrêter	to stop	se mettre à	to begin
s'asseoir	to sit down	se moquer de	to make fun of
s'attendre à	to await, to expect	s'occuper de	to take care of
se baisser	to lean over	se passer	to happen
se brosser	to brush	se peigner	to comb
se cacher	to hide	se rappeler	to remember
se coucher	to go to bed	se réjouir	to be happy
se décider	to decide	se reposer	to rest
se dépêcher	to hurry	se retourner	to turn around
se disputer	to argue	se résoudre à	to resolve to
se douter	to doubt	se réveiller	to wake up
s'échapper à	to escape from	se sauver	to save oneself
s'empêcher de	to prevent from	se servir de	to use
s'endormir	to go to sleep	se souvenir de	to remember
s'ennuyer	to be bored	se taire	to be quiet
s'étendre	to stretch out	se terminer	to end
s'étonner	to be surprised	se tromper	to be wrong
s'évanouir	to faint	se trouver	to find
s'excuser	to make an excuse	se vanter de	to brag
se fier à	to trust in		

For the moment, notice that there is very little similarity between the English use of a reflexive verb and the French requirement of one. Many of these verbs are used idiomatically; we will talk about that after you've worked on the conjugations.

When conjugated in compound tenses, all reflexive verbs use the auxiliary *être*.

LEARN THE PAST TENSE OF REFLEXIVE VERBS

To form the past tense of a reflexive verb, conjugate the verb *être* in the present tense and add the past participle of the verb as shown in the following table.

Conjugation of Reflexive Verbs: *passé composé*

se lever *(to get up)*	se coucher *(to go to bed)*
je me suis levé	*je me suis couché*
tu t'es levé	*tu t'es couché*
il s'est levé	*il s'est couché*
elle s'est levée	*elle s'est couchée*
on s'est levé	*on s'est couché*
nous nous sommes levés	*nous nous sommes couchés*
vous vous êtes levé	*vous vous êtes couché*
ils se sont levés	*ils se sont couchés*
elles se sont levées	*elles se sont couchées*

Although reflexive verbs are conjugated with *être* in compound tenses, the past participles of these verbs agree following the rule of agreement for verbs conjugated with *avoir*: The past participle agrees with a preceding direct object.

As strange as this might seem, the rule is strictly observed. In most cases, the reflexive pronoun is both a direct object and the same person and number as the subject. Therefore, in many cases it will appear as if the past participle is agreeing with the subject. However, with verbs that take an indirect object (such as *parler à, téléphoner à, écrire à*) the reflexive pronoun is an indirect object; therefore, there is no agreement of the past participle, as shown here:

se parler: Elles se sont parlé. (parler à une personne)

se téléphoner: Ils se sont téléphoné. (téléphoner à une personne)

Also, when these verbs are followed by a noun direct object, there is no agreement of the past participle:

- *Elle s'est brossé les cheveux. (Les cheveux* is the direct object: She brushed her hair.)
- *Ils se sont lavé les mains. (Les mains* is the direct object: They washed their hands.)

USE REFLEXIVE VERBS IN COMMANDS

When using reflexive verbs in commands, the reflexive pronoun follows the verb in positive commands and precedes the verb in negative commands. In addition, the pronoun *te* changes to *toi* in the positive command, as shown here:

- *Couche-toi!* (Go to bed!)
- *Ne te couche pas si tôt!* (Don't go to bed so early!)
- *Rappelez-vous!* (Remember!)
- *Dépêchons-nous!* (Let's hurry up!)
- *Ne vous inquiétez pas!* (Don't worry!)
- *Amuse-toi bien!* (Have a good time!)
- *Ne t'amuse pas trop!* (Don't have too good a time!)

You might want to review the formation of commands in Hour 5, "Express Yourself in the Present Indicative," so that you can compare the use of pronouns in commands of verbs that are reflexive with those that are not reflexive. For example, compare these two commands: *Levez-vous!* (Get [yourself] up!) *Levez-le!* (Lift it!) The first example is the command form of the reflexive verb *se lever*; the second example is the command form of the verb *lever*, which is not reflexive.

USE REFLEXIVE VERBS

Because the reflexive pronoun actually is an object pronoun, it occupies the same place in interrogative and negative sentences as the other object pronouns. Place it in front of the conjugated verb, as in the following examples:

GO TO ▶
Review the placement of object pronouns in Hour 14, "Free Time."

Interrogative:

- *Vous appelez-vous Claude?* (Is your name Claude?)
- *S'est-il brossé les dents?* (Did he brush his teeth?)
- *Se sont-ils levés de bonne heure?* (Did they get up early?)

 FYI In the interrogative, the subject pronoun is connected to the verb with a hyphen; the other pronoun is the reflexive pronoun.

Negative:

- *Il ne s'appelle pas Claude.* (His name is not Claude.)
- *Elle ne s'est pas brossé les cheveux.* (She did not brush her hair.)
- *Je ne me suis pas réveillé tôt ce matin.* (I didn't wake up early this morning.)

SPECIAL USES OF REFLEXIVE VERBS

Because some of the verbs in the preceding list are used idiomatically, you should use the following examples to guide you in using them correctly. Notice particularly that there are several *faux amis* (false friends) in the list, that is, the French verb resembles the English, but differs slightly in meaning; for example, *s'adresser* does not mean "to address yourself" but "to inquire."

- **s'abriter** *Je m'abrite sous un arbre.* (I take shelter under a tree.)
- **s'accoutumer à** *Je me suis accoutumé au mauvais temps.* (I got used to the bad weather.)
- **s'adresser à** *Tu dois t'adresser au guichet à gauche.* (You should inquire at the window to the left.)
- **s'en aller** *Nous nous en sommes allés.* (We went away.) Note that *aller* must be followed by an indication of where you're going, as in *Nous sommes allés à Paris.*
- **s'amuser** *Elle s'est bien amusée en France.* (She had a good time in France.)
- **s'appeler** *Il s'appelle Paul.* (His name is Paul.)
- **s'approcher** *Approchez-vous.* (Get closer.)
- **se brosser, se peigner, se laver** When these verbs are used with parts of the body (*les cheveux, les dents, les mains*, all covered in Hour 21, "Communicating in the Real World"), use the definite article instead

of the possessive adjectives (*mon, ton, son,* and so forth); for example, *Elle se brosse les cheveux.* (She brushes her hair.)

- *s'ennuyer*   *Je m'ennuie.* (I'm bored.)
- *s'évanouir*   *Pierre s'est évanoui.* (Peter fainted.)
- *s'excuser*   *Excusez-moi.* (Excuse me.)
- *s'habituer à*   *Je m'habitue, peu à peu, à la cuisine française.* (Little by little, I'm getting used to French cuisine.)
- *s'intéresser à*   *Ils s'intéressent aux sports.* (They are interested in sports.)
- *se méfier de*   *Je me méfie des chiens méchants.* (I watch out for mean dogs.)
- *se moquer de*   *Tu te moques de moi?* (Are you making fun of me?)
- *s'occuper de*   *On s'occupe de vous, Monsieur?* (Is someone helping you, sir?)
- *se passer*   *Qu'est-ce qui se passe?* (What's happening?)
- *se rappeler*   *Je ne me rappelle plus son nom.* (I don't remember his name.)
- *se servir de*   *Pour manger un sandwich en France, on se sert d'une fourchette.* (To eat a sandwich in France, one uses a fork.)
- *se tromper*   *Vous vous trompez!* (You're wrong.)

Note that the following verbs change their meaning when reflexive:

- *appeler quelqu'un* (to call someone)
- *s'appeler* (to be named)
- *demander quelque chose* (to ask for something)
- *se demander* (to wonder)
- *porter* (to carry; to wear [clothing])
- *se porter bien/mal* (to be well/sick)
- *trouver* (to find)
- *se trouver* (to be located)

LEARN VOCABULARY TO TALK ABOUT THE WORKPLACE

Now let's work on the new vocabulary for this hour: talking about the workplace. In the following tables you'll find words to describe your profession, the place where you work and the type of work you do.

Professions and Jobs

Professions and Jobs	Les professions et les emplois
accountant	*un comptable*
actor/actress	*un acteur/une actrice*
architect	*un/une architecte*
athlete	*un athlète, une athlète*
baker	*le boulanger, la boulangère*
banker	*le banquier*
barber/stylist	*le coiffeur, la coiffeuse*
bartender	*le barman*
businessman	*un homme d'affaires*
businesswoman	*une femme d'affaires*
butcher	*le boucher, la bouchère*
chef	*le chef*
civil servant	*le fonctionnaire, la fonctionnaire*
consultant	*le consultant*
customs officer	*le douanier*
dentist	*le dentiste*
director	*le directeur, la directrice*
doctor	*le médecin*
employer	*un employeur, une employeuse*
engineer	*un ingénieur*
farmer	*le fermier, la fermière*
fireman	*le pompier*
journalist	*le journaliste*
judge	*le juge*
lawyer	*un avocat, une avocate*
mailman	*le facteur*
mechanic	*le mécanicien, la mécanicienne*
pharmacist	*le pharmacien, la pharmacienne*
pilot	*le pilote*
policeman	*un agent de police*
politician	*un homme politique, une femme politique*
priest	*le prêtre*

Professions and Jobs	Les professions et les emplois
professor	*un professeur d'université*
reporter	*le journaliste*
salesman	*le vendeur, la vendeuse*
scientist	*le scientifique*
secretary	*le secrétaire, la secrétaire*
steward	*le steward*
stewardess	*l'hôtesse de l'air*
student	*un étudiant, une étudiante*
teacher	*un instituteur, une institutrice*
waiter	*le serveur (Monsieur)*
waitress	*la serveuse (Madame, Mademoiselle)*
writer	*un/une écrivain(e)*

Useful occupational phrases

To say …

- I work as a waiter.   *Je travaille comme serveur.*
- I work as a mecanic.   *Je travaille comme mécanicien.*

After the verb *être*, professions are used without an article, as in the following:

- I'm a doctor.   *Je suis médecin.*
- I'm a teacher.   *Je suis professeur.*
- I'm a student.   *Je suis étudiant(e).*

One works … (*on travaille …*)

- part-time   *à temps partiel*
- half-time   *à mi-temps*
- full-time   *à plein temps*
- freelance   *en freelance*

Or …

- I'm self-employed.   *Je suis à mon compte.*
- I'm unemployed.   *Je suis au chômage.*

Job-Related Vocabulary

Salary	Le salaire
fees (of artists, actors)	le cachet
fees (professional)	les honoraires (m.)
income tax	l'impôt sur le revenu (m.)
minimum wage	le Smic (salaire minimum interprofessionnel de croissance)
pay (of housekeepers, etc.)	les gages (m.)
raise	une augmentation de salaire
salary (worker's salary)	le salaire

Workplaces	Au travail
at home	à la maison
clinic	une clinique
college	une université
company	une entreprise, une maison
customer service	le service après-vente
factory	une usine
hotel	un hôtel
office	le bureau
retail business	la vente au détail
school	une école
wholesale business	la vente en gros

Types of Business	Les entreprises
agriculture	l'agriculture (f.)
clothing	la confection
commerce	le commerce
communications	la communication
design	le design
electrical engineering	le génie électrique
food industry	l'industrie alimentaire (f.)
industry	une industrie
information technology	l'informatique (f.)
medical industry	l'industrie médicale (f.)
publishing	l'édition (f.)
sales	la vente

Types of Business	Les entreprises
telecommunications	*les télécommunications* (f.)
tourism industry	*le tourisme*
transportation	*les transports* (m.)

Verbs	
to apply for a job	*poser sa candidature pour un emploi*
to attend a meeting	*aller à une réunion*
to be in a meeting	*être en réunion*
to earn	*gagner*
to fire (an employee)	*congédier (un employé)*
to have a (job) interview	*avoir un entretien*
to have a meeting	*avoir une réunion*
to hire (someone for a job)	*embaucher (quelqu'un)*
to lose one's job	*être démissionné(e)*
to manufacture, produce	*produire*
to mend, to repair	*réparer*
to pay, to pay for	*payer (je paie; nous payons)*
to retire	*prendre la retraite*
to search for a job	*postuler un emploi*
to sell	*vendre*
to travel for work	*aller en déplacement*

Let's end this hour by learning the final two pronouns in French: *y* and *en*.

USE THE PRONOUNS *Y* AND *EN*

At this point in your studies, you know the personal direct object (d.o.) and indirect object (i.o.) pronouns and you remember that they are used as the objects of a verb. To review, these pronouns are listed in the following table. The pronouns are placed in the table in the order they are used in a sentence; thus, *me, te* (singular familiar form), *nous, vous* (singular and plural formal form) precede *le, la, les*, which precede *lui, leur*.

GO TO ▶
Before continuing, review the object pronouns in Hour 14.

Personal Object Pronouns

Direct/Indirect	Direct	Indirect
me (me, to me)	*le* (him)	*lui* (to him, to her)
te (you, to you)	*la* (her)	*leur* (to them, m. and f.)
nous (us, to us)	*les* (them, m. and f.)	
vous (you, to you [singular and plural])		

You'll add two more indirect object pronouns to the preceding table. *Y*, meaning "there," replaces a noun referring to a thing and preceded by a preposition of place (*à*, *sur*, *dans*, *en*, and so forth).

- *Je vais à Paris demain.*

  J'y vais demain. (I'm arriving **there** tomorrow.)
- *J'ai acheté une très belle robe en France.*

  J'y ai acheté une très belle robe. (I bought a very pretty dress **there.**)
- *Il est déjà dans le train.*

  Il y est déjà. (He is already **there.**)

Y also is used idiomatically to mean "to get it" or "to understand," as in the following:

Vous y êtes? Oui, j'y suis. (Do you understand? Yes, I've got it.) (Literally: Are you there? Yes, I'm there.)

Y is also used in the expression *il y a* (there is, there are), as in the following:

- *Il y a 200 passagers dans l'avion.* (There are 200 passengers on the plane.)
- *Il y a une place libre dans le train.* (There is one free seat on the train.)

En, meaning "some," "of it," "of them," "from them," "from there," and "from here" replaces a noun referring to things (and sometimes people), preceded by the preposition *de*, as shown here:

- *Il est déjà sorti **du bureau.***

  Il en est déjà sorti. (He has already left from here.)
- *Avez-vous **de l'argent.** Oui, j'ai **de l'argent.***

  ***En** avez-vous? Oui, j'**en** ai.* (Do you have some? Yes, I have some.)

PROCEED WITH CAUTION

En should be avoided in referring to persons. Instead, use the preposition *de* + the disjunctive pronouns, as in *J'ai reçu une lettre de lui, d'elle, d'eux,* and so forth.

En also is used in the following instances:

1. With verbs that take the preposition *de* before a noun object, such as *se souvenir de* (to remember), *parler de* (to talk about), *se moquer de* (to make fun of), and so forth, as shown here:

   - *Tu te souviens **de ta jeunesse?** Oui, je me souviens **de ma jeunesse.***

   - *Tu t'en souviens? Oui, je m'en souviens.* (Do you remember it? Yes, I remember it.)

   - *Parlez-vous encore de vos problèmes? Oui, j'en parle encore.* (Are you still talking about your problems? Yes, I'm still talking **about them.**)

GO TO ▶
Review adverbs of quantity in the "How to Use Adverbs of Quantity" section in Hour 7, "Describe Your Surroundings."

2. With expressions of quantity and with numbers to mean "of them." When ending a French sentence with a number, you must use *en*, as shown here:

   - *Avez-vous beaucoup de problèmes? Oui, j'en ai beaucoup.* (Do you have a lot of problems? Yes, I have a lot [of them].)

   - *Combien de temps avez-vous? J'en ai beaucoup.* (How much time do you have? I have a lot [of it].)

   - *Combien de tickets as-tu? J'en ai trois.* (How many tickets do you have? I have three [of them].)

   Note that because both *y* and *en* are indirect object pronouns, the past participles of verbs conjugated with *avoir* do not agree with them, as shown here:

   - *J'en ai acheté trois.* (I bought three of them.)
   - *Ils en ont vu deux.* (They saw two of them.)
   - *Je suis allé en France.* (I went to France.)
   - *J'y suis allé.* (I went there [to France].)

3. In several common expressions:

   - *s'en aller* (to go away)
   - *en avoir assez* (to be fed up)
   - *en avoir marre* (to be fed up)

- *en avoir ras le bol* (to have it up to here)
- *en finir* (to get it over with)
- *en vouloir à* (to have a grudge against; be angry with someone)

As you complete this hour, review the agreement of past participles conjugated with *avoir* in Hour 8.

HOUR'S UP!

Merveilleux! Marvelous! With the completion of this hour, you know how to use reflexive verbs and all the object pronouns. You also have the vocabulary necessary to talk about your professional life. In the next hour, you'll be working on vocabulary and structures to use when you go shopping, but before going there, take a moment to review the material in this hour and test your mastery of it with the following quiz.

1. Which French sentence correctly translates the English phrase "I'm going to bed"?

   a. *Je lève le lit.*

   b. *Je me couche.*

   c. *Je lève.*

   d. *Je le lève.*

2. Which French sentence correctly translates the English phrase "They are talking to each other"?

   a. *Ils leur parlent.*

   b. *Il se parle.*

   c. *Ils se parlent.*

   d. *Ils parlent à eux.*

3. Which French infinitive correctly translates the English "to be wrong"?

   a. *se tromper*

   b. *se trouver mal*

   c. *se peigner*

   d. *avoir raison*

4. True or False: The past participle of reflexive verbs in compound tenses agrees with the subject.

5. True or False: The past participle of reflexive verbs in compound tenses agrees with a preceding direct object.

6. True or False: All reflexive verbs are conjugated with *être* in compound tenses.

7. Which French sentence correctly expresses the English phrase "Hurry up!"?

   a. *Dépêches!*

   b. *Tu te dépêches.*

   c. *Dépêche!*

   d. *Dépêche-toi!*

8. Which French sentence correctly expresses the English phrase "Don't worry!"?

   a. *Ne t'inquiète pas!*

   b. *Tu ne t'inquiètes pas!*

   c. *Inquiète-toi!*

   d. *Tu t'inquiètes!*

9. Which French sentence correctly expresses the English phrase "My name is Paul"?

   a. *J'appelle Paul.*

   b. *C'est Paul.*

   c. *Je m'appelle Paul.*

   d. *Son nom est Paul.*

10. Which French sentence correctly expresses the English phrase "I'm a doctor"?

    a. *Je suis un docteur.*

    b. *Je suis médecin.*

    c. *Je suis un médecin.*

    d. *J'ai un médecin.*

QUIZ

HOUR 19
Going Shopping

CHAPTER SUMMARY

LESSON PLAN:

In this hour you will learn ...

- How to use *pouvoir, devoir,* and *falloir.*
- How to use infinitives in new ways.
- How to use vocabulary to talk about going shopping.

In this hour you'll continue on the theme of stepping out by learning some facts about shopping in a French-speaking country and the vocabulary you'll need to make your purchases. You'll also learn more about three verbs you've already encountered: *pouvoir* (to be able to), *devoir* (to have to), and *falloir* (to be necessary). These three verbs change meaning depending on the tense in which they are conjugated. In most cases you will need to learn the various meanings of the verbs as vocabulary because there are no grammar rules to guide you.

LEARN TO SAY "CAN I?" AND "MAY I?"

French does not distinguish between the phrases "Can I?" and "May I?" Both are translated using the verb *pouvoir.* In addition to meaning "can" and "may," *pouvoir* has some special meanings depending on the tense in which it is conjugated. Following the conjugation below, you'll find examples of how the verb is used.

Let's review the conjugation of *pouvoir* (to be able, can) as shown in the following table.

Present Indicative and Present Subjunctive

Person	Present Indicative Singular	Plural	Present Subjunctive Singular	Plural
first	je peux	nous pouvons	que je puisse	que nous puissions
second	tu peux	vous pouvez	que tu puisses	que vous puissiez
third, masculine	il peut	ils peuvent	qu'il puisse	qu'ils puissent
third, feminine	elle peut	elles peuvent	qu'elle puisse	qu'elles puissent
third, generic	on peut		qu'on puisse	

The future stem for *pouvoir* is *pourr;* the past participle is *pu;* the present participle is *pouvant.*

When followed by an infinitive, *pouvoir* means "can," "may," "to be able to," or "could," depending on the tense used, as shown in the following.

Present tense: can, be able to

Je peux partir demain à midi. (I can [am able to] leave tomorrow at noon.)

Est-ce que je peux fumer? (May I smoke?)

FYI The English sense of "may" often is implicit in the French subjunctive, as in *Que Dieu vous bénisse.* (May God bless you.)

Future tense: will be able to

Je pourrai vous donner une réponse demain. (I will be able to give you an answer tomorrow.)

Present conditional: might

Il pourrait arriver demain soir. (He might arrive tomorrow evening.)

Past conditional: could have, might have

Ils auraient pu manquer le train. (They could have/might have missed the train.)

Passé composé: was able

Il n'a pas pu venir. (He was not able to come.)

If "can" means "have the right to," use the expression *avoir le droit de* (to have the right to):

> *Est-ce que je peux traverser la frontière sans passeport?* (Can I cross the border without a passport?)

> *Non, tu n'en as pas le droit.* (No, you can't [don't have the right to do that].)

(Note: Use *en* because the expression is *avoir le droit **de.***)

Pouvoir also is used in some fixed expressions:

> *Je n'y peux rien.* (I can't help it.)

> *Je n'en peux plus.* (I can't go on/continue.)

To translate "if I may/if I could," use *s'il vous plaît*, as in *Je voudrais vous parler, s'il vous plaît.* (I'd like to talk to you, if I may.)

LEARN TO SAY "MUST I?" AND "SHOULD I?"

"Must I?" and "Should I?" can both be translated by either *devoir* or *falloir*. However, since each verb also has other uses, they are not always interchangeable.

First let's look at *devoir*, a verb which changes meanings completely depending on the tense in which it is conjugated. Following the conjugation of the verb in the present tense, you'll find examples of how it is used in all the other tenses.

USE THE VERB *DEVOIR*

Person	Present Indicative Singular	Plural	Present Subjunctive Singular	Plural
first	je dois	nous devons	que je doive	que nous devions
second	tu dois	vous devez	que tu doives	que vous deviez
third, masculine	il doit	ils doivent	qu'il doive	qu'ils doivent
third, feminine	elle doit	elles doivent	qu'elle doive	qu'elles doivent
third, generic	on doit		qu'on doive	

The future stem of *devoir* is *devr*; the past participle is *dû*, *due* when feminine; the present participle is *devant*.

Used by itself, *devoir* means "to owe," as in the following:

- *Je vous dois 100 francs.* (I owe you 100 francs.)
- *Combien est-ce que je vous dois?* (How much do I owe you?)
- *Vous me devez 15 francs.* (You owe me 15 francs.)

When followed by an infinitive, *devoir* can indicate obligation (must, have to), intention (supposed to), or probability, depending on the tense used. You should use the following examples to guide you in the translations.

Present tense: must, have to, supposed to, probably is

Nous devons partir. (We have to/must leave.)

Nous devons partir demain. (We are supposed to leave tomorrow.)

Où est Jacques? Il doit être malade. (Where is Jack? He must be [and probably is] sick.)

Future tense: supposed to

Nous devrons partir demain. (We are to leave/are supposed to leave tomorrow.)

Passé composé: must have (and probably did)

Il a dû partir. (He must have left [and probably has].)

Present conditional: should/ought to

On ne devrait pas fumer. (One should not speak.)

Tu devrais boire beaucoup d'eau. (You should drink lots of water.)

GO TO ▶
Review the formation of the past conditional in Hour 17, "Eating Out."

Past conditional: should have, ought to have

Tu aurais dû me téléphoner. (You should have/ought to have phoned me.)

USE THE VERB *FALLOIR*

Falloir is used only in the third-person singular and means "to have to"; "to be necessary."

Falloir:

- Present indicative   *il faut* (*que* + subjunctive)
- Present subjunctive   *qu'il faille* (*que* + subjunctive)
- Future   *il faudra* (*que* + subjunctive)
- *Passé composé*   *il a fallu* (*que* + subjunctive)
- Imperfect   *il fallait* (*que* + subjunctive)
- Present participle   none

In the affirmative of the present tense, *falloir* + the present subjunctive is synonymous with *devoir* and means "must" or "have to," as shown here:

- *Je dois partir.* (I must leave.)
- *Il faut que je parte.* (I must leave.)
- *Vous devez parler français.* (You must speak French.)
- *Il faut que vous parliez français.* (You must speak French.)

Falloir also can be used with an infinitive and an indirect object pronoun to make a general statement about need. The pronoun identifies the person or persons concerned, as shown in the following:

- *Il nous a fallu acheter nos billets avant de partir en vacances.* (We needed to buy our tickets before leaving on vacation.)
- *Il me faut une nouvelle robe.* (I need a new dress.)

In the negative, *falloir* means "must not," as shown here:

- *Il ne faut pas se pencher par la fenêtre.* (One must not lean out the window.)
- *Il ne faut pas fumer dans l'avion.* (One must not smoke on the airplane.)

Because each of the verbs presented in the preceding has special meanings in various tenses, it is best to use the examples as models and learn them as vocabulary.

LEARN MORE ABOUT INFINITIVES

Now let's talk a bit more about infinitives and how their uses differ in French and English. To this point, you've learned the following about infinitives in French:

- French infinitives are single words; for example, *penser* (to think). (See Hour 2, "Describing Things.")

- Infinitives of regular verbs are used as the stem for creating the future tense and the present conditional mood, as in *Je chanterai* (I will sing); *Je chanterais.* (I would sing.) (See Hour 8, "Learn to Express Yourself in the Future.")

- Infinitives can follow a conjugated verb. Sometimes the prepositions *à* or *de* are used before an infinitive; other times no preposition is used, as in *J'aime chanter; Je commence à chanter; Je finis de chanter.* (See Hour 13, "Master the Prepositions.")

GO TO ▶
Now is a good time to review the use of the prepositions before infinitives discussed in Hour 13.

- Infinitives are used as the object of all prepositions except *en*, as in *sans parler* (without speaking); *Pour réussir, il faut étudier.* (To succeed, one must study.) (See Hour 15, "Around the House.")

In addition to these uses, the infinitive can be used in other ways, as discussed in the following sections.

INFINITIVE USED AS A NOUN

Some infinitives can be made into nouns simply by adding an article. These nouns are always masculine:

le boire (drinking)	*le manger* (eating)
le coucher (going to bed)	*le rire* (laughter)
le devoir (duty)	*le savoir* (knowledge)
le lever (getting up)	*le toucher* (touch)
le savoir-faire (know-how)	

Some infinitives also can be used where English might use a gerund (verbal noun, ending in *-ing*) or an infinitive, as in the following:

- *Apprendre, c'est comprendre.*   (To learn is to understand.)
- *Nager en hiver, c'est dangereux.*   (Swimming in winter is dangerous.)

INFINITIVE TO REPLACE THE SUBJUNCTIVE

When the main verb and the subordinate verb of a sentence have the same subject, French replaces the subordinate verb with an infinitive, if possible. Compare these two sentences:

- *J'espère que tu m'écriras bientôt.* (I hope that you will write to me soon.)
- *J'espère t'écrire bientôt.* (I hope to write to you soon.)

Although English permits the construction "I hope that I will write to you soon," French does not. Because both clauses would have the same person as the subject, you must use the infinitive in the second example. This rule is particularly important in the use of the subjunctive mood. You recall from your study of the subjunctive that you must have two different subjects to use the subjunctive in French. If you have the same subject (person and number) in both clauses, use an infinitive to replace the subordinate verb.

GO TO ▶
Review the rules for the use of the subjunctive in Hour 6, "Express Yourself in the Present Subjunctive."

In each of the following pairs of sentences, the second sentence uses an infinitive to avoid repetition of the same subject:

*Je veux que **tu** viennes demain soir.*

But:

Je veux venir demain soir.

*Il ne pense pas que **je** puisse le faire.*

But:

Il ne pense pas pouvoir le faire.

*Je lui écrirai pour qu'**il** sache ma réponse.*

But:

Je lui écrirai pour savoir sa réponse.

*Le **prof** explique le subjonctif afin que **nous** le comprenions.*

But:

J'étudie le subjonctif afin de le comprendre.

*Le **prof** est parti avant que **Suzanne** ait appris les résultats de l'examen.*

But:

Suzanne est partie avant d'apprendre les résultats de l'examen.

*Il a volé mon argent sans que **je** m'en sois aperçu.*

But:

J'ai perdu mon argent sans le savoir.

Here are some common conjunctions that require the subjunctive and the prepositions that replace them when you have a single subject:

Conjonction	Préposition
pour que (provided that)	*pour* (for)
afin que (in order that)	*afin de* (in order to)
avant que (before)	*avant de* (before)
sans que (without)	*sans* (without)
à moins que (unless)	*à moins de* (unless)
de peur que (for fear that)	*de peur de* (for fear of)

FYI The following conjunctions have no prepositional equivalent; therefore, they are followed by the subjunctive even when the subject of the two clauses is the same: *bien que* (although), *quoique* (although), *pourvu que* (provided that). An example is *Je voudrais aller en France bien que je n'aie pas de quoi faire le voyage.* (I would like to go to France, although I don't have the means to make the trip.)

INFINITIVE USED AS A COMMAND

In directions and legal language, the infinitive can be used to replace the imperative. You will often see the infinitive used this way in cookbooks, directions for how to use appliances (called *le mode d'emploi*), and general directions for product use, such as those found on commercially packaged food labels.

Pour ouvrir, tirer ici. (To open, pull here.)

D'abord, faire bouillir de l'eau. (First, boil some water.)

PAST INFINITIVES

In addition to the present infinitive, French has a past infinitive form composed of the appropriate auxiliary verb and the past particle, as in the following:

avoir parlé (having spoken)

être tombé (having fallen)

The past infinitive is always used following the preposition *après* (after) to mean "after having done something," as shown here:

Après avoir étudié, je me suis couché. (After studying/having studied, I went to bed.)

Après être parti, il a pleuré. (After leaving/having left, he cried.)

Now it's time to work on some new vocabulary to discuss shopping in French.

LEARN VOCABULARY TO TALK ABOUT GOING SHOPPING

Shopping in France is a wonderful way to spend a day, a week, or a month! However, there are some things you should know before hitting the stores and markets. Many French stores, even some large department stores, close between noon and 2:00 P.M. (so employees can enjoy the long lunch hour), and then remain open until 7:00 P.M. or later.

The American model of mega-stores and malls where everything from food to hardware is sold under one roof has come to France. Although such mass marketing is threatening the existence of the more traditional French specialty shops in urban areas, you can still find many privately owned and operated butcher shops, bakeries, wine shops, and book shops—even in the larger cities.

Certain regions of France are known for their specialties: *la haute couture* (high fashion) from Paris, *la faïence fine, la porcelaine* (china and porcelain) from Limoges, *les Truffes* (truffles) from le Périgord region in the south, true *Champagne* from the Champagne region, wine from the Bordeaux and Rhone river valleys, and so forth. All these regions now have *un site web* where you can use *le e-commerce* to make purchases *sur Internet*, known as *les achats sur le net*.

When shopping in small stores or at the traditional Saturday open-air markets, follow a few rules of politeness to make the experience more enjoyable:

- Always greet the owner or salesperson as *Monsieur* or *Madame*, as in *Bonjour, Madame*. On leaving, offer a cheery *Au revoir et merci, Monsieur*—even if you didn't purchase anything.

- In the vegetable and fruit markets, don't handle the produce. Ask the vendor to show you the merchandise.

- Don't be offended if you're not given individual service. Generally, shop owners will prefer to let you peruse the store quietly, respecting your right to look at all the merchandise at your own speed.

- Ask for help by saying *Je cherche* …. (I'm looking for ….)
- You might be greeted with *On s'occupe de vous, Monsieur/Madame?* (Is someone helping you?) If you are "just looking," you can reply with *Merci, mais je ne fais que regarder.* (Thank you, but I'm just looking.)

Finally, don't forget to keep all your receipts. Upon leaving France, you might qualify for a reimbursement of the luxury taxes you've paid (*la TVA: taxe sur la valeur ajoutée*).

The following table lists some useful vocabulary to help you make your purchases.

Vocabulary for Shopping

Clothing	Les vêtements
belt	*une ceinture*
blouse	*un chemisier*
coat	*un manteau*
dress	*une robe*
gloves	*les gants*
hat	*un chapeau*
jacket	*une veste*
jeans	*un blue-jean*
man's suit	*un costume*
pajamas	*un pyjama* (singular in French)
pants	*un pantalon* (singular in French)
pantyhose	*un collant*
raincoat	*un imperméable*
shirt	*une chemise*
shoes	*les chaussures* (f.)
shorts	*un short* (singular in French)
skirt	*une jupe*
slippers	*les pantoufles* (m.)
socks	*les chaussettes* (f.)
sweater	*un pull*
swimsuit	*un maillot*
tennis shoes	*les tennis* (m.)
tie	*une cravate*
T-shirt	*un tee-shirt*

Clothing	Les vêtements
underwear	les sous-vêtements (m.)
vest	un gilet
wallet	un portefeuille

Shops/Stores	Les magasins
bakery	la boulangerie
beautician	chez l'esthéticienne (f.)
butcher shop	la boucherie
department store	un grand magasin
fish shop	la poissonnerie
flea market	le marché aux puces
flower shop	le fleuriste
grocery store	une épicerie
hairdresser shop	chez le coiffeur
hardware store	une quincaillerie
market (open-air)	le marché
newspaper stand	un kiosque (à journaux)
pastry shop	la pâtisserie
pet shop	une boutique où on vend des animaux familiers
shoe shop	un magasin de chaussures
stationery shop	la papeterie
sweet shop/candy shop	la confiserie
tobacco shop	le tabac

In the Department Store	Au grand magasin
basement	le sous-sol
casual wear	les vêtements de sport (m.)
children's wear	les vêtements pour enfants (m.)
china/glassware	la vaisselle
computers	les ordinateurs (m.)
counter, checkout	la caisse
customer service	le service après-vente
department	le rayon
electrical appliances	les appareils électriques (m.)
elevator	l'ascenseur (m.)
entrance	l'entrée (f.)
escalator	l'escalator (m.)

continues

Vocabulary for Shopping   (continued)

In the Department Store	Au grand magasin
evening wear	*la tenue de soirée*
exit	*la sortie*
furniture	*les meubles* (m.)
gift	*un cadeau*
home furnishings	*la décoration d'intérieur*
kitchenware	*les ustensiles de cuisine* (m.), *la vaisselle*
leather goods	*la maroquinerie*
linens	*le linge de maison*
men's wear	*les vêtements pour hommes* (m.)
offices	*les bureaux* (m.)
package	*un colis*
perfumes	*la parfumerie*
photography	*la photographie*
restrooms	*les toilettes* (f.)
salesperson	*un vendeur, une vendeuse*
shelf	*un rayon*
shopping bag	*un sac*
stairs	*l'escalier* (m.)
suits	*les costumes* (m.)
toys	*les jouets* (m.)
underwear	*la lingerie*
women's wear	*les vêtements pour femmes* (m.)
Purchases	Les achats *(m.)*
ballpoint pen	*un stylo*
brush	*une brosse*
camera	*un appareil photo*
card	*une carte*
cologne	*l'eau de toilette* (f.)
comb	*un peigne*
dictionary	*un dictionnaire*
film	*une pellicule*
guidebook	*un guide*
jewelry	*la bijouterie*
make-up	*le maquillage*
map (city)	*un plan de ville*
map (country)	*une carte*

Purchases	Les achats (m.)
movie camera	une caméra
necklace	un collier
paper	le papier
pencil	un crayon
price	le prix
video camera	une caméscope
watch	une montre

Useful Phrases While Shopping

take-out	à emporter
How much is this?	C'est combien?
That's too much.	C'est trop (cher).
cheap	bon marché
expensive	cher/chère
That's a good price.	C'est un prix intéressant.
damaged	abîmé(e)
something cheaper	quelque chose de moins cher
something more expensive	quelque chose de plus cher
something smaller	quelque chose de plus petit
something larger	quelque chose de plus grand
something in (preferred) color	quelque chose en rouge, en vert, etc.
Where is that from?	Ça vient d'où?
Is this made in France?	C'est fabriqué en France?
What's it made of?	C'est fait en quoi?
Can I try it?	Je peux essayer?
That fits/doesn't fit.	Ça va./Ça ne va pas.
That doesn't suit me.	Ça ne me va pas.
I'll take it.	Je le/la prends.
Where do I pay?	Je paie où?
Do you take checks?	Prenez-vous les chèques?
Do you take credit cards?	Prenez-vous les cartes de crédit?
I'll pay in cash.	Je paie en espèce/en cash.
label (of the designer)	la marque (Lacoste, Cartier, etc.)
tag (in shirt, pants)	une étiquette
I don't have change.	Je n'ai pas de monnaie.
on sale	en solde
reduced price	réduction de prix

QUIZ

HOUR'S UP!

Vous devez être fier! You should be proud of yourself! In this hour you've mastered some difficult concepts using the verbs *pouvoir*, *devoir*, and *falloir* as well as learned how to shop for almost anything in French. As you've done in earlier hours, take a few moments to review the new structures and then confirm that you understand them by taking the following quiz. Then you must move on to the next hour! *Il faut continuer!*

1. Which sentence correctly translates the English "I will be able to leave tomorrow"?

   a. *Je peux partir demain.*

   b. *Je pourrai partir demain.*

   c. *J'aurais pu partir demain.*

   d. *Je pouvais partir demain.*

2. Which sentence correctly translates the English "I was not able to come"?

   a. *Je n'ai pas pu venir.*

   b. *Je ne pourrai pas venir.*

   c. *Je ne peux pas venir.*

   d. *Je ne viens pas.*

3. Which sentence correctly translates the English "I owe you 100 FF"?

   a. *J'ai dû vous donner 100 FF.*

   b. *Je vous donne 100 FF.*

   c. *Je vous devais 100 FF.*

   d. *Je vous dois 100 FF.*

4. Which sentence correctly translates the English "We are supposed to leave on Monday"?

   a. *Nous sommes partis lundi.*

   b. *Nous avons dû partir lundi.*

   c. *Nous devrons partir lundi.*

   d. *Nous partons lundi.*

5. Which sentence correctly translates the English "One should not smoke"?

    a. *On ne devrait pas fumer.*

    b. *Ne fumez pas!*

    c. *On ne fume pas.*

    d. *On ne peut pas fumer.*

6. *Falloir* often is synonymous with …

    a. *pouvoir*

    b. *savoir*

    c. *devoir*

    d. *vouloir*

7. Which sentence does not correctly use the verb *falloir?*

    a. *Il faut partir.*

    b. *Il nous faut partir.*

    c. *Il faut qu'on parte.*

    d. *Il faut que nous partons.*

8. Which sentence correctly translates the English "I hope that I see you tomorrow"?

    a. *J'espère que tu me verras demain.*

    b. *J'espère te voir demain.*

    c. *J'espère que je te verras demain.*

    d. *J'espère le voir demain.*

9. Which of the following conjunctions is not followed by the subjunctive?

    a. *parce que*

    b. *pour que*

    c. *sans que*

    d. *avant que*

10. Which sentence correctly translates the English "after having studied"?

    a. *après étudier*

    b. *après étudié*

    c. *après avoir étudié*

    d. *après que d'étudié*

QUIZ

HOUR 20

Campus Life

CHAPTER SUMMARY

LESSON PLAN:
In this hour you will learn …

- How to use idiomatic expressions.
- How to use common sayings and proverbs.
- How to use vocabulary to talk about campus life.

In this hour you'll learn some phrases and vocabulary to talk about life on campus. You also will learn a number of idiomatic expressions and some proverbs you can use to add some color and authenticity to your conversations.

Idiomatic expressions are often problematic because you simply must memorize their meanings and when it is appropriate to use them. So, it's best to think of these expressions as vocabulary items to be added to you notebook.

MASTER IDIOMATIC EXPRESSIONS

Idiomatic expressions are phrases or constructions that do not follow the particular usage or grammar of a language or that have a meaning other than the literal. For example, the phrases "there is/there are" are idiomatic expressions in English, used to point out or indicate the presence of something or someone, as in "There's the book"; "There are three people in the room."

You've already learned some idiomatic expressions in French:

- *Il est* for telling time, as in *Il est trois heures*.
- *Voici/voilà* meaning "here is/here are," as in *Voici ma voiture!* (Here's my car!) This expression must be accompanied by a gesture pointing out the person or object to which you are referring.
- *Il y a*, meaning "there is/there are," as in *Il y a deux élèves présents*. In contrast with *voici/ voilà*, *il y a* simply indicates that something exists but you are pointing out a specific thing or person; for example, *Il y a deux voitures dans la rue*. (There are two cars in the street.)

- *Il fait*, meaning "it is," for weather, as in *Il fait froid*. (It is cold.)
- *S'en aller*, meaning "to go away, to leave" as in *Je m'en vais maintenant*. (I'm leaving now.)

On the following pages you'll find a number of idiomatic expressions presented and explained. You cannot translate them literally, so you will have to learn them as vocabulary.

ÊTRE

Idiomatic use of *c'est/il est*

In formal or literary French, *c'est* and *il est* can replace *il y a*, as in the following:

Il est des moments difficiles dans la vie. (There are difficult moments in life.)

Idiomatic use of *il est*

Il est can be used idiomatically in the following ways:

- To express time:

  Quelle heure est-il? Il est trois heures. (What time is it? It is three o'clock.)

- To express an impersonal "it" [*il est* + adjective]:

  Il est bon de se coucher tôt. (It's good to go to bed early.)

- To describe the state of a thing (*il est* + adjective):

  Le café est chaud. Il est chaud. (The coffee is hot. It's hot.)

  Le coca est froid. Il est froid. (The cola is cold. It's cold.)

PROCEED WITH CAUTION

The verb *être* should not be used with *froid* or *chaud* (hot, cold) to describe a person. Doing so has strong sexual overtones.

AVOIR

Idiomatic use of *avoir* + noun

When referring to persons, English uses the verb "to be" and an adjective to describe feelings of hunger, thirst, and so forth: "I am hungry, I am thirsty."

French uses the verb *avoir* plus an adjective as follows:

- *Avoir faim* (to be hungry)
- *Avoir chaud* (to be hot)
- *Avoir froid* (to be cold)
- *Avoir peur* (to be afraid)
- *Avoir soif* (to be hungry)
- *J'ai froid et j'ai faim.* (I'm hungry and cold.)

The verb *avoir* is also used in the following common expressions:

- *Avoir besoin de* and *avoir envie de*: both express a need or desire; for example, *J'ai besoin d'un stylo et du papier.* (I need a pen and some paper.) *J'ai envie de partir.* (I want to leave.)
- *Il n'y a pas de quoi.* (Don't mention it. You're welcome.)
- *Avoir quelqu'un.* (To trick someone, to "get" someone); for example: *Il m'a eu!* (He got me!)

FAIRE

Idiomatic use of *il fait* + adjective or noun

To expresse weather, use *il fait* plus an adjective or a noun depending on the idiom:

- *Il fait beau.* (It's nice outside.)
- *Il fait chaud.* (It's hot.)
- *Il fait du brouillard.* (It's foggy.)
- *Il fait du soleil.* (It's sunny.)
- *Il fait du vent.* (It's windy.)
- *Il fait frais.* (It's cool.)
- *Il fait froid.* (It's cold.)
- *Il fait humide.* (It's humid.)

Idiomatic use of *il fait* + jour/nuit

To express daylight or nighttime:

- *Il fait jour.* (It's daylight.)
- *Il fait nuit.* (It's nighttime.)
- *Il fait sombre.* (It's dark outside.)
- *Il fait clair.* (It's light outside.)

Idiomatic use of *il* + impersonal verb

In addition to using the expression *il fait* + noun to describe the weather, you can use the impersonal subject pronoun *il* and a verb, as follows:

- *Il neige.* (It's snowing.)
- *Il pleut.* (It's raining.)
- *Il grêle.* (It's hailing.)
- *Il gèle.* (It's freezing.)

Note: *Il pleut des cordes.* (It's raining cats and dogs.)

VALOIR

Idiomatic use of *valoir mieux* + infinitive

This expression means "to be better to," as illustrated by these examples:

- *Il vaut mieux se taire.* (It's better to be quiet.)
- *Il vaudrait mieux partir demain.* (It would be better to leave tomorrow.)

SE PASSER AND ARRIVER

Idiomatic use of *il se passe* + noun and *il arrive* + noun

Both of these expressions mean "to happen" or "to occur":

- *Qu'est-ce qui se passe?* (What is happening?)
- *Il se passe des choses étranges.* (Strange things are happening.)
- *Il est arrivé un accident.* (An accident happened.)
- *Qu'est-ce qui est arrivé?* (What happened?)

PROCEED WITH CAUTION

Although both *se passer* and *arriver* can mean "to happen," they are not interchangeable. Use the examples as guides.

MORE IDIOMATIC EXPRESSIONS WITH ÊTRE

The following is a list of some very common sayings and proverbs that you can use to add color to your conversations. You will see that the French expression rarely parallels the English equivalent. For example, where we say

"Don't count your chickens before they hatch," the French say, "Don't sell the bear skin until you've killed the bear!" You've been forewarned! Never try to translate a proverb or idiom word for word.

- *Être tiré à quatre épingles* (spic and span)
- *Être (se mettre) sur son trente et un* (to be in [to put on] ones Sunday best)
- *Être dans le vent; être à la page* (to be up-to-date)
- *N'être pas né d'hier* (not to be born yesterday)
- *Être en jeu* (to be at stake)
- *C'est en forgeant qu'on devient forgeron.* (One learns by doing.)
- *Vous êtes bon comme du pain.* (You're as good as gold.)
- *Le remède est pire que le mal.* (The cure is worst than the cold.)
- *Tout est bien qui finit bien.* (All's well that ends well.)
- *Ce n'est que du vent.* (That's just hot air.)
- *La pilule est dure à avaler.* (That's a bitter pill to swallow.)
- *Ce fut le coup de foudre.* (That was love at first sight.)

STRICTLY DEFINED

Fut is the literary past (*le passé simple*) of *être*. (See Hour 24, "Understanding Formal Writing in French.")

- *Il n'en est pas question.* (It is out of the question/no way.)
- *Les affaires sont les affaires.* (Business is business.)
- *C'est à prendre ou à laisser.* (Take it or leave it.)

IDIOMATIC EXPRESSIONS WITH *AVOIR*

The following expressions using *avoir* are commonly used in conversation among friends, but they are too familiar to be used in formal writing or with persons you don't know well.

- *En avoir ras le bol* (to be fed up; to have it up to here)
- *Avoir vent de quelque chose* (to get wind of something)
- *Avoir quelque chose sur le bout de la langue* (to have something on the tip of one's tongue)
- *Avoir une dent contre* (someone) (to hold a grudge against [someone])

IDIOMATIC EXPRESSIONS WITH *FAIRE*

GO TO ▶

Both *avoir* and *faire* are used in a number of expressions referring to one's health (see Hour 22, "In Case of Emergency").

These expressions with *faire* are appropriate for use in any situation, casual or formal, where they make sense.

- *Tout bien réfléchi; réflexion faite* (on second thought)
- *Faire les cent pas* (to pace back and forth)
- *Faire la grasse matinée* (to sleep late)
- *Ce qui est fait est fait.* (What's done is done.)
- *C'est bien fait pour lui.* (That serves him right.)
- *Qui s'absente, se fait oublier* (long absent, soon forgotten)
- *On se couche comme on fait son lit.* (You make your bed, you lie in it.)
- *L'habit ne fait pas le moine.* (Clothes don't make the man.)
- *Les bons comptes font les bons amis.* (Good accounts make good friends.)

LEARN COMMON SAYINGS AND PROVERBS

The following list offers several common sayings, proverbs, and idiomatic expressions. Learning to use some of these expressions will add color and authenticity to your language. Notice that rarely are these expressions translated literally from one language to the other.

- *Après la pluie le beau temps.* (The calm after the storm.)
- *Beaucoup de bruit pour rien.* (Much ado about nothing.)
- *Ce qu'on ne peut curer, il faut l'endurer.* (What you can't change, you must endure.)
- *Cela donne à réfléchir.* (That's food for thought.)
- *Cela me dit quelque chose.* (That rings a bell.)
- *Cela s'arrose.* (Let's celebrate. Let's party.)
- *Cela se voit comme le nez au milieu de la figure.* (It's as plain as the nose on your face.)
- *Contre vents et marées* (through thick and thin)
- *Couper la poire en deux* (to meet halfway)
- *Couper les cheveux en quatre* (to split hairs)
- *Coûte que coûte* (at all costs/no matter what)
- *De gré ou de force* (whether you like it or not)

- *Envers et contre tout* (through hell or high water)
- *Joindre l'utile à l'agréable* (to combine business with pleasure)
- *Joindre les deux bouts* (to make ends meet)
- *Jouer franc jeu* (to play fair and square)
- *La fin justifie les moyens.* (The end justifies the means.)
- *Le chat parti, les souris dansent.* (When the cat's away, the mice will play.)
- *Les garçons seront toujours des garçons.* (Boys will be boys.)
- *Les murs ont des oreilles.* (The walls have ears.)
- *Les oiseaux du même plumage, s'assemblent sur le même rivage* or *Qui se ressemble, s'assemble.* (Birds of a feather flock together.)
- *Mettre les points sur les i* (to dot the i's)
- *Mieux vaut peu que rien* (better something than nothing)
- *Mieux vaut tard que jamais* (better late than never)
- *Moins nous serons, plus nous mangerons* (the fewer, the better)
- *Monter sur ses grands chevaux* (to get on ones high horse)
- *Ne pas arriver à la cheville* (not to hold a candle to)
- *Ne pas sourciller* (not bat an eye)
- *Oeil pour oeil, dent pour dent.* (An eye for an eye; a tooth for a tooth.)
- *Pas de nouvelles, bonnes nouvelles.* (No news is good news.)
- *Pierre qui roule n'amasse pas mousse.* (A rolling stone gathers no moss.)
- *Premier venu, premier servi.* (First come, first served.)
- *Prêter l'oreille à* (to lend one's ear to)
- *Qui trop embrasse, mal étreint.* (Take all, lose all.)
- *Qui veut, peut.* (If you want to, you can.)
- *Rira bien qui rira le dernier.* (She or he who laughs last laughs best.)
- *Se fâcher tout rouge* (mad as a hornet)
- *Se porter à merveille* (to feel as fit as a fiddle)
- *Se porter comme un charme* (to feel fine as wine)
- *Se répandre comme une traînée de poudre* (to spread like wildfire)
- *Tomber dans les pommes* (to pass out; to faint)
- *Un oiseau dans la main en vaut deux dans le bois.* (A bird in hand is worth two in the bush.)
- *Voir d'où vient le vent* (to see which way the wind is blowing)

- *Voir la vie en rose* (to see life through rose-colored glasses)
- *Voir rouge* (to see red, to be angry)
- *Tel père, tel fils.* (Like father, like son.)

LEARN VOCABULARY TO TALK ABOUT CAMPUS LIFE

The French educational system differs significantly from that of the United States. French children start school at *l'école maternelle* (nursery school), continue through *l'école primaire* (elementary school) and *le collège* (middle school), and finish at *le lycée* (high school) by *passer* (taking) a national examination called *le baccalauréat* (*le bac*). *Le bac*, divided into sections by subject matter (technical, mathematics, language, literature, and so forth), is taken in late June, and its scores determine whether students may continue their studies at the university or enter a *grande école* (professional graduate school).

By the time students take the *bac*, they have chosen their fields of specialty (*une spécialisation*) and, if they enter the university system, they begin specialized studies immediately. It takes two to four years to receive a diploma (*recevoir un diplôme*); then they can continue on to the Master's (*la maîtrise*) or doctoral (*le doctorat*) level.

The *grandes écoles* are specialized schools that students usually enter after a year of study (at a private *école préparatoire*) to prepare for entrance examinations (*les concours*). Only the elite enter these schools. Some of the best known are *l'École Polytechnique* (which specializes in engineering) and *la Haute École de Commerce de Paris* (H.E.C., pronounced *ahsh-ay-say*).

Students not pursuing a university diploma can enter technical schools to prepare for a career in the trades. Students pursuing degrees in medicine or law can enter *une école de médecine* (medical school) or *une école de droit* (law school).

The educational system is managed from the capital by a Minister of Education. Faculty are employed by the state. To teach below the university level, normally one must hold *une licence* (an advanced degree in education) and *le C.A.P.E.S* (pronounced *ka-pez*), for *le Certificat d'Aptitude pédagogique à l'Enseignement secondaire* (Certification of Teaching Ability at the Secondary Level). The doctorate typically is required for teachers at the university level.

Although school hours might vary among regions, the curriculum normally is set at the national level. Students have a half day off during the week (either Wednesday or Thursday) and then attend classes a half day on Saturdays.

Vocabulary to Talk About Campus Life

Around Campus	À l'université	Around Campus	À l'université
answer	une réponse	schedule	un horaire
appointment	un rendez-vous	stadium	le stade
campus	le campus	student (high school/university)	un étudiant, une étudiante
classroom	la salle de classe	student (lower grades)	un élève, une élève
computer	un ordinateur	syllabus	le plan du cours
correct, right	correct, juste	teacher	un instituteur, une institutrice
course	un cours	term paper	une dissertation
course of study	le cursus	test (oral/written)	un examen (oral/écrit) ; un test
dictation	une dictée	textbook	un texte
dictionary	un dictionnaire ; un dico	transcript	une relevé de notes
dissertation/thesis	une thèse	vacation (summer vacation)	les vacances (les grandes vacances) (f.)
e-mail	un message électronique ; le mel	dean	le doyen
examination	un examen	department (French, English, etc.)	la section (française, anglaise, etc.)
faculty	le professorat	department head	le cheffle directeur de …
grade	une note	lesson	la leçon
incorrect, wrong	incorrect	homework	les devoirs (m.)
meeting	un meeting ; une réunion	spelling	l'orthographe (f.)
notebook	un cahier	reading	une lecture
office hours	les heures (f.) de permanence	exercise	un exercice
paper	le papier	report	un rapport
pen	un stylo	term	le trimestre
pencil	un crayon	school year	l'année scolaire (f.)

continues

Vocabulary to Talk About Campus Life (continued)

Around Campus	À l'université	Around Campus	À l'université
professor	un professeur (m./f.)	beginning of school year	la rentrée
question	une question		
Places on Campus	*À l'université*	*Places on Campus*	*À l'université*
administrative offices	la direction, la présidence	residence hall	la résidence universitaire; la cité universitaire
auditorium	un amphithéâtre	snack bar	la cafétéria
bookstore	la librairie	stadium	le stade
coffee house/coffee shop/café	le café	swimming pool	la piscine
gymnasium	le gymnase	student cafeteria	le restaurant universitaire; le Resto-U
laboratory	le laboratoire	student center	le centre d'étudiants
library	la bibliothèque		
Educational Institutions	*Les institutions*	*Educational Institutions*	*Les institutions*
grade school	l'école primaire (f.)	nursery school	l'école maternelle (f.)
high school	le lycée	professional school	une grande école
institute (private)	un institut	school (of)	l'école (de, d') (f.)
middle school/junior high school	le collège	university	une université
Courses of University Study	*Les matières à l'université*	*Courses of University Study*	*Les matières à l'université*
major/minor	la première option; la deuxième option	biology	la biologie
accounting	la comptabilité	business	le business; les affaires
agriculture	l'agriculture (f.)	calculus	le calcul
		chemistry	la chimie

continues

Courses of University Study	Les matières à l'université	Courses of University Study	Les matières à l'université
algebra	l'algèbre (f.)	Chinese	le chinois
astronomy	l'astronomie (f.)	economics	l'économie (f.)
Bachelor of arts	être licencié(e)ès lettres	engineering	l'ingénierie
Bachelor of science	être licencié(e)ès sciences	engineering, civil	le génie civil
engineering, electrical	l'électrotechnique (f.)	management	le management; la gestion
engineering, mechanical	la mécanique	marketing	le marketing
English	l'anglais (m.)	mathematics	les mathématiques
foreign languages	les langues étrangères (f.)	medicine	la médecine
French	le français	philosophy	la philosophie
geography	la géographie	physics	la physique
geology	la géologie	political science	les sciences politiques
geometry	la géométrie	Portuguese	le portugais
German	l'allemand (m.)	psychology	la psychologie
history	l'histoire (f.)	religion	la religion
information sciences	l'informatique (f.)	Russian	le russe
Italian	l'italien (m.)	science	les sciences
Japanese	le japonais	sociology	la sociologie
Latin	le latin	Spanish	l'espagnol (m.)
law	le droit		

Vocabulary to Talk About Campus Life (continued)

Verbs

to answer a question	*répondre à une question*
to ask a question	*poser une question*
to be right; to have the right answer	*avoir raison*
to be wrong; to have the wrong answer	*se tromper; avoir tort*
to correct	*corriger*
to dictate	*dicter*
to educate	*éduquer; instruire*
to fail	*rater (un examen)*
to graduate	*recevoir un diplôme*
to have a college degree	*être diplômé(e)*
to have a Master's degree	*avoir une licence*
to learn	*apprendre*
to pass a course	*réussir à un cours*
to take a course	*passer un cours*
to take a test	*passer un examen*
to take notes	*prendre des notes*
to teach	*enseigner*
to write	*écrire*

HOUR'S UP!

Encore du bon travail! Again, good work! This hour completes Part 5, and the theme of stepping out. You only have four more hours to complete your studies so now is a good time to flip back through earlier hours and quickly review any structures that you found particularly difficult. Now go have a cup of coffee and relax a bit before undertaking the final hours. Oh, but before you do that, take this quiz to confirm your mastery of the idiomatic expressions presented in this hour.

1. In the following sentence, *il y a* can be replaced by which idiom: *Il y a des moments difficiles dans la vie.*

   a. *Voici*

   b. *Il est*

   c. *Il a*

   d. *C'est*

2. Complete this sentence with the correct verb: *Le café _____ chaud.*
   (The coffee is hot.)

   a. *est*

   b. *fait*

   c. *a*

   d. *se met*

3. Complete the sentence with the correct verb: *Il _____ faim.* (He's
   hungry.)

   a. *est*

   b. *se met*

   c. *a*

   d. *fait*

4. A synonym for *je veux partir* is:

   a. *je peux partir*

   b. *j'ai besoin de partir*

   c. *j'ai envie de partir*

   d. *je vais partir*

5. Which idiom best translates the following sentence: "Don't mention
   it"?

   a. *C'est de trop.*

   b. *Ne le mentionnez pas.*

   c. *Pardon.*

   d. *Il n'y a pas de quoi.*

6. Which of the following expressions does not refer to weather?

   a. *Il fait beau.*

   b. *Il a chaud.*

   c. *Il pleut.*

   d. *Il neige.*

7. *Il vaut mieux* means:

   a. It is better …

   b. It's good.

   c. It's going well.

   d. He's worth it.

8. Which of the following idioms means "He's fed up"?

    a. *Il cherche la petite bête.*

    b. *Il fait les cent pas.*

    c. *Il en a ras le bol.*

    d. *Il a fini.*

9. Which of the following idioms means "I'm getting mad"?

    a. *Je me fâche!*

    b. *Je me porte à merveille.*

    c. *Je suis tombé dans les pommes.*

    d. *Je vois la vie en rose.*

10. Which of the following means "high school"?

    a. *la grande école*

    b. *le lycée*

    c. *le collège*

    d. *l'école maternelle*

PART VI
The Real World

HOUR 21

Communicating in the Real World

T his hour focuses on communication in the real world with particular emphasis on structures to simplify your language while still communicating what you want to say. French literature and conversation are steeped in two very long traditions. The first is the constant search for *le mot juste* (just the right word) to express one's feelings and thoughts precisely. The second is conciseness. Every Frenchman is familiar with the classic definition of French as *simple, clair, et logique* (simple, clear, and logical). In fact, most French do try to say as much as possible with as few words as possible.

Also during this hour you'll learn to use "filler words" to give yourself time to find *le mot juste* when you're in the middle of a conversation. Then finally, you'll learn some slang expressions, most of which can be used in polite company.

LEARN CONVERSATIONAL SHORTCUTS

You've learned some fairly difficult constructions that are commonly used in both formal and informal speech, such as the subjunctive and the relative pronouns. Now that you understand how these structures work, let's talk about several ways to avoid them in the early stages of your language learning.

By offering alternatives, of course, we're not suggesting that you shouldn't continue to work on mastering the subjunctive and the relative pronouns. To the contrary, you should review these essential structures regularly and continue to practice them daily, for their proper use is

LESSON PLAN:

In this hour you will learn ...

- How to simplify your language in conversations.
- How to find the right word to express yourself correctly.
- How to use filler words and interjections.
- How to talk about parts of the human body, parts of an automobile, and parts of a computer.
- How to use slang expressions appropriately.

critical to your mastery of the language. However, it's always helpful to have a few linguistic tricks ready in case of emergency.

That said (*cela dit*), let's look at a few ways to avoid the subjunctive and the relative pronouns in conversation.

LEARN HOW TO SIMPLIFY YOUR LANGUAGE

The subjunctive mood, as you know, often is used in both familiar and formal speech. For example, on the playground you might hear children of four or five say to their playmates, *Mais, que voulez-vous qu'on fasse maintenant?* (But what do you want us to do now?) You've also seen (in Hours 6, 12, and 16) that there are numerous common verbs, conjunctions, and impersonal expressions that are followed by the subjunctive.

However, in most cases these verbs and expressions require the subjunctive only when you have a subordinate clause introduced by *que* and two different subjects in the sentence. So, your first hint for avoiding the subjunctive is this: Don't use a subordinate clause. The following offers a few examples to illustrate this method.

AVOIDING *FALLOIR* + SUBJUNCTIVE

To avoid *falloir* + subjunctive, state what you must do or what must be done, then add *c'est nécessaire*, or use a personal pronoun, as shown here:

- To avoid *Il faut que nous partions demain.*

  Use *Demain, nous partons. C'est (absolument) nécessaire.*

- To avoid *Il faut que nous partions demain.*

  Use *Il nous faut partir demain.*

 FYI You will notice that in some cases, by not using the subjunctive, you will lose the subtlety contained within the mood itself. Nevertheless, in many cases, you can come close to expressing the same idea and still avoid the subjunctive.

AVOIDING *VOULOIR, SOUHAITER, DÉTESTER, AIMER* + SUBJUNCTIVE

To avoid having to use the subjunctive after these four verbs, you can recast your sentence in one of the following three ways. By avoiding the subjunctive you'll lose some of the subtlety of the language, but you will still communicate your point.

1. Use the imperative softened with *s'il te plaît* or *s'il vous plaît*, if necessary.

2. Ask a polite question.

3. Reform the statement using *mais* (but).

Here are a few examples:

- To avoid *Paul, je voudrais que tu* **viennes** *dîner chez moi demain soir.*

  Use the imperative *Paul,* **viens** *dîner chez moi demain soir, s'il te plaît.* Or, add *si tu veux* (if you'd like), as in *Paul, si tu* **veux, viens** *dîner chez moi demain soir.*

- To avoid *Paul, je voudrais que tu* **viennes** *dîner chez moi demain soir.*

  Use a polite question *Paul, tu* **veux /peux** *venir dîner chez moi demain soir, s'il te plaît?*

- To avoid *Je déteste que vous me parliez comme ça.*

  Use *quand: Quand vous me parlez comme ça, je le déteste!*

AVOIDING A CONJUNCTION + SUBJUNCTIVE

To avoid a conjunction + subjunctive, use a conjunction that does not require the subjunctive, as in the following:

GO TO ▶
Review the formation and use of the subjunctive in Hours 6, 12, and 16.

- To avoid *Elle veut apprendre le français* **bien qu'elle n'ait pas** *le temps d'étudier.*

- Use *mais: Elle veut apprendre le français,* **mais elle n'a pas** *le temps d'étudier.*

AVOIDING THE SUBJUNCTIVE AFTER EXPRESSIONS OF EMOTION

To avoid the subjunctive after expressions of emotion (*je suis content que, je suis triste que,* and so forth) or an impersonal expression using *être* + adjective (*il est bon que, il est possible que,* and so forth), use the conjunction *et* or form two separate sentences, as shown here:

- To avoid: *Je suis très content* **que tu apprennes** *le français!*

  Use *et: Tu* **apprends** *le français* **et je suis** *très content!*

  Or, form two sentences: *Tu apprends le français. J'en suis très content!*

- To avoid: *Il est bon que tu sois content à Paris!*

  Form two sentences: *Tu es content à Paris. C'est bon!*

OTHER CASES

Finally, in some cases you can use a preposition plus a noun, which expresses the meaning of the subordinate clause, as shown here:

- To avoid: *Je vous téléphonerai **avant que vous n'arriviez.***

  Use *avant* + noun: *Je vous téléphonerai **avant votre arrivée.***

- To avoid: *à l'aéroport, il lisait **en attendant que sa femme parte** pour la France.*

  Use a noun + preposition: *à l'aéroport, il lisait **en attendant le départ de** sa femme pour la France.*

- To avoid: *Je crains qu'elle ne se mette en colère.*

  Use a noun: *Je crains sa colère.*

LEARN TO USE THE RIGHT WORD

As you've progressed through your studies, you've probably noticed that there are many English words that are very close to the French equivalent. These words are called *cognates*. However, there are many English words that resemble French words—and vice versa—whose meanings are quite different.

 FYI English and French words that resemble one another but have different meanings often are referred to as *faux amis* (false friends).

Using the wrong word in the wrong tense can lead to embarrassing *gaffes* or *faux pas* (literally: false steps), so it is important to be careful with words that appear to be the same in both English and French. Always consult your dictionary when in doubt.

To help you avoid some of the most common false cognates, here is a list of words to watch out for. In the column to the right is the word actually used in French to express the meaning of the English false friend.

List of Common False Cognates

French	English Meaning	English/French Equivalents
un agenda	appointment book	agenda: *l'ordre du jour*
une allée	driveway, walkway	alleyway: *une ruelle*
une apologie	praise, defense	apology: *des excuses* (f.)
une audience	formal hearing	audience: *le public*

French	English Meaning	English/French Equivalents
la balance	scales for weighing	sum, balance: *le solde*
blesser	to hurt, to injure	to bless: *bénir*
une caution	bail	a caution: *un avis*
une cave	cellar	a cave: *une grotte*
le change	money exchange	loose change: *la monnaie*
un/une enfant	child	infant, baby: *un bébé*
une escalope	cutlet	scallops: *les coquilles Saint-Jacques*
fat	conceited	fat: *gros/grosse*
fixer	to fasten	to fix, repair: *réparer*
gentil	nice, kind	gentle: *doux/douce*
large	wide	large, big: *grand*
une lecture	a reading	lecture: *une conférence*
la location	rent	location: *le site*
un magasin	a store	magazine: *un magazine*
un mémoire	a report, a memo	a memory: *un souvenir*
une nurse	a nanny	medical nurse: *un infirmier, une infirmière*
la parole	the word	prison parole: *libéré conditionnellement*
une phrase	a sentence	phrase: *une locution*
la rente	a pension	rent: *le loyer*
un stage	an internship	theater stage: *la scène*
un store	shades on a window	store: *un magasin*
sympathique	friendly	sympathetic: *compatissant(e)*
trivial	vulgar	trivial: *sans importance*
une veste	a jacket	vest: *un gilet*

MASTER THE USE OF FILLER WORDS

The most common words used to fill in the gaps of silence in a conversation are called *interjections*. These expressions often change with the times, but those in the following list have remained current.

STRICTLY DEFINED

Interjections are words or representations of sounds used in all languages to communicate feelings of surprise, pain, scorn, and so forth.

List of Common Interjections

English	French	English	French
Again!	*Bis! Encore!*	Ouch!	*Aïe!*
Ah!	*Ah!*	Quit it! Stop!	*Ça suffit!*
Ahem!	*Hum!*	(That's) ridiculous!	*(C'est) ridicule!*
Alas!	*Hélas!*	Shoot! Darn it!	*Mince! Mince alors!*
Bang (gun)!	*Pan!*	Shhhh!	*Chut!*
Boo!	*Hou!*	Watch out!	*Attention!*
Bravo!	*Bravo!*	Well, well!	*Ça alors!*
Crack!	*Crac!*	What?	*Hein?*
Darn it!	*Zut! Tonnerre!*	Whew!	*Ouf!*
Easy now! Go easy there!	*Doucement!*	Who cares!?	*Bof!?*
Great!	*Impec!*	Yuk!	*Pouah!*
Knock knock!	*Toc toc!*		

Learn Parts of the Human Body

Following is a list of the parts of the body. Work on this vocabulary now; you will need it in the next hour when you learn about visiting the doctor and the dentist.

Parts of the Human Body	Les parties du corps humain	Parts of the Human Body	Les parties du corps humain
ankle	*la cheville*	eyelid	*la paupière*
arm	*le bras*	face	*le visage, la figure*
back	*le dos*	finger	*le doigt*
body	*le corps*	finger, index	*l'index* (m.)
bone	*un os*	finger, little	*l'auriculaire* (m.)
calf	*le mollet*	finger, ring	*l'annulaire* (m.)
cheeks	*les joues* (f.)	fingernail	*un ongle*
chest	*la poitrine*	fist	*le poing*
chin	*le menton*	foot	*le pied*
ear	*une oreille*	forehead	*le front*
elbow	*le coude*	hair	*les cheveux* (m.)
eye(s)	*un oeil, les yeux*	hand	*la main*
eyebrows	*les sourcils* (m.)	head	*la tête*
eyelashes	*les cils*	heel	*le talon*

Parts of the Human Body	Les parties du corps humain	Parts of the Human Body	Les parties du corps humain
hips	*les hanches* (f.)	skull	*le crâne*
joint	*une articulation*	sole	*la plante des pieds*
knee	*le genou*	spine	*la colonne vertébrale*
leg	*la jambe*	stomach (external)	*le ventre*
lips	*les lèvres* (f.)	thigh	*la cuisse*
mouth	*la bouche*	throat	*la gorge*
neck	*le cou*	thumb	*le pouce*
nose	*le nez*	toe	*un orteil*
ribs	*les côtes* (f.)	tongue	*la langue*
shoulder	*une épaule*	tooth	*une dent*
skeleton	*le squelette*	waist	*la taille*
skin	*la peau*	wrist	*le poignet*
Internal Organs	Les organes internes	*Internal Organs*	Les organes internes
artery	*une artère*	lungs	*les poumons* (m.)
blood	*le sang*	muscle	*le muscle*
blood vessel	*le vaisseau sanguin*	nerves	*les nerfs* (m.)
brain	*le cerveau*	prostate	*la prostate*
heart	*le coeur*	pulse	*le pouls*
intestines	*les intestins* (m.)	stomach	*l'estomac* (m.)
kidneys	*les reins* (m.)	tendon	*le tendon*
ligament	*le ligament*	vein	*une veine*
liver	*le foie*		
Verbs			
to bleed	*saigner*		
to breathe	*respirer*		
to exercise	*faire de l'exercise*		
to hurt (in some body part)	*avoir mal* (*à la tête*, etc.)		

STRICTLY DEFINED

Le visage and *la face* mean "face" and are used to identify the body part. *La face* is used in the set expression *faire face à* (to face). *La figure* and *le visage* refer to one's *contenance* or the appearance of one's face.

La gorge also translates as "bosom," or "bust of a woman." A "bra" is *un soutien-gorge*.

Le ventre refers to the external abdominal area, or ones midsection; *l'estomac* (stomach) refers to the internal organ.

LEARN PARTS OF A CAR

Because you might travel by car when in France, here is some useful vocabulary for getting around and to use in case you need repairs or road assistance:

Parts of an Automobile	La voiture/une automobile
body	la carrosserie
brakes	les freins (m.)
brakes ABS	le freinage ABS
breakdown	une panne (de voiture)
bumper	le pare-chocs
clutch	l'embrayage (m.)
convertible (car)	une décapotable
door	la portière
engine	le moteur
four-wheel drive	le quatre-quatre
gas tank	le réservoir
gear	la vitesse
hatchback	un coupé
headlights	les phares (m.)
hood	le capot

Roads and Signs	Les routes et la signalisation
a minor road	une chemin communal
cul-de-sac	une impasse
curve, bend	un virage
departmental road	une route départementale

Parts of an Automobile	La voiture/une automobile
horsepower	la puissance
license	le permis de conduire
radiator	le radiateur
signal lights	les clignotants (m.)
speed	la vitesse
sports car	une voiture de sport
steering	la direction
steering wheel	le volant
tire	un pneu
transmission, automatic	une voiture automatique
trunk	le coffre
window	la vitre
windsheild	le pare-brise
windshield wipers	les essuie-glaces (m.)

Roads and Signs	Les routes et la signalisation
detour	une déviation
Do not pass.	Ne pas dépasser.
highway	une autoroute
lane	la voie

Roads and Signs	Les routes et la signalisation	Roads and Signs	Les routes et la signalisation
map (road/city)	une carte (routière/un plan de ville)	shoulder of road	la bande d'arrêt d'urgence
national road	une route nationale	speed limit	la limite de vitesse
one-way street	un sens unique	traffic jam	un embouteillage, un bouchon
road work	les travaux (m.)	traffic lights	les feux (m.)
road sign	les panneaux (m.)	two-way traffic	une route à double sens
At the Service Station	*À la station-service*	*At the Service Station*	*À la station-service*
break fluid	le liquide de frein	repair	la réparation
diesel fuel	le gasoil	super gasoline	le super
gasoline	l'essence	tire, flat	un pneu crevé
light bulb	une ampoule	tire pressure	la pression des pneus
pump	la pompe	unleaded gasoline	le sans plomb
puncture	une crevaison, un pneu crevé		
Miscellaneous			
accident	un accident		
carwash (machine)	le lavojet		
pile-up	un carambolage		
Verbs			
to break down	tomber en panne; avoir une panne	to run over	écraser
to change a tire	changer le pneu	to skid	déraper
to change gears	changer de vitesse	to slow down	ralentir
to drive	conduire	to speed up	accélérer
to pass	dépasser	to swerve	faire un écart
to reverse	faire marche arrière		

FYI Note that the words used to refer to a car door and car window are *la portière* and *la vitre;* not *la porte* and *la fenêtre. Une panne* generally means "a breakdown" or "stoppage," as in *une panne d'électricité* (an electrical failure, a blackout).

LEARN PARTS OF A COMPUTER

Computers are increasingly common in French homes, although they have not reached the level of use found in U.S. homes. Nevertheless, most French youth have access to a computer either through school libraries or at one of the many *cypercafés* located in urban areas. Because you will learn about doing business in France in a later hour, now is a good time to master this common vocabulary of the computer.

Computer Vocabulary

Using the Computer	Se servir d'un ordinateur	Using the Computer	Se servir d'un ordinateur
bug	*une bogue*	keyboard	*le clavier*
CD	*le CD, le CD-rom*	margin	*la marge*
cursor	*le curseur*	memory	*la mémoire*
database	*une base de données*	modem	*le modem*
diskette	*une disquette*	mouse	*la souris*
drive	*un lecteur de disquette*	plug	*la fiche*
DVD	*le DVD*	print format	*le format d'impression*
electronic mail	*le courrier électronique, le mel*	printer	*une imprimante*
file	*un fichier*	program	*un programme*
floppy disk	*une disquette*	tape	*une cassette*
folder	*un dossier*	terminal	*un ordinateur*
font (Times, etc.)	*la police* (Times, etc.)	virus	*un virus*
hard disk	*le disque dur*	window	*une fenêtre*
icon	*un icône*	word processing	*le traitement de texte*
key	*une touche*		
Verbs			
to bold	*mettre en gros caractères*	to download	*télécharger*
to click	*cliquer*	to edit	*éditer*
to close (a file, etc.)	*fermer*	to enter	*entrer*
to copy	*copier*	to export	*exporter*
to cut (text, etc.)	*couper*	to format	*formater*

Verbs

to import	importer	to select (all)	(tout) sélectionner
to install	installer	to turn off	éteindre
to paste (text, etc.)	coller	to turn on	allumer
to quit	quitter	to type	taper
to save	sauvegarder	to underline	souligner
to search	rechercher		

LEARN ABOUT SLANG

To complete this hour, let's learn a few slang expressions you can use to sound a bit more native. Be careful with these phrases; they should be used only with people with whom you feel comfortable.

PROCEED WITH CAUTION

Slang often can be offensive as well as amusing, so you should not attempt its use until you're certain of the sensibilities of those to whom you are speaking.

Slang, by its very nature, changes with the winds of the current mode. I've tried to include here only those phrases that seem to have withstood those winds. In the following table, words marked with an asterisk (*) should be avoided in polite company. You will hear much slang used among the young and between students, but you should not imitate or adopt it without first checking its current meaning with a trustworthy native speaker!

Common Slang Nouns

English	French
the bed, sack	le pieu
bike	un vélo
book	un bouquin
boring	barbant(e), rasoir, rasant(e)
brother	un frangin
car	une bagnole
clod, twit	une patate, une andouille
clothes	les fringues (f.), les nippes (f.)
cool, neat	cool, génial
cop	un flic
Crap!	Merde!*

continues

Common Slang Nouns (continued)

English	French
crazy, nuts	*dingue, timbré(e)*
Damn!	*La barbe!*
disgusting	*dégueulasse**
doctor	*un toubib*
exhausting	*crevant(e)*
fellow, guy	*un type, un gars, un mec**
food	*la bouffe**
francs (FF)	*les balles (f.)*
funny	*rigolo, rigolote*
girl, chick	*une nana**
half-wit	*débile*
I dare you!	*Chiche!*
I don't give a damn!	*Je m'en fiche!**
junkie	*un toxico*
kid	*un/une gosse*
lazy	*flemmard(e)*
mess, foul-up	*la pagaille*
money	*le fric*
Mr. What's His Name	*Monsieur Machin*
Ms. What's Her Name	*Madame Machin*
narcotic	*un stup (un stupéfiant)*
nose	*le pif**
okay	*d'ac (d'accord)*
parents	*les vieux*
phone call	*un coup de fil*
rat, bastard	*une vache**
really, very	*vachement, rudement*
Shut up!	*Ferme-la!**
silly goose	*une bécasse*
sister	*une frangine*
smoke, cig	*une sèche, une clope*
snag, small problem	*un pépin*
son	*un fiston*
teacher	*un prof*
thing-a-ma-gig	*un truc, un machin, un engin*
ugly	*moche*

English	French
upper crust	*le gratin*
What a bore/drag!	*Quelle barbe!*
work	*le boulot*
workplace	*la boîte*
yes	*ouais*
you ... so and so	*espèce de ...*
Verbs	
to be broke	*être fauché(e)*
to be in a hurry to	*avoir hâte de*
to be lucky	*avoir du bol*
to complain	*rouspéter*
to laugh	*rigoler*
to rip off	*pincer, chiper, piquer*
to shove off, leave	*filer*
to understand	*piger*
to watch out for	*faire gaffe à*
to work	*bosser*
to work hard	*bûcher*

FYI Although French has many colorful words referring to sexual and bodily functions, in general these terms are not nearly as offensive as their English counterparts.

HOUR'S UP!

Chouette! Neat! You've successfully completed another hour and this one was particularly enjoyable because you learned a lot of familiar language and easy ways to avoid complex constructions. The following hours in Part 6, "The Real World," will take you further into real, everyday French. Now take a moment to review the expressions and vocabulary presented in this hour and confirm your mastery of them by taking the following quiz.

QUIZ

1. Which of the following methods will not help you avoid using the subjunctive?

   a. using an infinitive

   b. using *quand, et, mais*

   c. using *pour que*

   d. using a noun

2. What is the best way to avoid using the subjunctive and still keep the essential meaning of the following sentence: *Il faut qu'il fasse son travail.*

   a. *Il lui faut faire son travail.*

   b. *Il faut le faire.*

   c. *Il faut travailler.*

   d. *Il faut qu'il travaille.*

3. Which of the following is not a *faux ami?*

   a. *une balance*

   b. *un agenda*

   c. *blesser*

   d. *la face*

4. Which of the following is a *faux ami?*

   a. *pensif*

   b. *un store*

   c. *ridicule*

   d. *un pyjama*

5. At a concert, if you like the performance, you might shout:

   a. *Aïe!*

   b. *Pan!*

   c. *Bis!*

   d. *Pouah!*

6. At the cinema, which of the following would most likely not be something you would shout?

   a. *Zut!*

   b. *Hou!*

   c. *Impec!*

   d. *Chut!*

7. Which of the following is not part of the human head?

   a. *le menton*

   b. *le mollet*

   c. *l'oeil*

   d. *les cils*

8. Which of the following is not part of the human torso?

    a. *l'orteil*

    b. *la poitrine*

    c. *le ventre*

    d. *le dos*

9. Where would you most likely put your luggage when leaving on a trip?

    a. *dans le capot*

    b. *dans le coffre*

    c. *sur le volant*

    d. *dans le réservoir*

10. When you're really bored, you might say:

    a. *Quelle barbe!*

    b. *Quel boulot!*

    c. *Quelle bécasse!*

    d. *Chiche!*

QUIZ

In Case of Emergency

Chapter Summary

LESSON PLAN:

In this hour, you will learn ...

- How to master the passive voice.
- How to avoid the passive voice.
- How to use the causative *faire* construction.
- How to use vocabulary to talk about medical and dental care.

In the previous hour, you entered the real world of the French language, learning vocabulary used in everyday situations, some slang, and a number of interjections and filler words. This hour continues exploring the real world by introducing you to structures and vocabulary relative to medical and emergency situations.

In addition to learning the new vocabulary, you'll master two new structures: the passive voice and the causative *faire* constructions. In English we use the passive voice to say that something is being done to the subject by someone or something else; for example, "The ball is hit by the batter." The passive voice is expressed in French much the same way as it is expressed in English but with several very important differences, which we will examine shortly.

The causative *faire* construction, also called the *faire faire* construction, is simply a way to say that you are having something done or made (by someone else, usually) rather than doing it yourself, as in this example: "I had the secretary make copies of these pages."

Both of these constructions use structures you've already mastered—they are just combined in different ways. You should have no problem mastering them during this hour.

MASTER THE PASSIVE VOICE

First let's review what we mean by active and passive *voices*. When a verb is in the active voice, the subject performs the action of the verb on the direct object of the verb, as in this example: "John found the money."

Voice is a form of the verb showing the connection between the subject and the verb. French verbs have three voices: active, passive, and pronominal, all of which are discussed in this hour.

When a verb is in the passive voice, the subject receives the action of the verb and the person (or thing) that performs the action becomes the *agent* of the verb, as in this example: "The money was found by John." The agent usually is identifiable in English through the use of the preposition "by."

Agent refers to the person or thing that performs the action in a passive construction. In English the preposition "by" precedes the agent; in French, the preposition may be either *par* or *de,* both of which would be translated "by."

Notice that the passive voice in French uses the verb *être* + the past participle of the appropriate verb. Whereas English uses the preposition "by" to identify the agent, French most often uses *par*. Because the verb *être* is used to form the passive voice, the past participle agrees in number and gender with the subject. Following are some examples of the use of the passive voice. Note carefully that these sentences are not in the past tense, even though they use a past participle. They are all in the present tense, passive voice.

- *Le sandwich* **est mangé par** *l'enfant.* (The sandwich is eaten by the child.)
- *La souris* **est mangée par** *le chat.* (The mouse is eaten by the cat.) (Note the agreement.)
- *Ces livres* **sont écrits par** *une femme.* (These books are written by a woman.) (Note the agreement.)

LEARN TO USE THE PASSIVE VOICE

The passive voice can be constructed in the tense appropriate to the meaning of the speaker. Following are a few examples. Note that the past participle agrees with the subject:

- *La maison* **a été** *vendue hier.* (The house was sold yesterday.)
- *L'argent* **a été** *trouvé par Jean.* (The money was found by John.) (The verb is the *passé composé* of *être*.)

- *Cette pièce **aurait été** écrite par un Américain.* (This play might have been written by an American.) (The verb is the past conditional of *être.*)

- *Ces articles **seront** lus par tout le monde.* (These articles will be read by everyone.) (The verb is the future of *être.*)

PROCEED WITH CAUTION

Don't be misled by the use of *avoir* in these examples. Remember that *avoir* is the auxiliary verb used to form the compound tenses of *être;* therefore, the verb being used in these passive constructions is *être,* conjugated in its compound tenses.

Cover the answers that follow each of these sentences and try making these active constructions into passive constructions:

- *La station-service vend l'essence.*

  L'essence est vendue par la station-service. (The gasoline is sold by the service station.)

- *Paul a acheté un ordinateur.*

  L'ordinateur a été acheté par Paul. (The computer was bought by Paul.)

- *Michèle a perdu sa voiture.*

  La voiture a été perdue par Michèle. (The car was lost by Michelle.)

- *Les étudiants finiront leurs compositions demain.*

  Les compositions seront finies par les étudiants demain. (The compositions will be finished by the students tomorrow.)

PROCEED WITH CAUTION

Note that when you change from the active to the passive voice, some changes must be made to the pronouns and articles. Thus, *leurs* becomes *les* in this example.

Although the preposition *par* usually is used with the passive voice, there are some exceptions:

- ***aimé de***   *L'enfant est beaucoup aimé **de** son père.*
- ***suivi de***   *Ce chapitre est suivi d'une table de matières.*
- ***accompagné de***   *La présidente est accompagnée **de** son mari.*
- ***entouré de***   *Le prof est entouré **de** ses élèves.*
- ***couvert de***   *La terre est couverte **de** neige.*
- ***rempli de***   *La boîte est remplie **de** suggestions.*

GO TO ▶
Review transitive and intransitive verbs in Hour 5, "Express Yourself in the Present Indicative."

When constructing a sentence in the passive voice, you must be very careful to use only transitive verbs. Intransitive verbs—those conjugated with *être* in compound tenses—cannot be used in the passive voice because they would make no sense. Study the following examples:

Intransitive Verbs	Transitive Verbs
Il est parti …	*Il est dit que …*
Il est arrivé …	*Il est écrit que …*
Il est allé …	*Il est aimé de tous.*

The verbs on the left in the preceding are intransitive verbs. When used with *être* in the present tense, you don't have the passive voice, but rather the past tense, as in *Il est parti*. ("He left"; not "He is left.") Remember that if you want to say, for example, "The child is left (by his mother) with the neighbor," you must use the transitive verb *laisser*, as in *L'enfant est laissé (par sa mère) au voisin.*

The verbs on the right in the preceding are transitive verbs; thus, the structures you see are the passive voice, as in "It is said that …"; "It is written that …"; and "He is loved by all."

Quickly review this distinction by identifying each of the following as either a passive construction of a transitive verb or the past tense of an intransitive verb.

French	Voice/Tense	English
Il est sorti.	past tense	He left.
Il est aimé.	passive voice	He is loved.
Vos achats sont arrivés.	past tense	Your purchases arrived.
L'argent est perdu.	passive voice	The money is lost.
Son père est mort.	past tense	His father died.
La souris a été tuée.	passive voice	The mouse has been killed.

PROCEED WITH CAUTION

When the English passive voice has a direct object associated with it, the French translation must use the active voice; for example, "He was given a dog." In French it's *on lui a donné un chien.* You cannot say *Il a été donné un chien!*

LEARN WHEN TO AVOID THE PASSIVE VOICE

As in English, French has a couple of ways to avoid the passive construction. Study the following methods:

1. Make the agent the subject of the sentence and use an active verb form:

   - *Le prix a été demandé par tout le monde.*
     Tout le monde a demandé le prix.

   - *L'éclipse a été vue par tout le monde.*
     Tout le monde a vu l'éclipse.

2. Use a reflexive or pronominal verb:

   - *La Nouvelle-Orléans est trouvée en Louisiane.*
     La Nouvelle-Orléans se trouve en Louisiane.

   - *Il est appelé Jean.* (rare)
     Il s'appelle Jean.

DOING SOMETHING VS. HAVING SOMETHING DONE

When you want to express that you are having something done instead of actually doing it yourself, you can use the *faire* followed by another infinitive; for example, *faire laver la voiture* (to have the car washed); *faire peindre la maison* (to have the house painted). Notice that the order of the French construction differs from the English and, where English uses a past participle, French uses an infinitive. This construction is called the causative *faire*, or the *faire faire* construction.

The order of the causative *faire* construction is as follows:

conjugated verb + infinitive + direct object

Study the following examples to see how this structure is used:

- *Le professeur fera lire les élèves.* (The teacher will have the students read.)
- *Notre voisin a fait peindre la maison.* (Our neighbor had the house painted.)
- *Nous ferons écrire les élèves.* (We'll have the students write.)
- *Ils faisaient imprimer des cartes postales.* (They used to have postcards printed.)

When the person who performs the action is indicated, that person is the indirect object of the verb.

- *Nous avons fait étudier sa leçon à Pauline.* (We had Pauline study her lesson.)
- *Nous ferons ranger leurs affaires aux enfants.* (We'll have the children put their things in order.)

When using object pronouns with this construction, the pronouns are placed in front of the verb *faire*; however, note that the past participle of the verb *faire* in this construction is invariable; that is, it does not agree with a preceding direct object:

- *Il la lui a fait faire.* (He had him do it.)
- *Je les leur ai fait taper.* (I had them type them.)

LEARN VOCABULARY TO TALK ABOUT ILLNESSES AND EMERGENCIES

Now that you've mastered the passive voice and the causative *faire* construction, it's time to enter some new vocabulary into your notebook. On the following pages you'll learn a number of words useful for discussing emergency health situations, and doctor or dentist visits.

AT THE DOCTOR'S OFFICE AND THE HOSPITAL

In case of emergency anywhere in France, you can contact one of the 105 offices of *le SAMU* (*Service d'Aide Médicale Urgente*—their emergency medical system). In Paris you can use a toll-free emergency telephone number (15) for direct public access to this service. All incoming calls are analyzed by a physician who dispatches the assistance required.

The following tables list relevant vocabulary should you need to seek medical services. Pharmacies are readily identifiable by a neon-green cross prominently displayed over the doorway. Medications, even nonprescription items such as aspirin, are only available through a pharmacy.

 To indicate that you suffer from something, use the verb *avoir* + noun, as in *j'ai le diabète; j'ai eu une crise cardiaque; il a une plaie profonde,* and so forth.

 French medications often come in powdered form (*en poudre*) or as a suppository (*un suppositoire*). Pharmacists will gladly recommend the best treatment for your cold, fever, and other minor aches and pains.

At the Doctor's Office/Hospital (*Chez le médecin/à l'hôpital*)

Illnesses	Les maladies	Illnesses	Les maladies
AIDS	*le Sida*	good health/bad health	*la bonne santé/la mauvaise santé*
appendicitis	*l'appendicite (f.)*	heart attack	*une crise cardiaque*
asthma	*l'asthme (m.)*	heartburn	*une crise de foie*
athlete's foot	*la mycose*	HIV negative	*séronégatif/séronégative*
bacteria	*la bactérie*	HIV positive	*séropositif/séropositive*
blister	*une ampoule*	illness	*une maladie*
blood pressure: high	*l'hypertension (f.)*	indigestion	*une indigestion*
blood pressure: low	*l'hypotension (f.)*	infection	*une infection*
broken leg/arm/ankle, etc.	*la jambe cassée, le bras cassé, etc.*	muscular pain	*la douleur articulaire*
bruise	*un bleu*	PMS	*le syndrome prémenstruel*
burn	*une brûlure*	rabies	*la rage*
cancer	*un cancer*	stroke	*une attaque d'apoplexie*
chronic	*chronique*	virus	*le virus*
constipation	*la constipation*	wound, sore, cut	*une plaie, une blessure*
diabetes	*le diabète*	deep (cut/wound)	*profond(e)(une plaie profonde)*
diarrhea	*la diarrhée*		
Medications/Treatments	*Les médicaments/les traitements*	*Medications/Treatments*	*Les médicaments/les traitements*
antibiotics	*les antibiotiques (f.)*	crutches	*les béquilles*
bandage	*un pansement*	dosage	*le dosage*
cast (plaster cast)	*le plâtre*	dose of	*une dose de*

continues

At the Doctor's Office/Hospital (*Chez le médecin/à l'hôpital*) (continued)

Medications/ Treatments	Les médicaments/ les traitements	Medications/ Treatments	Les médicaments/ les traitements
drops	les gouttes	remedy, cure	le remède
first aid	les premiers soins	shot, injection	une piqûre, une injection
healthy food	l'alimentation saine (f.)	syrup (for cough)	un sirop
lozenges	les pastilles (f.)	sleeping pills	les somnifères (f.)
medicine	un médicament	suppositories	les suppositoires (f.)
natural remedy	les médecines naturelles (f.)	tablet	un comprimé
operation	une opération	tranquillizers	les tranquillisants (m.)
pill	une pilule, un cachet	wheel chair	un fauteuil roulant
recuperation	le rétablissement	x-ray	une radio
Miscellaneous		*Miscellaneous*	
ambulance	une ambulance	nurse, female	une infirmière
appointment	le rendez-vous	nurse, male	un infirmier
blind	aveugle	optician	un opticien, une opticienne
chiropractor	le chiropracteur (m./f.)	orthopaedic surgeon	un orthopédiste (m./f.)
clinic	la clinique (privée)	osteopath	un ostéopathe (m./f.)
deaf	sourd(e)	patient	le malade, la malade
doctor	le médecin	pediatrician	le pédiatre, la pédiatre
handicapped	handicapé(e)	stretcher	le brancard
lame	boiteux, boiteuse	surgeon	le chirurgien, la chirurgienne
mute	muet, muette		

Verbs

to choke	*s'étouffer*
to cough	*tousser*
to diet	*faire un régime*
to faint	*s'évanouir*
to fast	*jeûner*
to feel better	*se sentir mieux*
to feel ill	*se sentir mal*
to feel sick (at stomach)	*avoir mal à l'estomac*
to feel well	*se sentir bien*
to get better	*aller mieux*
to have a cold	*avoir un rhume*
to have a cough	*avoir une toux*
to have a fever	*avoir la fièvre*
to have a headache, backache, etc.	*avoir mal à la tête, au dos, etc.*

Verbs

to have a runny nose	*avoir le nez qui coule*
to have a stuffed nose	*avoir le nez bouché*
to have a temperature	*avoir de la température*
to have the flu	*avoir la grippe*
to hurt	*faire mal; se faire mal*
to hurt (That hurts.)	*faire mal (Ça fait mal.)*
to infect	*infecter*
to make an appointment	*prendre rendez-vous*
to operate (on someone)	*opérer quelqu'un*
to sneeze	*éternuer*
to take one's pulse	*prendre le pouls*
to vaccinate	*vacciner*
to vomit	*vomir*

PROCEED WITH CAUTION

The verb *sentir* can mean "to touch" or "to smell." *Se sentir* means "to feel." *Je sens mauvais* means "I smell bad"; *Je me sens mal* means "I feel bad."

AT THE DENTIST'S OFFICE

If you find you're really in need of a doctor or dentist, first ask at the pharmacy closest to where you're staying. Often medical professionals will see travelers on an emergency basis if they are referred by someone local. The following table lists vocabulary you might need for a trip to a dentist.

Dental Vocabulary

At the Dentist's Office	Chez le dentiste
abscess	*un abcès*
braces	*un appareil dentaire*
cap	*une couronne*
dental floss	*le fil dentaire*
dentist	*le dentiste*
false teeth	*le dentier*
filling	*un plombage*
gum	*la gencive*
jaw	*la mâchoire*
molar	*la molaire*
root	*la racine*
sensitive tooth	*une dent sensible*
tooth	*la dent*
toothbrush	*une brosse à dents*
toothpaste	*le dentifrice*
toothpick	*un cure-dent*
wisdom tooth	*la dent de sagesse*
Verbs	
to break a tooth	*casser une dent*
to have a toothache	*avoir mal aux dents*
to lose a tooth	*perdre une dent*

HOUR'S UP!

Vous devez vous applaudir de vos efforts! You should give yourself a pat on the back for your efforts! Now that you've mastered the passive voice and the causative *faire* construction, you're in control of all the French grammatical structures. In your final two hours of study, you'll be working primarily on reading and writing the language. As you've done in the past, take a few moments to review the materials in the hour and then test your knowledge with the following quiz. *Et, bonne continuation!* Keep up the good work!

1. True or False: The passive voice always uses a form of the verb *être*.

2. True or False: In sentences using the passive voice, the subject receives the action of the verb.

3. The prepositions most closely associated with the passive voice are:

    a. *par/à*

    b. *par/de*

    c. *de/à*

    d. *à/sur*

4. Which of the following choices correctly changes this sentence from the passive voice to the active voice without changing the meaning of the original sentence: *Les clés ont été volées par les voleurs.*

    a. *Les voleurs volent les clés.*

    b. *Les voleurs voleront les clés.*

    c. *Les voleurs ont volé les clés.*

    d. *Les clés sont volées.*

5. Which of the following is not followed by a correct preposition?

    a. *accompagné par*

    b. *suivi de*

    c. *aimé de*

    d. *lu par*

6. Identify the tense of the verb in the following sentence: *Ils sont sortis par la porte d'entrée.*

    a. present tense, passive voice

    b. past tense

    c. present conditional

    d. future

7. Identify the tense of the verb in the following sentence: *Il est écrit dans mon livre de grammaire que …*

    a. past tense, active voice

    b. future tense

    c. present conditional

    d. present tense, passive voice

8. Which of the following methods can be used to avoid a passive construction?

    a. Use a reflexive verb.

    b. Use a conjunction + subjunctive.

    c. Change the subject to the object of the verb.

    d. None of these methods will work.

9. In which of the following sentences are the object pronouns not placed correctly?

    a. *Il la lui a fait faire.*

    b. *Il a fait les taper.*

    c. *Nous le faisons étudier.*

    d. *Nous le lui faisons étudier.*

10. Which of the following physical difficulties would a dentist most likely not treat?

    a. *un mal de dents*

    b. *une dent sensible*

    c. *une dent cassée*

    d. *une cuisse douloureuse*

QUIZ

HOUR 23

Managing Your Business

CHAPTER SUMMARY

LESSON PLAN:

In this hour you will learn …

- How to construct a curriculum vitae.
- How to write a cover letter.
- How to compose basic business correspondence.
- How to conduct business on the telephone.
- How to use new vocabulary to talk about banking and the stock market.

In this hour you'll learn how to construct a curriculum vitae (a CV) and a cover letter to present to a prospective employer. You'll also learn some of the conventions used in writing business correspondence.

Because much business is conducted on the telephone, we'll give you some expressions to use when making these kinds of contacts. You'll also learn enough vocabulary to engage someone in conversation about banking and the stock market.

Let's begin by looking at the format and content of a French curriculum vitae.

CONSTRUCT A CURRICULUM VITAE (CV)

The construction of a French CV follows many of the formatting conventions used in the United States: one page, typed, one-inch margins, and a professional font. The following outline of a typical CV can be filled in with the appropriate information. You can keep the headings as given or rearrange them within a category. Where the French might not be clear, English equivalents are given in brackets.

Sample CV

ETAT CIVIL (personal information)

- noms et prénoms (last name in capitals: SMITH, John)
- *date et lieu de naissance/ou âge* (le + day, month, year)
- *nationalité* (nationality: for example, *Américain/Américaine*)
- *service militaire* (for example, *Je suis libéré des obligations militaires*)
- *état civil* (for example, *marié[e], célibataire, divorcé[e], veuf/veuve*)
- *adresse* (address might include telephone number and e-mail address)

FORMATION (education)

- *diplômes, certificats* (degrees, certificates, and so forth)
- *stages* (internships)
- *d'autres expériences éducatives* (other educational experiences)
- *langue étrangère pratiquée* (Anglais: *lu, écrit, parlé*)

ETAT DES SERVICES PROFESSIONNELS (employment history)

- *emploi actuel* (current employment and address)
- *emplois précédents* (past employment and address)
- *expérience internationale*
- *rémunérations successives* (past salary; can be omitted)
- *salaire espéré* (desired salary; can be omitted)

DIVERS (miscellaneous: include appropriate information)

- *Je suis mobile sur toute la France* (ability to travel)
- *J'ai le Permis B et je dispose d'un véhicule* (licences and so forth)

RÉFÉRENCES (names and addresses of references)

ASSOCIATIONS (professional organizations, and so forth)

PASSE-TEMPS (hobbies and so forth)

PROCEED WITH CAUTION

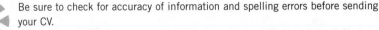

Be sure to check for accuracy of information and spelling errors before sending your CV.

Once you've completed the CV, you'll need to compose a cover letter.

LETTRE DE MOTIVATION

The CV is accompanied by *une lettre de motivation* (a cover letter) unless you drop in on a potential employer for *un entretien spontané* (an unscheduled interview). Although not recommended, the unscheduled interview is more common today as positions become harder to find, especially for young people entering the job market.

STRICTLY DEFINED

The cover letter often is handwritten in France because employers believe they can learn something about the applicants through their handwriting and the presentation of the letter. However, a typed *lettre de motivation* also is acceptable.

At the top of the letter, to the right or centered, is the date in this format: *le 2 février 2001*. Below the date, and aligned left, is the address to which you are sending the letter. Open the letter with *Monsieur* or *Madame*, followed by the full title or name, if possible. Typically the cover letter itself is short, preferably not more than 250 words, and has the following four parts:

1. A paragraph presenting the information from the *État civil* section of your CV (name, address, telephone, e-mail, and so forth).

2. A paragraph focusing on your understanding of the company to which you are applying. You might use a phrase such as *Je sais que votre entreprise fait figure de leader dans ...* (I know that your company is positioned as a leader in ...). Complete the sentence with a reference to the type of business performed by the company.

3. A paragraph highlighting your abilities; you might begin with *Titulaire d'une en maîtrise de gestion, je recherche actuellement un poste permettant de mettre en pratique ...* (As a young graduate with a Master's degree in management, I am seeking a position which will permit me to use ...). Complete the sentence with a reference to your particular skills, such as *mes connaissances en gestion* (my knowledge of management) or *mes connaissances en informatique* (my knowledge of computers).

4. A final paragraph explaining what you can do for the company; you might begin with *J'ai l'esprit d'initiative qui me permettra de ...* (My strong motivation allows me to ...). Complete the sentence with an infinitive that makes reference to contributing actively to the company; for example, *d'exploiter mes connaissances* or *d'apporter mon savoir-faire au sein de votre entreprise* (to share my expertise with/to bring my knowledge to your company).

The letter is ended using a formal convention of politeness. Because these closing sentences are highly conventional, you should not try to translate them. Here is one you can use in almost all cases, being sure to replace the *Monsieur/Madame* with the exact formula of address you used in opening of the letter:

> *Vous remerciant à l'avance de l'attention que vous porterez à ce document, je vous prie d'agréer, Monsieur/Madame, mes salutations distinguées.*

Sign the letter to the right of center, aligned with the date.

PROCEED WITH CAUTION

Your cover letter will say much about you, so you want it to be perfectly correct and to sound authentic. Always have an experienced native speaker review your letters before you send them out.

The language of most *lettres de motivation* is highly stylized by English standards. The following list outlines the formatting for a cover letter with some phrases and sentences you might work into each part of your letter. When a sentence is left open-ended in the examples, you should add the appropriate adjectives or nouns as cued by the English translations. Choose your wording carefully and be brief; a good *lettre de motivation* might only contain eight to ten sentences distributed in three to four short paragraphs.

The opening:

- *Pour faire suite à notre conversation téléphonique de la semaine dernière, j'ai le plaisir de vous faire parvenir ci-joint mon curriculum vitae.* (To follow up on our telephone conversation of last week, I'm pleased to send you my curriculum vitae.)

- *Je voudrais présenter ma candidature pour le poste de …* (I would like to apply for the position of …; complete the sentence with the type of position you seek.)

About yourself:

- *Je vous prie de bien vouloir étudier ma candidature à la formation de* (enter type of position) *dans votre établissement, candidature qui me tient tout particulièrement à cœur.* (Please consider my application for the posititon of ___ in your company, a position in which I am particularly interested.)

- *En effet, je suis actuellement engagé(e) dans une formation en …* (In fact, I am currently working on my degree in …; go to Hour 18, "At Work," for a list of professions.)

- *Au cours de ma formation actuelle, les stages ont été des points forts, par conséquent, j'ai une bonne connaissance de …* (In the course of my studies, my internships have been particularly instructive, therefore I have strong knowledge of …) (Complete the sentence with several nouns that indicate your areas of expertise developed during your internships. Be aware that French employers are more inclined to hire those who have actual work experience through part-time jobs or internships.)

- *De plus, la communication est dans ma nature.* (Moreover, I am by nature a good communicator.)

- *Enfin, je pense que ma personnalité est en plein accord avec ma motivation professionnelle.* (In conclusion, I believe that my professional motivation is reflected in my personality.)

- *Je sais m'adapter à …* (I know how to adapt to …) (Complete the sentence with one or more nouns indicating how you can adapt yourself; for example, *aux demandes d'un poste exigeant* [to the requirements of a demanding position], *aux besoins de votre entreprise* [to the needs of your company].)

- *En effet, je pense être ouvert(e) aux autres, dynamique et innovateur/innovatrice.* (In fact, I think that I am open to others, dynamic, and innovative.) (You should add adjectives describing your personality positively.)

- *J'ai le sens des responsabilités et de l'organisation.* (I am both responsible and organized.)

- *Mon adaptabilité me permet d'occuper des postes …* (My ability to adapt permits me to seek a position …) (You should complete the sentence with a phrase that highlights your adapability; for example, *où je peux travailler en équipe* [where I can work in a group] or *auxquels je peux apporter mes connaissances de la gestion et du marketing* [to which I can apply by knowledge of both management and marketing].)

About the job you're looking for:

- *Je veux devenir* (your desired profession), *car …* (I would like to become a ____, because …)

- *Je crois en une société basée en grande partie sur …* (I am attracted to a company that focuses on …) (Complete the sentence with a noun that defines the primary value you are seeking in a company; for example, *l'information* [information], *la communication* [communication], or *l'innovation* [innovation].)

- *C'est dans un cabinet dynamique que je désire apporter ma collaboration.* (I hope to work in a dynamic office.)

In closing:

- *J'espère vous avoir convaincu de …* (I hope that I have convinced you of …) (Complete the sentence with an appropriate noun or phrase; for example, *ma motivation; mon intérêt dans le poste que vous avez annoncé; mon fort désir de vous rencontrer le plus rapidement possible* [of my strong desire to meet with you as soon as possible].)

- *Je suis sûr(e) qu'un entretien vous permettra de mieux cerner mon expérience.* (I'm certain that an interview will permit you to better evaluate my experience.)

- *Je serais ravi de répondre à vos questions.* (I would be happy to respond to any questions you might have.)

- *Souhaitant vous convaincre de ma motivation, je me tiens à votre disposition pour un premier entretien.* (Hoping that I have convinced you of my interest in this position, I am available for an interview at your convenience.)

(Signature)

PROCEED WITH CAUTION

 U.S. conventions, such as *sincèrement* (sincerely) and *cordialement* (cordially), are appearing more and more commonly in French correspondence. However, such usage should be avoided in business writing.

If you are responding to business correspondence, there also are a number of conventions to follow, as discussed in the following section.

MASTER BUSINESS CONVENTIONS

Doing business successfully in any language is difficult; doing it in a language that is not native to you is extremely difficult. The many conventions of correspondence, formulas of politeness, and ways of conducting negotiations are far beyond the scope of this text. Nevertheless, you can acquaint yourself with a few of these conventions so you can feel comfortable when you encounter them in a business situation.

BASIC CORRESPONDENCE

A French business letter can be set up in several formats. The following sample business letter is one of the more traditional formats:

Sample Business Letter Form

[Letterhead]

New York, le 15 février, 2001   [Place of origin; date]

Monsieur Paul LEMARC   [Recipient's address]
Directeur des ventes
Maison Lemarc
30, blvd Victor Hugo
Paris
France

Objet: Demande de renseignements   [Subject of correspondence]

Monsieur le Directeur,   [Salutation]

En réponse à ...

....

[Body of the letter]

....

Veuillez agréer, Monsieur le Directeur, mes salutations distinguées.

        [Formula ending]

Signature   [Signature]

15, Broadway   [Address of sender]

New York, NY 10001

U.S.A.

p.j.   [Attachments]

HOW TO BEGIN A COMMERCIAL LETTER

By now you will be able to read the following sample openings for a commercial letter. These are merely formulas that you can find in many business writing texts; nevertheless, you can use them to compose a simple letter or to help you understand correspondence you might receive from abroad. Remember that this is conventional business language.

We regret ...

- *Je suis au regret de vous annoncer que ...* (I regret to inform you that ...) (Complete this sentence with a subject and a verb; for example, *nous ne pouvons pas répondre à votre demande* [we cannot respond to your order].)

- *Je vous prie de bien vouloir accepter mes excuses pour ...* (Please accept my apology for ...) (Complete this sentence with a noun; for example, *le delai de ma réponse à votre lettre* [the delay in my response to your letter].)

- *En réponse à la lettre que vous avez adressée à notre bureau, nous avons le regret de ...* (In response to the letter which you sent to our office, we regret to ...) (Complete this sentence with an appropriate infinitive; for example, *vous informer que ces articles ne sont plus disponibles* [to inform you that these items are no longer available].)

- *Nous sommes actuellement dans l'impossibilité de ...* (At the current time we are not able to ...) (Complete this sentence with an appropriate phrase beginning with an infinitive; for example, *expédier les marchandises que vous avez commandées* [to ship the merchandise you ordered].)

We have the pleasure ...

- *En réponse à votre demande d'emploi, nous avons le plaisir de vous informer que ...* (In response to your application for employment, we are pleased to inform you that ...) (Complete the sentence using a subject and a verb; for example, *nous vous offrons le poste de ___ dans notre entreprise* [we are offering you the position of ___ with our company].)

- *J'ai bien reçu votre invitation à ___ et je vous en remercie.* (I have received your invitation to ___ and thank you for it.)

- *Nous accusons réception de votre lettre du 30 mai et nous vous en remercions.* (We acknowledge receipt of your letter of May 30th and thank you for it.)

Neutral:

- *Nous désirons vous informer que ...* (We would like to inform you that ...) (Complete the sentence using a subject and a verb; for example, *nous sommes actuellement dans l'impossibilité de répondre à tous vos besoins* [we are unable to respond to all your needs at this time].)

- *À la suite de l'annonce parue dans le journal, j'aimerais ...* (In response to the announcement appearing in the newspaper, I would like to ...)

(Complete the sentence using an infinitive phrase; for example, *louer votre maison pour le mois de juin* [rent your house for the month of June]; *commander deux exemplaires de votre livre* [order two copies of your book].)

- *Pourriez-vous me faire parvenir la documentation relative à …* (Please send me the information dealing with …) (Complete the sentence with a noun; for example, *la douane* [customs]; *la taxe à la valeur ajoutée* [value added tax].)

- *Comme je vous l'ai proposé par téléphone …* (As I proposed to you on the telephone …) (Complete the sentence using a subject and a verb; for example, *notre entretien aura lieu lundi, le 20 mai* [our interview will be Monday, May 20]; *je confirme notre meeting pour demain à 10h* [I am confirming our meeting for tomorrow at 10:00 A.M.].)

TALKING ON THE TELEPHONE

Probably more business is conducted in France over the telephone than through correspondence. There are many conventions governing these conversations, so here are some basic vocabulary and structures to get you started.

Telephone Language

On the Telephone	Au téléphone
answering machine	*un répondeur*
beep	*le bip sonore*
busy (signal)	*occupé*
Can you call back?	*Vous pouvez rappeler?*
Can you please spell that?	*Épelez, s'il vous plaît.*
Can you repeat that?	*Répétez, s'il vous plaît.*
car phone	*un téléphone de voiture*
dial tone	*la tonalité*
Don't hang up. Hold, please.	*Ne quittez pas.*
Don't mention it.	*Je vous en prie.*
extension	*le poste*
fax	*un fax*
He/she's on the other line.	*Il/elle est en ligne.*
Hello (only on the phone).	*Allô.*
I dialed the wrong number.	*J'ai fait un faux numéro.*
May I leave a message?	*Puis-je laisser un message?*

continues

Telephone Language   (continued)

On the Telephone	Au téléphone
May I speak to …	*Puis-je parler à …*
message (phone)	*un message téléphonique*
phone book	*l'annuaire*
portable phone	*un portable*
switchboard	*le standard*
telephone	*le téléphone*
Thank you for calling.	*Je vous remercie.*
to call back	*rappeler*
to call	*appeler, faire un appel*
to make a collect call	*faire un appel en P.C.V.*
to telephone someone	*téléphoner à quelqu'un*

MASTER BUSINESS SITUATIONS

Two areas of particular interest to those doing business in France are banks (*la banque*) and the stock market (*la Bourse*). France is still a major banking power in the European Economic Community (EEC), and the French franc is among the most stable of currencies on the continent. However, the French stock market ranks third in importance behind the British and German markets and conducts its business almost entirely through electronic sales and exchanges. Nevertheless, the ups and downs of the French economy have a major effect on the overall health of the EEC. Beginning January 1999, the official currency of the EEC, the Euro, began circulating in France.

AT THE BANK

The major banking institutions today include *le Crédit Lyonnais, la Banque Nationale de Paris, le Crédit Commercial de France, le Crédit Industriel et Commercial,* and *le Crédit du Nord. La Banque de France* controls the national currency and is, of course, under the control of the state.

FYI The banking system in France dates back to the beginning of the nineteenth century when *La Banque de France* was created (January 18, 1800) by *le Premier Consul* Napoleon Bonaparte.

To open *un compte courant* (an account) you must be at least 18 years old and present yourself in person at the bank with the following documents:

une pièce d'identité (identification card) and *un certificat de domiciliation* (proof of residence), which can be a gas or telephone bill. If you are a student you also must present *un certificat de scolarité* (a certificate of full-time student status) as proof. To be issued *un chèquier* (a checkbook) you must have a job and receive *un salaire* (a paycheck).

If you are a salaried employee, you also are required by the French government to maintain a bank account, either with a commercial bank or with *la Poste* (the national postal service), which also serves as a bank. By law, all employers must deposit salary checks directly into the employee's banking or postal account. This system is designed to prevent both theft and tax evasion. Most French citizens maintain an account at a bank and also at the post office, known as *un CCP: Compte-Chèques Postal* (Postal Checking Account).

FYI A great deal of banking is done using ATMs, known as *les D.A.B.* (*distributeurs automatiques de billets*).

The following table lists some vocabulary to help you along at the bank. Most commercial banks in France provide the same services as U.S. banks: checking and savings accounts, credit cards, commercial and personal loans. Local banks also offer the best exchange rates when converting dollars to francs.

Banking Vocabulary

At the Bank	À la banque
amount	*le montant*
amount of check	*le montant du chèque*
bad check	*un chèque sans provision*
balance	*le solde*
bank card	*une carte bancaire*
bank charges	*les frais bancaires* (m.)
bank statement	*un relevé bancaire*
banking	*bancaire*
blank check	*un chèque en blanc*
checkbook	*un chéquier*
checking account	*un compte courant*
debit	*un débit*
deposit	*un dépôt*
endorse	*endosser*
I.D.	*une pièce d'identité*
passbook: savings	*un livret*

continues

Banking Vocabulary   (continued)

At the Bank	*À la banque*
payer of the check	*le tireur*
receipt	*un reçu*
receiver of the check	*le bénéficiaire*
savings account	*un compte d'épargne*
teller's window	*le guichet*
transfer	*un virement*
withdrawal: automatic	*un prélèvement automatique*
Verbs	
to cash a check	*toucher un chèque*
to check the balance	*vérifier le solde*
to debit	*débiter*
to deposit a check	*déposer un chèque*
to deposit money	*déposer de l'argent, verser de l'argent*
to open an account	*ouvrir un compte*
to stand in line	*faire la queue*
to transfer money	*virer de l'argent*
to withdraw	*retirer de l'argent*

ON THE STOCK MARKET

The French stock market (*la Bourse*) is not one of the major markets worldwide; however, its agents are major players in the European arena. Until recently, the Paris *Bourse* was located in the *Palais Brongniart*, in the middle of the city in which it was founded in 1826 by the Comte de Chabrol. Until 1987, the market agents worked around the well-known *corbeille* (basket) area in the center of the building, similar to the floor of the New York Stock Exchange. In June 1986, the market changed to a computerized system so that, presently, orders are entered directly into a nationally networked exchange. Gold is still quoted in the Brongniart Palace.

The principle French stock index is known as the CAC 40 (*Cotation assistée en continu* [Continuous Assisted Quotes]). It is composed of 40 stocks selected from the top 100 stocks and based on a monthly calculation of value. The French also carefully watch other indexes (*les indices*); in particular, *l'indice Dow Jones*, *l'indice NIKKEI* (Tokyo), *l'indice FTSE 100* (London), *les indices européens Stoxx* (Paris, Frankfort, Zurich), and *l'indice Dax* (Frankfort).

Buyers interested in less risk can invest in *les SICAV* (*sociétés d'investissement à capital variable*), which are mutual funds. Orders can be placed *par écrit* (in writing), *par téléphone* (by phone), *par fax* (by fax), and *par minitel* (by minitel computer system).

STRICTLY DEFINED

> **Minitel** is an intranet (within France) that is developed and supported by the government. It provides various online services, including telephone information, transportation schedules (train, plane), and entertainment announcements (concert schedules, movie times, and so forth). Subscription is free for these basic services; a small fee is charged for access to commercial sites.

The following table lists some vocabulary to talk about stocks and the stock market, in France or elsewhere.

Market Vocabulary

On the Stock Market	À la bourse
bond	*une obligation*
broker's fees	*des frais* (m.) *de courtage*
buyer	*un acheteur*
capital	*le capital*
commission	*une commission*
company quoted on the Exchange	*une société cotée en Bourse*
dividend	*un dividende*
exchange rate	*le cours d'échange*
fluctuation	*une fluctuation*
investment	*un investissement*
liquid assets	*la liquidité*
market index	*un indice boursier*
NAFTA	*l'ALENA* (*l'Accord de libre Échange Nord Américain*)
quote, quotation	*une cotation*
security	*une valeur boursière*
share	*une part de société*
stock	*une action*
transaction	*une transaction*

continues

Market Vocabulary   (continued)

Verbs		Verbs	
to buy	*acheter*	to invest	*investir*
to climb	*grimper*	to lower	*baisser*
to drop in value	*se dévaloriser*	to quote	*coter*
to earn	*rapport*	to resell	*revendre*
to exchange	*échanger*	to rise	*monter*
to fall	*tomber*	to sell	*vendre*
to finance	*financer*	to speculate	*spéculer*
to fluctuate	*fluctuer*	to transfer	*céder*
to get rid of	*se défaire de*	to transmit	*émettre*

LEARN VOCABULARY TO TALK BUSINESS

France is home to many companies with international reputations for the high quality of their products. Among the best known of these are: in the world of fashion, Yves Saint Laurent, Cardin, Chanel; in automotives, Peugeot, Michelin, Renault, Citroën; in food products, Danone, Vittel, Perrier; and in wines and liqueurs, Cointreau, Rothschild.

The following table lists some general vocabulary you can use to talk about doing business in France or at home.

Business Language

English	French
accounting	*la comptabilité*
advisor	*un conseiller*
agency	*une agence*
assets	*les atouts* (m.)
assets (total)	*le chiffre d'affaires*
auditor	*l'expert* (m.) *comptable*
board of directors	*le conseil d'administration*
boardroom	*la salle de conférences*
boss	*le patron*
business (private)	*une société privée*
buy-out	*le rachat*
CEO	*le P.-D.G.* (*président-directeur général*)
chamber of commerce	*une chambre de commerce*

English	French
companies	*les entreprises, les sociétés*
conference, meeting	*une conférence, une réunion*
director	*le directeur*
employee	*un employé, une employée*
factory	*une usine*
firm	*la firme, l'entreprise, la maison*
franchise	*une franchise*
incorporation	*S.A. (Société Anonyme)*
loss	*une perte*
management	*la gestion*
market	*le marché*
marketing	*le marketing*
office (branch)	*une succursale*
office (main, head)	*le siège social*
office supervisor	*le chef de bureau*
parking lot	*le parking*
pension	*la pension*
premises	*les locaux (m.)*
profit	*le profit, un bénéfice*
profit margin	*la marge bénéficiaire*
reception	*la réception*
sales	*les ventes*
sales rep	*le/la représentant(e)*
secretary	*le secrétaire, la secrétaire*
security guard	*le gardien*
store	*le magasin*
subsidiary	*une filiale*
utility (public)	*un service public*
warehouse	*un entrepôt*
worker	*un ouvrier, une ouvrière*

Verbs	
to apply for a position	*poser sa candidature*
to fire	*licencier*
to hire	*embaucher*
to manage	*gérer*
to retire	*prendre sa retraite*

QUIZ

HOUR'S UP!

J'ai le plaisir de vous informer que vous êtes arrivé à la fin de la leçon 23! I'm pleased to inform you that you have arrived at the end of Hour 23! Well done! At this point, you will be able to create your CV in French and compose a cover letter. With some luck, perhaps you'll be called for an interview! If you plan to do business in France, you can write a short business letter, converse on the phone, and talk about the banking system and the stock market. Good luck in your endeavors! Now it's time to review this new material and test your mastery of it with the following quiz.

1. On a French CV, which of the following would not appear under the heading *état civil?*

    a. *français*

    b. *divorcé*

    c. *veuf*

    d. *marié*

2. On a French CV, under which heading would you list a summer internship in Paris?

    a. *emploi actuel*

    b. *salaire espéré*

    c. *stages*

    d. *diplômes*

3. Under which heading would you list your love of golf?

    a. *service militaire*

    b. *lieu de naissance*

    c. *expériences internationales*

    d. *passe-temps*

4. A cover letter in France is called:

    a. *une référence*

    b. *une lettre de motivation*

    c. *un lettre d'emploi*

    d. *une couvre-lettre*

5. *Au cours de ma formation actuelle* means:

  a. Sailing through a great education

  b. My actual university courses are

  c. In the course of my present studies

  d. In my formative education

6. *Je serais ravi de répondre à vos questions* indicates that the writer is:

  a. ready to answer questions

  b. ravaged by worry

  c. sending his answers back to the employer who asked them

  d. discouraged

7. Where would the following sentence best fit in a cover letter? *Je voudrais présenter ma candidature …*

  a. At the end

  b. At the beginning

  c. In the second paragraph

  d. As a closing formula of politeness

8. Where would the following sentence best fit in a business letter? *En réponse à votre lettre …*

  a. At the end

  b. In the second paragraph

  c. At the beginning

  d. As a closing formula of politeness

9. Which of the following phrases is not typically associated with polite telephone conversations in France?

  a. *Je peux rappeler?*

  b. *Puis-je laisser un message.*

  c. *Ne quittez pas.*

  d. *Fermez-la.*

10. A checking account in French is:

  a. *un chéquier*

  b. *un livret*

  c. *un compte courant*

  d. *un dépôt*

QUIZ

Hour 24

Understanding Formal Writing in French

Chapter Summary

LESSON PLAN:

In this hour you will learn ...

- How to recognize literary tenses.
- How to read informally written literature.
- How to write informal notes.
- How to write formal correspondence.
- How to use new vocabulary to talk about literature and the arts.

Congratulations—you've reached the final hour! Soon you'll have completed your studies in this book. We've saved only a few important items until the very end; so in this hour you'll review some things, learn some final vocabulary, and explore a couple of verb forms that are used only in writing and literary works.

To this point, all the structures you've learned can be used in formal and familiar speech and writing. In this hour you'll learn the *passé simple* (simple past), which is used only in writing. However, it is used in all sorts of writing—from newspapers to novels to legal documents—so you will need to be able to recognize its forms if you want to read anything in French. Don't worry—I haven't been keeping much from you. In fact, the forms of the *passé simple* are quite easy to learn because they are based on forms you already know.

Additionally in this hour you'll learn how to write some formal and informal notes and to use some new vocabulary to talk about literature and the arts.

LEARN TO READ THE NEWSPAPER

As the *passé composé* is the past tense of conversation, the *passé simple* is the past tense of formal writing. It is used in writing where the oral language would use the *passé composé*. Both tenses are in contrast with the imperfect, which describes actions that took place over a period of time in the past.

The formation of the *passé simple* should not concern you too much, as most likely you will not be writing—only reading—it so I will present the forms quickly here. First, to the stem of the infinitive of the verb—that is, to the infinitive without the *–ir*, *-er*, or *-re* endings—add the endings shown in the following table.

Forming the *passé simple*

Person	-er	-ir	-re
first, singular	*-ai*	*-is*	*-is*
second, singular	*-as*	*-is*	*-is*
third, singular	*-a*	*-it*	*-it*
first, plural	*-âmes*	*-îmes*, *-ûmes*	*-îmes*
second, plural	*-âtes*	*-îtes*, *-ûtes*	*-îtes*
third, plural	*-èrent*	*-irent*, *-urent*	*-irent*

USE THE LITERARY TENSE

Now we will explore a few guidelines for the *passé simple*. You can see that the endings do not resemble any of those you've learned to this point. That's helpful information because if you see a verb with an unusual ending, such as *ils finirent*, *ils allèrent*, or *nous ouvrîmes*, and the context suggests the past, the verb probably is in the *passé simple*. As you will see shortly, there are quite a few irregular formations of the *passé simple*. Luckily, most of these irregular forms resemble in some way the past participle, which you've already learned.

Although the *passé simple* is formed in all six persons, only the third-person singular and plural are commonly used in writing; in fact, by far the third-person singular forms are the most common. Take a careful look at the following table of verbs and their conjugation in the third-person singular of the *passé simple*. To the right of the *passé simple* is the past participle of the verb.

Formation of the *passé simple* of Irregular Verbs

Infinitive	Third-Person Singular	Past Participle
acquérir	*il/elle acquit*	*acquis*
avoir	*il/elle eut*	*eu*
battre	*il/elle battit*	*battu*
boire	*il/elle but*	*bu*
conduire	*il/elle conduisit*	*conduit*
courir	*il/elle courut*	*couru*

Infinitive	Third-Person Singular	Past Participle
croire	il/elle crut	cru
devoir	il/elle dut	dû
dire	il/elle dit	dit
écrire	il/elle écrivit	écrit
être	il/elle fut	été
faire	il/elle fit	fait
falloir	il/elle fallut	fallu
lire	il/elle lut	lu
mettre	il/elle mit	mis
mourir	il/elle mourut	mort
naître	il/elle naquit	né
paraître	il/elle parut	paru
peindre	il/elle peignit	peint
plaire	il/elle plut	plu
pleuvoir	il/elle plut	plu
pouvoir	il/elle put	pu
prendre	il/elle prit	pris
recevoir	il/elle reçut	reçu
rompre	il/elle rompit	rompu
s'asseoir	il/elle s'assit	assis
savoir	il/elle sut	su
suffire	il/elle suffit	suffi
suivre	il/elle suivit	suivi
vivre	il/elle vécut	vécu
voir	il/elle vit	vu
vouloir	il/elle voulut	voulu

PROCEED WITH CAUTION

Note that *plaire* (to please) and *pleuvoir* (to rain) have the same form of the *passé simple* as well as the same past participle. Context will make the meaning clear: *Il **plut** en avril.* (It rained in April.) *Ce concert me **plut**.* (This concert pleased me.)

With the exception of five verbs (*être, faire, mourir, naître,* and *voir*), the *passé simple* closely resembles the past participle. Again, this is very helpful because all you need to do is recognize the verb and recognize that it is in the past tense.

LEARN TO READ LITERATURE

Here is an excerpt from a novella by Honoré de Balzac (*Le colonel Chabert*, 1832). Most of the verbs are in the *passé simple*. See if you can identify the infinitive of the verb forms shown in bold:

> *Ces diverses exclamations **partirent** à la fois au moment où le vieux plaideur **ferma** la porte avec cette sorte d'humilité qui dénature les mouvements de l'homme malheureux. L'inconnu **essaya** de sourire, mais les muscles de son visage se **détendirent** quand il **eut** vainement cherché quelques symptômes d'aménité sur les visages inexorablement insouciants des six clercs. Accoutumé sans doute à juger les hommes, il **s'adressa** fort poliment au saute-ruisseau, en espérant que ce pâtiras lui répondrait avec douceur.*

The verbs in bold are *partir*, *fermer*, *essayer*, *se détendre*, *avoir*, and *s'addresser*. Once you begin to associate the *passé simple* with your reading and the forms with the past participles you know, you should have no problem at all reading French at any level.

LEARN HOW TO WRITE INFORMAL NOTES

This section offers some guidance on how to compose invitations, requests for information, business cards, and formal business letters. You will notice that the language is stylized and conventional to the point that you cannot translate it directly into English.

INVITATIONS

An invitation should (of course) say what kind of event one is invited to and specify the time, date, hour, and location of the event. You might want to begin with the following set expression to compose your invitation:

> *Vous êtes très cordialement invité à (un dîner, une soirée, un anniversaire, des noces* [wedding anniversary]).

You might request that invited guests respond to your invitation by using one of the following phrases: *RSVP avant le* [insert date] *au* [insert telephone number]; or, *RSVP en cas d'empêchement* [regrets only]. RSVP is written without periods and stands for *Répondez s'il vous plaît*.

 You also might wish to indicate what attire would be appropriate, as in *Tenue de soirée* (evening dress) or *Cravate blanche* (white tie); *Smoking* (tuxedo) or *Cravate noire* (black tie); *Tenue de ville* (dressy casual); *Tenue décontractée* (very casual).

An invitation to a company party or dinner might include an open invitation to bring a guest, as in *Invitation pour deux personnes* or *Invitation valable pour deux personnes*, which is more business formal. If guests will need an invitation to enter, you can include this line: *Prière de se munir de la présente invitation* or—to be certain that they understand "no invitation, no entry"—*Carte strictement personnelle et exigée à l'entrée*. If you know the guests well you might end the invitation with *cordialement* or *Bien à vous* and your signature.

An invitation to a formal reception might look something like the following:

Monsieur Jean-Jacques Rousseau,

président de la Société [Company Name],

a l'honneur de vous inviter à un dîner [coquetel, soirée]

offert à l'occasion du lancement du nouveau répertoire de la société.

La réception aura lieu le [Date] à [Time] heures,

à [Location],

[Street Address, etc.]

Invitation pour deux personnes

RSVP avant [Date]

Téléphone: XX.XX.XX.XX.XX.

REQUESTS FOR INFORMATION

When requesting information, a brochure, or pamphlet you've seen announced in another publication, your request might resemble this one:

Madame/Monsieur,

À la suite de votre annonce dans [Name of publication], je vous saurais gré de me faire parvenir une exemplaire de [publication, brochure desired].

Vous en remerciant à l'avance, je vous prie d'agréer, Madame/ Monsieur, mes salutations distinguées.

Signature

Choose either *Madame* or *Monsieur* for your salutation. Do not, as is sometimes the case in the United States, use both *Monsieur/Madame* to mean "Dear Sir or Madame."

BUSINESS CARDS

The French *carte professionnelle* (business card) often is somewhat larger than its American counterpart and is not offered as freely as in the United States. A typical card might look like the following:

Marc LEBRUN
Professeur agrégé
Département de langues étrangères
Université de Paris X
15, rue de la Madeleine   Téléphone: XX.XX.XX.XX.XX
75003 Paris   Télécopie: XX.XX.XX.XX.XX
                                  C. élec.: M.lebrun@ute.sorbonne.fr

---

LEARN TO FORMAT A LETTER

In Hour 23, "Managing Your Business," I briefly introduced the format of a standard business letter. The following sample letter format is a more complete outline of how to compose a formal letter and some errors to avoid.

When composing your letter, keep these points in mind:

1. Do not abbreviate months of the year. If the letterhead does not contain an address, include it with the date.

2. Use a comma between the number and the street name in French addresses.

3. Spell out *Monsieur, Madame,* and so forth; never abbreviate them. They are properly followed by a period, not a colon (as in the U.S. style). You may abbreviate *avenue* (*av.*), *boulevard* (*bd.*), and *route* (*rte*).

4. The postal code appears before the city in French address, as in 75000 Paris; it appears under the city name in Canadian addresses.

FYI Many French businesses subscribe to a postal service called *CEDEX* (*Courrier d'Entreprise à Distribution Exceptionnelle* [Special Distribution of Business Mail]). The word *CEDEX*, followed by a numeric code, is placed after the city name, such as *75004 Paris CEDEX 13*. Letters bearing the *CEDEX* code receive priority handling.

5. Add an appropriate salutation at the end, such as:

- *Je vous prie d'agréer, Madame, mes salutations distinguées.*

- *Je vous prie de recevoir, Monsieur, mes meilleures salutations.*

- *Veuillez agréer, Monsieur, l'expression de mes sentiments les meilleurs.*

- *Veuillez recevoir, Madame, l'expression de mes sentiments distingués.*

- *Acceptez, Messieurs, l'assurance de mes sentiments dévoués.*

EN-TÊTE
[Company Logo]

Vedette
[Recipient Address]

Référenes
[Referencing]
A l'attention de:
[To the attention of:]

Objet:
[Object:]

Appel
[Mr./Ms, etc.]

Paragraphe
[Body]
Paragraphe
[Body]
Paragraphe
[Body]

Signature
[Signature]

Initiales d'identification
[Initials of typist]
Pièces jointes
[Attachments]
Copie conforme
[Carbon Copy]

Now that you've become acquainted with the *passé simple* and the format and style of some basic writing in French, it's time to work on your final list of vocabulary words. The following vocabulary will help you discuss literature and the arts.

LEARN VOCABULARY TO TALK ABOUT LITERATURE AND THE ARTS

Art and Literature (*Les arts et la littérature*)

English	French	English	French
architecture	l'architecture (f.)	landscape	un paysage
art	l'art	model	un modèle
art collection	une collection d'art	oil painting	une peinture à l'huile
art gallery	une galerie d'art	paint brush	un pinceau
artist	un artiste, une artiste	paints	les couleurs (f.)
baroque	baroque	pastels	les pastels
canvas	la toile	picture frame	le cadre
charcoal	le fusain	picture, painting	un tableau
classic	classique	portrait	un portrait
drawing	une dessin	sculpture	une sculpture
easel	le chevalet	sketch	un croquis
engraving	en gravure	still life	une nature morte
exhibition	une exposition	studio	un studio
Gothic	gothique	style	le style
illustrator	un illustrateur, une illustratrice	watercolor	une aquarelle
Verbs			
to carve	graver		
to paint	peindre		

Books and Magazines	Les livres et les magazines	Books and Magazines	Les livres et les magazines
ads	les petites annonces	horoscope	l'horoscope (m.)
article	un article	journalist	un journaliste
author	un auteur	magazine	un magazine
biographer	un biographe	novelist	un romancier
biography	une biographie	paperback	un livre de poche
cartoons	les BD (bandes dessinées)	poem	un poème
chapter	un chapitre	poet	un poète
column	la rubrique	poetry	la poésie
cover	la couverture	publisher	un éditeur, une éditrice
designer	le concepteur	puzzles	les jeux
detective novel	un roman policier	royalties	les droits d'auteur
editor	le rédacteur, la rédactrice	science-fiction novel	un roman de science-fiction
encyclopedia	une encyclopédie	serial	un feuilleton
feature story	l'article de fond (m.)	suspense novel	un roman à suspense
fiction	la fiction	textbook	un livre scolaire, un texte
front page	la une	travel guide	un guide
headlines	les gros titres	weather report	la météo
historian	un historien	writer	un écrivain
historical novel	un roman historique		

Theaters and Movies	Le théâtre et le cinéma	Theaters and Movies	Le théâtre et le cinéma
act	un acte	pornography	la porno
actor	un acteur	producer	le producteur
actress	une actrice	row	le rang
balcony	le balcon	scenery	le décor
curtain	les rideaux (m.)	screen	l'écran
detective film	un film policier	seat	le fauteuil
director	le metteur en scène	showing	une séance
film	un film	soundtrack	la bande-son, la bande sonore
horror film	un film d'horreur	stage	la scène
love story	un film d'amour	subtitled	sous-titré
movie star	une vedette	ticket office	le guichet
No one admitted under …	Interdit au moins de … ans	violence	la violence
opening night	la première	violent	violent
original language version	V.O. (version originale)	Western	un western
part	un rôle		
Verbs			
to applaud	applaudir		
to boo	huer		

STRICTLY DEFINED

"Fashion model" in French is **un mannequin;** "an art model" is **une maquette.**

You've been a wonderful student! Congratulations on finishing this text and on all you've learned in the past 24 hours. Of course, you'll need to continue to work on the vocabulary; practice the verb forms on a regular basis; and, hopefully, find a native French person with whom to have weekly conversations—that's the best way to improve your accuracy and pronunciation.

JUST A MINUTE

Un éditeur/une éditrice is "a publisher," i.e., the person who runs *une maison d'édition* (a publishing firm). A person who edits a text and works for *l'éditeur* is called *le rédacteur* or *la rédactrice.*

I hope to see you in Paris some day! *Bon voyage, à un de ces jours, j'espère!*

FYI The age required to see a film with strong adult content is 17, a rule that is strictly enforced.

HOUR'S UP!

1. True or False: The *passé simple* is the literary equivalent of the past subjunctive.

2. True or False: The *passé simple* is the literary equivalent of the *passé composé.*

3. Which of the following phrases is not in the *passé simple?*
   a. *il dut*
   b. *elle parle*
   c. *elle écouta*
   d. *il fit*

4. Which of the following phrases is in the *passé simple?*
   a. *elle veuille*
   b. *elle conduit*
   c. *il sait*
   d. *il crut*

5. True or False: The *passé simple* is commonly used with all the persons of the verb.

6. On a business letter, *la vedette* is:

   a. the recipient's address

   b. the sender's address

   c. the salutation

   d. the company logo

7. *Cedex* written on an address indicates:

   a. certified mail

   b. air mail

   c. a mail code

   d. city name

8. Which one of the following abbreviations is acceptable on a French business letter?

   a. *Mme.*

   b. *bd.*

   c. *fév.*

   d. *Fr.*

9. Someone who creates *un tableau* most likely would be:

   a. *un auteur*

   b. *un poète*

   c. *un acteur*

   d. *un peintre*

10. You most likely will find *les gros titres* on what?

    a. *la une*

    b. *une B.D.*

    c. *un chevalet*

    d. *une toile*

Key: verb (v.), preposition (prep.), conjunction (conj.), adverb (adv.), adjective (adj.). All French words preceded by an article are nouns.

ENGLISH/FRENCH

about (subject): *au sujet de*
about (approximately): *environ*
about (around): *autour de*
above: *dessus*
abreast of, level with: *à la hauteur de*
accident: *un accident*
accountant: *le comptable*
accounting: *la comptabilité*
act (v.): *agir*
actor/actress: *un acteur/une actrice*
advisor: *un conseiller*
after (conj.): *après que*
after (prep.): *après*
against: *contre*
agency: *une agence*
air conditioning: *la climatisation*
airplane: *l'avion*
airport: *l'aéroport*
alarm clock: *un réveil*
also: *aussi*
although (conj.): *bien que, quoique*
always: *toujours*
among: *parmi*
ankle: *la cheville*
answer a question (v.): *répondre à une question*
answer the phone (v.): *répondre au téléphone*
antique shop: *un magasin d'antiquités*
apartment: *un appartement*
apartment house: *un immeuble*
apple: *une pomme*
apply for a position (v.): *poser sa candidature*
apprentice: *un apprenti*
approximately: *environ*

apricot: *un abricot*
April: *avril*
archaeologist: *un archéologue*
architect: *un architecte*
arm: *le bras*
armchair: *un fauteuil*
around: *autour de*
arrive, happen (v.): *arriver*
artery: *une artère*
artist: *un artiste*
ashtray: *un cendrier*
ask a question (v.): *poser une question*
ask for (v.): *demander*
assets: *les atouts* (m.)
assets (total): *le chiffre d'affaires*
assistant: *un assistant/une assistante*
astrologer: *un astrologue*
astronaut: *un astronaute*
at home: *à la maison*
at the home/office of; among: *chez*
athlete: *un athlète, une athlète*
ATM: *un DAB*
attend, go to (v.): *assister à*
attic: *le grenier, la mansarde*
auditor: *l'expert* (m.) *comptable*
August: *août*
aunt: *une tante*
author: *un auteur*
auto racing: *les courses auto*
avenue: *une avenue*
back: *le dos*
back pay: *les arriérages de salaire*
backpack: *un sac à dos*
bad: *mauvais, mauvaise*
badly: *mal*

baker: *le boulanger, la boulangère*
balcony: *le balcon*
ballpoint pen: *un stylo*
banana: *une banane*
banker: *le banquier*
bar: *le bar*
barber: *le coiffeur, la coiffeuse*
bartender: *le barman*
baseball: *le base-ball*
basement: *le sous-sol*
basement apartment: *un appartement (de) sous-sol*
basil: *le basilic*
basketball: *le basket-ball*
bathrobe: *un peignoir*
bathroom (in a home): *la salle de bains*
bathroom (public): *les toilettes*
bathtub: *la baignoire*
bathwater: *le bain*
be born (v.): *naître*
be lost (v.): *être perdu*
be necessary (v.): *falloir*
be relaxed (v.): *être détendu(e)*
be right; have the right answer (v.): *avoir raison*
be wrong; have the wrong answer (v.): *se tromper; avoir tort*
because: *parce que*
become (v.): *devenir*
bed: *le lit*
bedroom: *la chambre*
beef: *le bœuf*
beer: *une bière*
before (conj.): *avant que*
before (prep.): *avant*
before (+ past inf.): *avant de*
behind: *derrière*
below: *dessous*
belt: *la ceinture*
bench: *un banc*
between: *entre*
bicycle: *une bicyclette, un vélo*
bidet: *le bidet*
big: *grand*
bike (v.): *faire du vélo*
bill (hotel): *la note*

bill (restaurant): *l'addition*
black: *noir, noire*
black currant: *le cassis*
blackberry: *la mûre*
blanket: *une couverture*
blinds: *les volets* (m.)
blood: *le sang*
blood vessel: *le vaisseau sanguin*
blouse: *le chemisier*
blue: *bleu, bleue*
board game: *un jeu de société*
board of directors: *le conseil d'administration*
boardroom: *la salle de conférences*
boat: *le bateau*
body: *le corps*
bone: *un os*
book: *un livre*
bookstore: *une librairie*
border: *la frontière*
boss: *le patron*
bottle: *une bouteille*
bottle of: *une bouteille de*
boulevard: *le boulevard*
bowl: *un bol*
bowl, for soup: *une assiette creuse*
boy: *un garçon*
brain: *le cerveau*
brandy: *le cognac*
bread: *le pain*
breakfast: *le petit-déjeuner*
brick; made of brick: *la brique; en brique*
bricklayer: *le maçon*
bridge (card game): *le bridge*
bridge (over river): *le pont*
broccoli: *le brocoli*
brother: *un frère*
brown: *brun, brune; marron*
brush: *une brosse*
Brussels sprouts: *les choux de Bruxelles*
builder: *un entrepreneur en bâtiment*
building: *un bâtiment, un édifice*
bull: *un taureau*
bus: *l'autobus, le bus*
bus (interurban): *le car*

bus stop: *un arrêt d'autobus*

business (private): *une société (privée)*

businessman: *un homme d'affaires*

butter: *le beurre*

buy (v.): *acheter*

buy-out: *le rachat*

by, through: *par*

cabbage: *le chou*

calf: *le mollet*

camcorder: *un caméscope*

camera: *un appareil photo*

can, be able to (v.): *pouvoir*

cancel (v.): *annuler*

cappuccino: *un cappuccino*

car: *une voiture*

card: *une carte*

carpet: *la moquette*

carrot: *une carotte*

carry (v.): *porter*

carton (of): *une brique de*

casual wear: *les vêtements de sport* (m.)

cauliflower: *le chou-fleur*

ceiling: *le plafond*

cellar: *la cave*

CEO: *le P.-D.G. (président-directeur général)*

chair: *une chaise*

chamber of commerce: *une chambre de commerce*

chamomile: *la camomille*

champagne: *le champagne*

change (pocket, loose): *la monnaie*

channel-surf (v.): *zapper*

check out (v.): *partir*

cheeks: *les joues* (f.)

cheese: *le fromage*

cherry: *la cerise*

chess: *un jeu d'échecs*

chessboard: *un échiquier* (m.)

chest: *la poitrine*

chicken: *la poule*

chicken (meat): *le poulet*

child: *un gosse, une gosse*

children's wear: *les vêtements pour enfants* (m.)

chin: *le menton*

china/glassware: *la vaisselle*

cinema: *le cinéma*

city hall: *la mairie, l'hôtel de ville*

clean: *propre*

clean the house (v.): *faire le ménage*

clinic: *une clinique*

closet: *le placard, une armoire*

club: *un club*

coat: *le manteau*

Coca-Cola: *un coca*

cod: *la morue*

coffee: *le café*

coffee cup: *une tasse à café*

coffee pot: *une cafetière*

coffee table: *une table basse*

coffee with milk: *un café crème*

college: *une université*

cologne: *l'eau de toilette* (f.)

comb: *un peigne*

come (v.): *venir*

comfortable: *à l'aise, bien* (used to describe persons, for example, *être bien dans une chaise confortable*)

companion: *le compagnon*

company: *une entreprise, une maison*

complaint: *une réclamation*

comprehend, understand (v.): *comprendre*

computer: *un ordinateur*

concert: *un concert*

condiments: *les condiments* (m.)

conductor (train): *le contrôleur*

conference, meeting: *une conférence, une réunion*

corner: *le coin*

correct (v.): *corriger*

corridor: *le corridor*

cost (v.): *coûter*

couch, sofa: *un sofa*

counter top: *le comptoir*

counter, check-out: *la caisse*

countryside: *la campagne*

cousin: *un cousin/une cousine*

cover (v.): *couvrir*

cow: *une vache*

crab: *le crabe*

cranberry: *la canneberge*
cream: *la crème*
credit card: *une carte de crédit*
crepes: *les crêpes* (m.)
croissant: *un croissant*
cup: *une tasse*
cure, heal (v.): *guérir*
curtains: *les rideaux* (m.)
customer service: *le service après-vente*
customs: *la douane*
cycling: *le cyclisme*
dance (ball): *une soirée (dansante)*
dance (v.): *danser*
date: *la date*
decaffeinated coffee: *un déca*
December: *décembre*
deck of cards: *un jeu de cartes*
den: *le living*
department (in a store): *le rayon*
department (of France): *un département*
dessert: *le dessert*
diary products: *les produits laitiers*
dictate (v.): *dicter*
dictionary: *un dictionnaire; un dico*
die (v.): *mourir*
dine out (v.): *aller au restaurant*
dining room: *la salle à manger*
dinner: *le dîner*
director: *le directeur*
dirty: *sale*
disco: *une discothèque*
dish: *un plat*
dishwasher: *lave-vaisselle*
do errands (v.): *faire les courses*
do nothing (v.): *ne rien faire*
do the dishes (v.): *faire la vaisselle*
do weight training (v.): *faire des *haltères* (m.)
do, make (v.): *faire*
doctor: *un médecin*
door: *la porte*
double bed: *un grand lit*
double boiler: *un bain-marie*
draught beer: *une pression*
draw (v.): *dessiner, tracer*

dream (v.): *rêver, songer*
dress: *la robe*
dresser: *le bureau*
drink: *une boisson*
drink (v.): *boire*
drive (v.): *conduire*
dry (adj.): *sec, sèche*
dry (v.): *sécher*
dryer: *le sèche-linge*
duck: *le canard*
during, while: *durant, pendant*
dust (v.): *épousseter*
ear: *une oreille*
early: *tôt*
eat (v.): *manger*
educate (v.): *éduquer; instruire*
egg: *un oeuf*
elbow: *le coude*
electrical appliances: *les appareils électriques* (m.)
elevator: *l'ascenseur* (m.)
employee: *un employé, une employée*
engineer: *un ingénieur*
enough: *assez*
enter (in) (v.): *entrer (dans)*
entrance: *l'entrée* (f.)
escalator: *l'escalator* (m.)
espresso: *un express, un café*
evening wear: *la tenue de soirée*
event: *une manifestation*
everywhere: *partout*
exchange money (v.): *changer de l'argent*
exercise (v.): *entraîner*
exit: *la sortie*
expensive: *cher, chère*
eye: *un oeil, les yeux*
eyebrows: *les sourcils* (m.)
eyelashes: *les cils*
eyelid: *la paupière*
face: *le visage, la figure*
facing, across from: *en face de*
factory: *une usine*
fail (v.): *rater (un examen)*
fall: *l'automne* (m.), *en automne*

fall (v.): *tomber*

false: *faux, fausse*

far: *loin*

far from (physical sense): *loin de*

farm: *une ferme*

fast (adj.): *rapide*

fast (adv.): *vite, rapidement*

fast (v.): *jeûner*

fasten (v.): *attacher*

father: *un père*

fats: *les matières grasses* (f.)

favorite: *favori, favorite*

fear: *la peur, la crainte*

fear (v.): *craindre, avoir peur de*

February: *février*

feel (touch) (v.): *sentir*

feel (well, ill, etc.) (v.): *se sentir*

fees (of artists, actors): *le cachet*

fees (professional; attorney): *les honoraires* (m.)

fennel: *le fenouil*

ferry: *le ferry, la navette*

few: *peu*

film (at the cinema): *un film*

film (for camera): *une pellicule*

film star: *une vedette*

find (v.): *trouver*

finger: *le doigt*

fingernail: *un ongle*

fire: *le feu*

fire (house fire): *un incendie*

Fire!: *Au feu!*

fire (v.): *licencier*

firm: *la firme, l'entreprise, la maison*

first course: *l'entrée*

first floor: *le rez-de-chaussée*

fish: *le poisson*

fishing: *faire de la pêche*

fist: *le poing*

flashlight: *une torche électrique*

flour: *la farine*

flower: *une fleur*

follow (v.): *suivre*

foolish: *fou, folle*

foot: *le pied*

football: *le football américain*

for: *pour*

for fear of (prep.): *de peur de*

for fear that (conj.): *de peur que*

forehead: *le front*

foreigner: *un étranger, une étrangère*

fork: *une fourchette*

franchise: *une franchise*

frank: *franc, franche*

fresh: *frais, fraîche*

Friday: *vendredi*

fridge: *le frigo*

friendly: *amical, sympa*

from (indicating a direction): *du côté de*

from, of, about: *de*

fruit: *le fruit*

fruit juice: *un jus de fruit*

full (glass): *plein, pleine*

full (hotel, etc.): *complet*

full (satisfied): *rassassié(e)*

furniture: *les meubles* (m.)

game: *un jeu*

garage: *le garage*

garden, yard: *le jardin*

garlic: *l'ail* (m.)

gentle: *gentil, gentille*

get bored (v.): *s'ennuyer*

gift: *un cadeau*

gin: *le gin*

girl, daughter: *une fille*

give (v.): *donner*

glass: *un verre*

gloves: *les gants*

go away (v.): *s'en aller*

go down (v.): *descendre*

go for a drive (v.): *faire une promenade en voiture*

go for a jog (v.): *faire du jogging*

go for a walk (v.): *faire une promenade*

go out with, date (v.): *sortir (avec)*

go sailing (v.): *faire de la voile*

go to bed (v.): *aller au lit, dormir*

go to/use the bathroom (no real equivalent): *aller prendre un bain; aller aux cabinets, etc.*

go to the beach (v.): *aller à la plage*

go up (v.): *monter*

go (v.): *aller*

goal: *le but*

golf: *le golf*

good: *bon, bonne*

goose: *l'oie* (f.)

grade school: *l'école primaire* (f.)

graduate (v.): *recevoir un diplôme*

grape: *un raisin*

grapefruit: *le pamplemousse*

green: *vert, verte*

green beans: *les haricots verts* (m.)

gross (salary): *brut*

grow (v.): *grandir*

guide: *le guide*

guidebook: *un guide*

hair: *les cheveux* (m.)

hair dryer: *un sèchoir-cheveux*

hairdresser: *la coiffeuse*

half-fat: *demi-écrémé*

ham: *le jambon*

hand: *la main*

handsome, pretty: *beau, bel, belle*

hang-gliding: *(le sport du) deltaplane*

hardly: *ne … guère*

hat: *le chapeau*

hate (v.): *détester, haïr*

have a college degree (v.): *être diplômé(e)*

have a Master's degree (v.): *avoir une licence*

head: *la tête*

hear (v.): *entendre*

heart: *le cœur*

heater: *le chauffage*

heel: *le talon*

help: *l'aide* (f.), *l'assistance* (f.)

help (v.): *aider*

Help!: *Au secours!*

herbs: *les fines herbes* (f.)

here: *ici*

high school: *le lycée*

hike: *une randonnée*

hiker: *un randonneur, une randonneuse (à pied)*

hips: *les hanches* (f.)

hire (v.): *embaucher*

hockey: *le hockey*

hold (v.): *tenir*

home furnishings: *la décoration d'intérieur*

hostel: *une auberge*

hot chocolate: *un chocolat chaud*

hotel: *un hôtel*

hotel desk: *la réception*

hotel phone operator: *le/la standardiste*

hour: *une heure*

house: *la maison*

how: *comment*

how much: *combien*

ice cream: *la glace*

ice cream, chocolate: *la glace au chocolat*

ice cream, vanilla: *la glace à la vanille*

ice rink: *une patinoire*

ice skates: *les patins à glace* (m.)

in, inside of: *dans*

in back of, behind: *derrière*

in front of: *devant*

in the back: *au fond*

in, on, to: *en*

in, on, to (countries, etc.): *en*

income tax: *l'impôt sur le revenu* (m.)

incorporation: *S.A. (Société Anonyme)*

infant: *un enfant, une enfant*

inside: *dedans*

instant coffee: *un nescafé*

institute (private): *un institut*

intestines: *les intestins* (m.)

jacket: *la veste*

January: *janvier*

jeans: *le blue-jean*

jewelry: *la bijouterie*

joint: *une articulation*

juice: *un jus (de pomme, etc.)*

July: *juillet*

June: *juin*

ketchup: *la sauce tomate*

kidneys: *les reins* (m.)

king: *un roi*

kiss: *un baiser, un bisou*

kiss (v.): *embrasser*

kitchen: *la cuisine*

kitchenware: *la vaisselle* (m.), *les ustensiles de cuisine* (m.)

kiwi: *le kiwi*

knee: *le genou*

knife: *un couteau*

knitting: *le tricot*

knock (at the door) (v.): *frapper (à la porte)*

know how to (v.): *savoir*

know, understand (v.): *connaître*

lady: *une dame*

lamb: *l'agneau* (m.)

lamb chop: *la côte d'agneau*

lamp: *la lampe*

lane, place, circle, etc.: *une rue*

langoustine: *la langoustine*

language: *la langue*

late: *tard*

later: *plus tard*

launderette: *la blanchisserie*

lawn: *la pelouse*

lawyer: *un avocat/une avocate*

lay, place, put (v.): *placer, mettre*

learn (v.): *apprendre*

lease: *un bail (à loyer)*

lease (v.): *louer*

leather goods: *la maroquinerie*

leave (v.): *partir*

leave (from) (v.): *partir de, quitter*

leave (something behind) (v.): *laisser*

leg: *la jambe*

leisure activities: *les loisirs* (m.)

leisure time: *le temps libre*

lemon: *le citron*

lemonade: *une limonade*

library: *la bibliothèque*

lie (tell falsehood) (v.): *mentir*

ligament: *le ligament*

light bulb: *une ampoule*

lime: *le citron vert*

linens: *le linge de maison*

lips: *les lèvres* (f.)

listen to (v.): *écouter (à la radio, etc.)*

live (in) (v.): *vivre (à), habiter (à, dans)*

liver: *le foie*

lobster: *le homard*

locker: *le casier*

long: *long, longue*

long-distance call: *un appel interurbain*

look for (v.): *chercher*

lose weight (v.): *maigrir*

loss: *une perte*

love, like (v.): *aimer*

luggage: *les bagages*

lunch: *le déjeuner*

lungs: *les poumons* (m.)

mackerel: *le maquereau*

magazine: *un magazine*

maid, housekeeper: *la femme de chambre*

main course: *le plat de résistance*

maitre d': *le maître d'hôtel*

make a meal (v.): *préparer un repas*

make-up: *le maquillage*

man, sir: *un homme, un monsieur*

manage (v.): *gérer*

management: *la gestion*

mango: *la mangue*

map (city): *un plan de ville*

map (country): *une carte*

March: *mars*

margarine: *la margarine*

market: *le marché*

marketing: *le marketing*

match: *un match (de football, etc.)*

mattress: *le matelas*

May: *mai*

meals: *les repas* (m.)

meat: *la viande*

meet (for the first time) (v.): *faire la connaissance de*

meet (in passing) (v.): *rencontrer*

melon: *un melon*

member: *un membre*

men's wear: *les vêtements pour hommes* (m.)

menu: *la carte*

metal; made of metal: *le métal; en métal*

middle school/junior high school: *le collège*

milk: *le lait*

mineral water: *l'eau minérale*

minimum wage: *le smic*

mirror: *le miroir*

misunderstanding: *une méprise*

modem: *un modem*

modern: *moderne*

Monday: *lundi*

money: *l'argent*

month: *un mois*

mortgage: *l'hypothèque* (f.)

mother: *une mère*

mountain bike: *un V.T.T. (vélo à tout terrain)*

mountaineering: *l'alpinisme* (m.)

mouth: *la bouche*

movie camera: *une caméra*

mow the lawn (v.): *tondre la pelouse*

much, a lot: *beaucoup*

muscle: *le muscle*

museum: *un musée*

music: *la musique*

musical instrument: *un instrument de musique*

must, to have to: *devoir*

mustard: *la moutarde*

napkin: *une serviette*

near, close to: *près de*

neck: *le cou*

necklace: *un collier*

neighborhood: *le quartier, le voisinage*

nerves: *les nerfs* (m.)

net (salary): *net*

new: *nouveau, nouvel, nouvelle*

newspaper: *un journal*

next day, the: *le lendemain*

next to, beside: *à côté de*

no more: *ne ... plus*

no one: *ne ... personne*

no smoking: *défense de fumer*

noisy: *bruyant*

nose: *le nez*

nothing: *ne ... rien*

November: *novembre*

now: *maintenant*

nursery school: *l'école maternelle* (f.)

nuts: *les noix* (f.)

October: *octobre*

offer (v.): *offrir*

office; offices: *le bureau* (m.); *les bureaux* (pl.)

office: *branche; une succursale*

office: *main, head; le siège social*

office supervisor: *le superviseur, le chef de bureau*

often: *souvent*

old: *vieux, vieil, vieille*

olive oil: *l'huile d'olive*

olives: *les olives*

Olympic Games: *les jeux Olympiques*

on (in a physical sense): *sur*

on condition of (prep.): *à condition de*

on condition that (conj.): *à condition que*

on the third (etc.) floor: *au troisième étage*

on the verge of: *prêt de*

one-story house: *une maison sans étage*

onion: *un oignon*

open (v.): *ouvrir*

opponent: *l'adversaire*

orange: *une orange*

orangeade: *une orangeade*

outside: *à l'extérieur, dehors*

outside of: *en dehors de*

outside of (physical sense): *hors de*

oven: *le four*

over there: *là-bas*

package: *un colis*

pajamas: *le pyjama* (singular in French)

pants: *la pantalon* (singular in French)

pantyhose: *le collant*

paper: *le papier*

parking lot: *le parking*

parsley: *le persil*

pass a course successfully (v.): *réussir à un cours*

passport: *le passeport*

pastry: *les pâtisseries* (f.)

pay (military, civil service): *le traitement*

pay (of housekeepers, etc.): *les gages* (m.)

pay (parlement, government): *l'indemnité* (f.)

paycheck: *un chèque de salaire*

pay day: *le jour de paie*

pay slip: *la feuille de paie*

pay (v.): *payer*

pay the bill (v.): *régler la note*

peach: *une pêche*

pear: *une poire*

peas: *les petits pois* (m.)

pencil: *un crayon*

pepper: *le poivre*

Pepsi: *un pepsi*

perch: *la perche*

performance: *un spectacle*

perfumes: *la parfumerie*

person: *une personne*

photography: *la photographie*

pillow: *un oreiller*

pineapple: *l'ananas* (m.)

pitcher, carafe: *une carafe*

place mat: *un set de table*

place setting: *le couvert*

plant: *la plante*

plate: *une assiette*

play (v.): *jouer (de la guitare, aux cartes)*

player: *un joueur*

plum: *la prune*

policeman: *un agent de police*

pork: *le porc*

pork chop: *la côte de porc*

post office: *la poste*

potato: *une pomme de terre*

poultry: *la volaille*

premises: *les locaux* (m.)

profit: *le profit, un bénéfice*

profit margin: *la marge bénéficiaire*

program, on TV: *une émission*

prostate: *la prostate*

provided that (conj.): *pourvu que*

public: *public, publique*

pulse: *le pouls*

put (v.): *mettre*

quail: *la caille*

queen: *une reine*

quickly: *tout de suite, rapidement*

quiet: *calme*

rabbit: *le lapin*

race: *un concours*

radiator: *le radiateur*

rain: *la pluie*

rain (v.): *pleuvoir*

raincoat: *un imperméable*

raise: *une augmentation de salaire*

raisin: *un raisin sec*

raspberry: *la framboise*

razor: *un rasoir*

read (v.): *lire*

reading: *une lecture*

receipt: *un reçu*

receive (v.): *recevoir*

reception: *la réception*

red: *rouge*

red currant: *la groseille*

red wine: *le vin rouge*

referee: *un arbitre*

reflect (v.): *réfléchir*

remain, stay (v.): *rester*

remote control: *un zappeur*

rent: *le loyer*

rent day: *le jour du terme*

rent (v.): *louer*

restaurant: *le restaurant*

restrooms: *les toilettes* (f.)

retail business: *la vente au détail*

retire (v.): *prendre sa retraite*

ribs: *les côtes* (f.)

rolls: *les petits pains*

roof: *le toit*

room (in a house): *la pièce*

room (in hotel): *la chambre*

rooster: *un coq*

rosemary: *le romarin*

round: *rond, ronde*

rug: *le tapis*

rugby: *le rugby*

rum: *le rhum*

run (v.): *courir*

runway: *la piste*

rye bread: *le pain de seigle*

safe (lockbox): *le coffre-fort*

safe (secure): *sauf, sauve*

sailing: *(faire de) la voile*

salad: *la salade*

salad oil: *l'huile* (f.)

salary (worker's salary): *le salaire*

sales: *les ventes*
sales rep: *un représentant, une représentante*
salesperson: *un vendeur, une vendeuse*
salmon: *le saumon*
salt: *le sel*
sandwich: *un sandwich*
sandwich with cheese: *un sandwich au fromage*
sandwich with ham: *un sandwich au jambon*
Saturday: *samedi*
sauce: *la sauce*
saucer: *une soucoupe*
sausage: *la saucisse*
say (v.): *dire*
scales (bathroom): *un pèse-personne*
scales (fish): *les écailles* (f.)
scales (in the market): *la balance*
scallops: *les coquilles Saint-Jacques* (f.)
school: *une école*
seafood: *les fruits de mer*
seat: *la place*
secretary: *le secrétaire, la secrétaire*
security guard: *le gardien*
see (v.): *voir*
sell (v.): *vendre*
September: *septembre*
series ("soap"): *un feuilleton*
serve (v.): *servir*
service charge, tip: *le service*
serving spoon: *une grande cuillère*
set the table (v.): *mettre la table*
sheet: *un drap*
shelf: *un rayon*
shellfish: *les crustacés* (m.)
shirt: *la chemise*
shoes: *les chaussures* (f.)
shop (v.): *faire du shopping*
shopping bag: *un sac*
shorts: *le short*
shoulder: *une épaule*
shower: *la douche*
shrimp: *la crevette*
sick, ill: *malade, avoir mal à (au)*
sideways: *de côté*
since, for: *depuis*

sink (bathroom): *un lavabo*
sink (kitchen): *un évier*
sister: *une sœur*
skeleton: *le squelette*
ski slope: *la piste*
ski (v.): *skier, faire du ski*
skiing: *le ski*
skin: *la peau*
skirt: *la jupe*
skull: *le crâne*
sleep (v.): *dormir*
slippers: *les pantoufles* (m.)
slowly: *lentement, doucement*
small town: *une petite ville*
snack: *le casse-croûte*
snails: *les escargots* (m.)
soap: *le savon*
soccer: *le football*
socks: *les chaussettes* (f.)
soft: *doux, douce*
sole (shoe): *la plante des pieds*
sometimes: *quelquefois*
son: *un fils*
soon: *bientôt*
soup bowl: *une assiette creuse*
sour cream: *la crème fraîche*
spine: *la colonne vertébrale*
spoon: *une cuillère*
sport: *un sport*
spring: *le printemps, au printemps*
squid: *l'encornet* (m.)
square (form): *carré*
square (town): *une place*
stadium: *un stade*
stairs: *l'escalier* (m.)
starter: *le hors-d'œuvre*
stereo: *une chaîne-stéréo*
steward: *le steward*
stewardess: *une hôtesse*
stomach: *l'estomac* (m.)
store: *le magasin*
storm (thunder): *une tempête, un orage*
stormy: *orageux, orageuse*
story; first floor: *l'étage; à l'étage*

story (history): *une histoire*

stranger: *un inconnu*

strawberry: *la fraise*

street: *une rue*

stroll (v.): *faire une promenade*

study (v.): *étudier*

subsidiary: *une filiale*

subway: *le métro*

succeed (v.): *réussir*

sugar: *le sucre*

suit (man's): *le costume*

suit (v.): *convenir à*

suitcase: *une valise*

summer: *l'été* (m.), *en été*

Sunday: *dimanche*

supper: *le souper*

sweater: *le pull*

swimming pool: *une piscine*

swimsuit: *le maillot*

table: *la table*

table cloth: *une nappe*

take (v.): *prendre*

take a bath (v.): *prendre un bain*

take a course (v.): *suivre un cours*

take a shower (v.): *prendre une douche*

take a test (v.): *passer un examen*

take notes (v.): *prendre des notes*

take-home pay: *le salaire reçu*

tap, faucet: *le robinet*

tea: *le thé*

tea bag: *un sachet de thé*

teach (v.): *enseigner*

teacher: *un professeur*

telephone: *le téléphone*

telephone (to) (v.): *téléphoner à*

television: *une télévision, la télé*

tendon: *le tendon*

tennis: *le tennis*

tennis shoes: *les tennis* (m.)

terrace: *la terrasse*

theater: *le théâtre*

then: *ensuite, puis*

there: *là*

thief: *un voleur*

Thief!: *Au voleur!*

thigh: *la cuisse*

think (v.): *penser*

throat: *la gorge*

throw (v.): *lancer*

thumb: *le pouce*

Thursday: *jeudi*

thyme: *le thym*

ticket: *un ticket, un billet*

tie: *la cravate*

time (general, as well as weather): *le temps*

time (one time, etc.): *une fois*

tip (in addition to service charge): *le pourboire*

tip (included in bill): *le service*

tip included: *service compris*

tip not included: *service non compris*

tip (v.): *laisser un pourboire*

tisane: *une tisane*

to, at, in: *à*

to, at, in (with places or place names): *à*

today: *aujourd'hui*

toe: *un orteil*

toilet tissue: *le papier hygiénique, le p.h.*

toilet water: *l'eau de toilette* (f.)

tomorrow: *demain*

tongue: *la langue*

tonight: *ce soir*

too: *trop*

tooth: *une dent*

toothpaste: *la pâte dentifrice*

tourist: *un/une touriste*

toothbrush: *une brosse à dents*

toward: *vers*

towel: *un drap de bain, une serviette*

town: *une ville*

toy: *un jouet*

track and field: *l'athlétisme*

train: *le train*

translate (v.): *traduire*

travel, trip: *un voyage, une excursion*

travel (v.): *voyager*

tree: *un arbre*

trout: *la truite*

T-shirt: *le tee-shirt*

Tuesday: *mardi*
tuna: *le thon*
turkey: *la dinde*
turn (v.): *tourner*
turnip: *le navet*
two-story house: *une maison avec étage*
umbrella: *un parapluie*
uncle: *un oncle*
under: *sous*
underwear: *la lingerie; le sous-vêtement*
unfriendly: *inamical*
United States: *les États-Unis* (m.)
university: *une université*
unless (conj.): *à moins que*
unless (prep.): *à moins de*
until (conj.): *jusqu'à ce que*
until (prep.): *jusqu'à*
upstairs: *à l'étage*
useful: *utile*
utility (public): *un service public*
vacant: *libre*
vase: *une vase*
VCR: *un magnétoscope*
veal: *le veau*
vegetables: *les légumes*
vein: *une veine*
venison: *la venaison*
very: *très*
vest: *le gilet*
victim: *une victime*
video camera: *un caméscope*
view: *une vue*
village: *un village*
vinegar: *le vinaigre*
visit (monuments) (v.): *visiter*
visit (persons) (v.): *aller voir; rendre visite à*
vodka: *la vodka*
waist: *la taille*
wait for (v.): *attendre*
waiter: *le serveur*
waitress: *la serveuse*
wall: *le mur*
wallet: *le portefeuille*
warehouse: *un entrepôt*

washcloth: *un gant de toilette*
washing machine: *une machine à laver*
watch: *une montre*
watch (v.): *regarder (la télé, etc.)*
water (some water): *l'eau (de l'eau)*
water closet: *les cabinets, le petit coin, le WC*
watercress: *le cresson*
Wednesday: *mercredi*
week: *une semaine*
well: *bien*
when: *quand*
where: *où*
whisky: *le whisky*
white: *blanc, blanche*
white bread: *le pain*
white wine: *un vin blanc*
who: *qui*
whole milk: *le lait entier*
wholesale business: *la vente en gros*
why: *pourquoi*
window: *la fenêtre*
wine: *le vin*
wine steward: *le sommelier*
winter: *l'hiver (m.), en hiver*
wish, want (v.): *vouloir*
with: *avec*
without (conj.): *sans que*
without (prep.): *sans*
woman: *une femme*
women's wear: *les vêtements pour femmes* (m.)
wood; wooden: *le bois; en bois*
work (v.): *travailler*
worker: *un ouvrier, une ouvrière*
workshop: *un atelier*
wrestling: *(le sport de) la lutte*
wrestling (tag team): *le catch à quatre*
wrist: *le poignet*
write (v.): *écrire*
year: *un an, une année*
yellow: *jaune*
yesterday: *hier*
yoga: *le yoga*
yogurt: *le yaourt*

APPENDIX B
Verb Conjugation Charts

The past participles of verbs conjugated with *être* in compound tenses agree with the subject pronoun.

aller

subject	present	passé composé	imperfect	future
je	vais	suis allé(e)	allais	irai
tu	vas	es allé(e)	allais	iras
il/on	va	est allé	allait	ira
elle	va	est allée	allait	ira
nous	allons	sommes allés	allions	irons
vous	allez	êtes allé	alliez	irez
ils	vont	sont allés	allaient	iront
elles	vont	sont allées	allaient	iront

subject	conditionnel	pres. subj.	simple past	imperative
j'	irais	aille	allai	
tu	irais	ailles	allas	va
il/elle/on	irait	aille	alla	
nous	irions	allions	allâmes	allons
vous	iriez	alliez	allâtes	allez
ils/elles	iraient	aillent	allèrent	

present participle: *allant*   past participle: *allé(e)*

future perfect: *je serai allé(e)*   past conditional: *je serais allé(e)*

pluperfect: *j'étais allé(e)*   past subj.: *je sois allé(e)*

avoir

subject	present	passé composé	imperfect	future
j'	ai	ai eu	avais	aurai
tu	as	as eu	avais	auras
il/elle/on	a	a eu	avait	aura
nous	avons	avons eu	avions	aurons
vous	avez	avez eu	aviez	aurez
ils/elles	ont	ont eu	avaient	auront

subject	conditionnel	pres. subj.	simple past	imperative
j'	aurais	aie	eus	
tu	aurais	aies	eus	aie
il/elle/on	aurait	ait	eut	
nous	aurions	ayons	eûmes	ayons
vous	auriez	ayez	eûtes	ayez
ils/elles	auraient	aient	eurent	

present participle: *ayant*   past participle: *eu*

future perfect: *j'aurai eu*   past conditional: *j'aurais eu*

pluperfect: *j'avais eu*   past subj.: *j'aie eu*

boire

subject	present	passé composé	imperfect	future
je	bois	ai bu	buvais	boirai
tu	bois	as bu	buvais	boiras
il/elle/on	boit	a bu	buvait	boira
nous	buvons	avons bu	buvions	boirons
vous	buvez	avez bu	buviez	boirez
ils/elles	boivent	ont bu	buvaient	boiront

subject	conditionnel	pres. subj.	simple past	imperative
je	boirais	boive	bus	
tu	boirais	boives	bus	bois
il/elle/on	boirait	boive	but	
nous	boirions	buvions	bûmes	buvons
vous	boiriez	buviez	bûtes	buvez
ils/elles	boiraient	boivent	burent	

present participle: *buvant*   past participle: *bu*

future perfect: *j'aurai bu*   past conditional: *j'aurais bu*

pluperfect: *j'avais bu*   past subj.: *j'aie bu*

connaître, naître*, reconnaître

subject	present	passé composé	imperfect	future
je	connais	ai connu	connaissais	connaîtrai
tu	connais	as connu	connaissais	connaîtras
il/elle/on	connaît	a connu	connaissait	connaîtra
nous	connaissons	avons connu	connaissions	connaîtrons
vous	connaissez	avez connu	connaissiez	connaîtrez
ils/elles	connaissent	ont connu	connaissaient	connaîtront

subject	conditionnel	pres. subj.	simple past	imperative
je	connaîtrais	connaisse	connus	
tu	connaîtrais	connaisses	connus	connais

subject	conditionnel	pres. subj.	simple past	imperative
il/elle/on	connaîtrait	connaisse	connut	
nous	connaîtrions	connaissions	connûmes	connaissons
vous	connaîtriez	connaissiez	connûtes	connaissez
ils/elles	connaîtraient	connaissent	connurent	

present participle: *connaissant*   past participle: *connu*

future perfect: *j'aurai connu*   past conditional: *j'aurais connu*

pluperfect: *j'avais connu*   past subj.: *j'aie connu*

*naître *is used primarily in the* passé composé *and is conjugated with* être *in compound tenses; past participle:* né(e)(s).

convaincre, vaincre

subject	present	passé composé	imperfect	future
je	convaincs	ai convaincu	convainquais	convaincrai
tu	convaincs	as convaincu	convainquais	convaincras
il/elle/on	convainc	a convaincu	convainquait	convaincra
nous	convainquons	avons convaincu	convainquions	convaincrons
vous	convainquez	avez convaincu	convainquiez	convaincrez
ils/elles	convainquent	ont convaincu	convainquaient	convaincront

subject	conditionnel	pres. subj.	simple past	imperative
je	convaincrais	convainque	convainquis	
tu	convaincrais	convainques	convainquis	convaincs
il/elle/on	convaincrait	convainque	convainquit	
nous	convaincrions	convainquions	convainquîmes	convainquons
vous	convaincriez	convainquiez	convainquîtes	convainquez
ils/elles	convaincraient	convainquent	convainquirent	

past participle: *convaincu*   past conditional: *j'aurais convaincu*

future perfect: *j'aurai convaincu*   past subj.: *j'aie convaincu*

pluperfect: *j'avais convaincu*

courir, parcourir

subject	present	passé composé	imperfect	future
je	cours	ai couru	courais	courrai
tu	cours	as couru	courais	courras
il/elle/on	court	a couru	courait	courra
nous	courons	avons couru	courions	courrons
vous	courez	avez couru	couriez	courrez
ils/elles	courent	ont couru	couraient	courront

subject	conditionnel	pres. subj.	simple past	imperative
je	courrais	coure	courus	
tu	courrais	coures	courus	cours
il/elle/on	courrait	coure	courut	
nous	courrions	courions	courûmes	courons
vous	courriez	couriez	courûtes	courez
ils/elles	courraient	courent	coururent	

present participle: *courant*   past participle: *couru*

future perfect: *j'aurai couru*   past conditional: *j'aurais couru*

pluperfect: *j'avais couru*   past subj.: *j'aie couru*

croire

subject	present	passé composé	imperfect	future
je	crois	ai cru	croyais	croirai
tu	crois	as cru	croyais	croiras
il/elle/on	croit	a cru	croyait	croira
nous	croyons	avons cru	croyions	croirons
vous	croyez	avez cru	croyiez	croirez
ils/elles	croient	ont cru	croyaient	croiront

subject	conditionnel	pres. subj.	simple past	imperative
je	croirais	croie	crus	
tu	croirais	croies	crus	crois
il/elle/on	croirait	croie	crut	
nous	croirions	croyions	crûmes	croyons
vous	croiriez	croyiez	crûtes	croyez
ils/elles	croiraient	croient	crurent	

present participle: *croyant*   past participle: *cru*

future perfect: *j'aurai cru*   past conditional: *j'aurais cru*

pluperfect: *j'avais cru*   past subj.: *j'aie cru*

conduire, détruire, construire, réduire, reproduire, séduire, traduire

subject	present	passé composé	imperfect	future
je	conduis	ai conduit	conduisais	conduirai
tu	conduis	as conduit	conduisais	conduiras
il/elle/on	conduit	a conduit	conduisait	conduira
nous	conduisons	avons conduit	conduisions	conduirons
vous	conduisez	avez conduit	conduisiez	conduirez
ils/elles	conduisent	ont conduit	conduisaient	conduiront

subject	conditionnel	pres. subj.	simple past	imperative
je	conduirais	conduise	conduisis	
tu	conduirais	conduises	conduisis	conduis
il/elle/on	conduirait	conduise	conduisit	
nous	conduirions	conduisions	conduisîmes	conduisons
vous	conduiriez	conduisiez	conduisîtes	conduisez
ils/elles	conduiraient	conduisent	conduisirent	

present participle: *conduisant* past participle: *conduit*

future perfect: *j'aurai conduit* past conditional: *j'aurais conduit*

pluperfect: *j'avais conduit* past subj.: *j'aie conduit*

coûter

Used primarily in the third person to mean "it costs/they cost."

subject	present	passé composé	imperfect	future
il/elle/cela	coûte	a coûté	coûtait	coûtera
ils/elles	coûtent	ont coûté	coûtaient	coûteront

subject	conditionnel	pres. subj.	simple past	imperative
il/elle/cela	coûterait	coûte	coûta	
ils/elles	coûteraient	coûtent	coûtèrent	

present participle: *coûtant* past participle: *coûté*

future perfect: *il/elle aura coûté* past conditional: *il/elle aurait coûté*

pluperfect: *il/elle avait coûté* past subj.: *il/elle ait coûté*

devoir

subject	present	passé composé	imperfect	future
je	dois	ai dû	devais	devrai
tu	dois	as dû	devais	devras
il/elle/on	doit	a dû	devait	devra
nous	devons	avons dû	devions	devrons
vous	devez	avez dû	deviez	devrez
ils/elles	doivent	ont dû	devaient	devront

subject	conditionnel	pres. subj.	simple past	imperative
je	devrais	doive	dus	
tu	devrais	doives	dus	dois
il/elle/on	devrait	doive	dut	
nous	devrions	devions	dûmes	devons
vous	devriez	deviez	dûtes	devez
ils/elles	devraient	doivent	durent	

present participle: *devant* past participle: *dû*

future perfect: *j'aurai dû* past conditional: *j'aurais dû*

pluperfect: *j'avais dû* past subj.: *j'aie dû*

dire, interdire, prédire

subject	present	passé composé	imperfect	future
je	dis	ai dit	disais	dirai
tu	dis	as dit	disais	diras
il/elle/on	dit	a dit	disait	dira
nous	disons	avons dit	disions	dirons
vous	dites	avez dit	disiez	direz
ils/elles	disent	ont dit	disaient	diront

subject	conditionnel	pres. subj.	simple past	imperative
je	dirais	dise	dis	
tu	dirais	dises	dis	dis
il/elle/on	dirait	dise	dit	
nous	dirions	disions	dîmes	disons
vous	diriez	disiez	dîtes	dites
ils/elles	diraient	disent	dirent	

present participle: *disant*   past participle: *dit*

future perfect: *j'aurai dit*   past conditional: *j'aurais dit*

pluperfect: *j'avais dit*   past subj.: *j'aie dit*

écrire, décrire, récrire

subject	present	passé composé	imperfect	future
j'	écris	ai écrit	écrivais	écrirai
tu	écris	as écrit	écrivais	écriras
il/elle/on	écrit	a écrit	écrivait	écrira
nous	écrivons	avons écrit	écrivions	écrirons
vous	écrivez	avez écrit	écriviez	écrirez
ils/elles	écrivent	ont écrit	écrivaient	écriront

subject	conditionnel	pres. subj.	simple past	imperative
j'	écrirais	écrive	écrivis	
tu	écrirais	écrives	écrivis	écris
il/elle/on	écrirait	écrive	écrivit	
nous	écririons	écrivions	écrivîmes	écrivons
vous	écririez	écriviez	écrivîtes	écrivez
ils/elles	écriraient	écrivent	écrivirent	

present participle: *écrivant*   past participle: *écrit*

future perfect: *j'aurai écrit*   past conditional: *j'aurais écrit*

pluperfect: *j'avais écrit*   past subj.: *j'aie écrit*

être

subject	present	passé composé	imperfect	future
je	suis	ai été	étais	serai
tu	es	as été	étais	seras
il/elle/on	est	a été	était	sera
nous	sommes	avons été	étions	serons
vous	êtes	avez été	étiez	serez
ils/elles	sont	ont été	étaient	seront
subject	conditionnel	pres. subj.	simple past	imperative
je	serais	sois	fus	
tu	serais	sois	fus	sois
il/elle/on	serait	soit	fut	
nous	serions	soyons	fûmes	soyons
vous	seriez	soyez	fûtes	soyez
ils/elles	seraient	soient	furent	

present participle: *étant*   past participle: *été*

future perfect: *j'aurai été*   past conditional: *aurais été*

pluperfect: *j'avais été*   past subj.: *j'aie été*

faire

subject	present	passé composé	imperfect	future
je	fais	ai fait	faisais	ferai
tu	fais	as fait	faisais	feras
il/elle/on	fait	a fait	faisait	fera
nous	faisons	avons fait	faisions	ferons
vous	faites	avez fait	faisiez	ferez
ils/elles	font	ont fait	faisaient	feront
subject	conditionnel	pres. subj.	simple past	imperative
je	ferais	fasse	fis	
tu	ferais	fasses	fis	fais
il/elle/on	ferait	fasse	fit	
nous	ferions	fassions	fîmes	faisons
vous	feriez	fassiez	fîtes	faites
ils/elles	feraient	fassent	firent	

present participle: *faisant*   past participle: *fait*

future perfect: *j'aurai fait*   past conditional: *j'aurais fait*

pluperfect: *j'avais fait*   past subj.: *j'aie fait*

falloir

Used only in the third person singular with an impersonal subject (*il*) to mean "it is necessary."

subject	present	passé composé	imperfect	future
il	faut	a fallu	fallait	faudra
subject	conditionnel	pres. subj.	simple past	imperative
il	faudrait	faille	fallut	

past participle: *fallu*　　　　past conditional: *il aurait fallu*

future perfect: *il aura fallu*　　past subj.: *il ait fallu*

pluperfect: *il avait fallu*

lire

subject	present	passé composé	imperfect	future
je	lis	ai lu	lisais	lirai
tu	lis	as lu	lisais	liras
il/elle/on	lit	a lu	lisait	lira
nous	lisons	avons lu	lisions	lirons
vous	lisez	avez lu	lisiez	lirez
ils/elles	lisent	ont lu	lisaient	liront
subject	conditionnel	pres. subj.	simple past	imperative
je	lirais	lise	lus	
tu	lirais	lises	lus	lis
il/elle/on	lirait	lise	lut	
nous	lirions	lisions	lûmes	lisons
vous	liriez	lisiez	lûtes	lisez
il/elles	liraient	lisent	lurent	

present participle: *lisant*　　　　past participle: *lu*

future perfect: *j'aurai lu*　　　　past conditional: *j'aurais lu*

pluperfect: *j'avais lu*　　　　　past subj.: *j'aie lu*

mourir*

subject	present	passé composé	imperfect	future
je	meurs	suis mort(e)	mourais	mourrai
tu	meurs	es mort(e)	mourais	mourras
il/elle/on	meurt	est mort(e)	mourait	mourra
nous	mourons	sommes mort(e)s	mourions	mourrons
vous	mourez	êtes mort(e)(s)	mouriez	mourrez
ils/elles	meurent	sont mort(e)s	mouraient	mourront

*Conjugated with être in compound tenses.

subject	conditionnel	pres. subj.	simple past	imperative
je	mourrais	meure	mourus	
tu	mourrais	meures	mourus	meurs
il/elle/on	mourrait	meure	mourut	
nous	mourrions	mourions	mourûmes	mourons
vous	mourriez	mouriez	mourûtes	mourez
ils/elles	mourraient	meurent	moururent	

present participle: *mourant*   past participle: *mort(e)(s)*

future perfect: *je serai mort(e)*   past conditional: *je serais mort(e)*

pluperfect: *j'étais mort(e)*   past subj.: *je sois mort(e)*

ouvrir, découvrir, couvrir, offrir, souffrir

subject	present	passé composé	imperfect	future
j'	ouvre	ai ouvert	ouvrais	ouvrirai
tu	ouvres	as ouvert	ouvrais	ouvriras
il/elle/on	ouvre	a ouvert	ouvrait	ouvrira
nous	ouvrons	avons ouvert	ouvrions	ouvrirons
vous	ouvrez	avez ouvert	ouvriez	ouvrirez
ils/elles	ouvrent	ont ouvert	ouvraient	ouvriront

subject	conditionnel	pres. subj.	simple past	imperative
j'	ouvrirais	ouvre	ouvris	
tu	ouvrirais	ouvres	ouvris	ouvre
il/elle/on	ouvrirait	ouvre	ouvrit	
nous	ouvririons	ouvrions	ouvrîmes	ouvrons
vous	ouvririez	ouvriez	ouvrîtes	ouvrez
ils/elles	ouvriraient	ouvrent	ouvrirent	

present participle: *ouvrant*   past participle: *ouvert*

future perfect: *j'aurai ouvert*   past conditional: *j'aurais ouvert*

pluperfect: *j'avais ouvert*   past subj.: *j'aie ouvert*

partir*, sortir*, servir, dormir, s'endormir*, sentir, se sentir*, ressentir, pressentir, mentir

subject	present	passé composé	imperfect	future
je	pars	suis parti(e)	partais	partirai
tu	pars	es parti(e)	partais	partiras
il/on	part	est parti	partait	partira
elle	part	est partie	partait	partira
nous	partons	sommes partis	partions	partirons
vous	partez	êtes parti	partiez	partirez
ils	partent	sont partis	partaient	partiront
elles	partent	sont parties	partaient	partiront

subject	conditionnel	pres. subj.	simple past	imperative
je	partirais	parte	partis	
tu	partirais	partes	partis	pars
il/elle/on	partirait	parte	partit	
nous	partirions	partions	partîmes	partons
vous	partiriez	partiez	partîtes	partez
ils/elles	partiraient	partent	partirent	

present participle: *partant* past participle: *parti*

future perfect: *je serai parti(e)* past conditional: *je serais parti(e)*

pluperfect: *j'étais parti(e)* past subj.: *je sois parti(e)*

peindre, craindre, joindre, se plaindre*

subject	present	passé composé	imperfect	future
je	peins	ai peint	peignais	peindrai
tu	peins	as peint	peignais	peindras
il/elle/on	peint	a peint	peignait	peindra
nous	peignons	avons peint	peignions	peindrons
vous	peignez	avez peint	peigniez	peindrez
ils/elles	peignent	ont peint	peignaient	peindront

subject	conditionnel	pres. subj.	simple past	imperative
je	peindrais	peigne	peignis	
tu	peindrais	peignes	peignis	peins
il/elle/on	peindrait	peigne	peignit	
nous	peindrions	peignions	peignîmes	peignons
vous	peindriez	peigniez	peignîtes	peignez
ils/elles	peindraient	peignent	peignirent	

present participle: *peignant* past participle: *peint*

future perfect: *j'aurai peint* past conditional: *j'aurais peint*

pluperfect: *j'avais peint* past subj.: *j'aie peint*

*Reflexive verb conjugated with être in compound tenses.

pouvoir

subject	present	passé composé	imperfect	future
je	peux (puis)	ai pu	pouvais	pourrai
tu	peux	as pu	pouvais	pourras
il/elle/on	peut	a pu	pouvait	pourra
nous	pouvons	avons pu	pouvions	pourrons
vous	pouvez	avez pu	pouviez	pourrez
ils/elles	peuvent	ont pu	pouvaient	pourront

subject	conditionnel	pres. subj.	simple past	imperative
je	pourrais	puisse	pus	
tu	pourrais	puisses	pus	
il/elle/on	pourrait	puisse	put	
nous	pourrions	puissions	pûmes	
vous	pourriez	puissiez	pûtes	
ils/elles	pourraient	puissent	purent	

present participle: *pouvant* past participle: *pu*

future perfect: *j'aurai pu* past conditional: *j'aurais pu*

pluperfect: *j'avais pu* past subj.: *j'aie pu*

prendre, apprendre, comprendre, entreprendre, reprendre, surprendre

subject	present	passé composé	imperfect	future
je	prends	ai pris	prenais	prendrai
tu	prends	as pris	prenais	prendras
il/elle/on	prend	a pris	prenait	prendra
nous	prenons	avons pris	prenions	prendrons
vous	prenez	avez pris	preniez	prendrez
ils/elles	prennent	ont pris	prenaient	prendront

subject	conditionnel	pres. subj.	simple past	imperative
je	prendrais	prenne	pris	
tu	prendrais	prennes	pris	prends
il/elle/on	prendrait	prenne	prit	
nous	prendrions	prenions	prîmes	prenons
vous	prendriez	preniez	prîtes	prenez
ils/elles	prendraient	prennent	prirent	

present participle: *prenant* past participle: *pris*

future perfect: *j'aurai pris* past conditional: *j'aurais pris*

pluperfect: *j'avais pris* past subj.: *j'aie pris*

mettre, promettre, admettre, commettre, compromettre, omettre, permettre, soumettre, transmettre, battre (past participle: *battu*), combattre (past participle: *combattu*), débattre (past participle: *débattu*)

subject	present	passé composé	imperfect	future
je	mets	ai mis	mettais	mettrai
tu	mets	as mis	mettais	mettras
il/elle/on	met	a mis	mettait	mettra
nous	mettons	avons mis	mettions	mettrons
vous	mettez	avez mis	mettiez	mettrez
ils/elles	mettent	ont mis	mettaient	mettront

subject	conditionnel	pres. subj.	simple past	imperative
je	mettrais	mette	mis	
tu	mettrais	mettes	mis	mets
il/elle/on	mettrait	mette	mit	
nous	mettrions	mettions	mîmes	mettons
vous	mettriez	mettiez	mîtes	mettez
ils/elles	mettraient	mettent	mirent	

present participle: *mettant*   past participle: *mis*
future perfect: *j'aurai mis*   past conditional: *j'aurais mis*
pluperfect: *j'avais mis*   past subj.: *j'aie mis*

recevoir, apercevoir (past participle: *aperçu*), décevoir (past participle: *déçu*)

subject	present	passé composé	imperfect	future
je	reçois	ai reçu	recevais	recevrai
tu	reçois	as reçu	recevais	recevras
il/elle/on	reçoit	a reçu	recevait	recevra
nous	recevons	avons reçu	recevions	recevrons
vous	recevez	avez reçu	receviez	recevrez
ils/elles	reçoivent	ont reçu	recevaient	recevront

subject	conditionnel	pres. subj.	simple past	imperative
je	recevrais	reçoive	reçus	
tu	recevrais	reçoives	reçus	reçois
il/elle/on	recevrait	reçoive	reçut	
nous	recevrions	recevions	reçûmes	recevons
vous	recevriez	receviez	reçûtes	recevez
ils/elles	recevraient	reçoivent	reçurent	

present participle: *recevant*   past participle: *reçu*
future perfect: *j'aurai reçu*   past conditional: *j'aurais reçu*
pluperfect: *j'avais reçu*   past subj.: *j'aie reçu*

rire, sourire

subject	present	passé composé	imperfect	future
je	ris	ai ri	riais	rirai
tu	ris	as ri	riais	riras
il/elle/on	rit	a ri	riait	rira
nous	rions	avons ri	riions	rirons
vous	riez	avez ri	riiez	rirez
ils/elles	rient	ont ri	riaient	riront

subject	conditionnel	pres. subj.	simple past	imperative
je	rirais	rie	ris	
tu	rirais	ries	ris	ris
il/elle/on	rirait	rie	rit	
nous	ririons	riions	rîmes	rions
vous	ririez	riiez	rîtes	riez
ils/elles	riraient	rient	rirent	

present participle: *riant* past participle: *ri*
future perfect: *j'aurai ri* past conditional: *j'aurais ri*
pluperfect: *j'avais ri* past subj.: *j'aie ri*

savoir

subject	present	passé composé	imperfect	future
je	sais	ai su	savais	saurai
tu	sais	as su	savais	sauras
il/elle/on	sait	a su	savait	saura
nous	savons	avons su	savions	saurons
vous	savez	avez su	saviez	saurez
ils/elles	savent	ont su	savaient	sauront

subject	conditionnel	pres. subj.	simple past	imperative
je	saurais	sache	sus	
tu	saurais	saches	sus	sache
il/elle/on	saurait	sache	sut	
nous	saurions	sachions	sûmes	sachons
vous	sauriez	sachiez	sûtes	sachez
ils/elles	sauraient	sachent	surent	

present participle: *sachant* past participle: *su*
future perfect: *j'aurai su* past conditional: *j'aurais su*
pluperfect: *j'avais su* past subj.: *j'aie su*

suivre, poursuivre

subject	present	passé composé	imperfect	future
je	suis	ai suivi	suivais	suivrai
tu	suis	as suivi	suivais	suivras
il/elle/on	suit	a suivi	suivait	suivra
nous	suivons	avons suivi	suivions	suivrons
vous	suivez	avez suivi	suiviez	suivrez
ils/elles	suivent	ont suivi	suivaient	suivront

subject	conditionnel	pres. subj.	simple past	imperative
je	suivrais	suive	suivis	
tu	suivrais	suives	suivis	suis
il/elle	suivrait	suive	suivit	
nous	suivrions	suivions	suivîmes	suivons
vous	suivriez	suiviez	suivîtes	suivez
ils/elles	suivraient	suivent	suivirent	

present participle: *suivant*　　past participle: *suivi*

future perfect: *j'aurai suivi*　　past conditional: *j'aurais suivi*

pluperfect: *j'avais suivi*　　past subj.: *j'aie suivi*

valoir

Used in the third person and in impersonal expressions such as *valoir mieux* (*Il vaut mieux*).

subject	present	passé composé	imperfect	future
il/elle/cela	vaut	a valu	valait	vaudra
ils/elles	valent	ont valu	valaient	vaudront

subject	conditionnel	pres. subj.	simple past	imperative
il/elle/cela	vaudrait	vaille	valut	
ils/elles	vaudraient	vaillent	valurent	

present participle: *valant*　　past participle: *valu*

future perfect: *il/elle aura valu*　　past conditional: *il/elle aurait valu*

pluperfect: *il/elle avait valu*　　past subj.: *il/elle ait valu*

venir*, devenir*, intervenir*, parvenir*, revenir*, se souvenir*, tenir**, appartenir**, obtenir**, retenir**, soutenir**

subject	present	passé composé	imperfect	future
je	viens	suis venu(e)	venais	viendrai
tu	viens	es venu(e)	venais	viendras
il/on	vient	est venu	venait	viendra
elle	vient	est venue	venait	viendra
nous	venons	sommes venu(e)s	venions	viendrons
vous	venez	êtes venu(e)(s)	veniez	viendrez
ils	viennent	sont venus	venaient	viendront
elles	viennent	sont venues	venaient	viendront

subject	conditionnel	pres. subj.	simple past	imperative
je	viendrais	vienne	vins	
tu	viendrais	viennes	vins	viens
il/elle/on	viendrait	vienne	vint	

subject	conditionnel	pres. subj.	simple past	imperative
nous	viendrions	venions	vînmes	venons
vous	viendriez	veniez	vîntes	venez
ils/elles	viendraient	viennent	vinrent	

present participle: *venant*   past participle: *venu*

future perfect: *je serai venu(e)*   past conditional: *je serais venu(e)*

pluperfect: *j'étais venu(e)*   past subj.: *je sois venu(e)*

*venir, devenir, intervenir, parvenir, revenir, se souvenir: *conjugated with* être *in compound tenses.*

**tenir, appartenir, obtenir, retenir, soutenir: *conjugated with* avoir *in compound tenses.*

vivre, revivre, survivre

subject	present	passé composé	imperfect	future
je	vis	ai vécu	vivais	vivrai
tu	vis	as vécu	vivais	vivras
il/elle/on	vit	a vécu	vivait	vivra
nous	vivons	avons vécu	vivions	vivrons
vous	vivez	avez vécu	viviez	vivrez
ils/elles	vivent	ont vécu	vivaient	vivront

subject	conditionnel	pres. subj.	simple past	imperative
je	vivrais	vive	vécus	
tu	vivrais	vives	vécus	vis
il/elle/on	vivrait	vive	vécut	
nous	vivrions	vivions	vécûmes	vivons
vous	vivriez	viviez	vécûtes	vivez
ils/elles	vivraient	vivent	vécurent	

present participle: *vivant*   past participle: *vécu*

future perfect: *j'aurai vécu*   past conditional: *j'aurais vécu*

pluperfect: *j'avais vécu*   past subj.: *j'aie vécu*

voir, prévoir, revoir

subject	present	passé composé	imperfect	future
je	vois	ai vu	voyais	verrai
tu	vois	as vu	voyais	verras
il/elle/on	voit	a vu	voyait	verra
nous	voyons	avons vu	voyions	verrons
vous	voyez	avez vu	voyiez	verrez
ils/elles	voient	ont vu	voyaient	verront

subject	conditionnel	pres. subj.	simple past	imperative
je	verrais	voie	vis	
tu	verrais	voies	vis	vois
il/elle/on	verrait	voie	vit	
nous	verrions	voyions	vîmes	voyons
vous	verriez	voyiez	vîtes	voyez
ils/elles	verraient	voient	virent	

present participle: *voyant*   past participle: *vu*

future perfect: *j'aurai vu*   past conditional: *j'aurais vu*

pluperfect: *j'avais vu*   past subj.: *j'aie vu*

vouloir

subject	present	passé composé	imperfect	future
je	veux	ai voulu	voulais	voudrai
tu	veux	as voulu	voulais	voudras
il/elle/on	veut	a voulu	voulait	voudra
nous	voulons	avons voulu	voulions	voudrons
vous	voulez	avez voulu	vouliez	voudrez
ils/elles	veulent	ont voulu	voulaient	voudront

subject	conditionnel	pres. subj.	simple past	imperative
je	voudrais	veuille	voulus	
tu	voudrais	veuilles	voulus	veux (veuille)
il/elle/on	voudrait	veuille	voulut	
nous	voudrions	voulions	voulûmes	voulons
vous	voudriez	vouliez	voulûtes	voulez (veuillez)
ils/elles	voudraient	veulent	voulurent	

present participle: *voulant*   past participle: *voulu*

future perfect: *j'aurai voulu*   past conditional: *j'aurais voulu*

pluperfect: *j'avais voulu*   past subj.: *j'aie voulu*

APPENDIX C
Answer Key

HOUR 1
1. False
2. False
3. True
4. False
5. c
6. d
7. c
8. b
9. b
10. d

HOUR 2
1. c
2. b
3. c
4. b
5. d
6. a
7. b
8. d
9. a
10. a

HOUR 3
1. False
2. True
3. False
4. True
5. b
6. a
7. d
8. b
9. c
10. a

HOUR 4
1. False
2. False
3. True
4. c
5. a
6. b
7. d
8. a
9. b
10. c

HOUR 5
1. d
2. b
3. a
4. d
5. b
6. c
7. d
8. c
9. a
10. b

HOUR 6
1. a
2. c
3. c
4. c
5. a
6. d
7. c
8. b
9. b
10. d

HOUR 7
1. a
2. c
3. d
4. True
5. False
6. c
7. a
8. b
9. a
10. b

HOUR 8
1. b
2. d
3. a
4. c
5. a
6. b
7. d
8. b
9. c
10. d

HOUR 9
1. d
2. a
3. b
4. b
5. a
6. True
7. d
8. b
9. True
10. True

HOUR 10
1. a
2. b
3. True
4. True
5. False
6. c
7. d
8. b
9. c
10. a

HOUR 11
1. False
2. c
3. b
4. c
5. c
6. d
7. c
8. b
9. a
10. d

HOUR 12
1. b
2. c
3. a
4. d
5. c
6. a
7. b
8. d
9. c
10. a

Hour 13

1. a
2. b
3. c
4. b
5. d
6. a
7. c
8. c
9. a
10. c

Hour 14

1. False
2. True
3. True
4. d
5. b
6. d
7. c
8. a
9. c
10. True

Hour 15

1. b
2. a
3. c
4. d
5. a
6. c
7. b
8. a
9. d
10. c

Hour 16

1. a
2. c
3. b
4. d
5. c
6. a
7. b
8. d
9. c
10. a

Hour 17

1. b
2. c
3. d
4. a
5. b
6. b
7. b
8. c
9. d
10. a

Hour 18

1. b
2. c
3. a
4. True
5. True
6. True
7. d
8. a
9. c
10. b

Hour 19

1. b
2. a
3. d
4. c
5. a
6. c
7. d
8. b
9. a
10. c

Hour 20

1. b
2. a
3. c
4. c
5. d
6. b
7. a
8. c
9. a
10. b

Hour 21

1. c
2. a
3. d
4. b
5. c
6. a
7. b
8. a
9. b
10. a

Hour 22

1. True
2. True
3. b
4. c
5. a
6. b
7. d
8. a
9. b
10. d

Hour 23

1. a
2. c
3. d
4. b
5. c
6. a
7. b
8. c
9. d
10. c

Hour 24

1. False
2. True
3. b
4. d
5. False
6. a
7. c
8. b
9. d
10. a

Index